CASES IN

INTERNATIONAL RELATIONS

PRINCIPLES AND APPLICATIONS

—■—

NINTH EDITION

—■—

DONALD M. SNOW

THE UNIVERSITY OF ALABAMA

ROWMAN &
LITTLEFIELD

Lanham · Boulder · New York · London

Published by Rowman & Littlefield
An imprint of The Rowman & Littlefield Publishing Group, Inc.
4501 Forbes Boulevard, Suite 200, Lanham, Maryland 20706
www.rowman.com

86-90 Paul Street, London EC2A 4NE

British Library Cataloguing in Publication Information Available

Library of Congress Cataloging-in-Publication Data

Names: Snow, Donald M., 1943– author.
Title: Cases in international relations : principles and application / Donald M. Snow.
Description: Ninth edition. | Lanham, Maryland : Rowman & Littlefield, 2022. | Includes
  bibliographical references and index.
Identifiers: LCCN 2021050208 (print) | LCCN 2021050209 (ebook) | ISBN 9781538153437
  (cloth) | ISBN 9781538153444 (paperback) | ISBN 9781538153451 (epub)
Subjects: LCSH: International relations—Case studies.
Classification: LCC JZ1242 .S658 2022 (print) | LCC JZ1242 (ebook) | DDC 327—dc23
LC record available at https://lccn.loc.gov/2021050208
LC ebook record available at https://lccn.loc.gov/2021050209

Contents

Preface

This book is, and through its various editions always has been, about explaining basic concepts, forces, and dynamics in international relations and how these principles help shape and guide applications to contemporary situations. As such, it has two basic missions: providing basic instruction in important dynamics of how international relations work (hopefully in a lively and engaging manner) and providing updated and relevant information and interpretation of major events helping to shape the world. These have been the goals since the first edition appeared in 2002; they remain for this, the ninth edition. After some experimentation with formats, I have adopted a "formula" of sorts, where each case study begins with a principle of operation of the international system followed by an example of events that illustrate the principle and controversies surrounding it. This division is reflected in the overall table of contents: the first nine chapters deal with underlying international relations principles, whereas the last nine chapters focus on substantive problems. The purpose is to create a coherence often missing in supplemental texts. I would like to think that, in addition to being a "reader" to accompany a comprehensive text, it could be used as a text on its own supplemented by other materials.

Like all books going through multiple editions, this one has evolved over time. This edition is distinguished by two major structural changes from previous editions. Both affect the cases in this volume. First, there are more cases than before. Most of the previous editions had fourteen cases, and the eighth and this ninth edition have eighteen. The length of each case has been reduced from about 9,000 words to a little over 6,000 words, leaving the final product about the same length as earlier editions. This restructuring replicates the organization of my *Cases in U.S. National Security*, published in 2018. The shorter chapters are more reader friendly, in the sense that each chapter can be read in one easy sitting. Second, the expansion in number of cases allows an expansion of the topics covered, thereby enhancing the book's comprehensiveness. I hope the reader will find the additions interesting, informative, and readable, and that what has been lost in the depth of past cases will be compensated for by greater topic coverage.

New to This Edition

The new configuration of the table of contents has provided both the opportunity and necessity of adding additional topics, reconfiguring some others, and eliminating yet others—particularly applications that have become less relevant since the last edition was published. There is, for instance, much less coverage of the Islamic State than in the earlier editions, for the simple reason that its star rose and then fell (largely for reasons laid out in the last edition). The eliminated chapters have been replaced by new chapters reflecting more contemporary

v

problems, like the problems posed by the COVID pandemic and global warming. The whole manuscript has been updated to reflect events through mid-2021.

The text also introduces some new ideas and forces in the international mix. An illustrative list includes the world's struggle with the COVID pandemic, the evolving threat posed by climate change, and the problem of cyberwar. There is more, but it is a broad and I hope rich menu. Dig in!

Features

What distinguishes this effort from other supplementary texts in the field? One answer is that all the chapters included in the volume are original papers written by the author specifically for this volume. The reason for doing so was to allow for more timely coverage of ongoing situations than is possible with the publication lag time of scholarly journals and their availability to readers and other compendia. It also allows casting the cases in a common format that makes it easier to compare the contents of the various cases without wading through disparate styles and formats of various authors and publications. In addition, journal articles are written for academic peers rather than more-or-less lay students, meaning they are generally rendered in language and theoretical trappings that are less than accessible to student readers. Finally, writing original chapters facilitates updating and modifying materials as events and dynamics change, which hopefully adds to the freshness, accuracy, and timeliness of the materials contained in these pages. Presenting the most contemporary set of portraits possible has certainly been a major purpose of this and earlier editions.

A word about what this book is—and is not—is appropriate at this point. It is a case book, presenting a series of individual instances of dynamics and trends within the international arena. The effort is neither inclusive nor encyclopedic; it covers selected concepts and events, not the universe of international concerns. A series of eighteen important, underlying concepts and principles of the international system have been chosen and discussed, and the discussion of these principles has been applied to contemporary, important, and interesting real-life examples. The result is not a systematic overview of the international system or its history, which is the province of core textbooks in the field. Likewise, it does not offer a unifying theoretical explanatory framework of international politics, a task that more specialized books purporting grand "theories" of international relations propound. Rather, the intent is to introduce and apply some basic concepts about international relations and how they apply in real situations.

Acknowledgments

This edition of the book is once again dedicated to my good friend and colleague, the late D. Eugene Brown. Gene and I met in 1989 at the U.S. Army War College, where we both served as visiting professors and shared an office for two years before he returned to his permanent home at Lebanon Valley College in Annville, Pennsylvania, and I returned to the University of Alabama in Tuscaloosa. In the ensuing decade, we were collaborators on several book projects; *Cases in International Relations*, which was mostly Gene's idea, was to be a continuation, even culmination, of those efforts. Unfortunately, Gene left us before the original project was complete. His shadow remains, I hope with a smile on his face.

I have also received generous and very helpful assistance from the team at Rowman & Littlefield. In particular, I would like to thank two members of the Rowman & Littlefield team. My editors, Susan McEachern and Michael Kerns, obtained the reversion of rights to me for the seventh edition and encouraged me throughout the writing process. Alden Perkins did her usual professional job turning the manuscript into a book, our fourth project together. Special thanks go to Elizabeth Von Buhr, who cheerfully and efficiently came to my aid when my lack of knowledge and empathy with the dynamics of electronic infernal machines left me in a bewildered panic (a recurrent burden on her). Thanks for everything, guys!

Lastly, I would like to thank the reviewers of the ninth edition: Dan Caldwell (Pepperdine University) and Alfredo Carnevali (Montclair State University).

DONALD M. SNOW
PROFESSOR EMERITUS
UNIVERSITY OF ALABAMA

PART I
Conceptual Framework

1

Sovereignty

Defining Territorial Integrity and Jurisdiction on the West Bank

Sovereignty—supreme authority—has been the most central concept and operational principle of the international order since the Peace of Westphalia ended the Thirty Years' War in 1648. Since then, sovereignty has been defined territorially as possessed by states. This has meant that state sovereignty is the principle on which world political order is grounded. Within sovereign states, there can be no authority greater than that of the state. In principle, it is absolute in scope. In practice there are infringements on the total control of the state. Sovereignty is a controversial operational concept that is used to justify armed violence and can be a shield behind which atrocity is sometimes committed. Established sovereignty does, however, endow its possessor with international legitimacy, making it a valued commodity among possessing political actors.

Sovereignty is pervasive, is jealously guarded by its state possessors, and is a fundamental pillar of world politics. Some states are more obsessed with protecting their sovereignty than others, but it is important to all states. The most powerful states have the most to lose if others can infringe on their sovereignty, and they tend to be the strongest champions of state sovereignty. China and the United States are the purest examples of this dynamic in contemporary international politics.

The pervasiveness of sovereignty extends to virtually all aspects of international interactions, and it is so important that a systematic examination of international relations must begin by understanding the concept and how it intrudes on so many of the dealings of international actors. One area where claims of sovereignty are most foundational occurs when multiple states claim jurisdiction over the same territory and where the claimants are unwilling to relax or compromise their claims, resulting in especially bitter conflict that can, at worst, devolve to armed conflict between them. In contemporary international relations, an example is the contest between Israel and the Palestinians over the West Bank of the Jordan River, a part of sovereign Jordan until 1967, when it was occupied by Israel in the Six-Day War. The Israelis and the Palestinians have each claimed sovereign primacy ever since.

Principle: The Concept of Sovereignty

Any discussion of the underlying philosophy, structure, or operation of international relations begins with the concept of sovereignty. Defined as "supreme authority," it is the operational base of both international and domestic political life, although with quite opposite effects on the two realms. Ever since it emerged as the bedrock organizational principle of world politics in 1648, it is, and has always been, a somewhat controversial foundation for world affairs. Controversy has surrounded matters such as the location of sovereignty (who has it?) and the extent of power that it conveys to its possessors (what can the sovereign do—and not do?), and concepts have changed over time. Disagreements about sovereignty are prominent parts of some debates about the evolving international order, and the assault on its basic function is part of international dialogue.

Sovereignty emerged as a defining concept at a time when modern political states did not exist except in limited places such as France and England. During this period, questions of political authority still revolved around whether people owed their ultimate loyalty and even existence to sectarian authority represented most prominently by the Catholic Church or to secular monarchs in the locales where they resided. One of the most important elements of the Peace of Westphalia (the collective name given to the series of treaties that ended the Thirty Years' War) was to wrest political control from the church and to transfer that power to secular authorities. This transfer was accompanied by the effective installation of sovereignty as the basis of relations among secular political communities. A primary outcome of this "marriage" was to associate sovereignty with territorial political jurisdictions. Because those territories were essentially all ruled by absolute monarchs, the conjunction effectively created the precedent that the power of the sovereign was absolute. This association is symbolized by the fact that the monarchs of the time were also known as sovereigns.

Sovereignty has changed over time. Reflecting the political period in which it became the bellwether concept of an evolving secular state-based system, sovereignty began as a principle that legitimized and promoted authoritarian rule. That principle was challenged with the rise of democratic thought, suggesting that sovereignty was a characteristic not only of the ruler but the ruled as well. From this challenge arose the modern notion of popular sovereignty.

Origins and Evolution

Understanding how and why sovereignty came to be the major organizing principle of international relations begins with an enigma. The heart of sovereignty is territorial supremacy—whoever has sovereignty has ultimate authority over the physical territory where it is claimed and enforced. This means that in the domestic affairs of sovereign entities, sovereignty provides the basis for political *order* by endowing its possessors with the ability to develop and enforce rules and laws that produce some form of political system. It does not predetermine *who* within the jurisdiction has sovereignty or the *extent* to which it can be exercised. In domestic affairs, it is the basis for order.

The impact of sovereignty on the relations *between* sovereign territories (in modern terms, the world's states or countries) is quite the opposite. The supreme authority that sovereignty creates means that there can be no other entity that can claim or exercise any form of authority over another state, and this principle implies states cannot interfere in one another's affairs. Although this principle was never taken quite literally in practice, the result was that international relations (the interactions between states) was effectively a state of *anarchy* (the absence of government) where no state could legally be impelled to do things it did not want or that might offend others within their sovereign domains. The only recourse that a political authority aggrieved by the actions of another sovereign state was through *self-help*, which often effectively meant the recourse to arms.

The fact that sovereignty created the justification both for order and disorder was not a concern of its early chroniclers and enthusiasts. The concept was first introduced by the French philosopher Jean Bodin in his 1576 book *De Republica*. Bodin's major concern was to promote the consolidation of the authority of the king of France over his realm. The problem that he sought to alleviate was the practice by lower feudal lords within France of effectively claiming sovereignty over their realms by charging tolls to cross their territories.

To deal with this situation, Bodin countered with the concept of sovereignty, which he defined as "supreme authority over citizens and subjects, *unrestrained by law*" (emphasis added). Bodin was a staunch monarchist, and he felt the italicized element was necessary to keep the monarch from being hamstrung by parochial laws in his quest to establish the power of the monarchy and to spread its sway over the entire country. The notion of exemption from law has fallen from common conceptions of sovereignty, but its implications remain and are part of ongoing disagreements on the meaning and controversies surrounding the concept. If the sovereign is indeed above the law, then nothing he or she does can possibly be illegal, at least when committed within the sovereign jurisdiction over which the sovereign reigns. The claim by Richard Nixon during the Watergate scandal that "if the President does it, it cannot be illegal" is an example; so is Robert Mueller's 2019 determination that President Trump could not be tried for a crime while he was in office and in controversies over his legal status since he left office.

Bodin was not concerned about sovereignty's extension to forming the basis of international relations. That extension occurred as the state system evolved and the structure of the modern state emerged in an increasing number of European states. The major publicist of this extension was the Dutch scholar Hugo Grotius, who is generally acknowledged as the father of the idea of international law. He first proclaimed state sovereignty as a fundamental principle of international relations in his 1625 book *On the Law of War and Peace*, and by the eighteenth century it was accepted as both a principle of domestic and international relations.

By the nineteenth century, the modern state system was taking form, and this change entailed implications for both the questions raised earlier: with whom does sovereignty exist within sovereign jurisdictions? And how extensive are the legitimate powers that reside in the holder of sovereignty? Both remain basic questions.

The question of the locus of sovereignty was a product of greater citizen participation in the political process within evolving countries, and especially within emerging democracies. When monarchism was universal and was accompanied by the belief that the monarch was supreme over his or her realm, it was natural to assume monarchical control over the state. When political philosophers like the Englishman John Locke and his French counterpart Jean-Jacques Rousseau made the counterclaim that the sovereign's powers were limited and could be abridged by the people, the question of the locus of sovereignty was joined. The premise of both the American and French Revolutions was that the people were the source of fundamental political legitimacy, which translated into the idea of popular sovereignty. The heart of this notion, which gradually took hold as the state system matured in Europe, was that the people were sovereign and that they voluntarily relinquished parts of that sovereignty to the state to legitimize state power and to ensure domestic order.

The idea of popular restraint suggested that there were limits on the unrestricted extent of the freedom of states to act as they might want to. Within democratizing states, the major limit (or restraint) on sovereign authority was what the people would tolerate. This expression was asserted gradually: after a republican form of government was established in the United States, other states during the nineteenth century, notably France (which alternated between democratic and authoritarian rule before 1870) and Great Britain, which gradually expanded political rights, began to democratize more broadly, and this trend spread. The symbolic acts of embracing this notion in domestic politics were the UN Charter and various declarations after World War II, although full implementation of the concept has not yet occurred universally.

Changing Conceptions of Sovereignty

Developing and applying changing conceptions of sovereignty to the relations *among* sovereigns has been difficult. Sovereignty as the basic principle of international relations remains largely conceptually intact, although its pervasive dominance has been selectively diluted through voluntary forfeitures by organs like the European Union. Most of the attempts at change come from international efforts to limit the degree of control and even persecution to which states can subject their citizens (extensions of the idea of popular sovereignty) like the UN Declaration on Human Rights and the Convention on Genocide, both of which the United States did not ratify until the 1990s (they were first drafted in the 1940s). The nature and implications of sovereignty remain controversial in contemporary international politics for different reasons. Three of them are worth noting as examples.

The first is the connection between sovereignty and war. One of the commonly stated objections to sovereignty is that the concept justifies and even glorifies war to settle difference between states—a consequence of international anarchy. Conflict–resolving methods like domestic justice systems with mandatory jurisdiction are unavailable for most purposes. In a system of sovereign states, after all, there is no authority to enforce international norms on states or to enforce judgments resolving disputes that arise between them. Such mechanisms are conspicuously (and purposely) missing in the relations among states. Because there can be no superior authority to that of the sovereign, no one can enforce anything against a sovereign (at least in principle). The reason is simple: states have what are generally referred to as *vital interests*, conditions on which they will not voluntarily compromise, and are thus unwilling to empower any authority that could dilute that power (the concept of national interest is the basis of chapter 2).

The second objection to sovereignty is the degree of control it gives states over their citizens, including the right to suppress and even murder individuals and groups. The assertion of this objection is largely contemporary, a postwar phenomenon reflecting global outrage to the genocide during the Holocaust. The notion of absolute sovereignty implies that the sovereign state has total control over those who reside within its legal boundaries. Taken literally, this means the sovereign can do anything he or she wants or can do to those citizens—including killing all or parts of the population—with no outside legal sanction or basis for interference in any atrocities arising from that treatment.

That scenario, of course, describes the Holocaust carried out by Nazi Germany against the Jewish and Roma (sometimes referred to as Gypsy) population of Germany and other countries it occupied. Rejection of this practice represents, at least implicitly, an affirmation and advocacy of popular sovereignty. It has also been the subject of attacks that argue the assertion that government control over its citizenry is fundamental to the conceptual underpinning of the state system, and that, despite the merits of protecting people from atrocity, it should be opposed on the basis that it erodes and undermines the basic conceptual underpinning of the state system.

The third, and somewhat mitigating, factor is that sovereignty in practice has never been as absolute as it is in theory. The degrees of control in the nineteenth century were not actually total, and they are less so today. Countries can and do regularly interfere with the affairs of other countries. The attempts by Russia to influence the 2016 American presidential election were presented as something unusual and extreme, but they were not. During the Cold War, the Soviet Union regularly attempted to influence American elections by manipulating relations to make different candidates they favored or opposed look good or bad, and the United States also has a long history of interfering with elections through the use of clandestine intelligence operations to do things like financing campaigns either to elect or defeat candidates and, in the most extreme cases, to carry out "wet operations" to eliminate disfavored politicians from some countries, notably in the Western Hemisphere, and in the 1940s in places like Iran. The phenomenon of sovereignty-violating interference is examined in chapter 9.

The United States is by no means the only country that engages in these kinds of violations of the state sovereignty of other countries. It is a kind of general rule that large states—those with considerable and extensive interests and the means to realize them—are more likely to cross the sovereign rights line in other countries than weaker and smaller states that lack both those levels of interests and those means. To paraphrase an old saw, with regards to the maintenance of sovereignty, the powerful states do what they can and the weak states suffer what they must.

The U.S. Position

The United States has been one of the chief proponents of the retention of maximum sovereign rights for the government. Most of the assault has focused on human rights abuses—from genocide to torture—in the form of international conventions and treaties, mostly sponsored and sanctioned under the United Nations. In general, these treaties specify things governments cannot do and prescribe penalties, up to and including criminal penalties for the leaders of countries breaking the international agreements. They also specify that acceptance includes incorporation of prohibitions within domestic laws, a clear infringement on the "right" of countries to do anything they please within their sovereign jurisdictions. As an example, the Convention against Terrorism makes the suborning or commission of torture a war crime, and its acceptance by the United States has meant that torture is a crime under American law as well. American resistance to assaults on sovereignty based in jurisdictional infringement often puts the United States at odds with its closest allies and in incongruous positions, as the West Bank case illustrates.

Characteristics of Sovereignty

Sovereignty has become more controversial in the contemporary world than it was when absolute rulers declared themselves sovereigns and their claims were accepted by other similar rulers and when political distinctions were less important to national populations than they are today. In the modern world, there are often multiple claimants to sovereign status, each of which has arguments that support its claim. The West Bank is a prime example. There are several criteria that are used to reinforce claims to supreme authority. Some conflict with one another and they change in emphasis, making an iteration of qualities of sovereignty necessary to understanding that changing role. To this end, a fully sovereign state must possess four characteristics: a recognized territory and population, recognized jurisdiction and legitimate authority over the territory and its inhabitants, autonomy from external control, and recognition by other states. A state is only considered sovereign if it possesses all these characteristics. The requirements are cumulative and related. If any of these characteristics is lost or falls under question, the entity's sovereignty is compromised and can be questioned. Each characteristic is sufficiently important to warrant examination.

Territory and Population

States are inherently physical places, the delineation of which is based on political boundaries on a map. For sovereignty to be established, there must be a recognized place over which that sovereignty can be claimed and a population that resides in that area. For this latter reason, for instance, it has always been controversial whether claims of sovereignty can be made for Antarctica, which has no permanent human population. One way to solve this problem is to colonize that area with people who become permanent residents. There is no accepted process or criteria for legitimizing this method.

Accepted Jurisdiction and Legitimate Authority

Successfully claiming sovereignty also requires that the claimant has a legitimate basis for that possession that supersedes the claims of any other body and that the claimant can politically exercise control: legitimacy and authority. These characteristics are most often called into question when a group seizes another territory and attempts to rule as a sovereign. Seizures that are the result of invasion are illegal under international law and undermine legitimacy. This situation has been particularly contentious regarding the West Bank.

Autonomy from Outside Control

This characteristic refers specifically to the independence of whoever claims sovereignty from outside forces. This situation occurs when a country is invaded and conquered, and the invader puts a puppet regime in nominal charge of governance. The puppet regime may claim that it is sovereign, but its claims are unlikely to be accepted by other sovereign states. The German-installed Vichy Regime in France during World War II, which consisted of French Nazi collaborators, was an example.

Recognition by Other States

The acceptance that a physical territory and its rulers possess the other characteristics leads to the bestowal by other states of the claimant's status as a sovereign state. The symbols of that acceptance include such things as formal recognition of governments, the exchange of diplomatic personnel and establishment of embassies, and regular interaction between the sovereign state and its counterparts.

Although the content and meaning of sovereignty is in a constant state of flux or adjustment, it retains considerable force as a conditioning parameter about how countries deal with one another and even *if* they interact. Almost all the situations derive from questions about whether different states possess all the elements of sovereignty or whether they can successfully protect their sovereignty from outside intrusion.

Contemporary Issues and Limits

Virtually no one overtly opposes the primacy of sovereignty as the basic means by which the international system operates. Legitimacy and authority must exist at some level to avoid total anarchy, and the alternatives to a system of sovereign states would have to transfer sovereignty either to a larger, more inclusive authority or to a smaller, more atomized series of authorities. The first possibility is to transfer power to larger bodies such as international organizations or associations of states. The UN system represents a very limited example of the international organization alternative; the European Union is an example where members confer sovereignty to elements of a voluntary association. Secession and the formation of new sovereign states represents the atomization direction.

Until recently, those who would transfer elements of sovereignty to larger bodies have had the upper hand. There has, however, been a political backlash in both Europe and the United States that these "internationalists" (to borrow a designation developed in chapter 7) have dangerously encroached on national sovereignty in ways these "unilateralists" find dangerous. In a December 4, 2018, speech in Brussels, American secretary of state Michael Pompeo warned of the invidious impact of organizations like the United Nations, the European Union, the Organization of American States, the African Union, and even the World Bank and the International Monetary Fund because they can pose potential sovereignty and national security dangers to their members on these grounds.

The issue of sovereignty thus has become entangled in the widening debate about the future direction of international relations (see chapter 5). The discussions tend to focus on the most adamant defenders of national sovereignty against those who believe that some relaxation of that principle can lead to a more prosperous, safe, and even just international system than one where absolute sovereignty holds sway.

The debate can, of course, be overstated. The assertion that states do not violate one another's sovereignty has always been somewhat fictitious, and modern electronics and cyber capabilities have made the "impenetrability" of state sovereignty even more suspect (see chapter 12). Sovereignty as the premier principle for organizing the political order within and between states has remained the basis for operation in the international system, because where it can be applied, it provides an order that simplifies international interactions between states. The United States and Canada both recognize one another's sovereign control over accepted territory, and this removes some possible disagreements from the table. The possessor(s) of sovereignty and the physical territory over which that sovereignty can be exercised, however, is under increasing siege in an international system where there are more claimants to that sovereignty than before, a problem that could become even greater as world population continues to increase. Sovereignty remains a useful principle that simplifies international life when its parameters are agreed upon, but there are also areas where the definitions arising from sovereign claims are the basis for conflict, not its resolution. There is no place in the world that better illustrates this dilemma than the West Bank of the Jordan River, an area sovereignty over which has been hotly contested since the end of World War II.

Application: Defining Territorial Inequality and Jurisdiction on the West Bank

The status and disposition of the West Bank of the Jordan River has been the most visible symbol of conflict between Israel and most countries of the Islamic Middle East since 1947, when the creation of the state of Israel was proclaimed and all sides began the rush to claim this piece of strategically and demographically valuable piece of real estate. In purely physical terms, it is a small piece of land: it is bounded by pre-1967 Israel on the Mediterranean side and extends eastward to the western bank of the Jordan River (hence its name). It occupies about 5,400 square miles of land primarily suited for agriculture and is about the size of Delaware. At the time of partition, it had about three million inhabitants, about 75 percent of whom were Palestinians and the rest mostly Israelis. When the disagreement began, this territory was claimed by Jordan, a status it maintained until 1967, when it was conquered and occupied by Israel as one of the outcomes of the Six-Day War of 1967. Its status has been the hoariest issue dividing Israel and the Palestinian people ever since. The West Bank is the key to solving the question of Palestinian statehood and thus arguably to stabilization of the Middle East.

The heart of the issue is to whom does the West Bank "belong." Put a slightly different way, who has the legitimate claim to sovereign jurisdiction over this piece of land and the people who live on it. It is a difficult question to answer, and the various claimants have different interpretations, as does much of the international community. The consequences of who legitimately can claim sovereignty would determine whose land the West Bank is. To understand the difficulty this situation creates requires looking at the sovereignty question as it existed in 1947 and how it has evolved since then.

The Context

The area known as the West Bank has a long and convoluted history, none of which clearly leads to the authoritative assertion of sovereignty by any of the groups claiming primacy over the land. The area was part of the Ottoman Empire from 1517 to 1917, and it remained part of the successor state of Turkey until 1923, when that country renounced its claim. The area became part of the British Mandate (see Anderson), which made no claim of sovereign control. The current impasse was joined after World War II. In 1947, the United Nations and other international entities (including the United States) recommended the West Bank, which had large Palestinian and Jewish populations, be designated as the base for a future Arab state. In 1948, contiguous Jordan occupied the West Bank, followed by annexing to the country in 1950.

The West Bank remained a part of Jordan until 1967, when the Israelis captured and occupied territory in the Six-Day War, thereby effectively removing the Jordanians from the physical equation regarding ownership and sovereignty. The loss was very damaging for Jordan, which had derived 40 percent of the Gross National Product (GNP) from the area, mostly from growing fruits and other agricultural goods, but they were in no physical position to pursue their claims and eventually quit doing so. The withdrawal of Jordan from the equation left the Palestinians and the Israelis as the remaining claimants to the land, a status effectively enshrined by United Nations Security Council Resolution 242 in 1967, a document that is still cited as authority, particularly by the Palestinians.

The status of the West Bank has been in a state of legal, jurisdictional limbo ever since. At the risk of oversimplifying a dizzyingly complex set of arguments, there are two positions on who has the stronger claim. Most of the international community considers the current situation as a "belligerent occupation" by Israel. Because maintenance of this situation for over a half century is considered excessive by most outsiders and because most international groups consider the Palestinians to be the rightful tenants, Israel prefers to consider the area "disputed territory," which is somewhat more questionable given progressive settlement by Jewish immigrants on the West Bank (an action generally considered illegal as grounds for establishing sovereignty under international law). As of February 2020, roughly 70 percent of the members of the United Nations (134 of 193) recognized the West Bank as part of Palestine rather than as Israeli-occupied territories.

None of the actions and positions of affected parties provides a definitive answer to the question of which group is the rightful possessor of sovereignty over the West Bank. The result is to leave the roughly 3.3 million inhabitants of the West Bank (about 2.75 million Palestinians, almost 400,000 Israelis, and about 200,000 Israeli settlers in East Jerusalem) in jurisdictional limbo. This situation would be clarified if one group or another could effectively claim and enforce sovereignty, but that is not the case. Most of the international community supports the idea of Palestinian possession, but since the territory is occupied and effectively ruled by Israel, their claims cannot be implemented and enforced. The Israelis exercise de facto sovereignty over the West Bank, but they do not proclaim that status due to international objections. The result is a jurisdictional impasse.

Reasons for Deadlock

The reason for the ongoing impasse speaks to one of the primary attractions of sovereignty to state authorities. In simplest terms, a favorable outcome to West Bank status is too important to both sides for them to be willing to accept an unfavorable outcome to their claim. As a result, there is no international decision body that has the authority to issue such judgments. In this case, the scarcity of territory in the region is simply too great for either side to accept willingly an unfavorable judgment on their claim. There is simply not enough land for there to be a viable Palestinian state without the West Bank, and Israel's dreams of relocating greater numbers of Jewish immigrants to their state is impossible without some relocation to the West Bank (see Snow, *The Middle East and American National Security: Forever Conflict and War*, for a discussion). The fact that East Jerusalem, claimed by both sides as its capital, is part of any comprehensive West Bank solution adds to the dilemma.

These problems are fundamental and interrelated, and they are basically real estate concerns. The claims that the Israelis and the Palestinians have on the West Bank are mutually exclusive. The Trump administration endorsed a plan whereby the two groups subdivided the land and authority over it, but it was only acceptable to Israel. Under current circumstances, the West Bank is divided into 167 Palestinian "islands" under the internal control of the Palestinian National Authority for civil rule and 230 Israeli settlements, over which the government of Israel exercises de facto total control. The Israeli settlements are in the choicest locations (high ground, guaranteed access to water), and Israel maintains military control of the area. The result is a map of settlements that looks like a crazy quilt and is totally unacceptable to the Palestinians. Neither side has shown any interest in a compromise solution, the content of which is hard to envisage. American support of this arrangement will likely be revised by the Biden administration.

The heart of the problem is clear: scarcity. There is simply not enough territory available for both sides to realize their objectives. Israelis do not believe they can provide acceptable security for their country without effective control of the West Bank and that Palestinian control would also thwart the Israeli goal of immigration to implement the policy of a Greater Israel. The Palestinians likewise have no reasonable prospect of forming a viable state without the West Bank as its core. Scarcity is simply reality, and the only way the question can be resolved is for one side or the other ultimately to gain sovereign control of that land. That requires, as a basic matter, determining which side has a superior claim to being the sovereign over the disputed land.

The West Bank as a Sovereignty Question

Does it help clarify the rightful disposition of the West Bank to think of the problem in terms of the criteria for sovereignty laid out in the first section of the chapter? All claimants to sovereign status will make the argument that their advocacy is superior in terms of meeting the largely legal requirements for possession of sovereignty. The establishment of the legitimacy of one party or another based in sovereignty is, after all, a legal question and thus it is likely a litigious process. The problem is common to international law generally (and at least partly the result of sovereignty as the value base of the system), and thus the legal outcomes do not always prevail.

The criteria for possession of sovereignty by one side or another over the West Bank illustrates this dynamic. The first characteristic is the possession of a physical territory and population. The West Bank clearly has both, but they are divided. There are both Jewish and Muslim inhabitants on the West Bank, and early post–World War II discussions suggested a multinational solution that has not stood up with time and geopolitical change. The multinational composition of the area broke down when many Palestinians panicked and fled the new Israeli state into parts of Jordan, including the West Bank. The international community generally accepts the notion that the West Bank is the heart of Palestine, thus sovereignty resides with the Palestinians. The Israelis, who have physically occupied and controlled the territory for a half century, disagree, and while they do not claim sovereignty over the West Bank, they view the territory as "disputed," thus subject to litigation.

The second characteristic is accepted jurisdiction and legitimate authority over the territory, and disagreement on this matter is at the heart of the conflict in sovereignty terms. Israel exercises direct authority over most of the West Bank, but acceptance of that status is generally lacking among the Palestinian majority. The Israelis have sought to bolster their physical claim to legitimate status through immigration onto the West Bank and into the Jewish settlements, but this is widely viewed as a ploy to make it physically impossible to form a Palestinian state incorporating those settlements. The Israelis exercise jurisdiction and authority; whether that exercise is legitimate and accepted is a matter of controversy and is at the heart of the conferral of sovereignty by the international community.

The third characteristic is autonomy from outside control. This provision is basically intended to prevent a conqueror from taking over a country and installing a puppet regime, for which it then claims sovereign rights. Since World War II, the practice of doing this has essentially disappeared, and the conquest of territory is prohibited under the UN Charter, among other places. In the context of the West Bank, it is sometimes alleged by anti-Israeli forces that the recruitment and movement of Jewish immigrants from Europe to Israeli-controlled areas of the West Bank comes close to or violates this rejoinder, and if that criticism is accepted, it further weakens Israeli claims to parts of the West Bank.

The final characteristic is the most straightforward, stating that for a state to be considered sovereign, it must be recognized as such by other sovereign states. As noted earlier in this section, most UN members recognize the Palestinians as the sovereign force on the West Bank, and since there can be only one recognized sovereign in any territory, that negates any claims the Israelis might propose regarding their own sovereign position there.

Conclusions

Sovereignty is the chief organizing concept of international relations, but it is also contradictory in application some of the time. The basic function of claiming sovereign control and having it recognized by other states is protective for whoever achieves it. Sovereignty, in effect, places a conceptual fence around the possessor that says that outsiders cannot intrude upon the affairs of the sovereign. Sovereignty is, after all, *supreme* authority, and whoever meets the criteria of sovereignty over a given piece of territory and its inhabitants wields great power within the affected realm.

Because of these characteristics, sovereignty is also a very conservative force that makes changes in the status quo more difficult than it might otherwise be. The case of the West Bank is a clear illustration. The Palestinians and their international supporters ground their claim to the land in sovereignty and thus the rightful possession of the West Bank as the lawful site of the core of the sovereign state of Palestine. Faced with overwhelming international support for the Palestinian claim of sovereignty, the Israelis generally avoid the sovereignty question, instead basing their continued presence in the unsettled nature of the area's status while further developing and inhabiting the West Bank with refugees and what appear to be very permanent settlements that have led some to conclude that they have accomplished a de facto if not legally sanctioned annexation and thereby left the sovereignty question moot. Sovereignty forms the basis of the Palestinian claim, but their inability to enforce sovereignty also provides a cover that allows the Israelis to ignore those opinions. Supreme authority protects Israel and blocks a pro-Palestinian settlement. The only definitive outcomes are for Palestine to renounce its claim or for the international community to somehow force Israel to accept the international position on Palestine. Creating either solution is easier said than done.

Study/Discussion Questions

1. Define sovereignty. When did the concept emerge as a central tenet of international relations? Who were Bodin, Grotius, Locke, and Rousseau, and how did each contribute to the development of sovereignty?

2. Sovereignty has opposite effects on domestic and international relations. What are the differences? Explain the implications for international politics.

3. How has the concept of sovereignty evolved as both a dictate in domestic and international affairs? What is the U.S. position on sovereignty? Why?

4. What are the characteristics of a sovereign state? Why is sovereignty so important to those states that they sometimes go to great lengths to protect that sovereignty?

5. What and where is the West Bank? Why is it a major international and Middle Eastern concern?

6. How does the West Bank question become a matter of sovereignty? What are the Israeli and Palestinian positions on the relevance of sovereignty to West Bank status?

7. Why is a favorable outcome to West Bank sovereignty so important to both sides? Elaborate.

8. How does the impasse surrounding West Bank sovereignty illustrate the ambivalent impact of the concept in international relations?

Bibliography

Anderson, Scott. *Lawrence in Arabia: War, Deceit, Imperial Folly, and the Making of the Modern Middle East.* New York: Anchor Books, 2013.

Armstrong, Karen. *Jerusalem: One City, Three Faiths.* London: Ballantine Books, 2011.

Avashi, Bernard. "Confederation: The One Possible Arab-Palestinian Solution." *New York Review of Books*, February 3, 2018.

Benn, Aluf. "Netanyahu's Referendum: What's at Stake for the Israeli Prime Minister in the Early Election." *Foreign Affairs* (online), February 6, 2019.

Bodin, Jean. *Six Books on the Commonwealth.* Oxford, UK: Basil Blackwell, 1955.

Bregman, Ahron. *Cursed Victory: A History of Israel and the Occupied Territories, 1967 to the Present.* Trenton, TX: Pegasus, 2015.

Brown, Nathan J. "The Occupation at Fifty: A Permanent State of Ambiguity." *Current History* 116, no. 704 (December 2017): 345–51.

Carter, Jimmy. *Palestine: Peace Not Apartheid.* New York: Simon and Schuster, 2006.

Cusimano, Mary Ann, ed. *Beyond Sovereignty.* Bedford, MA: Bedford St. Martin's Press, 1999.

Dowty, Alan. *Israel/Palestine* (fourth edition). London: Polity Press, 2017.

Elshtain, Jean Bethke. *Sovereignty: God, State, and Self* (reprint edition). New York: Basic Books, 2012.

Freedman, Robert, ed. *Israel and the United States: Six Decades of U.S.-Israeli Relations*. New York and London: Routledge, 2018.

Grimm, Dieter (translated by Belinda Cooper). *Sovereignty: The Origin and Future of a Political and Legal Concept* (Columbia Studies in Political Thought/Political History). New York: Columbia University Press, 2015.

Grotius, Hugo. *On the Law of War and Peace*. New York: Cambridge University Press, 2012 (originally published 1625).

———. *The Rights of War and Peace: Including the Law of Nature and Nations*. New York: M. W. Dunne, 1981.

Harms, Gregory, and Todd M. Ferry. *The Palestinian-Israeli Conflict: A Basic Introduction*. London: Pluto Press, 2017.

Harris, Gardiner. "Pompeo Takes Aim at Global Institutions." *New York Times* (online), December 5, 2018.

Hashami, Sohail, ed. *State Sovereignty and Persistence in International Relations*. University Park, PA: Penn State University Press, 1997.

Hobbs, Thomas. *Leviathan*. Oxford, UK: Clarendon, 1989.

Jackson, Robert. *Sovereignty: The Evolution of an Idea*. New York: Polity Press. 2007.

Krasner, Stephen D. *Sovereignty: Organized Hypocrisy*. Princeton, NJ: Princeton University Press, 1999.

Locke, John. *Two Treatises on Government*. New York: Cambridge University Press, 1988.

Lyons, Gene M., and Michael Mastanduno, eds. *Beyond Westphalia: State Sovereignty and International Relations*. Baltimore, MD: Johns Hopkins University Press, 1995.

Morgan, Edmund S. *Inventing the People: The Rise of Popular Sovereignty in England and America* (revised edition). New York: W. W. Norton, 1989.

Muravchik, Joshua. *Making David into Goliath: How the World Turned against Israel*. New York: Encounter, 2016.

Rousseau, Jean-Jacques. *The Collected Works of Jean-Jacques Rousseau*. Hanover, NH: University Press of New England, 1990.

Shavit, Ari. *Promised Land: The Triumph and Tragedy of Israel*. New York: Spiegel and Grau, 2015.

Snow, Donald M. *The Middle East and American National Security: Forever Conflict and War?* Lanham, MD: Rowman & Littlefield, 2021.

———. *National Security* (seventh edition). London and New York: Routledge, 2020.

Van Creveld, Martin L. *The Land of Blood and Honey: The Rise of Modern Israel*. New York: Thomas Dunne, 2010.

2

National Interests and Power

Competing with China

Interests represent a second primary concept in international relations. They have an ambivalent relationship to sovereignty. Sovereignty means those interests are defined in national terms, making the determination and protection of national interests the key operational dictate and definition of sovereignty. At the same time, the pursuit of interests sometimes causes states to violate the sovereignty of other states.

The basic term "interests" has multiple meanings in different contexts, but the base of the concept comes from the French term *raison d'etat* (reason of state), which establishes national interests (the values of the sovereign states) above those of other claimants. In practice, determining interests is not so easy because people within and between states disagree fundamentally on the content and relative importance of interests as they affect themselves and other states. Moreover, interests come into conflict with those of other individuals and states, and they often are not amenable to easy resolution. The competitive pursuit of national interests by the world's sovereign states is thus highly controversial, ambiguous, and conflict-producing.

The interplay of conflicting interests is at the heart of much diplomatic activity, whether amicably conducted or more conflictual. Ultimately, resolving conflicts of national interests requires some or all the parties do things they would rather not do, which is the definition of power.

The resolution of conflicts of interest is often idiosyncratic, influenced by a complex of factors that is unique to the relations of affected states at different times. The application in this chapter between China and the United States reflects both change and uniqueness. Their relationship has been contentious since the communists gained control of the country in 1949 after a long civil war and turned violent when China sent "volunteers" into the Korean War to aid the North Koreans against the Americans in 1951. They remained antagonistic until the Chinese began to allow limited free enterprise in the early 1970s under Deng Xiaoping, a process in which the Americans enthusiastically participated. The have become military rivals in the twenty-first century. They are true "frenemies" (part friends, part enemies).

Principle: National Interest and Power

The term "national interest" occupies a virtually sacrosanct position in international political language. These interests represent the hierarchical values that states have. National interests and sovereignty are inextricably intertwined. Sovereignty dictates that the interests a state has are its most important concern and are called "vital interests." Preserving the status of important interests is the highest national priority and thus the supreme national interest. This attachment endows the concept of national interest with a virtually absolute importance and need for obeisance in even the most heated and contentious discussions. The primacy and necessity of preserving and promoting national interests is at the heart of international conflicts and their resolution. The use of force is one of the ways these conflicts may be resolved.

National interests are controversial. It is easy to state the definition of what constitutes an interest; the application of that definition to the substance of actual situations is difficult. The idea that there *are* conditions that serve national values is virtually unassailable; *what* those conditions may be in general or in the context of often ambiguous situations is quite another matter, and it is the basis for lively domestic and international debates about national interest that are subjective in nature and often difficult to resolve.

The Non-Intersubjective Nature of National Interest

Phrasing any issue in terms of the national interest gives it an aura of great importance and gravitas, because many people equate national interest and national security. Arguing something is in the national interest suggests that it is contributing to that most vital of national interests—the country's security from harm. Sometimes that equation is valid and sustainable, but at other times it is not so clearly the case, for one or both of two reasons. One is that the issue may not really be important enough for this elevation, and the other is that the position the advocate has on the issue may or may not be the best way to attain the goal. The abstract idea of national interest may be rock solid, but the proposed actions made in its name may not be.

There is a formalistic way to state this problem: *intersubjectivity*. The term comes from the philosophy of science, and it refers to whether all observers can view the same phenomenon in the same way. A useful synonym for the term is objectivity, and it means that for something to be intersubjective, it must be viewable in the same way by all observers. The statement that former president Donald Trump is a Republican is intersubjective; it is a fact that his membership in the Republican party can be viewed by everyone as true. The statement that Trump was a good (or bad) president or Republican is not intersubjective, because it requires a subjective interpretation that goes beyond objective fact to opinion, and people hold different opinions on things.

Questions of national interest are very much of this nature. Their core begins from some generally objective observation (a statement of fact), to which two additional characteristics, neither of them objective, are added. One is whether the issue is in fact a matter of interest and what degree of importance should be attached to doing something about it. The second characteristic consists of a prescription for appropriate action to alleviate whatever problem the situation creates. The first observation is generally objective: its truth or falsity can be demonstrated objectively. The other questions are subjective, because it is a matter of opinion what the nature and extent of the problem is and what needs to be done about it.

One can make questions of what is and is not in the national interest look more chaotic and contentious than they in fact are. Determining interests is an ongoing exercise within governments and analysts where there is broad agreement on the general categories of those interests and at least in general about how to handle them. The content of what is in the national interest does not change as much as do challenges to that interest and what those changes may portend. The key concept is the idea of vital interests, the sole property of sovereign states.

Operationalizing the National Interest: The Key Role of Vital Interests

Scholars and policy makers alike seek to make national interests more concrete and objective. No one doubts that national interests exist and are supreme in a system of sovereign states. Likewise, everyone agrees that not all interests are equally important, that the consequences of their non-realization differ depending on their relative importance, and that different levels and kinds of national exertion are appropriate to attain or maintain them.

A basic distinction is often made between those interests that are *vital* (VIs) for the country to realize and those that are *less-than-vital* (LTVs). VIs are generally defined as conditions that are so important to the state that it will not willingly compromise on their attainment. Achieving those interests may not always be within the power of the state, but they are the baseline of a country's sense of security. This definition helps explain why states will not allow an authority superior to themselves to adjudicate their differences, because a verdict against them could affect their vital interests and would be unacceptable and likely would be resisted or disobeyed. LTV interests, on the other hand, are matters of descending but lesser importance to the state that would cause varying but not basic discomfort or inconvenience to the state and whose non-realization may not be entirely intolerable.

The VI-LTV distinction is critical because it is generally considered the effective boundary between those situations where the state will and will not consider the recourse to violence to attain them. In simplest terms, some VIs may be potentially worth going to war over to ensure; LTVs do not normally justify the recourse to force. This distinction is less sharp than the simple statement may imply; there will always be disagreement about the worthiness and appropriateness of force in a specific situation. For this reason, it may be better to think of the boundary between VIs and LTVs as a "confidence interval" within which disagreement exists rather than as a sharp line.

These distinctions are important enough that they bear further elaboration both analytically and as a guide for political action. The late Donald Nuechterlein, in a 1991 text, laid out a more elaborate way of distinguishing interests based in a four-by-four matrix reproduced as table 2.1.

The two dimensions are hierarchical in descending order of importance to the state. On the intensity dimension, the survival of the state is clearly its most intense interest, and the inability to secure that survival leaves attaining other interests moot. Not all vital interests entail challenges to national survival, but they are important enough that states will engage in serious, including military, efforts to attain them. Other problems, like those associated with occasionally deep and intractable economic conflicts such as those arising between the United States and China, may fall into this category. The differentiations are not precise or clearly intersubjective, but major interests are matters that would inconvenience and trouble a state (the terms of an international trade agreement might be an example) but whose non-realization would be tolerable. Peripheral interests attach to conditions the state might disfavor but to which it can adapt. The U.S. periodic border dispute with Mexico probably belongs between vital and major intensity.

The other dimension refers to the content of interests. It is also hierarchically arranged. Clearly, matters of homeland security are of the most basic nature and can be either survival or vital in intensity, depending on how extensive the threat is. Conquests of states clearly qualify as survival in intensity; the annexation of a small part of national territory may be vital but not survival-threatening. Because the commodiousness of life within a state is related to its economic standing, economic well-being is also important, and it probably can take on the characteristic of vital or major importance depending on the situation. A favorable world order and the promotion of American values are presumably at a lower order of vitality.

The Nuechterlein matrix may help clarify some thinking about the relative priority of securing certain national interests, but it does not resolve all matters nor provide ironclad guidance over what the country should do all of the time. All situations are unique, meaning some judgments must be made in all cases, and people will disagree about the nature and importance of given challenges to interests: into what pair of categories from the matrix does an individual situation fall? How important is it? Based on this assessment, what quality of actions are justifiable to realize the affected interest and which are not? Clearly, the most important consequential differentiation involves the boundary between VIs and LTV interests. As noted, this line is really a confidence interval (or band), because not everyone accepts the same frontier at which an interest passes from LTV to vital, and vice versa.

Table 2.1.   Nuechterlein National Interest Matrix

Basic Interest at Stake	Intensity of Interest			
	Survival	Vital	Major	Peripheral
Homeland Defense				
Economic Well-Being				
Favorable World Order				
Values Promotion				

National and Other Levels of Interest

The concepts of sovereignty and national interest are intertwined in another way that leads some to question the idea that national interest, like sovereignty, should be as supreme and overriding as it is. The objection suggests that state sovereignty has pernicious effects and has its parallel in the definition of the supremacy of national interest as opposed to the interests of individuals and the interests that go beyond those of states (international interests).

The obvious implication of elevating national interest to conceptual supremacy is that as a result, interests at other levels occupy a lesser priority and importance, a consequence with which not everyone agrees. They are asserting other levels of interest that some argue are of equally or even greater importance than those of national interest.

Objections come from both ends of a spectrum from interests that affect individual humans to those that affect the human condition. At one extreme are *individual* interests, the most important of which center on individual human rights and the conditions that maximize (or minimize) the survival and prosperity of individuals. At the other end of the spectrum are *international* interests, those conditions and actions that contribute to or detract from maximum survivability and prosperity for everyone. The levels problem exists because the pursuit of one level may come at the expense of the others. More specifically, the pursuit of national interest as the supreme value may endanger or preclude the pursuit of individual or international interests.

Individual interests represent an extension of the arguments for popular sovereignty that can be endangered by an unfettered pursuit of national interests in several ways. Probably the most obvious is when national interests collide with those of another state, are sufficiently important to both that they cannot compromise on them, and thus result in the resort to armed violence. In that circumstance, individuals may well be involuntarily required to fight in the ensuing hostilities, a participation to which those placed in harm's way may object and which certainly infringes on the pursuit of the individual right to survive.

The other competing level is international interests, conditions that transcend national boundaries and which can only be addressed by international efforts. This level becomes a concern and source of international tension and disagreement particularly when efforts to pursue national interests result in international effects that both make the disagreement over national interests greater and endanger the interests of humans as a species.

Possibly the most notable political science example of the clash of national and international interest levels is a construct called the *security dilemma*. This idea was first articulated by John H. Herz in a 1951 book and referred to the situation where one state, feeling insecure in its security relationship with another state, takes actions to increase its sense of security. In the classic depiction, the threatened state builds up its military power to cancel a perceived inferiority, and this action creates a similar reaction by the other state (the dynamic is often referred to as the action-reaction phenomenon) which, in the classic example, did not previously harbor animosity to the threatened state. It interprets the other's buildup as a hostile act and increases its own armament which, in turn, causes the other state to arm even more, and the situation spirals into an arms race in which both states end up being less secure than they were in the first place. This dynamic, as pointed out by scholars like Jervis and Waltz, is most destabilizing when nuclear weapons are the currency of the arms race. Waltz's *Theory of International Politics*, reprinted in 2010 before his 2013 death, remains a classic statement.

National interests are more controversial than many who emphasize them lead people to believe. The concept flows from the notion of a world of sovereign states each concerned almost exclusively with its own narrowly defined well-being. Raising national interest to supremacy, however, accentuates conflict and competition between its members and adds to the use of power—including military force—that may be invoked to get other states to do what they would prefer not to do. The concept in application is also much more fluid than its apparent immutability suggests. Interests and conflicts between them do change, as the contemporary relations between the United States and China demonstrate.

Application: Competing with China, the Ultimate "Frenemy"

The interests that states have and which interact and conflict with the interests of other states are the basis of a great deal of international relations in practice. In the bilateral relations between states, there are generally some areas where interests coincide and lead to cooperation, and there are other areas where the parties disagree, sometimes strenuously enough to strain relations between them. When such incompatibilities arise (as they often do), reconciliation of differences becomes an interest in and of itself. It is a complex, often bewildering process that is itself highly contentious both within and between the conflicting parties. It also describes well how the United States and China manage their interactions. Given their sizes and capabilities, that interaction of interests is arguably the most consequential dynamic in world politics.

Interests are thus competitive, ambivalent, and interactive. Competition arises because the two states hold and promote competing and contradictory values that must somehow be reconciled. Few international values and interactions are unanimously held by all states. Ambivalence arises from trying to assess best outcomes for the parties, a process on which there is always disagreement. They are interactive, because the pursuit of an interest by one state will often produce adverse effects on other states. The security dilemma is a particularly vivid example.

This confusing process is particularly important when the states involved are arguably the most powerful states in the world and where a serious deterioration in their interest interaction could, at worst, deteriorate to war, a prospect that has (arguably somewhat hysterically) been used to describe the direction of U.S.-Chinese relations. That relationship is evolving, and it has, particularly since the rise of Deng Xiaoping, had elements of both conflict and cooperation. On his nightly show on Comedy Central between 2005 and 2014 (*The Colbert Report*), comedian/talk show host Stephen Colbert revived a term originally devised in 1953 to describe the relationship. He described the two countries as "frenemies," friends on some matters and enemies on others. Keeping their interests on the friendly side of the dichotomy has become a key dynamic of contemporary international relations.

The United States and China: A Sketch

During the twilight of a Trump administration that had become increasingly unilateralist and antagonistic toward its Chinese frenemy, relations appeared to deteriorate, some would argue radically, from the friendly to the antagonistic end of the spectrum of relationship to the point that particularly militant unilateralists even spoke of an increasing likelihood of war between the world's two most powerful countries. Given that both states are major nuclear weapons possessors and that violence between them could devolve to nuclear exchange that would threaten the mutual interest both have in survival, such a path in the relationship is clearly irrational and potentially in the *worst* interest of both. That does not mean their relationship has not become more conflictual, even confrontational, only that the harshest hyperbole serves neither.

The two countries are the two most powerful countries in the world, meaning their interests and how they conflict—especially with one another—is at the heart of contemporary geopolitics. The emergence of China as the primary competitor with the United States is the major international change from the late twentieth to the twenty-first century. When the Soviet Union imploded in 1991, the United States emerged as the sole major power in the system—a period of pax Americana that followed the Cold War. In the wake of 9/11 and other shifts, China's star has risen to the point of arguable co-equality with that of the United States, and the erratic international behavior of the Trump administration added to the change in the relative positions and interest pursuit by the two countries. Returning the relationship to its old or a more favorable new configuration is a high priority of the Biden incumbency.

Competition between the two countries has been building since the Chinese system began reforming itself in the wake of the death of People's Republic of China (PRC) founding leader Mao Zedung in 1976. It accelerated under the economic leadership of Deng Xiaoping and has turned decidedly more geopolitical since Xi Jinping achieved control in the last decade. The net result of change has been to make China a far more formidable rival than it had been, meaning Chinese pursuit of interests at odds with those of the United States has increased. The major questions are how ominous these trends are and where they are headed.

The import of change has been evident for some time. Henry Kissinger, a prime architect of the opening of China in 1972, argued in a 2016 *Atlantic* interview with Jeffrey Goldberg that "our relationship with China will shape the international order in the long term. The United States and China will be the world's most consequential countries." The net result, Campbell and Ratner maintain, is that "Washington now faces its most dynamic and formidable competitor in modern history." That challenge is largely manifested in the clash of national interests and their interaction in a bilateral relationship that has historically not been among the world's most stable and predictable. To understand the pattern of their interaction, one must begin by looking at the erratic history of U.S.-PRC relations and at the comparison of the two countries as the system's "superpowers" in contemporary international relations. This leads to the crucial question of interests of the two countries that come into conflict with one another. The bottom line of the comparisons is to allow an interests-driven assessment of the likely direction of U.S.-Chinese relations in at least the near future.

The Schizophrenic Nature of the United States and China Relationship

The United States and China could hardly be more unalike, and their stark differences help explain why their relationship has been erratic and changing. The history of relations between them is short and has been schizophrenic, and it has been evolving rapidly over the last half century. To capture its bizarre nature, between 1949 (when the PRC finally consolidated its control over the Chinese mainland) and 1972, the United States steadfastly refused to acknowledge the existence of that regime, instead pretending that the Nationalist regime of Chiang Kai-shek, which had lost the Chinese civil war and was forced to flee to Taiwan/Formosa, was the only legitimate regime of both the mainland and Taiwan. The effect was to deny the political existence of over one-quarter of humankind, and it was a fiction that persisted until 1972, when then president Richard M. Nixon, the staunchest anti-communist to occupy the White House, used a visit to Beijing by the U.S. table tennis team as a ruse to open relations. Once the barrier was broken, relations exploded between the two countries largely based on economic interaction. The result was an increasingly close relationship that carried over into the second decade of the twenty-first century and the emergence of a militantly geopolitical Chinese regime whose expansive definition of the Chinese national interest has largely defined an increasingly conflictual view of the interaction between the two countries.

The Contemporary Comparison and Trends

A statistical comparison of the two countries makes them appear similar and comparable, although such comparisons can be misleading given the incomparable historical experience and possible geopolitical trajectories of the two countries. In sheer size, they are similar, with land masses that are comparable. The United States has the fourth largest land mass in the world, whereas China is fifth. The Chinese population in 2020 was 1.394 billion, largest in the world, whereas the American population of 332 million was third among sovereign countries. The Chinese GDP had risen to make the Chinese economy the largest in the world, followed by that of the United States. Translated into per capita figures, China ranks ninety-sixth in the world, whereas the United States GDP per capita figure is nineteenth. As a percentage of GDP, American defense spending at 3.42 percent of GDP is considerably higher than that of China at 1.87 percent. (All figures are from the *CIA World Factbook, 2020–2021*.)

These measures provide the contemporary condition of relations between the two countries. Their roots are far deeper, although the details do not concern us here. China is the world's oldest continuous civilization and during its heyday dominated the world. The Chinese, to some extent by self-assessment, considered themselves so superior to other civilizations that they decided to isolate themselves from the "barbarians," defined as anybody who was not Han Chinese; the Great Wall is the great symbol of their self-imposed isolation. The isolationist decision was, however, double-edged in effect: it kept the barbarians out, but as other, primarily Western, civilizations thrived, it also excluded outside ideas. China stagnated and became comparatively weak.

The culmination of this process emerged in the nineteenth century, which is known in China as the Century of Humiliation. It began when the West (notably Britain) occupied parts of China during the Opium War of 1839–1842. China had become so weak it could not successfully resist Western intrusion. The humiliation continued into the twentieth century. During World War II, the Chinese could not successfully repulse the occupation of large parts of the country by a hostile Asian rival—Japan—and the humiliation continued until the Chinese Communists overcame Chiang Kai-shek's nationalists and won the civil war in 1949. China has been at least nominally communist ever since.

The American role in the experience was marginal at best. During the nineteenth century, some American missionaries sought to convert resentful Chinese to Christianity, but the Americans largely stayed on the outside, favoring but not decisively aiding their Nationalist Chinese allies (an association that helped poison U.S.-PRC relations until the 1970s). The two countries interacted during the Korean War, when Chinese "volunteers" entered that fray against South Korea and the United States–led United Nations.

The contemporary relationship emerged in the 1970s and continues to evolve. The first step was the opening of relations by Richard Nixon in 1972, culminating in full recognition of the PRC by President Carter in 1979. As that process was unfolding, Mao died in 1976, and he was succeeded by Deng Xiaoping.

Deng came to power intent on reasserting Chinese world prominence by reestablishing a vibrant China capable of competing with the world, essentially a revival of the Chinese interest in being treated as *the* most prominent world power. This desire would manifest itself in a greater geopolitical set of ambitions in the 2010s under Xi, but its roots were found in the need to make China a more competitive society than it had been. The vehicle was the Four Modernizations.

The Deng program encompassed four areas of modernization—agriculture, science and technology, economic strength, and the military. All were areas of perceived Chinese backwardness: a marginally productive rural peasant agricultural sector, an inferior scientific and technological foundation, inadequate economic power to enhance its program, and a military structure that could not establish Chinese preeminence as a geopolitical force. The most consequential modernization was the economy, the expansion of which was necessary to induce change in the other areas. The heart of economic reform added generous amounts of capitalist practices to Marxist principles. The major vehicle was the creation of so-called Special Economic Zones (SEZs), areas where Western entrepreneurs could set up businesses in cooperation with Chinese counterparts. The SEZs were mutually beneficial: Western (including American) businesses could move manufacturing ventures to China and benefit from lower labor costs, and Chinese entrepreneurs could benefit from Western capital and expertise. The SEZs became the engine of Chinese resurgence to the point that the Chinese economy has, as noted, surpassed the U.S. economy and caused some of the concern about the contemporary competition. Without the modernizations and American enthusiastic complicity in their implementation, the conflict of interest between the two countries might look considerably different, including less menacing.

The rise of China started by Deng has created great concern about the future of Chinese and American relations, the relative power and ability of the United States to compete with China in world geopolitics, and even the prospect of war between them. These concerns are not baseless, but they can also be overstated. Chinese growth has been spectacular, but it is not without limits. The economy has slowed in recent years, and the Chinese population is both aging and shrinking. An older population is less productive and will place real strains on the social security system, and the workforce is shrinking. Mitter reports that starting in 2029, the population will decline by about five million a year, and the Chinese are unlikely to compensate with immigrants (the classic American solution). Energy problems plague China during its transition away from fossil fuels, and China faces serious water problems (dropping water tables). Moreover, any shooting conflict between the two countries could escalate to nuclear war, the danger of which is a serious brake on precipitous actions. China and the United States face significant conflicts of interest and disagreement; it is probably imprudent to be hysterical about them.

Conflicts of Interest: Economics and Geopolitics

There are serious disagreements and conflicts between the two countries describable in terms of conflicts of interest. As is often the case, the most troublesome of these disagreements are in the areas of geopolitics and economics. The two areas are also related to one another. Economic success can provide resources for additional military capabilities with which to realize interests, and military action or its threat can provide opportunities for economic expansion. It is this synergism in the interaction of interests that may be the most distinctive aspect of the clash of interests between the United States and China.

Economics. Until the rise of Ji, the economic challenge posed by China to American economic interests was the most prominent aspect of the interaction. Mitter in January 2021 listed four primary goals of the Chinese Communist Party (CCP), and they were heavily economic in content: firming up CCP control of Chinese society, encouraging consumerism at home and abroad, expanding global influence, and developing and exporting China's most advanced technologies. This emphasis is particularly aggressive in the area of climate control, where the Chinese have developed and are marketing emissions control technology worldwide, some more advanced than American efforts. The Trump administration was basically hostile to Paris limits on greenhouse problems (which he viewed as an international effort to disadvantage the United States economically), but the Biden administration has both moved to return the United States to the climate accord and to reestablish preeminence in the international competition over spreading the associated technologies worldwide. While China has made inroads in this competition, some of the problems China will encounter (see last section) could tilt the scales back in American favor.

Geopolitics: The other major area of interest collision is over premier influence in Asia between the two powers. By virtue of geographic position, China seeks to reassert its historic role as the dominant, even suzerain, power in East Asia, spreading from Siberia southward to Southeast Asia and westward at least to the Indian subcontinent and beyond along trade routes from east to west. U.S. interests in this area are more hortatory than geopolitical: the Americans decry Chinese aggressiveness toward the Uighurs in central Asian China and worry about Chinese penetration of the oil-rich Middle East. Of those interests, penetration of the Persian Gulf is historically the most important, but as the world moves away from dependence on fossil fuels (including Middle East reserves), that factor could moderate somewhat.

The real point of interest intersection and conflict is along the Pacific Rim. Largely as a result of the outcome of World War II in the Pacific, the United States developed primary interests in the states along the east coast of the Pacific: Japan, South Korea, and Taiwan are the most obvious examples of countries with close political and economic-geopolitical bonds with the United States. All are major economic partners of the Americans, and there are close politico-military interests for the United States in each. Until the economic and more recently geopolitical rise of China, control of the coastline was largely moot; China now challenges the economies of these American allies, and this threat to American interests could expand as Chinese military, and especially naval, power increases.

There are three specific points of geopolitical interest incompatibility along the Pacific Rim. The *Korean peninsula, and especially North Korea*, has been the most prominent since 1950. The premier Chinese interest in the peninsula is ensuring that there is no hostile country on its boundaries, and this means supporting a North Korean regime with which China is otherwise not close. Talk of unifying the peninsula into one Korea or in expanded U.S. relations with North Korea are particularly troubling to the Chinese. The political future of the Koreas is a major point of interest conflict between the two countries.

Taiwan is the second point of contention. When the Chinese civil war ended in 1949 with communist victory, the American-backed nationalist government of Chiang Kai-shek fled across the Formosan Strait to Taiwan, where they established themselves as an alternate government. Ever since, the mainland communists and the nationalists have both maintained that they are the legitimate government of both the PRC and Taiwan. Prior to 1972, the United States supported the Taiwanese claim, and the issue remains unresolved. It is, however, true that much of the developmental capital in the PRC comes from Taiwanese sources, and that the recent PRC treatment of Hong Kong has made Taiwanese independence more of an issue than it might otherwise be.

More recently, the fate of the *South China Sea* has been a source of disagreement with some military content. The issue is straightforward: the Chinese government claims the South China Sea, including petroleum deposits beneath its surface, as part of Chinese territorial waters despite lying outside the twelve-mile limit that is the international limit on control of bodies of water touching a country's shores. The United States in particular refuses to honor China's territorial claims, and American and Chinese vessels and aircraft regularly confront one another over or on its surface.

Prospects for Future Interaction: Conclusions

There are clear areas where the interests of the United States and China collide that define the issues between them, but they have remained manageable because conflict deterioration serves neither country: proper relations represent a more important interest than the possible outcome of any deterioration in relations. As a result, differences are managed. Commerce between them is more important than the benefits of confrontation, and international flash points like the buffer between China and Western powers, like South Korea, have greater salience than honoring South Korean desires for peninsular reunification, for instance.

In the final years of the Trump administration, relations cooled between the two powers to the point where one heard the possibility of war between the two openly discussed. The lens of interests suggests these prospects were remote, even nonsensical. The added variable is nuclear weapons. Both China and the United States possess nuclear arsenals which, if unleashed against one another, would destroy both. What national interest could possibly be served by following a course of action that would result in national destruction? At least for nuclear-armed countries in competition with other nuclear powers, the dynamic of survival-motivated prudence suggests that the nuclear genie can moderate rather than exacerbate conflicts of interest. It also suggests the variation in the "instruments of power" states can invoke in support of national goals, the subject of the next chapter.

Study/Discussion Questions

1. Define the terms "interest" and "national" and how they are combined as a basic principle of international relations. Why are they so important?
2. What does it mean to say national interests are non-intersubjective? How does this make them controversial in political discussions?
3. What is the Nuechterlein matrix? Describe it and how difficult it can be to apply in individual situations.

Emphasize the VI-LTV interest distinction in your discussion.
4. What is a conflict of interest? Apply the concept to individuals and states. Also, what is the problem of levels of interest? What are the competing levels? How may they conflict with national interests?
5. What is a frenemy? Why is the term used to describe contemporary U.S. relations with China?

6. Why has the U.S.-PRC relationship been referred to as schizophrenic? Describe that relationship over time in these terms.
7. Describe the evolution of China from the Century of Humiliation through the Four Modernizations.

Why is that progression important to understanding contemporary Chinese policies and goals?
8. Describe the major aspects of U.S.-Chinese conflicts of interest. Are any likely to lead to war? Why or why not?

Bibliography

Allison, Graham T. *Destined for War: Can America and China Escape Thucydides' Trap?* Boston, MA: Houghton-Mifflin, 2017.
———, and Dimitri K. Simes. "The National Interest." *The National Interest*, 2017.
Art, Robert, and Kenneth A. Waltz, eds. *The Use of Force: Military Power and International Politics* (seventh edition). Lanham, MD: Rowman & Littlefield, 2009.
Blanchette, Jude. "Xi's Gamble: The Race to Consolidate Power and Stave Off Disaster." *Foreign Affairs* 100, no. 4 (July/August 2021): 10–19.
Brown, Kerry. *CEO China: The Rise of Xi Jinping*. London: I. B. Tauris, 2016.
Campbell, Charles. "China Steps Closer to Despotism as Xi Becomes Leader for Life." *Time* 191, no. 10 (March 12, 2018): 5–6.
Campbell, Kurt M., and Ely Ratner. "The China Reckoning: How Beijing Defied American Expectations." *Foreign Affairs* 92, no. 2 (March/April 2018): 60–70.
Central Intelligence Agency. *CIA World Factbook, 2020–2021*. New York: Skyhorse Publishing, 2021.
Christensen, Thomas J. *The China Challenge: Shaping the Choices of a Rising Power*. New York: W. W. Norton, 2015.
Davis, Bob, and Lingling Wei. *Superpower Showdown: How the Battle between Trump and Xi Threatens a New Cold War*. New York: Harper Business, 2020.
Eberstadt, Nicholas, and Ashton Verdery. "China's Shrinking Families: The Demographic Trend That Could Curtail Beijing's Ambitions." *Foreign Affairs* (online), April 7, 2021.
Economy, Elizabeth. *The Third Revolution: Xi Jinping and the New Chinese State*. Oxford, UK: Oxford University Press, 2018.
———, and Michael Levi. *By All Means Necessary: How China's Resources Quest Is Changing the World*. Oxford, UK: Oxford University Press, 2014.
French, Howard W. "China's Twilight Years: As Immigrants Replenish America, China's Population Is Shrinking and Aging." *Atlantic* 317, no. 5 (June 2016): 15–17.
Friedman, Thomas L. "The First Law of Petropolitics." *Foreign Policy* (May/June 2006), 28–36.
Fromkin, David. *The Independence of Nations*. New York: Praeger Special Studies, 1981.
Goldstein, Lyle G. *Meeting China Halfway: How to Defuse US-China Rivalry*. Washington, DC: Georgetown University Press, 2015.
Hardy, Alfredo Toro. *China versus the US: Who Will Prevail?* Singapore: World Scientific Publishing Co., 2020.
Heikkila, Eric J. *China from a US Policy Perspective*. New York and London: Routledge, 2020.
Heilman, Sebastian. *China's Political System*. Lanham, MD: Rowman & Littlefield, 2016.
Herz, John H. *Political Realism and Political Idealism*. Chicago, IL: University of Chicago Press, 1951.

Jervis, Robert. *Perception and Misperception in International Politics*. Princeton, NJ: University of Princeton Press, 1978.

Joseph, William A. *China: An Introduction* (third edition). Oxford, UK: Oxford University Press, 2019.

Kaplan, Robert D. *The Coming Anarchy: Shattering Dreams of the Post Cold War*. New York: Random House, 2000.

Krasner, Stephen D. *Defending the National Interest: Raw Materials Investments and U.S. Foreign Policy*. Princeton, NJ: Princeton University Press, 1978.

Lampton, David M., Selina Ho, and Cheng-Chwee Kuik. *Rivers of Iron: Railroads and Chinese Power in Southeast Asia*. Berkeley: University of California Press, 2020.

Lanteigne, Marc. *Chinese Foreign Policy: An Introduction* (third edition). New York and London: Routledge, 2015.

McDougal, Walter A. *The Tragedy of U.S. Foreign Policy: How America's Civil Religion Betrayed the National Interest*. New Haven, CT: Yale University Press, 2016.

Mitter, Rana. "The World China Wants: How Power Will—and Won't—Reshape Chinese Ambitions." *Foreign Affairs* 100, no. 1 (January/February 2021): 161–74.

Nuechterlein, Donald. *America Recommitted: United States National Interests in a Reconstructed World*. Lexington: University of Kentucky Press, 1991.

Pei, Minxin. *China's Gang Capitalism: The Dynamics of Regime Decay*. Cambridge, MA: Harvard University Press, 2016.

Shambaugh, David, ed. *China and the World*. Oxford, UK: University of Oxford Press, 2020.

———. *China's Future*. Cambridge, UK: Polity Books, 2016.

———. *Where Great Powers Meet: America and China in Southeast Asia*. Oxford, UK: Oxford University Press, 2020.

Snow, Donald M. *Regional Cases in U.S. Foreign Policy* (second edition). Lanham, MD: Rowman & Littlefield, 2018.

———. *National Security* (seventh edition). New York and London: Routledge, 2020.

Sutter, Robert G. *Chinese Foreign Relations: Power and Policy since the Cold War*. Lanham, MD: Rowman & Littlefield, 2016.

———. *US-China Relations: Perilous Past, Uncertain Future*. Lanham, MD: Rowman & Littlefield, 2017.

Waltz, Kenneth. *Theory of International Politics* (revised edition). Long Grove, IL: Waveland Press, 2010.

Xuetong, Yan. "Becoming Strong: The New Chinese Foreign Policy." *Foreign Affairs* 100, no. 4 (July/August 2021): 40–47.

3

The Instruments of Power

Trying to End the Syrian Civil War

The first two chapters have laid out much of the basis for organizing and understanding the basic dynamics of international relations. The bedrock principle, of course, is sovereignty, which makes the international order anarchic if not necessarily chaotic. The definition of state interests as supreme and the nonnegotiability of some matters of interests—vital interests—means the ultimate method states possess to retain or expand that which they deem to be most important to them is through self-help. Some challenge this construction, but it remains intact.

The major method through which states realize their interests is the exercise of power, and this had led many analysts to refer to international politics as *power politics*. In an anarchical system, the member states have conditions of existence on which they will not willingly compromise if they can avoid doing so, because those conditions are deemed vital to the state's acceptable situation in the world. It means they succeed to the extent they possess the relevant ability to get other states to do what they deem vital to their interests, even if those conditions are antithetical to the equally strongly held interests of others.

The generic term for how states array their resources to impose or convince others to do what they want is known as the *instruments of power*. Broadly, this term refers to the accumulation of capabilities that the state has at its avail to convince or coerce others to accept their will. There are various categories of instruments, and one of them, diplomacy, is introduced in the next chapter. There is some disagreement about the kinds of capability that should be considered in classifying the instruments of power, and the list expands as new forces associated with technology expand the list of potential instruments.

Controversy surrounds the instruments of power concept in some quarters, because one instrument, arguably the most important or ultimate category, is the recourse to military force. Those who seek a world in which differences between countries are increasingly settled by nonviolent means decry the implicit emphasis the concept places on the threat or use of force. The realist paradigm has been a leading construct for understanding the conflictual nature of international relations and is still the dominant paradigm in most policy circles, and it illustrates this dominance with considerable clarity. At the same time, there are enough countervailing limits on the application of the instruments to suggest that their influence is not universal or straightforward in all situations, making that application difficult.

The Syrian Civil War has raged since 2011, when it erupted as one theater of the largely abortive Arab Spring, and it demonstrates the complexity and difficulty of applying the instruments of power construct. The carnage in that conflict has been horrendous, including over a half-million killed and over half the population forced into being internal or external refugees, according to August 2020 U.S. Institute of Peace estimates. Reaching a peace settlement to begin the process or returning normalcy to the country and its citizenry would seem an obvious goal to which applications of power would seem an approach, but this has not been the case. Prominent reasons include the conflict of multiple basic interests and thus the inability for potentially helpful states to agree either on desired outcomes or accepted instrumental means to accomplish them.

Principle: The Instruments of Power

Power, the ability to get someone to do something they otherwise would not do, is a vital building block in understanding how international politics works. In one sense, all politics—domestic and international—are power based, because the heart of politics is the allocation of scarce resources among individuals and groups with different claims on those resources. The difference between domestic and international politics is contextual. Domestic politics normally proceeds within a framework of rules and practices (e.g., laws and institutions) that specify how allocations will occur and includes mechanisms for enforcing whatever choices are made. The purposeful anarchy of international politics creates a contrasting context within which there are no authoritative structures to allocate how resource conflicts are to be resolved and, in most cases, no authoritative means to enforce divisions of resources peacefully.

The result is that international politics are inherently based in power: states achieve their goals to the extent they can do so themselves—known as the principle of self-help. Lacking institutions to resolve differences and enforce the outcomes, the result is the need to have power to ensure favorable outcomes.

The basic concept of power is ubiquitous and ambiguous. Power is used so generally to describe relationships in international relations that it is difficult to imagine situations that do not have a power element. At the same time, there is disagreement about what power *is*. The most common academic debate is between power as a physical commodity or attribute and power as a relationship. The first emphasis tends to look at the attributes that a state possesses—the amount of military power is an obvious example. This approach produces concrete measures of the attributes a state has at its avail and thus allows countries to be ranked according to how much power they have. It facilitates guessing how a conflict between states will come out based on a comparison of measures of power and also allows quantification of power attributes, an important emphasis in much modern international political analysis. Viewing power in relational terms is more subjective and less observable. It emphasizes the *perception* of relevant comparisons of power in determining the outcome of conflicts. It operates more at the psychological level of participants acting based on their perceptions of relevant factors.

The Vietnam War between 1965 and 1973 (the period of American active combat in that country) illustrates the distinction. The American purpose in intervening in that country's civil war was to assist the government of the Republic of Vietnam (RVN, or South Vietnam) to prevail in the southern half of the country, whereas the opposition members of the National Liberation Front (the military component of which was the Viet Cong) and the armed forces of the Democratic Republic of Vietnam (DRV, or North Vietnam) sought to avoid that outcome and to unify the country under their control. Because these outcomes were mutually exclusive and neither side would accept the other's victory, power would have to be imposed on one side by the other; the United States sought to augment the power of the RVN by intervening with a military force that numbered over 500,000 at its zenith.

By any objective power comparison, the United States and the RVN should have prevailed, but they did not. The application of the military instrument of power, after all, matched the world's most powerful country in military terms with an opponent that American president Lyndon B. Johnson depicted as a "piddling, piss-ant little country" (quoted in Chua). How could the United States have lost? The answer is that it applied the instruments of power incorrectly.

The mistake shows why comparisons of power are ambiguous. The comparison showing the United States and the RVN could not lose was based on viewing power as a property rather than a relationship and was incorrect, for at least three reasons that point to power as a relational concept. First, it failed to reflect an analysis of the situation correctly. The Vietnam War was more than a territorial struggle—it was a clash over the future shape of the Southeast Asian peninsula. The Americans saw it as a territorial contest, whereas many Vietnamese saw it as an opportunity to rid themselves of a Chinese minority that controlled 70 to 80 percent of the country's wealth and was despised for it. As Chua puts it, "In effect, the U.S.-backed regime was asking the South Vietnamese to fight and die—and kill their northern brethren—in order to keep the Chinese rich." This led to the second reason: the war was simply more important to North Vietnamese than it was to the United States and the RVN. Third, the United States was backing the wrong side and in fact had little stake in the outcome. It had a lesser resolve and eventually tired of the contest and left. The United States and its ally won the power comparison of material power, but it lost the relational battle for "the hearts and minds of men," which ultimately proved more important.

The point is that comparisons of power must take various factors into account, and some will prove more prescient than others in concrete applications. If there is a concrete, irrefutable formula for applying the instruments of power that would allow predictions of outcomes with great accuracy, we do not know it at this time. As a result, the application of the instruments of power remains subjective, as much an art as a science.

Delineating the Instruments of Power

There is general agreement about what the concept of instruments of power is, and there is also agreement that the problem is increasing. From the early days of the modern state system, there were generally three universally acknowledged instruments: the military, economic, and political/diplomatic. These reflected the kinds of capabilities states possessed and could harness to achieve national ends. That list expanded during the twentieth century to include categories like information, intellectual prowess, financial strength, and even the sophistication of law enforcement power in different places. Citing categories from the *U.S. Army War College Guide to National Security Issues*, *Wikipedia* adds other categories, including geography, resources, population, and psychological strength. The list is expandable—for instance, cybercapability (see chapter 12) could easily be added, and there will undoubtedly be more.

No list is thus comprehensive, but one can list and briefly describe the accepted candidates and how they can potentially be applied in different situations. The three traditional instruments have formed the basis for most calculations until recently. They can be thought of as ascending in potential severity, and each has a series of suboptions that can be applied in different circumstances.

Diplomacy, as discussed in chapter 4, is the most "civilized" form. Its core is the use of persuasion by national diplomats and other political figures to convince an opponent to accept an outcome that one favors. To be effective, diplomacy requires a level of civility and willingness to compromise that has declined in an environment where partisan political practice, and notably political actors with little or no diplomatic training or understanding, have intruded.

Recourse to the economic instrument has increased as the use of traditional diplomacy has waned. The most common form of economic action is the threat or imposition of some form of economic sanctions against an opponent that will not conform to some demand. Freezing access to a country's funds held in another country (a favorite American tactic against Iran) is an example. The idea is to create enough economic discomfort that the recipient will relent to the demands of the sanctioning party. The effectiveness of sanctions is mixed at best. As well, targets are often more resistant to being coerced by these actions than anticipated. For another, quite often sanctions have an adverse effect on the party imposing them, and relenting is hard to disguise as anything other than capitulation, an admission states are reluctant to make.

The third traditional instrument is military power. It is generally based in the threat to cause physical injury or harm if the other party fails to comply to whatever demand the threatening party issues. It is, in most cases, the most volatile form of threat, because if the threat is not honored, it may require carrying out military action, in which case both sides are likely to suffer to some degree. Military threats by nuclear weapons–possessing states have the further danger that, no matter how unlikely the prospect may be in any given situation, escalation is always possible. Less extreme uses of the military instrument include restrictions on arms sales or pulling back from military commitments.

In addition to this traditional trinity, information has become an accepted part of the arsenal of instruments. The collection of information about rivals is, of course, a venerable practice generally thought of as the product of espionage of one sort or another, but modern technology has expanded this concept. Electronic technology and the whole area of cyberspace has expanded the ability of states to interfere in the activities of opponents, as with the Russian electronic interference in the 2016 American presidential election; this is a precedent likely to spread more widely to other countries like China and will be an ongoing source of influence on the interactions between affected countries.

Limits of Power

Determining the utility of the instruments of power in specific situations is not a simple matter of counting how much of a given capability those engaged in a relationship possess and assuming whoever has the most capability will prevail. The comparison is not irrelevant, but its importance varies by situation.

The application of the instruments is both psychological and situation-specific. The decision to accede to a demand (have power exercised against it) or not is a psychological decision that entails calculations on both sides. At least three factors are relevant to that specificity. All are leavened by the tendency, especially by the world's most powerful countries and least experienced leaders, to overestimate the utility and effectiveness of the instruments.

Situation-specificity refers to the relevance of a given element of power to a specific application. The United States, for instance, is by most measures the most powerful country in the world, and the ultimate expression of that strength is nuclear weapons. But for what applications of power are those weapons effective instruments for convincing other states to accede to American interests? The answer is that the utility is circumscribed and specific to situations where those weapons are relevant—which are limited in number. By any measure, for instance, the United States has overwhelmingly more military power than almost any small African state. So what? Can the United States threaten to initiate a nuclear war against Upper Volta or a conventional invasion of Burkino Faso? It could issue such a threat, but nobody (and especially those at whom the threat was directed) would believe the threat or be overly influenced by it. The situation would simply not warrant carrying out the threat.

If they are to be effective, the use of threats to employ the instruments of power must be believable and their consequences acceptable. Is it believable that many states would be willing to carry out major threats against very weak states knowing that such an action would be almost universally condemned by the international community? If outcomes are viewed as important enough, some states (Russia, for instance, in its annexation of Crimea) might take actions that are broadly condemned by others, but that dynamic is circumscribed. The willingness to carry out some actions because of possessing certain amounts of power are limited by the costs in terms of prestige and humanity that might be entailed. Possessing and using the instruments of power is not a simple matter of standing bare-chested on a parapet and loudly extolling one's power. It is also a matter of determining when and how that power may or may not be relevant to the situation at hand.

As it winds down toward an uncertain ending, a slice of the problem of applying relevant power to achieve the peace in the Syrian Civil War illustrates the difficulty of a straightforward application of the instruments to resolve international difficulties. That aspect of the problem is the fate of the Kurds, whose quest for statehood is the subject of chapter 16. The Kurds have been among the most valiant and effective fighters in the conflict which is, in their estimation, one theater of their goal of establishing a Kurdish state from several Middle Eastern states, none of which wants them to succeed. Among the states most opposed to the Kurds is Turkey, and one of the possible outcomes of the peace that will at some point come into being in Syria could be a concerted Turkish military drive to break, even to destroy, the Kurdish independence movement by decimating the Kurds. The United States has had a modest but crucial presence in eastern Syria, where the Kurds have primarily been the effective opponents of ISIS.

The positions taken by Turkey and the United States and the very public way in which they have been presented virtually precludes a diplomatic solution (which is characteristic of the entire Syrian problem). The two sides have taken extreme opposite positions on the Kurds. The United States insists on an ironclad guarantee of Kurdish security, an insistence clearly aimed at the Turks. The Turks adamantly refuse, citing their strongly stated position that the Kurds are terrorists whose goal is to overthrow the Turkish government. Because the positions of both sides are public, any concession by either side will be viewed domestically in their countries as a defeat by some. Where is the possibility of resolution? The Kurds, of course, are stuck in the middle of the confrontation, largely powerless to influence the outcome of what is an existential problem for them.

The Americans and the Kurds have been cooperative forces in the eastern region of Syria that the Kurds call Rojava and claimed as part of Kurdistan. This territory abuts Southern Turkey, where Kurdish separatists have operated to subvert the Turkish government as part of their national aspirations. The Turkish government has rejected the American demand as collusion with Kurdish "terrorists." The result is loggerheads, where some form of power must be effectively exerted by either the United States or Turkey. The Kurds, not unusually in their history, are caught in the middle.

The question is how to resolve this problem. It is only one part of the overall complicated set of factors and forces seeking to end a terribly bloody civil uprising that has been going on for over a decade and that has decimated Syria to the point that it is not clear how that country can ever be made whole again. The effort shows how deeply conflicted interests among interested partners create an enormous tangle of instruments of power trying to settle the conflict.

Application: Ending the Syrian Civil War

The Syrian Civil War has been one of the bloodiest, most tragic events of recent political history. It began, as summarized in *Cases in U.S. National Security*, as part of the so-called Arab Spring, which broke out in Tunisia in 2010 to protest corrupt, autocratic rule in the Middle East. The movement did not achieve most of its lofty goals, but it did spin off movements in various other regional countries. It occurred most tragically in Syria.

The offshoot that became the civil war began in March 2011 in Syria in the form of protests against the autocratic rule of Bashar al-Assad, the Shiite Alawite who had succeeded his father, Hafiz, but had not instituted reforms he had promised when he took office. The immediate spark occurred when teenagers were arrested for spray-painting antigovernment slogans on buildings. Police reacted harshly, arresting fifteen of the protesters, and one died under suspicious circumstances, igniting protests and violence among the Sunni Syrians, who constitute about 70 percent of the country's population. The situation quickly devolved into violent clashes, as hastily assembled Sunni militias took up arms to protest the government's action. What I have described elsewhere as "the perfect maelstrom" was set spinning in the process. It continued to swirl as the government moved to quash the resistance, and suffering remained the norm for the beleaguered Syrian people.

The tragedy for the Syrians is well chronicled but in summary provides context for the disaster in need of resolution. On the eve of the violence, the Syrian population was about 21 million. Of that number, an estimated 510,000 had been killed by March 2018 according to Syrian Observatory for Human Rights, quoted in *The World Almanac and Book of Facts*, 2019 edition. In addition, the 2020 U.S. Institute of Peace (USIP) study indicates at least 6 million Syrians have been driven from their homes into exile and at least 6.6 million are internal refugees. Estimates of what it will take to rebuild the country vary from a quarter trillion to more than a trillion dollars. All estimates are no more than refined speculation given the fluidity of the situation and the extent of physical devastation. Stated roughly, however, over half the prewar Syrian Civil War population has died or been displaced by the war, and most of the country lies in ruins. In human terms, it is a tragedy that has cried out for alleviation. It is, however, caught up in a power struggle between various conflicting sides with differing objectives, none of which has adequate relevant power to impose a solution, and especially one that meets the needs of the Syrians and outsiders with some interest in the outcome.

Issues and Interested Parties

There are two sets of parties who have an interest in the outcome of the Syrian conflict and who have, with varying success, tried to force an outcome to their favor. The first set are internal, and the primary groupings are the government of Bashar al-Assad and the various opposition groups seeking to overthrow him. According to the USIP study, these include "the Syrian rebels, the self-styled Islamic State, Al-Qaeda affiliated terrorist organizations, Kurdish-led organizations, and foreign militias including Hezbollah." The second set are outside countries and movements, all of which seek a different Syrian outcome featuring a Syrian government that will be sympathetic to their positions. The USIP study lists Russia, Iran, Turkey, and the United States as countries that have "intervened." The positions and support these groups represent contradict one another. None of these internal or external groups has demonstrated that they have adequate power to overcome the power of those that oppose them.

There are other factors that inhibit either internal or international efforts to bring the Syrian nightmare to an end. It is certainly in the interests of the Syrian population to end their horror, whether they have remained in their homes or been forced into a form of relocation. Unfortunately, there are strong, countervailing interests and forces at both levels that insist on their preferred outcome and have enough power to prevent the other side from successfully applying its own instruments of power.

The internal situation is conceptually the most straightforward. The al-Assad government represents a minority of the population; the Shiites, of whom the ruling Alawites are a part, represent about 15 percent of the population, compared to the 70 percent of the population that is Sunni and from which most of the opposition groups are drawn. This comparison appears to favor the rebels, but it is misleading. Historically, the Alawites have dominated the professional Syrian military, and they are much better organized and equipped than their opposition. The government, for instance, controls the Syrian Air Force, whereas what airpower the opposition can call upon must be supplied by outsiders. Moreover, the opposition groups are weakened by their internal divisions—many of the opposition groups hate other opposition groups nearly as much as they hate the government. Cooperation has been virtually nonexistent, and outsiders seeking to find some group or leader that can unite the opposition and provide the basis for a new government have largely failed. The United States, for instance, tried in the early stages of the war to identify a rebel group or coalition to which it could direct aid to oppose the government, but it could never identify a group it considered reliable and which would not end up losing their weapons to ISIS. Because of this lack of coordination among groups, they have not succeeded despite what would seem formidable demographic odds against the government. Since 2018, there have been widespread reports that the government was on the verge of prevailing and crushing the last organized resistance to its rule, and this outcome seems increasingly likely. The major impediments to achieving this end, however, have come from outside forces which, for one reason or another, oppose an outcome in which their "side" does not prevail. No side has demonstrated the requisite power to impose its preferred settlement, although the Assad forces have come close.

Support for the government illustrates the point. In broad terms, outside help and support has come from three sources. One is Iran (including its ally Hezbollah). Their connection is partly the result of shared adherence to Shiite Islam but also contains an important element of Iranian geopolitics. The Alawite government of al-Assad provides a Shiite entry point for Iran into the Mediterranean Middle East. This provides a platform for aspiring regional power Iran to expand its influence in the region generally, but more specifically to give it a stronger physical link to Hezbollah, whose terrorist campaign against Israel is part of Iran's attempt to cause the Israelis to abandon the West Bank to the Palestinians, a cause that Iran also supports. This linkage has benefited the Syrian government: Iran has allegedly provided "volunteers" from Iran and other Shiite areas to augment Syrian forces and help maintain a favorable balance of power for the government.

The second major supporter for al-Assad has been Russia. Syria provides Russia with a physical entry point into the region that it would not otherwise have. The arrangement is reminiscent of then-Soviet policy during the Cold War. The key physical gem in the relationship for the Russians is their naval base in Northern Syria at Tartus, which is located within the Alawite region of the country, thereby reinforcing the bond between Damascus and Moscow.

The third supporter has been Turkey, a country whose support has been the most blatantly geopolitical and least sincerely pro-Syrian. Virtually the sole interest the Turks have in the outcome is whether it will strengthen the Kurds. That concern, of course, centers along the Turkish-Syrian border area claimed by the Kurds as Rojava and parts of the Kurdish Autonomous Region of Iraq that also borders on Turkey. The Turks view the Kurds as their prime enemy in the region, and although they are at best ambivalent about the close relationship between the Syrians and Iran, they more fear Kurdish benefit from the outcome of the civil war as the greater of two evils. Most particularly, they fear that if al-Assad is overthrown, the ensuing chaos in Syria could allow the Kurds to consolidate their hold on Rojava, which they would then use as a launching pad for attacks (which they deem terrorist) against Turkey in support of Turkish Kurdish separatists.

The motives and methods of those supporting the Damascus regime are disparate. Those of the Iranians and the Turks, who are themselves rivals and historic enemies, are almost entirely geopolitical. Each has an agenda motivated by personal gain (the extension of Iranian influence, Turkish frustration of the Kurds) and has little to do with the well-being of the Syrians. The Iranians have religious ties with the Alawites as an added incentive and have been the most active, in terms of personnel and financial/military assistance, whereas the Turks have been more restrained physically because of their North Atlantic Treaty Organization ties and the fear that any active intervention might cause the region to erupt. The Russians are the true opportunists in the equation, and they have also provided the most active assistance to the al-Assad regime. They have provided airpower to assist in suppression of the rebels and military equipment to regime forces, in addition to issuing warnings against American air actions that might cause a confrontation between them. They have also provided valuable diplomatic cover against international condemnation of Syrian chemical attacks against civilians in 2012, 2013, and 2018 in forums like the UN Security Council.

Outside support for the rebels has been spottier and less effective. The large reason for this is that there is not *a* resistance but a whole series of fragmented, feuding groups, none of which receive much general support. The fact that ISIS arose as one of those groups further taints the effort and makes outsiders, including the United States, reluctant to do much beyond counseling a negotiated settlement and keeping a token training force in the east. Because 70 percent of the Syrian citizenry is Sunni, one might expect more assistance from major Sunni states but, except for some private assistance from Saudi Arabia and the Gulf states, little has been forthcoming. The Trump administration, with its basically isolationist view of U.S. activism in the world (see chapter 7), showed notable reluctance to take any leadership role in an intractable conflict they maintain is really none of the United States' business. The possession of usable military power within Syria continues to favor the government augmented by its outside allies and against the Syrian rebels. As of mid-2021, it appeared the Assad government had gained the decisive upper hand and thus was likely to retain power. Like essentially all Syrian politics, however, the situation is subject to change.

Conclusion

The instruments of power concept is simultaneously beguiling and deceptive. The dynamic it measures—how much power one state has compared to another by various measures—is appealing because it apparently allows one to predict likely outcomes of conflicts between two (or more) states when they come into conflict over some mutually desired outcome in situations of scarcity where they cannot both (or all) have all the resource they want. Knowing which side has the most power helps to predict who will prevail.

The calculation can and often proves to be deceptive. The problem is, in important ways, a matter of measurement. The concept of instruments leads one to measure those attributes that are physical, concrete, and easily measurable, and that can be misleading. It does not, for instance, account well for intangible but often critical factors like will and determination, among other psychological elements. To return to the Vietnam example, the Vietnamese had no objective physical chance against the mighty United States, but they prevailed. The reason, simply put, was that the outcome was more important to them than it was to the Americans—they wanted to win much more than did the Americans, and they succeeded. A whole genre of military strategy, what is called asymmetrical warfare, is dedicated to the development and application of ways that an inferior military force (one with less of the military instrument) can prevail over an objectively superior force (see chapter 8). It does not work all the time, but it does enough of the time that it is adopted by those in an objectively inferior position. The same kind of analysis applies to the other instruments as well.

The American role has been enigmatic and changing. Under President Obama, the Americans initially supported the Sunni rebels in Syria, but that support was limited because their primary means of support was the provision of military supplies and equipment, and they could not find any group they were confident would keep that aid out of the hands of ISIS. Trump had closer ties with the Russians and backed away from commitments, especially if they might entail sending even limited numbers of forces into the country. Biden's policy is likely to return to a strong anti-Assad stance, but it may be too late to make much difference.

Measuring outcomes is problematical when there are multiple participants with differing motivations and preferred outcomes. No outsider favors the suffering that has been going on in Syria since 2011, but the various state and nonstate actors have clearly differing preferences they would like to see as the outcome, and they are applying their power to realize their vision. On the ground, the government forces seem close to imposing their preferred outcome, but achieving it is problematic in a situation where there are so many actors with differing commitments and capabilities that contradict and cancel out one another. Determining which instruments of power possessed by which participants will prevail is not a simple matter of putting the measurable power of two opponents in the two sides of a scale and seeing which is heavier. The instruments offer one kind of measure that is important but not always decisive. Before reaching judgments, it is necessary to incorporate both the physical and measurable elements of power and the less tangible but, in certain circumstances, equally or more important intangibles. When the situation features multiple interested outside parties with contradictory values that contrast, the result can be particularly confounding.

The COVID-19 crisis also illustrates how extraneous, unpredictable factors can complicate traditional calculations. The pandemic began its spread at a time when many observers believed the Syrian fighting might be coming to an end, but the health crisis has interrupted that process by adding another, especially lethal, element to the situation. As an example, the USIP study states that "in-person dialogue activities in northeast Syria are not possible due to security and health risks." At the same time, COVID has ravaged Syria and overwhelmed its already overtaxed medical capabilities, and recovery from its effects only adds to the mountainous burdens of national recovery and reconstitution.

There is an old saying that, in paraphrase, suggests that for every concrete, complicated problem, there is an answer that is simple, straightforward—and wrong. That may not be the case for all applications of the instruments of power concept, but neat projections of outcomes based on who has the most measurable power are not foolproof either. Indeed, solutions based on applying the instruments of power may result in more destruction and suffering than they solve or alleviate, which has occurred in Syria. Talking and negotiating, the staples of diplomacy, may provide an attractive alternative, as examined in chapter 4.

Study/Discussion Questions

1. Why is international politics an exercise in power? What controversies surround the concept and its application?

2. Why is it difficult but tempting to devise instruments of power to measure national power and the ability of states to exercise power in their favor?

3. What categories appear on various lists of instruments of power? List and briefly describe each.

4. Why is it difficult to apply the instruments of power to concrete situations? Use the Vietnam War and the U.S. policy of protecting the Kurds from Turkey as examples.

5. Describe the Syrian Civil War. How did it start, how has it progressed, and why have efforts to end it failed?

6. What countries and groups have supported the Syrian government and its opponents in their efforts in the civil war? Do their efforts lead to a uniform application of the instruments of power?

7. What are the possible outcomes of the Syrian conflict? Can recourse to the instruments of power help predict the eventual outcome with any precision? Why or why not?

8. Why did the text describe the use of the instruments of power concept as both beguiling and deceptive? Do you agree with that assessment?

Bibliography

Abboud, Samer N. *Syria: Hot Spots in Global Politics*. Cambridge, MA: Polity Press, 2015.

Abouzeid, Rania. *No Turning Back: Life, Loss, and Hope in Wartime Syria*. New York: W. W. Norton, 2018.

Ajami, Fouad. *The Syrian Rebellion*. Palo Alto, CA: Hoover Institution Press, 2012.

Art, Robert J., and Kelly M. Greenhill, eds. *The Use of Force: Military Power and International Politics* (eighth edition). Lanham, MD: Rowman & Littlefield, 2015.

Chua, Amy. *Political Tribes: Group Instinct and the Fate of Nations*. New York: Penguin Press, 2018.

"The Current Situation in Syria: A United States Institute of Peace Fact Sheet." Washington, DC: U.S. Institute of Peace, August 26, 2020.

Dagher, Sam. *Assad or We Burn the Country. How One Family's Lust for Power Destroyed Syria*. Boston, MA: Little Brown, 2019.

D'Anieri, Paul. *International Political Power and Purpose in Global Affairs* (fourth edition). Boston, MA: Cengage, 2016.

Drew, Dennis M., and Donald M. Snow. *Making Twenty-First-Century Strategy: An Introduction to Modern National Security Processes and Problems*. Montgomery, AL: Air University Press, 2006.

Feldman, Noah. *The Arab Winter: A Tragedy*. Princeton, NJ: Princeton University Press, 2020.

Ford, Robert S. "Keeping Out of Syria: The Least Bad Option." *Foreign Affairs* 96, no. 6 (November/December 2017): 16–22.

Fromkin, David. *The Independence of Nations*. New York: Praeger Special Studies, 1981.

Ghosn, Faten. "The Hard Road Ahead for Syrian Reconstruction." *Current History* 117, no. 803 (December 2018): 331–37.

Goldsmith, Leon. *Cycle of Fear: Syria's Alawites in War and Peace*. London: Hurst Publications, 2015.

Hisham, Marwan. *Brothers of the Gun: A Memoir of the Syrian Civil War*. New York: One World, 2018.

Jablonsky, David. "National Power," in J. Boone Bartholomees, ed. *The U.S. Army War College Guide to National Security Issues*, Volume 1: Theory of War and Strategy. Carlisle Barracks, PA: U.S. Army War College, 2010.

Liddell Hart, B. H. *Strategy*. New York: Meridian Press, 1991.

McHugo, John. *Syria: A Recent History*. London: Saqi Books, 2015.

Morgenthau, Hans J. *Power among Nations* (seventh edition). Revised by Kenneth W. Thompson and W. David Clinton. New York: McGraw-Hill Educational, 2005.

Nuechterlein, Donald E. *America Recommitted: United States National Interests in a Restructured World*. Lexington: University of Kentucky Press, 1991.

Phillips, Christopher. *The Battle for Syria: International Rivalry in the Middle East*. New Haven, CT: Yale University Press, 2020.

Rabinovitch, Itaman, and Carmit Valensi. *Syrian Requiem: The Civil War and Its Aftermath*. Princeton, NJ: Princeton University Press, 2021.

Reilly, James N. *A Shattered Land: The Modern History of Syria*. Boulder, CO: Lynne Rienner, 2018.

Schelling, Thomas G. *Arms and Influence*. New Haven, CT: Yale University Press, 1966.

Schmidinger, Jordi. *Rojava: Revolution, War, and the Future of Syria's Kurds*. London: Pluto Press, 2018.

Snow, Donald M. *Cases in U.S. National Security: Concepts and Processes*. Lanham, MD: Rowman & Littlefield, 2019 (see especially chapter 10, "Syria: The Perfect Maelstrom").

———. *The Middle East, Oil, and the U.S. National Security Policy*. Lanham, MD: Rowman & Littlefield, 2016.

———. *The Middle East and American National Security. Ending Forever Wars*. Lanham, MD: Rowman & Littlefield, 2021.

Sorenson, David S. *Syria Is Rising: The Dynamics of the Syrian Civil War*. Westport, CT: Praeger Security International, 2016.

Stares, Paul B. *Preventive Engagement: How America Can Avoid War, Stay Strong, and Keep the Peace*. New York: Columbia University Press, 2018.

Tejel, Jordi. *Syria's Kurds: Politics and Society*. New York and London: Routledge, 2008.

Thucydides. *The History of the Peloponnesian Wars*. New York: Penguin Books, 1954.

Van Dam, Nikolas. *Destroying a Nation: The Civil War in Syria*. London: I. B. Tauris, 2017.

Waltz, Kenneth. *Realism and International Politics*. New York: Routledge, 2006.

The World Almanac and Book of Facts 2019. New York: World Almanac Books, 2019.

Worley, D. Robert. *Orchestrating the Instruments of Power: A Critical Examination of the U.S. National Security System*. Washington, DC: Potomac Books, 2015.

Yassin-Kassala, Robin, and Leila Al-Shami. *Burning Country: Syrians in Revolution and War* (second edition). London: Pluto Press, 2018.

4

Diplomacy
Negotiating the U.S.-Mexican Border

States have a variety of ways for dealing with one another. These range from the use of armed force to the more cooperative methods. The use of envoys from the leaders of countries (or their representatives, known as plenipotentiaries) to interact verbally with one another (what is called diplomacy) began with the first interactions between different human groups as they encountered one another. In most cases, their initial interactions were probably hostile, fearful, or both, as both (or all) sides encountered people whose appearance and means of communication were alien and incomprehensible. The problem for both was what to do about this new and probably unwanted set of other humans, and the first reactions probably included the instinct to attack and vanquish the intruders or, alternatively, somehow to communicate with them, try to find out if their intents were hostile or fearful like their own, and to try to reach some form of accord with them. The first reaction was the prototype for war; the second was the spark of human interaction which, in the relations between groups, became diplomacy. Both processes have developed and been greatly sophisticated since. The threat of nuclear war has acted as a governor on violent resolution to many, but not all, encounters. Recent international interactions have also raised questions about both the utility and methods of diplomacy. During the single Trump term, much of what passed for the diplomatic spotlight shone on the 1,933-mile-long border between the United States and Mexico.

Understanding what is happening in the realm of diplomacy begins by examining what the term means. Most definitions emphasize two distinct aspects of what constitutes diplomacy. The first is what diplomacy does, and it emphasizes the goal of diplomacy, which is, in the words of the *Cambridge English Dictionary*, "the management of the relations between countries." Other definitions add that doing so is a "profession" or "an art or practice." The second definition emphasizes the salient characteristics and methods of those who practice diplomacy. They emphasize what is often thought of as acting "diplomatically." It is depicted as "skill in dealing with people without offending them" or "skill in handling affairs without arousing hostility." The two meanings are related: the first describes the purposes of diplomacy and the second how diplomats ought to go about that task.

It is the second meaning that is in some dispute in contemporary terms. Traditional diplomacy was largely conducted in private settings involving diplomatic professionals for whom discretion and social correctness were paramount. This meant that the public was generally unaware of the content of intergovernmental discussions and thus was unable to determine if their side had "won" or "lost" the outcome, only that an accord had been reached in which both sides argued their interests had been served by the outcome. This method, private diplomacy, stands in stark contrast to methods associated with so-called public diplomacy. The epitome of this new practice was the bombastic style of the Trump administration, which unsettled the diplomatic community and changed the way countries deal with one another. These changes and their impact are the subject of this chapter, illustrated by international efforts somehow to negotiate and finance the unsuccessful controversial border wall between the United States and Mexico, a project shelved by the Biden administration. The border wall project may be dead, but the lessons of how its negotiation was mishandled is not. Biden, with more extensive diplomatic experience than his predecessor, has sought a return to more traditional methods (the second definition of diplomacy cited above).

Principle: The Art of Diplomacy

Diplomatic practices and traditions are the accumulated product of a long evolution of human experience in intergroup interaction. The Greeks, Romans, Chinese, and Egyptians are all known to have developed ad hoc ways to regularize encounters between them. Thucydides' *A History of the Peloponnesian Wars*, a fifth-century BC account of wars between Athens and Sparta, is one of the first systematic explorations of how the Greek city-states dealt with one another. Machiavelli's *The Prince*, an account of sixteenth-century power politics, is another famous account of the accumulating practice of what became diplomatic standards. Probably the first principles that underlay the practice were connected to reciprocity and diplomatic immunity. Before these were accepted rules of interchange, negotiators could never be sure of their fate if they ventured into hostile territory to negotiate, making the profession of diplomacy decidedly perilous. The principle of reciprocity, which roughly means that the treatment of other diplomats is governed by the treatment one might expect to be accorded one's own emissaries, and diplomatic immunity, which granted safe passage and treatment to foreign emissaries, were the necessary preconditions to developing some sort of diplomatic process.

Evolution of the Diplomatic Art

The differing experience of groups from contrasting cultures, locales, and backgrounds congealed to produce what became the modern practice of diplomacy in Europe during the fourteenth and fifteenth centuries. What is now looked upon as *classic diplomacy* is most often associated with the long process that created the Peace of Westphalia that ended the Thirty Years' War in 1648. That process was elaborated in subsequent centuries to form much of the basis of modern diplomacy. A cardinal principle of that process was governmental secrecy in how states dealt with one another, a practice that was tolerable when most countries were not democratic and thus popular support for and information about diplomatic practice was not necessary or expected by the population. World War I, which was arguably the result of practices associated with secret diplomacy, created outrage over this veil of secrecy and ushered in change to something that has been labeled *modern diplomacy*. The assault of the modernizers was led by American president Woodrow Wilson, a former political science professor, and its implementation under the banner of "open covenants openly arrived at" helped shape diplomacy for the rest of the twentieth century. The wave of populism of the early twenty-first century helped spawn another "revolution" in how *postmodern* diplomacy is conducted. The distinction of this contemporary model seems to be public discussions of methods and outcomes in electronic media. Assessing the import and likely permanence and impact of this latter phenomenon requires looking at least briefly at the other stages of diplomatic evolution.

The heart of diplomacy is face-to-face interactions between governments on matters of mutual concern. Historically, the role of accredited diplomats—ambassadors and their staffs being the most prominent example—was crucial. Diplomats exercised considerable discretion in how they worked and what they concluded because the physical distance between national capitals and the primitive nature of communications technology meant it was impractical, even impossible, for diplomats in the field to communicate events and ask for instructions from their governments. Plenipotentiaries were thus given considerable latitude in their actions. Depending on the distance between the capitals of two states engaged in a diplomatic negotiation, the time necessary to communicate with the national capital and get a response could be weeks, even months, often with considerable possible impact. The United States, for instance, declared war on Great Britain in 1812 two weeks after all the issues dividing them had been successfully resolved: the word had simply not made its way back to Washington in time. Similarly, the most famous military clash of that war, the Battle of New Orleans, took place several weeks after the truce formally ended the war.

Modern electronic technology has had a major impact on the structure of diplomacy. Diplomats and their central governments can now communicate with one another instantaneously, so that the discretion of diplomats has been greatly reduced. In addition, diplomatic missions used to be a prime source of information, but much of that function has been eclipsed by global electronic media that collect and disseminate news much faster than before. In a classic example during the George W. Bush administration, Secretary of State Colin Powell called an ambassador in a foreign country and asked for information from the embassy about an ongoing crisis. The ambassador said he knew nothing about the situation and asked Powell what his source was. The secretary replied that he was watching the unfolding events on CNN.

There are two major impacts of these changes on modern diplomacy. First, the ambassador has effectively ceased being the country's chief negotiator with foreign governments, since his/her activities can now be closely monitored and instructions provided to the embassy in real time. The ambassador is thus not a policy maker in the classic sense. Second, electronic speed has allowed, even facilitated, the direct intervention of the chief executive and presidential staff in diplomatic efforts. The president can keep apprised of many world events (admittedly at an unclassified level) by watching television and can communicate directly with other world leaders by picking up the telephone.

Classic Diplomacy

Classic diplomacy was developed and evolved in a different environment than that of today, and thus evolution and change are to be expected. The basic purpose of diplomacy—resolving differences hopefully in a mutually satisfactory manner short of the employment of violence—remains the same. What is important to note is the principles that have evolved and form the basis of modern practice and how changes in the international environment have had an impact on those methods of doing business.

Classic diplomacy evolved in Europe—especially the Italian states and France—when absolute sovereignty was the norm including, importantly, the equation of the sovereign condition with the monarch. The relations between sovereign states were considered the king's business. Generally, the interactions between monarchs had little effect on the citizenry, which did not believe it had a right to question those interactions until the rise of popular sovereignty began to broaden conceptions about the national interest—notably where it resided and who had a voice in it. As a result, international diplomacy could be conducted outside the spotlight that illuminates modern interstate relations, including the popular politicization of those actions.

The absence of public scrutiny and concern created a veil behind which the negotiations between states could be conducted. It was a profoundly political process in that its purpose was to resolve differences between states on matters of disagreement where the two (or more) sides desired mutually exclusive outcomes that required either or both to accept results they would rather not accept. How difficult this process might be varied, of course, depending on how important the outcomes might be to either or both. The more important the interests involved were, the more difficult the resulting bargaining might be. Unlike the more contemporary world, those interests and bargaining were unknown to the public. This dynamic is important because of the impact it had on reaching solutions where the sides did not get everything they initially wanted.

Secrecy provided the context for bargaining and, most importantly, compromises that were the central purpose and outcome of the process. In most situations, the two sides would enter with opposing demands which often could not simultaneously be accommodated. In this situation, there were only two ways to resolve the situation: one side could physically coerce or convince the other side to accept its position through the threat or use of violence, or they could compromise and reach a solution where both got part of but not all they wanted. Because the reason for pursuing diplomacy was normally to avoid military clashes, negotiating and reaching a compromise where each got part of but not all they wanted was the main goal.

Secrecy made compromise feasible. At the end of successful negotiations, both sides would announce a settlement including the claim that they had "won"—they had accomplished what they set out to attain. The nature of compromise is that both sides relent on some desired outcome to allow the other to get something it can claim as success. Both sides get less than they wanted, meaning the claim of "victory" is normally exaggerated, but it worked because secrecy meant outsiders did not know initial positions and thus could not judge if they were achieved. This allows both sides to claim a victory their populations may demand, thus settling the dispute.

Modern Diplomacy

Citizen participation in the political system changed the traditional environment. It was the result both of political democratization that reflected the changing nature of the locus of sovereignty and growing public perceptions of the corruption of the classic situation culminating in the series of secret treaties and protocols that helped lead to World War I. That war was a massive bloodletting from which hardly any European was exempt. The old system was blamed, and democratization seemed an inevitable consequence.

U.S. president Woodrow Wilson was the primary symbol of the assault on the old system. Wilson's classic text *Constitutional Government* was an early advocacy of political democracy and a founding building block of the study of comparative politics. The chief thesis of Wilson's text was the inherent superiority of democracy to other forms of government, and Wilson believed that the application of democratic principles to diplomatic practices would produce a superior, and especially more peaceful, international order.

Because American entrance into the "Great War" had proven crucial to breaking the deadlock in Western Europe, Wilson was a leading figure at the Versailles Conference, where he worked tirelessly to move the diplomatic process to a more open and popular level. Both the diplomatic process and its outcomes in terms of various kinds of international agreements should, in his view, be open to public scrutiny that would eliminate the pattern of secret agreements secretly negotiated and implemented. His basic belief and hope were that the result would be a more peaceful world. He maintained that the people at large would be much more reluctant to enter arrangements that led them to war than was possible when only a few people could reach those decisions. The crown jewel of this revolution in diplomacy was the first universal political international organization, the League of Nations.

The Wilsonian experiment ultimately failed, the chief symbol of which was its inability to prevent the slide into World War II. The idea of democratic participation and parameter setting on the diplomatic enterprise was not universally embraced by states that did not join the democratizing world system (Imperial Japan was a prime example) and thus clung to both the traditional values and methods. In a few cases like those of Germany and Italy, democratic processes were even used to bring antidemocratic elements to power who perpetuated the classic model. After World War II, the Cold War confrontation further impeded the universal development of a more democratic diplomatic set of practices, at least in the relations between the superpowers.

Enough of the democratic model did seep into diplomatic practice to sow the seeds of the current transition away from classic diplomacy and the erosion of its more beneficial values on both diplomatic and domestic political processes. The opening of the diplomatic process politicized diplomacy in ways to which the international system is still adjusting. Democratizing diplomacy has had the unintended consequence of politicizing the methods, and particularly the expectations that surround international relations and the resolution of the kinds of disputes that formerly would be dealt with quietly by employing compromise that allowed for both sides to claim accomplishment from the same outcome. This dynamic has been largely missing in both domestic and international relations in the early twenty-first century.

Postmodern (Contemporary) Diplomacy

In 1996, Eugene Brown and I published an international relations textbook, one of the features of which was an examination of the evolution of diplomatic practices. We identified four trends we associated with "modern diplomacy," and the categories serve to frame the more contemporary period, especially the apparent merger of diplomatic methods with the domestic ways of politics. With some modifications and updates, the four observations still serve as useful ways to discuss contemporary diplomatic practice. They are summarized in table 4.1.

The first characteristic is the proliferation of different kinds of diplomatic players. This is largely a reflection of changes in the basic structure of the international system. In the classic system, diplomacy was the exclusive province of a small group of monarchical court members who were internationally recruited (it was normal for nationals from several countries to be included in any country's diplomatic corps), and they shared common outlooks, values, methods, and goals. After World War II, democratization entailed the injection of more narrowly national viewpoints that made the system less universal and, in terms of values, more parochial because diplomacy was conducted exclusively by citizens of the countries negotiating. These diplomats did not share as fully the orientation to the process and its values that earlier practitioners held.

Contemporary practice has further expanded this trend in two ways with major effects on the structure and conduct of diplomacy. One is the addition of new countries from regions that had not historically been part of diplomatic practices and which either had different values or were inexperienced in diplomatic practices. The Democratic People's Republic of Korea (or North Korea) is an example. The second is the addition of nonstate actors, groups within or among states whose goals are sufficiently unlike those of traditional actors that

Table 4.1. Characteristics of Contemporary Diplomacy

1. Expansion and diversification of the range of diplomatic players.
2. Declining autonomy of ambassadors and embassies due to centralization of decision making in national capitals.
3. Public opinion pressure for greater openness and political accountability in diplomacy.
4. Growing importance of summit diplomacy.

their goals do not conform to traditional norms. Revolutionary groups seeking to overthrow or change national boundaries by force are examples.

The second characteristic is the continuing declining role of ambassadors in actual decision making. This decline is largely the result of improved communication that makes it easier for national governments to communicate and even negotiate with counterpart leaders, thereby allowing a leader so inclined virtually to ignore the advice of a professional diplomatic corps and its accumulated knowledge about the countries and issues with which they must deal. The Trump incumbency provided a prime example of this trend.

The third characteristic is public demands for greater openness and accountability in diplomatic practice. This phenomenon is part of the Wilsonian influence, the purpose of which was to create a brake on secret alliances and other elite-dominated activities. A basically unintended result, however, has been to politicize the conduct of diplomacy and, in the most deleterious sense, to inject a highly partisan element into the system that interferes with the ability to negotiate, both because the influence can be fickle and because other states with which one is negotiating may be inhibited or confused by the vagaries of the domestic politics of those with whom they are interacting.

Possibly the most dramatic, transformational change has been the degree to which heads of state now personally conduct diplomacy among themselves—summit diplomacy. This trend, which has been growing and reached a kind of zenith in the United States with the presidency of Donald J. Trump, has several aspects. First, it can effectively cut the professional diplomats out of the negotiating process. The diplomatic corps may remain a vital link due to its procedural and substantive expertise, but it also may be possible for national leaders to ignore their advisors and conduct negotiations on subjects they do not fully understand. A classic case involved the 1986 summit between Ronald Reagan and Mikhail Gorbachev, where the two leaders agreed privately on total nuclear disarmament before aides managed to intervene and terminate the discussions (see Oberdorfer). Second, negotiations conducted in this manner tend to be more media-driven "photo ops" than serious, detailed discussions that produce detailed, concrete resolutions of problems. Summit diplomacy, in other words, tends to simplify inherently complicated, contentious problems, and along with the greater politicization inherent in executive-level involvement, often to produce inadequate outcomes. Trump's 2017 summit with the Democratic People's Republic of Korea's Kim Jong-un in Singapore is one of many examples. These influences—simplification and politicization—were also demonstrated by the political and diplomatic conflict between the United States and Mexico over their shared border.

Application: Negotiations and the U.S.-Mexico Border ("The Trump Wall")

The 1,933-mile land border between the United States and Mexico is the most enduring source of international, and thus diplomatic, interaction and disagreement between the two North American powers, and it became a highly politicized issue since Donald J. Trump became the forty-fifth American president in 2017. His obsession with building a physical barrier of some kind became a signature political issue that transformed what has been a diplomatic problem into a highly charged political problem, thereby moving the nature of any resolution process away from diplomatic practice and distorting its nature into the realm of partisan politics. The process itself distorted traditional patterns as well. There were no quiet, behind-the-scenes negotiations where the parties hammered out agreements with which they could live. Instead, Trump simply stated a wall would be built and that Mexico would pay for it. The Mexicans refused, and the issue festered during the Trump incumbency. The issue was effectively settled when new president Biden announced on January 20, 2021, that he would spend no additional funds on "Trump's Wall."

The border problem is venerable. Disagreement about where the line should be and who should control what parts of it goes back at least to the nineteenth century, when large parts of what is now the American Southwest was ceded to the United States as part of the Louisiana Purchase in 1803, and it has resurfaced periodically since: as part of the conflict over the Texas Republic and its annexation to the United States in the 1840s, to the Mexican War and its settlement in 1848, and forward into the early twentieth century when the United States admitted Mexican-touching New Mexico and Arizona into the Union and Pancho Villa and his bandits raided across the border.

The problem is unique and extensive. The frontier between the two countries is the longest land border between a member of the "developed" and the "developing" worlds, meaning there are very different standards of living on either side of the frontier that serve to draw people across it in search of economic benefit. This dynamic in turn makes the function of the border more problematical than it might otherwise be: is it, in Nevins' terms, more a gateway to facilitate movement or a line of control (barrier) to restrict that movement? The broad answer is that it is both. Its length and the broadly differing terrain and barriers along it make it difficult to fashion and enforce a policy emphasizing both the gateway and barrier functions. The border between the United States and Canada is primarily a gateway; the U.S.-Mexico border is both gateway and barrier. It is thus more complicated.

Aspects of the Border Dispute

The current political debate on erecting a physical barrier oversimplifies the issue, ignoring major aspects of the border's function than the atavism of essentially closing the border suggests. The current policy debate focuses on the problem of immigration by illegal undesirables and the problems they pose. The real dynamics of the problem are more complex and probably best served by international negotiation—diplomacy—that the political effort has virtually precluded. Traditional analyses (including my own) have focused on three essentially international problems: the question of immigration (see chapter 15), the narcotics trade that crosses the border, and terror. Evidence of the terrorist penetration is so minimal that it does not merit consideration beyond saying it is possible but has not been convincingly observed. Immigration and drugs are largely domestic American problems; they are also international problems, some of the solutions to which require diplomatic attention and resolution. They also provide a context for framing the diplomatic issues surrounding the wall.

The Immigration Problem

That there is a constant influx of foreigners into the United States from south of the U.S.-Mexico border is a consequence of being where the less-developed world rubs against its more prosperous neighbor. It is a situation that has existed since the two countries were formed, and it probably reached its zenith in the 1990s, when implementation of the North American Free Trade Agreement stimulated the economy, producing jobs in the United States for which there were inadequate workers and thus stimulating an influx of workers to fill the void, many of whom were undocumented or "illegal."

These immigrants can be classified into three groups. The vast majority are *economic immigrants*, people who travel to the United States to make a better living than they can in their native countries; many send remittances back to their relatives and help to boost local economies. Their virtue is that they are, by and large, hardworking and honest. They can further be divided into those seeking permanent residence in the country and seasonal workers who come into the United States for jobs like food harvesting and return home after their jobs are completed. They perform tasks Americans do not want: the so-called 3-D jobs (dirty, dangerous, and difficult). Moreover, their crime rates are well below those of the general American population. Second are the *political immigrants*, asylum seekers fleeing oppression and even death in their home countries, a problem largely associated with the Central American states (Nicaragua, Guatemala, and El Salvador).

The third group, *criminal immigrants*, are the real problem. This group consists mainly of people associated with criminal cartels and organizations engaged in the narcotics business, and they migrate to organize the sale of and profit from the sale of narcotics to Americans. These "narco-gangs," many of whose members are Mexican, pose the real threat to which border security advocates refer when they advocate great line of control measures. The irony is that these measures—like the "wall"—are primarily effective against the immigrants who will not commit crimes if admitted and quite ineffective against the criminal elements, who possess monetary and other resources to surmount or bypass any barriers.

Is a stronger line of control the answer to the immigration part of the issue? A barrier may slow the rate of infiltration, but it is not clear that it is effective against the real problem, which is the crime and violence associated with criminal insurgents. As officials like Utah senator Mitt Romney point out, if one wants to cut the flow of economic immigrants, the answer is to attack their incentive, which is the availability of jobs. It violates American law to employ undocumented workers, and Romney argues that enforcing existing laws (arresting and trying employers who hire illegal workers) would reduce the jobs and the flow. The Trump administration never implemented effective procedures for doing so. Similarly, the reason the drug lords are active is because Americans represent a ready market for their wares. A quarter century ago, one part of the solution was "demand side," reducing the market for drugs through efforts to reduce drug usage through education and the like, especially in urban areas where the problem (and thus the profits) is concentrated. The wall proposal did not directly address this problem.

Drugs

If there is a core security issue of which the southern border is a central part, it is the flow of illegal narcotic drugs (especially heroin and cocaine) northward into the United States. It dates to the post–American Civil War period, when wounded veterans suffering long-term effects from their war wounds turned to narcotics from South America to ease their pain, and the practice was repeated by World War I veterans. Today, between 70 and 90 percent of the illegal drugs entering the United States come across the Mexican border. Almost all make the transit through regular points of entry, normally as physically small parts of loads of cargo in eighteen-wheeler tractor trailer trucks that the border patrol cannot adequately inspect.

The drug traffic is at the heart of whatever crisis exists surrounding the border in two ways. First, it fuels a sizable part of the drug epidemic in the United States, a public health and crime problem of significant proportions that has existed for at least three decades. Second, almost all the crime and violence associated with illegal immigration is a direct consequence of drug trafficking, because narcotics traffickers, not economic immigrants, commit virtually all the crime that forms what President Trump labeled the "national emergency" resulting from illegal migration.

Conclusion: Diplomacy and Border Security

Border security has been a venerable issue between the United States and Mexico at least since the Louisiana Purchase of 1803, and periodically it reenters the public debate. It did so in 2016, when then-candidate Donald J. Trump announced a campaign pledge to create a barrier that would have the effect of sealing the 1,933-mile land border between the two countries. Like previous attempts at regulation, it has basically failed, and under the Biden administration, its pursuit has been assigned to Vice President Kamala Harris.

There are at least two underlying reasons for this failure. The first is that the goal is not equally shared by the two countries. Border control is, and has been, an effort by the United States to regulate and limit the flow of people and goods northward, and it has no reciprocal emphasis from north to south beyond issues like the flow of illegal American weapons to Mexican drug cartels. Instead, the emphasis is on migration northward (especially of undocumented Mexicans, many of whom wish to become American citizens) and illicit goods like narcotic drugs. There is no Mexican equivalent. The border issue is quintessentially an American policy interest, not a shared, bilateral concern.

This leads to the second reason for failure, and it is at the heart of the current situation: the failure of diplomacy. Because the United States is the more powerful of the two countries, it is tempted simply to impose its unilateral solutions to border issues rather than to negotiate them with a coequal sovereign state. It is not so much a failure of diplomacy as it is a failure to engage in meaningful diplomatic interaction. The Trump administration was either unaware of the international diplomatic framework that should have been honored or simply chose to ignore the rules and protocols. In either case, its actions made the wall proposal a dead letter in Mexico City from the beginning. It was at heart a failure of diplomacy.

The death knell of the proposal was inadvertently sounded during the 2016 U.S. presidential campaign in its initial introduction. Candidate Trump announced that not only would the wall be built, but that Mexico would pay for the construction. This demand apparently came as a surprise to the Mexican government, which was apparently officially unaware of it before it was articulated. The requirement was not negotiated or approved by Mexico, which consequently could offer no counterproposal that it could argue showed Mexico got something it wanted from the deal. The Mexicans argued they would do no such thing as paying for a project they had not agreed to in diplomatic negotiations with the Americans. They have not backed down from Trump's humiliating, undiplomatic unilateral demand. The wall proposal was thus DOA (dead on arrival).

Think of the contemporary border debate in these terms. It began with the highly public announcement by the American candidate that there would be a border barrier the length of the frontier and that Mexico would pay for it. Mexico immediately fired back they certainly would not pay for the wall and implied they would not cooperate with its construction. Regardless of the merits of either position, they were the kind of differences one pursues in private, because announcing them publicly removes any ability for compromise without "losing" in the estimation of its own countrymen. Could Trump back away from an augmented line of control without appearing to "lose," regardless of the merits of any other parts of the proposal? Could Mexico participate in financing the wall without a similar loss of face? The answer in both cases was negative, and the large reason is that diplomatic principles were ignored and violated from the start. Had the initial positions/demands been made in private, there might have been the possibility of a compromise in which both could claim something valuable, turning the outcome into a mutually acceptable win-win situation rather a win-lose proposal that was made. The former was the framework for diplomatic success, the latter for failure.

The outcome of the wall proposal was a quintessential, textbook failure of diplomacy. One can argue that diplomacy would not have produced an agreement slowing or reversing the flow of people and illicit goods going north because Mexico lacked incentives that might have been built into a diplomatic accord, and that is also possible. It is also beside the point, since there is no public record that such an approach was tried in this case. By announcing his intention unilaterally as a campaign promise, Trump derailed the diplomatic process. Diplomacy did not fail; it was never tried.

The effort that was tried was unilateral, limited, and political. Erecting a true barrier across the extent of the border from Texas to California was always implausible because of natural barriers like terrain (the Trump advocacy always maintained only less than half the boundary needed barriers), and funding was never available for more than token construction. In December 2020, according to FactCheck.org, the United States had built 438 miles of the "border wall system." Of that figure, 365 miles was replacements for old, dilapidated fences, while 40 miles of new primary walls and 33 miles of secondary walls were constructed. In August 2020, then candidate Joe Biden declared "there will not be another foot of wall construction in my administration." The diplomatic process did not fail. Rather, the process was ignored and distorted in ways that assured that failure.

Diplomacy has been the backbone method by which states have sought to solve their problems with one another in a nonviolent manner for well over two millennia. The protocols and methods that have evolved over time are detailed and go beyond present concerns, but their underlying rationale does not. Diplomacy is, at heart, a quiet enterprise wherein the participants negotiate to reach mutually acceptable—if not always optimal—resolutions to their differences. The key element is compromise, the willingness to accept less than one might want in order to facilitate an outcome where both sides can claim success and be satisfied with the outcome. The intrusion of public political posturing upsets, even destroys, the heart of that process. Compromise becomes a dirty word, because partisans do not get everything they want and deride the diplomats who failed to achieve resolutions in which they attain all their desires—outcomes that would almost certainly be unacceptable to the other side and thus guarantee that no resolution occurs at all.

The border security debate centering on a border wall between the United States and Mexico illustrates the distortion that failing to engage in quiet diplomacy can create. At one level, there is the question of whether a physical barrier solves the problem of border security between the two countries, a legitimate national interest for which an arguably faulty implementing strategy was advocated. In the process of a highly politicized debate in the United States, the possibility of quiet diplomatic interaction between the two states to their potential mutual benefit was abandoned and the possibility of compromise forfeited. That this was the case was the real shame of the situation, and it is a failure one hopes will not be repeated.

Study/Discussion Questions

1. What is diplomacy? What are the three stages through which it has evolved since 1648? Why is this evolution important?

2. What are the four characteristics of modern diplomacy identified in the text? Describe each and why it is important.

3. How have diplomacy and politics comingled in the contemporary world? How has that phenomenon affected the contemporary conduct of international relations?

4. Would a return to older and more prominent roles for diplomacy improve American interaction

with the world and the outcomes of diplomatic situations involving the United States? Use the wall as an example.

5. What are the basic issues that divide the United States and Mexico surrounding their mutual border? Place the wall imbroglio in historic context.

6. Discuss the immigration problem along the border. Discuss the vari-ous kinds of immigrants that cross the border. Do current policy efforts reflect the problem?

7. What is the nature of the drug crisis as a border security problem? Is drug (and drug dealer) penetration the real border issue? Discuss.

8. Why was the Trump initiative to build a wall between the United States and Mexico a failure of diplomacy? Explain.

Bibliography

Andreas, Peter. *Border Games: Policing the U.S.-Mexico Divide*. Ithaca, NY: Cornell University Press, 2009.

Berridge, G. R. *Diplomacy: Theory and Practice* (fifth edition). London: Palgrave, 2015.

Black, Jeremy. *A History of Diplomacy*. Chicago, IL: University of Chicago Press, 2010.

Bonner, Robert C. "The New Cocaine Cowboys: How to Defeat Mexico's Drug Cartels." *Foreign Affairs* 89, no. 4 (July/August 2010): 35–47.

Camp, Roderic. *Politics in Mexico: Consolidation or Decline?* New York: Oxford University Press, 2013.

Carpenter, Ted Galen. *The Fire Next Door: Mexico's Drug Violence and the Danger to America*. Washington, DC: Cato Institute Press, 2012.

Cooper, Andrew F., and Jorge Heine. *The Oxford Handbook of Modern Diplomacy* (Oxford Handbooks). Oxford, UK: Oxford University Press, 2015.

Dorman, Shawn. *Inside a U.S. Embassy: The Essential Guide to the Foreign Service* (third edition). Washington, DC: Potomac Books, 2011.

Edmunds-Poli, Emily, and David A. Shirk. *Contemporary Mexican Politics* (third edition). Lanham, MD: Rowman & Littlefield, 2015.

Farley, Robert. "Trump's Border Wall: Where Does It Stand?" FactCheck.org, December 20, 2020.

Farrow, Ronan. *War on Peace: The End of Diplomacy and the Decline of American Influence*. New York: W. W. Norton, 2018.

Ganster, Paul, and David E. Lorey. *The Mexican Border Today: Conflict and Cooperation in Historical Perspective*. Lanham, MD: Rowman & Littlefield, 2015.

Kennan, George F., and John Mearsheimer. *American Diplomacy: Sixtieth Anniversary Expanded Edition*. New York: Simon and Schuster, 2012.

Kerr, Pauline, and Geoffrey Wiseman. *Diplomacy in a Globalizing World*. Oxford, UK: Oxford University Press, 2017.

Kissinger, Henry A. *Diplomacy*. New York: Touchstone Books, 2011.

———. *A World Restored: Metternich, Castlereagh, and the Problem of Peace*. New York: Touchstone Books, 1999.

Kopp, Harry W., and John K. Naland. *Career Diplomacy: Life and Work in the U.S. Foreign Service* (third edition). Washington, DC: Georgetown University Press, 2017.

Kralev, Nicholas. *America's Other Army: The U.S. Foreign Service and Twenty-First-Century Diplomacy* (second edition). New York: CreateSpace Independent Publishing Platform, 2015.

Lasswell, Mark, ed. *Fight for Liberty: Defending Democracy in a World of Trump.* New York: PublicAffairs, 2018.

Longo, Matthew. *The Politics of Borders: Sovereignty, Security, and the Citizen after 9/11.* New York: Cambridge University Press, 2017.

Machiavelli, Niccolo. *The Prince.* New York: Millennium Press, 2018 (originally published 1532).

Nevins, Joseph. *Gatekeepers and Beyond: The War on "Illegals" and the Remaking of the U.S.-Mexico Border* (second edition). New York: Routledge, 2010.

Oberdorfer, Don. *The Turn: From the Cold War to a New Era: The United States and the Soviet Union, 1983–1990.* New York: Poseidon Press, 1991.

O'Neil, Shannon. "The Real War in Mexico: How Democracy Can Defeat the Drug Cartels." *Foreign Affairs* 88, no. 4 (July/August 2009): 63–77.

Payan, Terry. *The Three U.S.-Mexico Border Wars: Drugs, Immigration, and Homeland Security* (second edition). Westport, CT: Praeger Security International, 2016.

Phelps, James R., and Jeffrey Dailey. *Border Security* (second edition). Durham, NC: Carolina Academic Press, 2018.

Rana, Kishan S., and Giles Scott-Smith. *Twenty-First-Century Diplomacy: A Practitioner's Guide.* New York: Continuum, 2011.

Shifter, Michael. "Latin America's Drug Problem." *Current History* 106, no. 697 (February 2007): 58–63.

Snow, Donald M. *Regional Cases in U.S. Foreign Policy* (second edition). Lanham, MD: Rowman & Littlefield, 2018.

———, and Eugene Brown. *The Contours of Power: An Introduction to Contemporary International Relations.* New York: St. Martin's Press, 1996.

Thucydides. *A History of the Peloponnesian Wars.* New York: Penguin Books, 1954.

U.S. Government and U.S. Military. *Decision Model for U.S.-Mexican Border Security, Measures—President Trump's Proposed Border Wall, History of Security Infrastructure by ICE, CBP, DHS, Intelligence Community, Law Enforcement.* Washington, DC: U.S. Government, 2017.

Walt, Stephen. *The Hell of Good Intentions: America's Foreign Policy Elite and the Decline of American Primacy.* New York: Farrar, Straus, and Giroux, 2018.

Wilson, Woodrow. *Constitutional Government: A Study in American Politics.* New York: Amazon Digital Services, 2017 (originally published 1885).

PART II
Methods and Mechanics

5

Globalization, Protectionism, and Trade

Free Trade or Not?

The exchange of goods and services among people and political units is as old as human interaction generally. It has evolved into a main emphasis in economics and internal and international politics. Economic protectionism and globalization have been the competing philosophies in the debate about economic international relations. After the end of the Cold War, free trade under the banner of globalization became the reigning concept in the debate about international economic policy. More recently, protectionism has reappeared on the horizon. Trade, the most prominent current indicator of international economic relations, has clear economic consequences, but it also has political impacts. Economic issues are often exaggerated and politicized by both champions and opponents, which has arguably been the case in contemporary discussions. Donald Trump was a vocal advocate of protectionism. His successor, Joseph Biden, is more clearly identified with globalization.

How to deal with economic interactions is a prominent part of the broader debate over the levels of interaction and connectivity that a political unit has with other states and the question of its philosophical orientation toward other world countries (the broader subject of chapter 7). Generally, the debate is over whether a country should maximize or minimize the extent to which it is dependent on domestic or foreign sources of goods and services to maximize the national interest of the economic well-being of the country and its citizens. In the contemporary American debate, it has focused particularly on economic relations with major trading partners like the European Union.

The momentum to open the international economic system to more international trade was, in many ways, a post–World War II reaction to the perceived role of restrictions on trade before that great bloodletting. In the period between the world wars, countries enacted strict limits on international trade that worsened the slide toward the second global conflict of the twentieth century. Protectionism was blamed for much of this result and created an inexorable demand for a more open, globalized system in 1945.

The modern issue of trade congealed over whether to import goods and services that were also produced domestically, especially if foreign goods were cheaper and of comparable or better quality. That question is near the top of the agenda in contemporary discussions of trade and is manifested in disagreements on the subject from questions of barriers to trade to environmental impacts of importation versus domestic production. Since the economic downturn of 2008, the contribution of trade to prosperity has been a point of concern, particularly in areas such as employment and fairness of competition.

Whether to allow the unfettered movement of goods and services internationally (free trade) or to place restrictions of one kind or another on that flow is a central element in contemporary international relations. The removal of remaining barriers to trade was the centerpiece of the economic globalization movement of the 1990s, one of the engines designed to draw countries into closer collaboration by entwining them in the global prosperity of that decade. The global economic downturn at the turn of the millennium, the rise of the global war on terror, and COVID removed some of the luster from the free trade issue and relegated it to a less prominent place on the international political agenda. The policy question of the 2020s is whether globalization will return to prominence or whether the movement toward restrictions that arose in the second half of the 2010s will continue. This debate affects the actions both of individual states and combinations of states. This chapter emphasizes how the debate has affected the largest and most successful of free trade efforts, the European Union, and reactions to it, notably Brexit (the British decision to leave the European Union).

Principle: Globalization and Terms of Trade

The basic poles in the free trade debate have been between those seeking to expand trade (free traders) and those seeking to restrict trade (protectionists). Nestled between the extremes are those who advocate freer, but not necessarily totally free, trade (who often portray themselves as fair traders). All three emphases are vibrant parts of contemporary arguments.

The debates tend to be emotional and hyperbolic. A major conjunction in the debate is between trade practices and jobs, a clearly critical concern for almost everyone. From both economic and political perspectives, a key question is whether policies promoting one or another trading philosophy create, destroy, or have no effect on employment generally or on individual categories of jobs. The result is to add a clearly emotional element to the debate that is exploited by partisans on all sides of the issue. There is some concern that some philosophies may affect groups differently—the creation of greater wealth inequalities, for instance. The trends have been intensified by the economic effects and human pressures of the global pandemic.

Trade Advocacies

The economic aspect of the trade debate has been, and continues to be, asymmetrical. Proponents on both sides tend to talk past one another, meaning interchange often devolves into monologues. The arguments promoting free and expanded trade tend to be mainly abstract, impersonal, and macroeconomic. Free trade is advocated because it unleashes basic economic principles like comparative advantage that make overall economies (national or international) stronger and economic conditions within and between countries more vital and prosperous. Advocates maintain that arrangements promoting trade have had a net positive impact on the global economy. Because they also expand production, they promote closer, friendlier relations between the participants. Additionally, they intertwine the economies of trade partners in ways that make conflict between them impractical and self-destructive.

Anti–free trade arguments, on the other hand, tend to be specific, personal, and microeconomic. Cries to restrict trade tend to be posed in terms of the adverse impact that expanding trade opportunities has on individuals, groups, industrial sectors, and even geographical regions within countries. Trade is not about economic theories; rather, it is about people's jobs and livelihoods. Thus, opponents emphasize things like jobs lost by individuals in individual industries to make their points.

Fair trade is a third alternative. Fair traders seek a compromise between the extremes, advocating selective trade reductions in conformance with the principle of free trade but seeking to minimize negative microeconomic impact where they might occur. Frequently, fair traders emphasize the need for compensatory actions for those individuals adversely affected by what they basically see as the beneficial impacts from free trade. They also oppose actions by trade partners that artificially inflate their competitive advantage at the expense of others. Violations of fair trade standards were frequent complaints of many anti–free trade members of the Trump administration—especially against China.

The overall debate is intensely political at both the domestic and international levels. Within American national politics, the asymmetry is often reflected between branches of the federal government. Historically, the executive branch of government, more concerned with the overall health of the economy and somewhat more removed from the impact on specific individuals or groups, has tended to be more free trade–oriented and macroeconomic. Members of Congress, whose constituents are the people whose jobs are endangered when foreign goods and services enter the country more freely, tend to be more microeconomically oriented.

At the international level, the debate tends to get intermingled with preferences for the general orientation toward political interactions with the world. As discussed in chapter 7, two positions have dominated the global argument. *Internationalists* generally advocate a maximum engagement in the international system, believing such involvement is systemically beneficial and promotes cooperative interactions among states. Free trade and globalization are the economic manifestation of that reasoning. *Unilateralists* advocate a minimal and more nationally controlled level of involvement in the world. The "America First" movement under Trump reflected this orientation.

The terms of this debate are not purely economic. Pro-trade advocates of the 1990s, for instance, argued that the globalization process produces political as well as economic benefits. One of the major reasons for promoting trade with China was to draw that country more intimately into the global political system. At the same time, anti–free trade arguments have expanded to include strictly noneconomic concerns ranging from environmental degradation to compromises of sovereignty, and more recently immigration as well as politico economic arguments about the effects on different groups within societies.

Trade can also become a political weapon. In 2019, President Trump framed implementing the imposition of tariffs on countries with which the United States had other disagreements. Some were based in economic practices (tariffs on Chinese goods) and some were political (threatened tariffs on Mexico over border security). Tariffs are levies (taxes) against goods entering a country and are adamantly opposed by free traders. Their use reached a zenith during the protectionist 1930s, and they were identified as one of the culprits in the slide to World War II. They have been in general disfavor since, until Trump's attempt to employ them as an instrument of power.

This introduction frames the structure of the section, which has two purposes. The first purpose is historical, tracing the process whereby free trade has been grounded in the advocacy and opposition to free trade. Finally, it will attempt to apply this institutional framework and the positions of the two sides to the current, ongoing debate on the issue. The arguments apply both to individual countries and to international units like the European Union. These distinctions help frame the debate over "free trade or not."

Institutionalizing Trade

As noted, post–World War II planners agreed a major reason for the war was economic conditions during the Great Depression that nurtured protectionism and produced economic chaos facilitating the descent into the maelstrom of global war. They were determined not to allow these conditions to return.

There were two geographic thrusts in this effort. One of these was universalist, seeking to create arrangements and institutions with global membership, reach, and economic effect. The United States took the lead in this effort, putting forth and advocating the proposals that became known as the Bretton Woods system, named after the New Hampshire town in which they were negotiated beginning in 1944. The major outcomes were two international organizations, the International Bank for Reconstruction and Development (or World Bank) and the International Monetary Fund (IMF), both aimed at reducing or eliminating protectionism. Both were limited in their reach and were not explicitly forms of economic integration, and both remain important efforts to promote economic cooperation through free trade. That emphasis was deferred until 1995, when it came into being in the form of the World Trade Organization (WTO). It has a worldwide but not universal membership.

The WTO has now existed for over a quarter century. Its membership has increased from approximately seventy in 1995 to 164 as of July 29, 2016 (according to its website). In addition, twenty-four nonmember countries participate in the organization (observers have five years to apply for full membership). These states include Iraq, Iran, and Afghanistan. The headquarters, including the secretariat, are in Lausanne, Switzerland. The WTO has established itself as a leading international economic organization in the process.

Its brief tenure has been filled with more controversy and a great deal more publicity than functional international organizations (those that deal with a specific policy area rather than generalist organizations like the United Nations) usually attract or desire. In some ways, the acceptance of or opposition to the WTO reflects the status of globalization, whose central principle of free trade it exemplifies. When the charter came into effect in 1995, globalization was at its apex and the new WTO activated reactions only from most ardent opponents. After 9/11, international attention shifted to the problem of terrorism, taking the spotlight off globalization and the WTO. Free trade has continued to grow, but the acceptance of its values and their institutionalization have become more controversial. The "America First" orientation of the Trump administration accelerated anti–free trade policy advocacy, a policy direction the Biden administration seeks to reverse.

The other, and more successful, approach to economic integration has been regional. Regional organizations, as the name implies, are physically bounded and, in practice, all have been associations of countries with similar interests and pasts, and this has facilitated both the development and progress of these schemes. The most successful by far has been the European Union (EU), and all others are compared to the European Union in terms of progress toward internationalism. To understand the comparative evolution, one needs to look at these forms of association as well.

Forms of Economic Integration

The movement to promote greater international trade has had two related thrusts, one economic and one political, since it burst upon the global scene as a dominant theme in the 1990s. Both trends illustrate the postwar evolution of trade promotion and share two assumptions: that greater trade will increase productivity and prosperity and that the resulting economic globalization will also promote economically induced interdependence that will contribute to political stability and peace. Economic integration is the quintessential expression of globalism; resistance to it flows from unilateralist preferences. The European Union is the expression of globalism; Brexit exemplifies the rejection of globalism.

The economic dimension is based on how extensive the commitments are and thus how much increased trade they produce. The motivation to enter into economic arrangements is idiosyncratic, but it combines economic and political motives. The economic appeal, on which much of the process is premised, is to create greater prosperity through economic expansion, including easier trade, and at the macro level, this has generally been achieved. The beneficial effects may be selective, with some groups benefiting more than others—a source of potential backlash. Politically, the motives are geopolitical, as they were in the case of the European Union.

Forms of Increased Cooperation

The process of economic integration has progressed through four steps of increasing extensiveness and effect. All are premised on increasing reductions in barriers to trade and commerce within the physical area in question. The "deeper" the commitment involved, the greater the need for political structures to regulate the process, an inevitable cause of friction. The extreme negative reaction is symbolized by the British decision to divorce itself from the European Union, a process currently being completed.

Free trade agreements stand at the base of economic integration schemes. The purpose of these arrangements is to stimulate economic activity among the contracting members. They do so by lowering or eliminating barriers to trade among the contracting members, usually in the form of tariff reductions or eliminations. Free trade agreements do not, however, impose uniform regulations on the terms of goods and services entering the area. These are set by the individual members and raise the problem of so-called indirect importation, whereby an exporter avoids tariffs and the like on its goods with one member of the arrangement by trading with another member that does not have that barrier. Once inside the free trade area, goods can move freely among the members, allowing those goods to be sent to the original destination without penalty. The import of automobile parts for American cars from countries like China through Mexico, allowed under NAFTA, is an example.

The second step is a *customs union*. In this arrangement, the members add a common external tariff (or quotas) to all goods and services entering all member states, thereby eliminating indirect importation into the area. The effects are greater interaction among the members, the further reduction of goods coming into the area from the outside (which increases economic exchange among members), and greater unity among the members, if they can agree politically on the effects.

When a free trade area and a customs union are created in the same area, the third step is to create a *single* or *common market*. This action combines the dynamics of each previous form and aims to create the free circulation of goods, capital, people, and services within the market area. This is accomplished by reducing, preferably to zero, all trade barriers among members (a free trade area) and by creating common external barriers for goods and services coming from the outside (a customs union). This was the original form that the European Economic Community took in the 1960s and was the launching pad from which the European Union was formed.

The fourth and, at least to this point, ultimate form of integration is an *economic union*. At the purely economic level, the creation of an economic union culminates the process of economic integration. It is a two-step process that becomes progressively more complicated and controversial as it becomes more political.

The first step in creating an economic union is the formation of a *monetary union*, a financial institution that can issue a common currency and make monetary policy binding on all the members. The process becomes more politically controversial at this point, because the second step requires creating political bodies with the authority to make policy binding on all the members, a direct infringement on the national sovereignty of individual members. It is notable that most of the controversy within the European Union has arisen since the process of creating the monetary union began. When an arrangement combines a single common market and a monetary union, a full economic union has been created.

Economic union adds a political element to the mix that creates or inten-sifies politically based opposition. These misgivings are generally unimportant in the early stages of free trade movements, where economic benefits are most obvious and the effects of transfer of political powers like the authority to set monetary policy are not obvious. When these transfers do occur, they impinge on national sovereignty in the affected areas and trigger opposition on purely political grounds. In the EU case, this meant transferring part of economic deci-sion power from national capitals to EU headquarters in Brussels. Brexit was largely a reaction to this dynamic. In American politics, that same kind of fear of centralized power helped enhance the appeal of unilateralism during the Trump administration.

The major objections to free trade thus do not come over abstract princi-ples, but from their application. Another key element in opposition arises from the presumption that all countries (or whatever entities are part of a free trading arrangement) will in fact find areas of production at which they have a compar-ative advantage. This is not always the case, and countries lacking comparative advantage (generally the least developed units) thus tend to avoid involvement to the extent they can. It also presumes that areas of uncompetitive production can be replaced with compensatory equivalent areas where comparative advantage can be developed to replace uncompetitive enterprises. It is central to microeco-nomic (protectionist) objections to free trade that this does not always occur.

This contrast in macro-level versus micro-level benefits also helps explain why free trade is more popular among economic elites than the general pop-ulation and why the issue has become a flash point in economic debates since 2016 in the United States. The economic elites—investors, entrepreneurs, and the like—are all more likely to be insulated from negative micro-level impacts but more affected by broader, macro-level effects like the overall impact on the stock market. If these macro-level indicators are expanding, then those elites are likely to benefit and be supportive. Negative micro-level effects have a direct impact on the jobs of individual voters, and candidates for public office are likely to reflect the suffering that displaced individuals and industries feel. These latter effects were a pillar of Trump administration policy.

Politics and economics can be separated only in the most general sense. Whether trade is good depends on who benefits. Because economic elites tend to receive benefits from the macroeconomic activities that trading associations produce, it is not surprising that internationalists are likely to be free traders who favor trading agreements. Because the impact of those arrangements tends to favor some forms of economic activity and punish others, it is also unsurprising that people adversely affected would favor isolationist solutions that would shield them from negative personal effects.

Like all economic ideas and their institutionalization, trade arrangements are thus inextricably economic and political, and attempts to argue them exclu-sively on one ground or the other are fundamentally feckless. Politics involves the authoritative allocation of scarce resources, and economic resources like wealth and economic power are prime subjects for politically determined decisions with both political and economic consequences. To argue the case for or against trade arrangements on "purely" economic criteria distorts reality. Whether macroeconomic or microeconomic consequences should be supreme, for instance, is a political determination, because some of those consequences affect who gains or loses scarce economic benefits. Politics and economics are inextricably intertwined, and this is true of both the European Union and reactions to it like Brexit.

Application: The European Union and Brexit

The European Union has been the most prominent and pervasive trade-based international economic arrangement since World War II. The European Union is the only trade-based organization to achieve the status of an economic union. That accomplishment, however, has brought with it political problems, notably Brexit, that it had previously avoided. The Brexit phenomenon raises at least some questions about the future both of EU and other globalization-based arrangements, including the long-term durability of the arrangement and whether the experience will impede the development of similar arrangements elsewhere in the future.

The European Union Experience

The process that has evolved into the European Union reversed the politics/economics order of evolution. The original idea that became the union was to create an economic structure that would bring together the principal combatants of World War II under a common banner and, in the process, make future wars between them impossible. The original effort was so successful economically and politically that it created the momentum that led the Europeans through the four steps of the economic association process. The institutionalization of that process reached its seventieth anniversary in 2020 as a movement.

Europe had exploded into two horrific continent-wide wars in the twentieth century that had decimated the continent and left most of its combatants prostrate and at the apparent mercy of the Soviet Union poised at their doorstep. Their only powerful ally was the United States, which was both the bulwark of their defense and the only available source of funds to rebuild the continent. Thus, Europeans faced two most difficult problems: how to recover and how to defend themselves. With American participation, the two tasks were effectively combined in what became the European Union movement. The first task was how to make war between the principal members unlikely or impossible; the second was how to rebuild them economically and militarily to create a prosperous peace.

The Integration Process
The impetus for what became the European Union had its origins in wartime discussions about the post–World War II order. There was consensus that a major reason for the war had been exclusionary economic nationalism in the form of high barriers against the movement of goods and services across borders, and this belief resulted in a postwar determination to open the global economic

system in the direction of some form of free trade to avoid the worst possible outcomes of an economically isolationist system. The Bretton Woods universalist system was one thrust of the determination to change that configuration. What became the European Union was its first and most powerful regional expression.

The genesis was something called the Schumann Plan, named after French foreign minister Robert Schumann. His proposal addressed both the free trade issue and the causes of war by proposing a European Coal and Steel Community (ECSC) in 1951. The organization's members were the six original members of the EU movement: France, Germany, Italy, and the Benelux countries (Belgium, the Netherlands, and Luxembourg). The major provision of ECSC was to pool the coal and iron ore resources of France and Germany so that neither could independently produce steel that could become the basis for a new military competition. The European Coal and Steel Community was wildly successful and popular, and it spawned interest in wider forms of cooperation. The result was the negotiation of the Treaties of Rome in 1957 that created the European Economic Community among the six countries. Expansion began in 1973 with the addition of three countries that had historically tried to be aloof from European geopolitics, Denmark, Ireland, and the United Kingdom. That process has led to the gradual expansion of the European Union to its current twenty-seven members (before British withdrawal). As Moravcsik summarizes the evolution, "The EU has enjoyed an astonishingly successful run." Its population is over 500 million in a territory half the size of the United States, and its economy is the world's third largest (behind China and the United States).

The final step in the integration process, implementing the Lisbon Treaty of 2009, was to create the monetary and thus the full economic union. It has been the most problematic and difficult step, reintroducing national politics into this remarkably successful economic enterprise. The major problem has been that a full monetary union that includes a common currency must also have political decision bodies coterminous with the union, and this entails increased community-wide decision powers wrested from national governments. The strengthening of the union thus entails some weakening of the independent powers of the members. This transfer of authority to community institutions extends to other areas like the movement of peoples within the union area and the dilution of sovereign control over some traditionally national functions.

Brexit

Politics and economics can clash, and the clearest example has been Brexit. The term, of course, is shorthand for "British exit" from the European Union, the outcome of a 2016 referendum where the citizens narrowly decided to become the only state ever to exercise the option to leave the union. Their reasoning was mainly political based on the loss of British sovereignty over monetary policy implicit in the Lisbon Treaty: monetary decisions affecting the lives of UK citizens would be made at EU headquarters in Brussels, not in London. In addition, an increase in EU authority over immigrants played a role. Free movement across borders had long been part of the European Union, but as a result of immigration problems caused by Syrians fleeing their civil war, the European

Union voted on December 18, 2015, to supplant national control over who entered the EU area with an EU force, the European Border and Coast Guard, to catch illegal immigrants. This act enraged many, but especially the British, and, in Muller's estimate, "led to an unprecedented politicization of the EU."

If there was to be a reaction to increased EU assumption of physical and symbolic function historically performed by individual states, the United Kingdom was the most likely candidate. Great Britain is, after all, physically separated from the rest of Europe by the English Channel and the North Sea. The separation has always been both physical and political psychologically. Physically, of course, the separation has always made it more difficult to invade the United Kingdom than it would be if the watery barrier were not there. Imagine, for instance, how World War II would have been different if the Germans could have marched directly from France to the United Kingdom without getting their boots wet. Geography has thus insulated Britain from much of the violence of the continent over time.

The psychological and political dimension has also been part of the equation. Being physically separated from the continent has allowed the British to be part of Europe without being a physical part of the continent. In foreign policy, a major consequence has been to facilitate the British view of their relationship to the continent as the balancer of power who could intervene to determine the outcomes of conflicts in their—and they would argue—Europe's best interests. Politically, this physical position has always made Britain more powerful and consequential than it otherwise would have been. Britain clearly relished its self-appointed role as the balancer of power in a European-centered world system.

The evolution of the European Union to a full economic union undercut this self-role and activated the anti-EU sentiment that led to the successful referendum in 2016. Britain was not an original member of the EU movement, having joined the European Economic Community (EEC) in 1973, a reflection of its position as a "special" member. Being a member of the European Union meant being a full member of Europe, a status that troubled many of its citizens, and the movement toward full union threatened to erode that special relationship infinitely more. The breaking point for many was the EU decision in 2015 to take control of immigration. The British, much to the chagrin of many who had previously regretted the compromise of physical access to the islands posed by the railroad tunnel between France and the United Kingdom (the so-called chunnel), were further appalled by the prospect that bureaucrats in Brussels (EU headquarters) and not Britishers would determine who could enter their country. These kinds of concerns helped to pave the way for Brexit.

Brexit and Globalization

The divorce of the European Union and Great Britain has become a long and tortured process that continues to evolve and unfold. The movement was largely stimulated by the British Conservative Party and reflected growing disaffection in Britain with British membership and participation in the European Union. The major theme of those who favored British disengagement was what many citizens believed was British forfeiture of sovereign control over its territory and especially who would be allowed to settle on that territory, actions that threatened the "special relationship" between the island nation and the mainland. These concerns included the erosion of British sovereignty to the union, increasing EU regulations with negative economic and political impacts, and especially immigration issues that many English citizens deemed essential to their lifestyle. These causes were basically political, not economic. As implementation of Brexit has occurred in 2020 and 2021, the impacts have become more directly economic in terms like tariffs and other barriers between the European Union and the United Kingdom.

Brexit was adopted in a national referendum on June 23, 2016, by a narrow electoral margin. Over thirty million British citizens voted in the referendum, with 52 percent favoring leaving the European Union and 48 percent opposing the action. England and Wales favored separation, whereas Scotland voted to remain a member. The process of implementation has been the subject of negotiation ever since, and the divorce is supposed to be completed by the end of 2021.

What does Brexit suggest about sentiment for globalization or protectionism more broadly? The Brexit experience is not a direct repudiation of globalism per se, although that sentiment has proceeded during the second half of the 2010s, a period dominated by the isolationism of the Trump administration in the United States. It may have been more a reaction to extrapolating globalization principles like free movement of immigrants to places where labor is in short supply (see chapter 15). British Brexit supporters seem to have reacted negatively to the consequences of this globalization extension—the loss of control over immigration as a political and cultural question, not on economic grounds per se. Loss of control of its borders, a long-held British obsession, was the culprit, a byproduct of the globalization process, not globalization per se. If there is a lesson in this, it is when politics and economics collide, economics does not always prevail.

Will the 2020s be different? The Brexit divorce will be in place, and it may well have negative economic effects in the United Kingdom that may trigger a backlash and sentiment to return, which will not be greeted initially well by the remaining members. The transition in Washington from an American isolationist to a more globalist administration may change the general "atmospherics" back toward greater support for the kind of economic relations that marked the globalization-dominated 1990s, but the United States economy no longer dominates the global economy the way it did then. Any change probably requires a new condominium between Washington and Beijing that may or may not occur. Just before President Biden was inaugurated, there were press reports that Xi Jinping wanted to reopen a dialogue with the new regime in Washington (see chapter 2), so who knows?

Conclusion: Brexit and the Future

As the Brexit case illustrates, advocacy or opposition to free trade and its institutionalization has never been an easy or straightforward proposition. At the abstract, theoretical level of international macroeconomics, the case for free trade is convincing, and it is not surprising that many of the defenses of free trade spring from these theoretical arguments. At the applied level of the impact of free trade on individuals and groups (the microeconomic level), the proposition creates more ambivalence. Individual consumers benefit when comparative advantage produces goods and services at lower cost and higher quality through free trade than they otherwise would. Imagine, for instance, the impact on Christmas gift spending if all goods made in China were eliminated. At the same time, removing protection can terminate employment for those in the less-efficient industries. The theory of comparative advantage says that displaced people should find alternative employment in more competitive fields, but that outcome is almost always easier to accomplish in the abstract than in reality.

Institutionalizing free trade is a related but not synonymous question. One can reasonably take one of three positions on the desirability of free trade per se: one can favor free trade unconditionally, one can oppose it equally unconditionally, or one can favor free trade with some restrictions, the heart of fair trade. For the "pure" positions, the answer to whether some organization should be established to promote and enforce free trade is straightforward and flows directly from one's basic position—virtually regardless of empirical circumstances. From either extreme, the debate is pointless and the facts are almost beside the point.

The free trade movement is under some level of siege that is partly the result of excessive expectations when globalization burst upon the scene toward the end of the last century. Its virtues and positive impacts were exaggerated, as were its negative effects. Stimulating economic activity by reducing barriers to trade across state boundaries became the mantra of the 1990s, and it did produce positive outcomes. The hype, however, was greater than the dynamics of trade deserved or could sustain. The Trump protectionist backlash during his single term reflected that dynamic. The Biden position is more globalist; it may or may not be more successful.

That overselling is apparent in the institutions created in trade's name. The European Union has progressed steadily through the integration process because the organization's efforts benefit EU members. It became controversial only when it became political. As Crowie concludes, "The economic impact of the trade deal is far more ambiguous and significantly less interesting than its political impact. Indeed, it is less of a trade deal than an icon to be smashed or revered."

Study/Discussion Questions

1. What are the reasons for trade? What are the basic positions on trade that have evolved? Describe them, including how politics and economics intertwine in trade discussions.

2. What are the three contemporary positions on trade? Describe each, including its genesis and relationship to basic foreign policy schools of thought.

3. How did World War II affect thinking about trade? What perceptions of why the war occurred led to an emphasis on free trade?

4. Globalization embodying free trade was dominant in the 1990s but has receded in dominance since. Discuss the premises and evolution of the free trade–protectionist debate of the 2010s.

5. Free trade is more than simple economics. Discuss it as an economic and a political phenomenon, including macroeconomic and microeconomic effects and basic argument for and against it.
6. What is the European Union? Discuss its origins, structure, functions, and controversies associated with it.
7. The relationship between the economic arguments on trade and

its political dynamics have had an increasing impact on thinking about and conducting trade in recent years. How? Use the European Union to illustrate your points.
8. What is Brexit? What were the reasons it came about? How does it illustrate the dynamic relationship between globalization and politics?

Bibliography

Bauman, Zygmunt. *Globalization: The Human Consequences.* New York: Columbia University Press, 1998.

Brickerton, Chris. *The European Union: A Citizen's Guide.* New York: Pelican, 2016.

Clarke, Harold D., Michael Goodwin, and Paul Whiteley. *Brexit: Why Britain Voted to Leave the European Union.* Cambridge, UK: Cambridge University Press, 2017.

Clausing, Kimberly. *Open: The Progressive Case for Free Trade, Immigration, and Global Capital.* Cambridge, MA: Harvard University Press, 2020.

Coombs, Kevin. "The Brexit Breakup Gets Messier: The United Kingdom and the EU Will Be Tied to Each Other for Years to Come." *Foreign Affairs Snapshot* (online), March 27, 2019.

Crowie, Jefferson. "What Trump Gets Wrong about NAFTA: The Deal Is Not the Source of America's Problems." *Foreign Affairs Snapshot* (online), May 4, 2017.

Davies, Stephen. *The Economics and Politics of Brexit: The Realignment of British Public Life.* Great Barrington, MA: American Institute for Economic Research 2020.

Delanty, Gerard. "The EU's Indistinct Identity." *Current History* 115, no. 779 (March 2016): 117–19.

Dinan, Desmond. *Europe Recast: A History of the European Union.* Boulder, CO: Lynne Rienner, 2014.

Dregner, Daniel W. *U.S. Trade Strategy: Free Versus Fair.* New York: Council on Foreign Relations Press, 2006.

Dunt, Jan. *Brexit: What the Hell Happens Now? Everything You Need to Know about Britain's Divorce from Europe.* London: Canbury, 2016.

Evans, Geoffrey, and Anond Menon. *Brexit and British Politics.* Cambridge, UK: Polity, 2017.

Friedman, Thomas L. *The Lexus and the Olive Tree: Understanding Globalization.* New York: Farrar, Straus and Giroux, 1999.

Gumbel, Peter. *Citizens of Everywhere: Searching for Identity in an Age of Brexit.* London: Haus Publishing, 2020.

Irwin, Douglas A. "The False Promise of Protectionism: Trump's Trade Policy Could Backfire." *Foreign Affairs* 96, no. 3 (May/June 2017): 56–65.

———. *Free Trade Under Fire* (fifth edition). Princeton, NJ: Princeton University Press, 2020.

McCormick, John. *European Union Politics.* London: Palgrave Macmillan, 2015.

————. *Understanding the European Union: A Concise Introduction*. London: Palgrave Macmillan, 2002.

Moravcsik, Andrew. "Europe: The Second Superpower." *Current History* 109, no. 725 (March 2010): 91–98.

Muller, Jan-Werner. "The EU's Democratic Deficit and the Public Sphere." *Current History* 115, no. 779 (March 2016): 83–88.

Naim, Moises. "Think Again: Globalization." *Foreign Policy* (March/April 2009): 28–34.

Norris, Pippa, and Ronald Inglehart. *Cultural Backlash: Trump, Brexit, and Authoritarian Populism*. Oxford, UK: University of Oxford Press, 2019.

O'Connor, David E. *Demystifying the Global Economy: A Guide for Students*. Westport, CT: Greenwood Press, 2002.

Oliver, Craig. *Unleashing Demons: The Inside Story of Brexit*. London: Hodder and Stoughton, 2016.

Olsen, Jonathan. *The European Union: Politics and Policy* (seventh edition). New York and London: Routledge, 2020.

O'Rourke, Kevin. *A Short History of Brexit: From Reentry to Backstop*. New York: Pelican Press, 2019.

Panagariya, Arvind. *Free Trade and Prosperity: How Openness Helps the Developing Countries Grow Richer and Combat Poverty*. Oxford, UK: University of Oxford Press, 2019.

Pinder, John, and Simon Usherwood. *The European Union: A Very Short Introduction* (fourth edition). Oxford, UK: University of Oxford Press, 2018.

Rodrik, Dani. *The Globalization Paradox: Democracy and the Future of the World Economy*. New York: W. W. Norton, 2010.

————. *Straight Talk on Trade: Ideas for a Sane World Economy*. Princeton, NJ: Princeton University Press Reprint Edition, 2017.

Rothgeb, John M. J. *Trade Policy: Balancing Economic Dreams and Political Realities*. Washington, DC: CQ Press, 2001.

Shah, Anup. "Free Trade and Globalization." *Global Issues* (online), July 25, 2009.

Shipman, Tim. *All Out War: The Full Story of How Brexit Sunk Britain's Political Class*. New York: HarperCollins, 2016.

Snow, Donald M. *Cases in International Relations* (sixth edition). New York: Pearson, 2015.

Soros, George. *The Tragedy of the European Union: Disintegration or Revival*. New York: PublicAffairs, 2014.

6

Rising and Declining Powers
Iran and Russia

The role of power in international relations is pervasive and forms much of the context in which states conduct their relations with one another. Power is, however, an elusive and multifunctional attribute. Definitions of what constitutes power and how its different forms apply in different situations are inherently subjective and controversial. In ordering this ambiguity, the most important, powerful states are those with the largest amounts of the widest variety of "instruments of power" (chapter 3). Understanding the role and function of power is further complicated because power is both an attribute that states possess and an object of some international power situations: states, in other words, use power to get more power that they can use in other situations, including with those that seek to increase their power. Much of this process is based on states' reputations: what states are considered most powerful.

The relative power that different states possess absolutely and compared to other states changes. Over time, some states become more powerful and others become less so. Those whose power is increasing are referred to as *rising powers*, whereas states whose power is comparatively shrinking are called *declining powers*. The process of rise and decline is historic and perpetual. States emerge, rise, expand, and ultimately decline, replaced in the hierarchy of power by others. The pattern and causes differ from epoch to epoch, but the general phenomenon seems immutable.

Since the 1991 collapse of the Cold War, it has been widely asserted that another cycle of change is occurring. The most obvious manifestation came when the Soviet Union collapsed and the successor Russian Federation emerged as a much weaker power, a state in obvious decline. This left the United States the "sole superpower" for the balance of the twentieth century and arguably beyond. Russia has not accepted this reduction in status with magnanimity. As declining states usually do, the Russians have sought to reassert their historic status with limited success. Their task of image building has been made more difficult by comparisons to a clearly ascendent China.

An interesting case of a rising power is Iran. As discussed more fully in chapter 11, Iran considers itself to be the pivotal state in the Middle East, but other states—notably the United States and Israel—have sought to deny Iran's rise in power status. American actions especially sought to blunt Iran's rise in power during the Trump years.

Principle: Rising and Declining Power

Power is a basic element of international relations. The basis of much of the attempt to grasp, measure, and assess the role of power in the international system has already been introduced, but one additional element is the competition among states for being considered powerful and how states can try to enhance their power or avoid the perception that it is eroding. The concepts of rising and declining power contribute to that understanding.

For most Americans, this is a relatively new consideration. Since the end of the Second World War, the United States has been the preeminent state in the world, its comparative power basically unchallenged across the spectrum of measures of national power. That status has come under some question in the twenty-first century, as new competitors like China have arisen to challenge that preeminence. This has been unsettling for some Americans and has become a part of the foreign policy dialogue. The result has been to examine the issue of American status in the world and whether that status is changing.

The idea of rising and declining powers can help clarify and condition these concerns. The simple fact is that preeminent positions in the international realm change. Most of the countries that were the most important and powerful in 1900, for instance, no longer have that status, although many are prosperous and in comfortable, even enviable, international positions. Countries rise to positions of enhanced importance in the world, in a few cases become the preeminent territorial entities in the system, and they remain so for a time. In the long run, however, new states or other entities arise and challenge that supremacy.

The comparison of the most important or powerful countries in the world is an important consideration in a political system where power remains an important determinant of national success and the ability to realize national security interests. Power is a difficult, often even gauzy concept that is hard to pin down and the applications of which can be hard to predict. Nonetheless, power is important, and the reputation of states in power terms is important both to their status and their ability to succeed. This makes the determination of who is and is not powerful important, as well as whether the power of individual states is waxing or waning. The relative power of states and whether that power is increasing (rising) or decreasing (declining) has international currency. Power, in other words, is to some extent a reputation based on a belief that others hold.

Ranking Powers

The comparison of national power among states is a controversial, imperfect, and subjective process. Wanting to know where a country ranks in the international hierarchy of influence is a natural phenomenon in a power-driven system, and states will always seek to maximize their relative status. The process of estimation is both subjective and prone to disagreement. That said, one can make distinctions along two bases, recognizing their imprecision. These dimensions can be thought of as comparative status and direction.

The first concern is national reputation. It is an estimate of how other states regard the ability of a country to influence events regionally or globally. At the top of the contemporary list are countries with nuclear weapons, and especially large nuclear arsenals. During the Cold War, the United States and the Soviet Union were the acknowledged superpowers. When the Soviet Union imploded, the United States was considered the sole superpower for the balance of the last century, even though the Russians maintained control of the Soviet arsenal. Superpowers are also generally thought of as countries whose interests and influence are global in nature.

The category below superpower consists of *major* or *great* powers. This category is composed of countries that were the greatest powers before superpower status eclipsed them. The countries of the pre–World War II European balance are the obvious examples. The great powers are still consequential globally and especially within their regions, but their power is more limited than that of the most powerful states. Beneath this category are the most important *regional* states, also sometimes referred to as *pivotal*. The influence of these states is mostly limited to the physical regions of which they are part, but when superpowers or major powers encounter them in their regions, the pivotal state's influence must be accounted for. Iran and Vietnam in their regions are examples. At the bottom of the ranking are the *regional powers*, generally smaller and less powerful states lacking the personal ability to influence matters outside the narrow physical area of which they are a part.

The other designation, which forms the basis for this chapter, is the direction in which the power of states is headed relative to the power of others. Rising powers are states whose power and reputation is ascendant, including their ability to influence international affairs. Iran is also an example, with ambitions to become a premier pivotal state or even a great power. Declining powers are countries whose ability to influence events has decreased relative to that of other states.

The rise of new powers always seems to follow major dislocations in previous arrangements, and the contemporary period has been no exception. The United States never aspired to be the unilateral world power in the sense of seeking a hegemonic level of power, but changes in the world power equation lifted it to that status. The rising power of the current century is China, which clearly alters the geopolitical map of global politics. Whether China's ascension will be achieved peacefully and productively will depend to some degree on the ability of the major participants to avoid the dangers that sometimes accompany the rise and decline of states.

The Dangers of Rising Powers: Thucydides' Trap

Because they represent changes in the relative power of states, the rise or decline of new states can be an unsettling phenomenon. Part of the problem is uncertainty. How much and in what ways will a rising power upset the existing order, especially to the detriment of powers whose relative places they will challenge and even supplant? What will be the nature of the change the rising power tries to implement, and how will that affect others in the system? If a rising state eclipses the position of other powers, what will the effect be on those affected? Possibly of the greatest importance, how will those being challenged react to these changes? More to the point, what will they do in the face of perceived threat both before and while it is occurring?

It is not a new question. The first major exposition of this phenomenon was recorded by the Greek historian Thucydides in the fifth century BCE. His *History of the Peloponnesian War* chronicled the long war between Athens and Sparta for supremacy, and the trigger for that conflict was the changing power relationship between the two city-states. As he described it, "It was the rise of Athens and the fear that this instilled in Sparta that made war inevitable."

The Harvard political scientist Graham Allison labeled this dynamic the "Thucydides' trap" in a 2017 *Foreign Affairs* article as a warning about the direction and growing drift in U.S.-Chinese relations. The "trap" arises from the degree of threat that a country experiences when a challenge arises from another, and especially a rival, state. It can trigger what is sometimes called an "action-reaction phenomenon." That situation is where one party (A) to a competition perceives a threat from the growth in power of a rival (B) and responds by building its power to a greater level than the rising competitor. The rising power (A) sees this change, views it as threatening and aggressive, and responds with another increase in power, which in turn induces the other party (B) further to increase its power. The resulting spiral may create a classic arms race that can lead to war—the trap.

Not all rising power situations result in war. The Cold War competition between the United States and the Soviet Union was clearly the result of a rising power challenging an established premier power, a prime feature of which was a classic arms race. Thucydides' trap was not sprung in this case, because each side came to realize that nuclear war between them would threaten both their existences.

The major purpose of Allison's argument is to try to manage the ongoing shift in relative power among the major powers. Change may be perpetual in the international system, but its intensity varies considerably. The end of World War II created a power vacuum that caused the decline of the pre-1939 powers and the rise of the United States, the Soviet Union, and eventually China to major significance in the international system. The implosion of the Soviet Union created another major change by vastly depreciating the power of one superpower and initiating a process to see what replaced the Soviet vacuum at the top. The result has been the current period of major rise represented by China and the adaptation to decline of Russia, a process that the Russians seek desperately to reverse. These kinds of dynamics are not confined to the superpowers of the system but can extend to regional conflict areas as well.

Application: Iran and Russia

It is widely believed that effective power in the world has been moving eastward in the twenty-first century. The major focus of that shift has, of course, been on the economic and military growth of China, but it also extends to regional arenas like the Middle East, where Iran is the leading aspirant to a broader role in regional geopolitics and considers itself as the pivotal state in the area. Russia is equally obviously a power in decline that struggles both to obscure that trend and seeks to regain its Cold War status against long-term odds.

Iran, a Rising Regional Power

Iran, the modern successor to Persia, is an enigmatic place. It is the largest and most populous country in the Arabian Middle East (for present purposes extending from the Russian and Turkish borders on the north to the southern border of the Arab Peninsula as it laps on the Indian Ocean and from the Afghani and Pakistani border westward to the Mediterranean Sea). Although Sunni and Shia Muslims make up virtually the entire population, Jewish Israel has become the dominant military force in the region largely thanks to its nuclear arsenal (see chapter 10), and the Israelis became a major geopolitical actor in the region during the Trump years, when the United States served as a mediating force in the overtures between the Israelis and several Persian Gulf states led by Saudi Arabia in an apparent attempt at encircling and further isolating Iran as well as supporting Israeli policy in the region—and notably toward Iran—virtually uncritically. The area is nominally referred to as Arab, indicating the ethnicity of Saudi and other Arab peninsular states, but the Persian Iranians, the major protagonists in the region, share neither Arab ethnicity nor adherence to the majority Sunni sect of Islam.

The region has been important to the world (including the United States) because of two major characteristics, both of which are changing. One is that Iran is one of the major oil-possessing and oil-producing countries in the world, and it sits astride the Persian Gulf supply route to the world. Despite American economic sanctions, it was the world's fourth largest producer in 2017 at about 4.5 million barrels per day. That production would increase greatly—and Iranian wealth and influence with it—should the American embargo be relaxed or lifted by the Biden administration. It should be noted that the boycott of Iranian oil has not been a constant in Iran's relations with the region. Under the Shah's rule, for instance, the Iranian navy patrolled the Gulf and assured that oil (including their own) had safe transit out of the region to destinations that included the United States and Israel. Sanctions are largely a byproduct of the deterioration of Iranian relations with the United States after the Iranian Revolution of 1979.

The other complicating factor has been Israel. Although Iran and Israel are bitter opponents today, that has not always been the case. The Persian Empire was the first country to recognize the original Israeli state over a millennium ago, and during the series of attempts by Arab states between 1948 and 1973 to attack, defeat, and even destroy the Jewish state, the Shah's Iran was the one state in the region that did not join the assault. The enormous enmity between Israel and Iran emerged after the 1979 revolution. A major part of that antagonism is the result of Israel's nuclear weapons possession and its use of their arsenal as a hidden cudgel over other states in the region, notably Iran. Much of Israeli opposition to Tehran arises from the fear that Iran might seek to "go nuclear," thereby denying Israel its status as the only regional nuclear power.

Is Iran Rising?

By any regional yardstick, Iran is the largest and arguably the most important state in its region of the Middle East. Given that international interest in the Arab world revolves around petroleum energy, it makes Iran an important world power as well. Since the Iranian Revolution of 1979 radicalized Iranian politics, Iran has been viewed and treated as a pariah state, a designation it finds abhorrent. Iran's aspiration in the region, extended to the international system at large, is to be recognized as the dominant regional power. Iran considers itself to be the rising, pivotal Levantine state and wants that status recognized.

The bases of an Iranian claim to rising power status begins with geography and demography. Iran is physically the second largest state in the Arab Middle East following the much less populous Saudi Arabia, which is much larger physically than Iran but has a population less than half that of Iran. Iran is slightly larger physically than Alaska and is the eighteenth largest country in the world. It has the region's largest population with over eighty-three million, followed by Iraq (about forty million) and Saudi Arabia (around thirty-three million). Iran is the world's largest state with a Shiite majority and is by far the largest non-Arab state in the region. The only larger states in the general region are Pakistan to the east and Egypt to the west. Among the Persian Gulf/Arab states, Iran's sheer size is striking. Were Iran's economy to be unfettered from American-led sanctions, it would also be an economic powerhouse regionally as well.

History and location reinforce Iran's position as a rising, pivotal state. As noted, it is the world's second oldest civilization, its geopolitical prowess interrupted by three centuries of Ottoman rule. It was part of the geopolitical struggle after World War I to reconstitute the region, and its attempt to regain its interrupted sway is clearly part of its campaign to be considered pivotal.

Iran's struggle to reassert itself has been impeded by both internal and external opposition. The internal struggle has been between those who have sought to modernize Iran's power by Westernizing it and transforming it into a Western-style country and traditional Shiites. The rise to power, rule, and fall of the Shah represents the modernizing approach in close cooperation with the United States, and it produced a Westernized elite that still exists in the country as a suppressed minority. Like most religiously dominated Muslim countries, the Westernization and modernization that accompanied the thrust of what the Shah deemed the "White Revolution" was profoundly opposed by the very conservative Shiite religious hierarchy and their mostly rural supporters, and these groups formed the core of support for the Iranian Revolution of 1979 and remain in power as an elite deeply suspicious of the West—and especially the United States, a status reinforced by the Iranian presidential election of 2021.

The Ambivalent American Influence

The relationship between the United States and Iran has been schizophrenic. After World War II, the Americans developed a largely oil-driven interest in preventing Soviet penetration into Iran, and arguably the first episode of what became the Cold War played out in the Azerbaijans—the Soviet socialist republic and the Iranian province—where the United States moved militarily to prevent a Soviet occupation seen as a stepping-stone to Persian Gulf oil. The Americans aligned themselves (see Kinzer, *The Brothers*) closely with the Shah between 1950 and his flight from the country in 1979 and were his principal supporters and especially mentors in attempting to Westernize the country. Although generally unrecognized at the time, this placed the Americans in fundamental opposition to the Shiite masses who opposed Reza Pahlevi, and this fissure did not become apparent to Americans until the Shah fled into American exile in 1979. The seeds of enmity emerged as the Americans refused to remand the Shah to revolutionary forces in Iran, to which the Iranians responded by occupying the American embassy in Tehran for 444 days. The relationship has thus been adversarial ever since.

The American relationship with Iran has gone through two distinct post–World War II phases. The first began with the courtship of Reza Pahlevi and participation in the coup that overthrew Mohammed Mossadegh, the only fully democratically elected leader of Iran, and replaced him with the Shah in 1950. The next three decades witnessed a political "romance" between the two countries, wherein the Americans became the chief advisors of the White Revolution and Iran protected the flow of oil to the West. It seemed a very symbiotic relationship, but it also masked the considerable internal opposition to the Shah for his Westernization of the country and his autocratic rule that suppressed large portions of the population outside Tehran and offended religiously conservative Shia. The Americans ignored both trends. The Shia did, however, form the basis of support for the Iranian Revolution of 1979, which was both an anti-Shah *and* anti-American uprising.

The Current Opposition

Iran's unique geopolitical situation and mutually poisonous relationship with the United States defines both the geopolitical predicament in which Tehran finds itself and the problems it must overcome before its status as a rising power is generally accepted. The outcome of the revolution has contributed to this dilemma by spawning an Iranian regime that is both militant and obstinate, thereby making reconciliation with others more difficult. That said, it faces three interrelated problems that hinder acceptance of its status. These are the inter-Islamic regional balance of power among the states of the region, the poisonous, violent relationship with Israel highlighted by Israeli nuclear weapons, and restoration of some normalcy in the less adversarial relationship with the United States. Each must change for Iran to be recognized as a rising power.

The first problem deals with the Islamic balance of power in the region. The chief protagonists are Iran as leader of the Shiite world and Saudi Arabia as leader of the Sunni states. Each side has tried to isolate the other: the Saudis with their nascent encirclement of Iran featuring rapprochement with Israel, and the Iranians by mobilizing support in the Shiite crescent of Iran, Iraq, Syria, and Lebanon (see Snow, *The Middle East and American National Security*). The Saudi effort is by necessity more political than military, because the Saudi armed forces are no match for Iran's. The Saudis have long relied on the United States for their effective defense, as they did in the 1990–1991 Gulf War confrontation with Iraq. The relationship Saudi Arabia has negotiated with Israel implicitly creates a bond between the two that arguably extends to Israeli nuclear weapons.

Iranian-Israeli relations are the second, and arguably most volatile and dangerous, part of the puzzle. Israeli nuclear weapons are the key implicit underpinning of their security posture, providing Israel with a source of protection it would not otherwise enjoy. Israel is thus the military hegemon of the Middle East, but that position holds only if Israel maintains a regional nuclear monopoly. Iran, on the other hand, is the only other state that could rapidly go nuclear if it chose to do so, which would destroy that monopoly. Despite other rhetoric from Jerusalem, preventing proliferation in the form of an Iranian nuclear capability is the key element in Israeli security strategy, and the Israelis have demonstrated they will be utterly ruthless in maintaining their monopoly, as the recent assassination of the top Iranian nuclear scientist demonstrates. On the other hand, breaking that monopoly is the key to Iran's claim as a rising, pivotal state. It is a fundamental problem, and Middle Eastern peace probably hinges on its resolution, either by Israeli nuclear disarmament or Iranian nuclearization. The Trump administration did not address this issue other than through unilateral denunciations of Iran; the Biden administration is likely to be less ritually anti-Iranian.

The resolution or containment of the first two problems depends on dealing with the third, which is relaxation—even return to something like normalcy—in U.S.-Iranian relations. The two countries have not had relations since 1979 and have regularly pilloried one another rhetorically and in terms of policy. Animosity was especially venomous during the Trump years, when U.S. policy closely (and consciously?) mirrored Israeli policy. The major issues between the two countries are continued American sequestering of Iranian financial assets in the United States and the return of the Americans to the treaty by which Iran agrees not to expand their nuclear program. Some of Biden's closest advisors, including Secretary of State Tony Blinken, helped craft the Joint Comprehensive Plan of Action (JCPOA, as the nuclear deal is known) and wants American participation reinstated, and loosening American control of Iranian monetary assets could be part of that arrangement.

Russia, a Declining State with Ambitions

The Russian profile in the contemporary world has been that of a state in decline. During the Cold War, the Soviet Union/Russia was clearly the "senior partner" of the communist world against the West. Russia stagnated and began the process of economic decline two decades before it physically dissolved, and it struggled with postcommunist chaos until the rise of Vladimir Putin to leadership in 2000. Russia has tried to piggyback a geopolitical resurgence on oil revenues, but these efforts have been partially subverted by downward fluctuations in petroleum prices. Mirroring centuries of Russian history, Putin has attempted to use expansionist policies to reassert Russia's claims to superpower status. It has been only a partial success and continues in the shadow of negative trends, especially demographic, in the Russian future.

States was enlisted to help get part of the former Soviet nuclear arsenal out of the Soviet Socialist Republics, where the loyalty and responsibility of newly independent regimes was suspect, and to engage in some inspection of those weapons to guard against nuclear accidents. This was the situation Vladimir Putin inherited when he became president in 2000.

The Limits of Russian Power and Prospects

A declining Russia was beset by two major problems that continue to bedevil Putin's dream of reasserting Russian status as a superpower. One is demographic: the Russian population was halved by the breakup of the USSR and has declined more since. The other is economic: Putin has addicted Russia to an economy dominated by oil sales, and the result is a petrolist state with all its inherent problems, including dependence on a wildly vacillating market for that resource.

The demographic problem is straightforward and dire. Using U.S. Census Bureau figures, the 2019 *World Almanac and Book of Facts* documents the Russian population decline. In 1990, the last year of the Soviet Union, its population stood at about 300 million (compared to 290 million for the United States). In 2018, the estimate was 142 million, and by 2050, it is projected at 129 million. By contrast, the U.S. projections are over 330 million today and extrapolated to 398 million in 2050, three times that of Russia. Russia's population used to be third largest in the world; it is now ninth and falling. Factors in this dismal prospect include declining fertility rates and shortened life expectancies. Because only 7 percent of Russian land is arable, it also has trouble feeding itself. Proposed solutions include greater immigration and expansion into new territories. Neither is likely to work well.

The other problem is economic. Putin tied Russia's economy to oil revenues, making the country an effective petrolist state, with all the vagaries attached, including boom and bust cycles based on the global price of oil, corruption, and a government dependent on oil revenues. When oil prices are high, the system appears to work, because there is a surplus of money to spend on citizen welfare and government expansion. When oil prices fall, discontentment and associated problems return. People get less benefits, the corruption associated with petrolism increases, and the system becomes what is sometimes called a kleptocracy. The price of oil collapsed in the early 2010s, and in a two-year period, Russian gross domestic product fell from 2 to 1.2 trillion (U.S. gross domestic product at the time was over 16 trillion).

Putin's dream is clearly a return to great-/superpower status, and both demographic and economic dynamics are heavy anchors weighing it down. Clearly, Putin wants to rekindle the prestige of the Soviet days, and his long-term success and popularity are largely dependent on a return to glory for the highly nationalistic Russians. Putin witnessed the precipitous decline of his country in the 1990s, and he is struggling to reverse that status. He has, in typical Russian fashion, chosen expansion as his preferred method—into the Crimea and Eastern Ukraine for now.

Putin's Russia may be a modern Potemkin Village, but it is still an important state whose continued decline can only further destabilize world politics. Nuclear

The Russian Saga

Russia has always been an enigmatic place. It sits astride the eastern part of Europe and has spread across Asia to the Pacific, making it the world's largest country in land mass, even since half the Soviet Union disappeared and the USSR dissolved. Its sheer size makes it a consequential place, but it has remained culturally and politically, as well as physically, at the fringes of a world order it seeks to join, even dominate, as a fully accepted member. Much of Russia's political history has been the quest for acceptance as a great power. It achieved that status after World War II; it lost it after the Soviet Union dissolved.

Although much about Russia is mysterious from the outside (Winston Churchill's depiction of the USSR as "a riddle wrapped in a mystery inside an enigma"), its broad contours are not. By most material standards, Russia has always trailed behind the other major powers, and it continues to do so today. Its claim to status is its size, and it has sought to augment its claim to world power status through relentless expansion. The sheer size and resultant power of the Soviet Union represented its high-water mark in international political terms. Along with the United States, it was the only major participant in World War II to emerge as a significant power, and its development of a large nuclear arsenal allowed it to rise to the status it had fought so long to achieve.

Unfortunately for the Russians, part of the image was an illusion, a false front that obscured flawed foundations. The Soviet Union's claim to leadership in the world was almost entirely military. Its political system was harsh and authoritarian and eventually lost the support of the people both within its borders and in places like Eastern Europe that were effectively vassal states. The economy was essentially a developing world construct in structure and performance, leading to its depiction by some as a "frozen banana republic with nuclear weapons."

Despite efforts to obscure the fact, the fatal weakness of the Soviet system was evident to some by the early 1970s. Soviet academic economists called it the Era of Stagnation: by 1973, the only economic sector not in decline was vodka production. Soviet academic economists adopted Mikhail Gorbachev and his wife, Raisa (a colleague at Moscow State University), to publicize this fate, which helped lead to Gorbachev's ascension to power. This crisis was most strikingly obvious in science and technology (a traditional Russian strength), and especially computer development, where the Soviets lagged progressively further behind. These trends led Gorbachev in two fateful policy directives. First, he determined that he must end the Cold War and try to rejoin the world order to gain access to funds and technology. Second, in 1989, he ended a debilitating military adventure in Afghanistan. The result demonstrated the weakness of the iron fist and encouraged defections from both the Soviet Union and among its satellites. I discussed this progression in a three-edition series of books in the 1990s collectively titled *The Shape of the Future*.

The end of the Cold War began Russia's decline from superpower to a lesser status. Russia was plunged into essentially a state of economic and political chaos in the 1990s with which Boris Yeltsin, the new leader, could not successfully cope. The economy collapsed, leaving many Russians in abject poverty and misery. Former Soviet authority and power declined to the point that the United weapons mean it remains a dangerous state. It has under its permafrost and Arctic waters some of the world's largest stores of energy, which the world needs. It is still a potentially aggressive, expansionist, and politically destabilizing place—it is Russia, after all, and that alone causes it to be described, possibly hyperbolically, as a "rising revisionist power." The question is what can be done to make it a power with a status it can embrace that does not trigger Thucydides' trap.

Conclusion

International power status is clearly in a period of transition. The Soviet Union disintegrated in 1991, and China has emerged as a preeminent power. In the Middle East, Iran clearly aspires to a more prominent role. The concept of rising and declining states is an intuitively appealing way to depict these changes and how those countries affected have responded to them.

Periods of transition are always unsettling to those involved, and the trajectory of change is seldom linear or entirely predictable. Russia is not what it used to be, and it wants to return to its former status. It is not clear what its path to redemption is or whether a rise to its former status is even possible. The Iranian situation is different. Iran aspires to be recognized as a rising power, but that recognition is denied by regional rivals like Saudi Arabia and Israel and extra-regionally by the United States. If Russia seeks to regain its former status, Iran seeks to have its status recognized.

The United States stands in the middle of this turbulence. The competition with a Soviet superpower dominated the post–World War II period, and a weaker Russia clearly resents and works to subvert its contemporary invidious comparison with American status. Iran has been both an American friend and foe at different times. Since 1979, it has been the enemy, a status that impedes global recognition of its preferred status. A change in American attitudes is an important element in Iran's ascent. The Iranian election results in June 2021 do not change that assessment.

Thucydides remains relevant. Athens and Sparta came in conflict because one was rising and the other feared the consequences of that rise and reacted to blunt it, activating a process that ended in war. The contemporary situation is distinguished by rising and declining forces in both directions. Avoiding Thucydides' trap is arguably more imperative now, because all the parties who could become entrapped in its dynamics are affected by nuclear arsenals the resort to which could be catastrophic. That makes avoiding the trap even more imperative.

Study/Discussion Questions

1. What are rising and declining states? Why is the distinction important in the conduct of international relations?

2. What are the categories of powers through which states ascend (rise) or descend (decline)? Briefly describe each, including examples.

3. What is Thucydides' trap? How does it work? Why is it important, especially in the context of rising and declining states?

4. Describe Iran as a rising state. How has it risen, what problems does it pose, and what are the barriers to its continuing ascent?

5. Describe Russia as a declining state. What caused it to decline? What are its prospects of reversing that decline over the short and long haul? What problems does it pose?

6. Which state, Iran or Russia, poses the greatest threat to international peace and stability due to its process of rise/decline? Defend your choice.

7. Iran's rise is regional rather than global. What are the basic sources of opposition to Iran's rise in the region and beyond?

8. Why are these changes in status important to the United States? What is the American status in these terms? How does each change pose a different problem to the United States in terms of avoiding Thucydides' trap?

Bibliography

Abrahamian, Ervand. *A History of Modern Iran* (revised and updated second edition). Cambridge, UK: Cambridge University Press, 2018.

Alawi, Ali. *Iran and Palestine: Past, Future.* New York and London: Routledge, 2019.

Allison, Graham T. *Destined for War: Can America and China Escape Thucydides' Trap?* Boston, MA: Houghton-Mifflin, 2017.

Amanat, Abbas, Derek Perkins, et al. *Iran: A Modern History.* New Haven, CT: Yale University Press, 2019.

Art, Robert A., and Kenneth N. Waltz, eds. *The Uses of Force: Military Power and International Politics* (seventh edition). Lanham, MD: Rowman & Littlefield, 2009.

Aslan, Reza. *No God but God: The Origins, Evolution, and Future of Islam* (updated edition). New York: Random House Trade Paperbacks, 2011.

Axworthy, Michael. *A History of Iran: Empire of the Mind.* New York: Basic Books, 2016.

Bakhtiari, Bahman. "Iran's Conservative Revival." *Current History* 106, no. 696 (January 2007): 11–16.

Ben-Joseph, Uri. "Why Israel Should Trade Its Nukes: Stop Iran's Centrifuge by Accepting a Nuclear-Free Middle East." *Foreign Affairs* (online), October 25, 2012.

Biden, Joseph S. Jr., and Michael Carpenter. "How to Stand Up to the Kremlin: Defending Democracy against Its Enemies." *Foreign Affairs* 97, no. 1 (January/February 2018): 44–57.

Central Intelligence Agency. *The CIA World Factbook, 2020–2021.* New York: Skyhorse Publications, 2020.

Committee on Foreign Relations, U.S. Senate. *Strategic Assessment of U.S.-Russian Relations.* New York: CreateSpace, 2018.

Dawisha, Karen. *Putin's Kleptocracy: Who Owns Russia?* New York: Simon and Schuster, 2014.

Frantzman, Seth. *After ISIS: America, Iran, and the Struggle for the Middle East.* Jerusalem: Gefen Publishing House, 2019.

Friedman, Thomas J. "The First Law of Petropolitics." *Foreign Policy* (May/June 2006): 28–36.

Fromkin, David. *A Peace to End All Peace: The Fall of the Ottoman Empire and the Creation of the Modern Middle East* (twentieth anniversary edition). New York: Holt, 2009.

Ghattas, Kim. *Saudi Arabia, Iran, and the Forty-Year Rivalry That Unraveled the Culture, Religion, and Collective Memory in the Middle East*. New York: Holt, 2019.

Goldberg, Jeffrey. "How Iran Could Save the Middle East." *The Atlantic* 304 (August 2009): 66–68.

———. "The Lessons of Henry Kissinger." *Atlantic* 218, no. 5 (December 2016): 50–56.

Gorbachev, Mikhail. *The New Russia*. Cambridge, UK: Polity Press, 2016.

Hiro, Dilip. *Cold War in the Islamic World: Saudi Arabia, Iran, and the Struggle for Supremacy*. Oxford, UK: Oxford University Press, 2019.

Hitchcock, Mark. *Israel and Iran: Wars and Rumors of Wars*. Irvine, CA: Harvest House, 2013.

Kaplan, Robert D. "Living with a Nuclear Iran." *The Atlantic* 306, no. 2 (September 2010): 70–72.

Kazemzedeh, Massoud. *Iran's Foreign Policy: Elite Factionalism, Ideology and the Nuclear Weapons Program*. New York and London: Routledge, 2020.

Kinzer, Stephen. *The Brothers: John Foster Dulles, Allen Dulles, and Their Secret World War*. New York: Times Books, 2013.

———. *Iran, Turkey, and America's Future*. New York: Times Books, 2010.

Legvold, Robert. *Return to Cold War*. Cambridge, UK: Polity Press, 2016.

Mandelbaum, Michael. "The New Containment: Handling Russia, China, and Iran." *Foreign Affairs* 98, no. 2 (March/April 2019): 123–31.

Nalbandov, Robert. *Not by Bread Alone: Russian Foreign Policy under Putin*. Washington, DC: Potomac Books, 2016.

Owen, John M. "From Calvin to the Caliphate: What Europe's Religious Wars Tell Us about the Modern Middle East." *Foreign Affairs* 94, no. 3 (May/June 2015): 77–89.

Parsi, Trita. *Treacherous Alliance: The Secret Dealings of Israel, Iran, and the United States*. New Haven, CT: Yale University Press, 2008.

Polk, William R. *Understanding Iran: Everything You Need to Know from the Present to the Islamic Revolution, from Cyrus to Ahmadinejad*. New York: Palgrave Macmillan Trade, 2011.

Riedel, Bruce. *How America's Wars in the Middle East Began*. Washington, DC: Brookings Institution Press, 2019.

Shaked, Ayelet. "Ministering Justice: A Conversation." *Foreign Affairs* 95, no. 4 (July/August 2016): 2–8.

Sick, Gary G. *All Fall Down: America's Tragic Encounter with Iran*. New York: Random House, 1985.

Snow, Donald M. *Cases in U.S. National Security: Concepts and Processes*. Lanham, MD: Rowman & Littlefield, 2019.

———. *Regional Cases in U.S. Foreign Policy* (second edition). Lanham, MD: Rowman & Littlefield, 2018.

———. *The Middle East and American National Security: Ending Forever Wars*. Lanham, MD: Rowman & Littlefield, 2021.

———. *The Shape of the Future: The Post–Cold War World* (three volumes). Armonk, NY: M. E. Sharpe, 1991, 1995, 1999.

Stent, Angela. *The Limits of Partnership: U.S.-Russian Relations in the Twenty-First Century*. Princeton, NJ: Princeton University Press, 2015.

Thucydides. *The History of the Peloponnesian War*. New York: Penguin, 1954 (originally published in the fourth century BCE).

Toal, Bernard. *Near Abroad: Putin, the West, and the Contest over Ukraine and the Caucasus*. Oxford, UK: Oxford University Press, 2017.

Trenin, Dmitri. *Should We Fear Russia?* Cambridge, UK: Polity Press, 2016.

———. *What Is Russia Up to in the Middle East?* Washington, DC: Potomac Books, 2017.

Tsygankov, Andrei. *Russia's Foreign Policy: Change and Continuity in National Identity* (fourth edition). Lanham, MD: Rowman & Littlefield, 2016.

Uskowi, Nader. *Temperature Rising: Iran's Revolutionary Guards and Wars in the Middle East*. Lanham, MD: Rowman & Littlefield, 2018.

Waltz, Kenneth N. "Why Iran Should Get the Bomb." *Foreign Affairs* 91, no. 4 (July/August 2012): 2–5.

The World Almanac and Book of Facts, 2019. New York: World Almanac Books, 2019.

Yadlin, Amos, and Ebtesman el-Ketbi. "The United States Should Move Forward, Not Back, on Iran: A Return to the Nuclear Accord Would Be a Strategic Mistake." *Foreign Affairs* (online), January 27, 2021.

Zarif, Muhammad Javad. "Iran Wants the Nuclear Deal It Made: Don't Ask Tehran to Meet New Demands." *Foreign Affairs* (online), January 22, 2021.

7

Internationalism and Unilateralism

Evaluating the Fate of NATO

The early twenty-first century has produced a growing amount of speculation about the nature and distribution of power in the international system. Under the leadership of Vladimir Putin, Russia has mounted an attempt to reassert its twentieth-century role since he assumed the presidency, as discussed in chapter 6. China has risen to possess the world's largest economy (see chapter 2) and has shown signs of geopolitical expansionism around the world. The United States, on the other hand, has demonstrated some signs of geopolitical recession. The challenge of reacting to the 9/11 attack arguably began this process, and it was accentuated by the isolationism of the Trump presidency. The liberal internationalist consensus crafted after World War II seems increasingly under siege. If so, what does this trend portend for the United States and the international order? If it is malevolent in effect, can it be reversed? What does it mean for venerable monuments of the international system like the North Atlantic Treaty Organization (NATO)?

The internationalist order has never been universally embraced. In the 2010s, the challengers have become increasingly bold, vocal, and powerful. The most common banner under which this opposition is expressed is that of nationalism, and one way the challenge is often phrased is as an intellectual contest between internationalism and unilateralism. This construction played a major role in the Brexit decision by the United Kingdom to leave the quintessential expression of a more cooperative order, the European Union (see chapter 5), and it was a major theme of the Trump administration during its four years in office. The contrast between the two approaches marks the clearest foreign policy difference between President Biden and his predecessor.

Both approaches have common and contrasting bases. Both, for instance, have the promotion of the interests of the state as their main goal. They fundamentally disagree about whether this goal is more effectively pursued through collective action that seeks to enlist the international system in joint actions that promote mutual security and prosperity (going it together) or through unilateral actions wherein the benefit of others is far less important than benefits for the individual country trying to maximize its utilities (going it alone). Both approaches have been pursued in the past and present; preference for one or another has always been a matter of time, circumstance, and the predilections of their enthusiasts.

The liberal internationalist order has been the dominant paradigm for most of the world for just over a century. Its genesis was in nineteenth-century Europe and paralleled the democratization of the continent. It is generally associated with British prime minister Lord Palmerston. The liberal order was not well established enough to prevent the dynamics leading to World War I, and in its wake, it was revived by President Woodrow Wilson at the Versailles peace negotiations in 1918 that led to the founding of the first contemporary universal manifestation of internationalism, the League of Nations.

The League experiment failed. The Great Depression that began in 1929 was a major cause of that failure, as desperate countries turned their economies inward to protect their national populations, and one victim was cooperation among them. Internationalist sentiments and efforts collapsed as a result, replaced by unilateralist, isolationist alternatives that helped create tensions contributing to the slide to World War II, the largest bloodletting in human history. In that war's wake, the internationalists reemerged and took leadership virtually by default in reasserting internationalism and building an institutional framework reflecting their return. Symbolized by the single term of Donald J. Trump, that consensus has been under some assault again. How it evolves will affect the balance of power in the world order.

Fluctuations between periods when one conceptualization or the other has dominated policy outcomes in world capitals occur periodically, often associated with how prosperous various members of the international system feel and how positively they view the future. Internationalism is inherently a more optimistic philosophy that is premised on the notion that both its champions and those associated with them will prosper by cooperating with one another. That has been the prevailing American assessment from the end of World War II until the recent past. Unilateralism, on the other hand, is inherently more suspicious and pessimistic, based in an adversarial view of international interactions and seeking maximum unilateral control over relations. The two philosophies are currently at rhetorical "war" for dominance. How the situation evolved to this point and what it means for venerable institutions like NATO are featured concerns that will occupy our attention.

Principle: Internationalism or Isolationism

The designations and interpretations of the two approaches for dealing with other countries are not precise. Internationalism tends to be associated with political liberalism. It is premised on the underlying notion that cooperation between sovereign entities can yield better results than individual, adversarial approaches. This premise leads to a positive predilection toward international agreements binding states in cooperative effort in areas as diverse as economic trade agreements to common efforts to control climate change. Isolationists, on the other hand, have a more pessimistic view of human nature and are more prone to view arrangements where states forfeit political power with suspicion, even disdain.

This basic distinction reflects views on the sanctity of sovereignty. Those who favor international approaches to problems believe that transcending political boundaries is an acceptable compromise, whereas isolationists tend to be more jealous defenders of the absolute sanctity of sovereignty as the bedrock guarantor of political independence. Sometimes the dialogue between enthusiasts of the positions can be spirited, even mean-spirited. In a recent *Foreign Affairs* article, Kirshner refers to the isolationist position as "knuckle dragging America firstism," and isolationists refer to internationalists as "socialists" or worse.

The debate between internationalism and unilateralism and American participation in that debate first surfaced in the early twentieth century. It was not a coincidence. The United States had been very consciously isolationist before 1900, reflecting a combination of disdain for European politics and a perceived need for protection to shield its fledgling economy. By the early 1900s, the United States was clearly a rising power, a status solidified by its late but decisive intervention in World War I. During the "Roaring Twenties" that followed the war, it was an enthusiastic international participant in a globalizing world order. When the Great Depression destroyed that prosperous edifice, the United States retreated to its traditional isolationism.

The debate joined after World War I has continued. The first American-led effort to institute internationalism failed, and scholars and others have long debated why the League collapsed. A variety of reasons have been put forward. They all reflect philosophical differences between supporters of the two basic positions that are both symbolically and physically present in the current debate. They are worth considering because of their resemblance to the past.

Since World War I, the United States has been a featured actor in the debate between internationalism and nationalist-based isolationism. The heart of the debate is, and always has been, over whether American interaction and entanglement with international affairs should be limited or extensive, which reflects a judgment about whether American interests are best served by differing levels of involvement in international affairs. For most of early American history, there was a consensus on isolation—going it alone—as the appropriate approach both to development of the United States across the continent and to isolate Americans from what many viewed as the taint of European politics.

World War I broke the historical consensus and introduced the internationalist element into the equation. It thus began a debate over the best approach for the country that has continued to the present. Following World War I, the debate ended with a return to isolationism in the United States. World War II was widely blamed, justly or not, on American retreat from international affairs. The argument is that if the United States had been an active, committed member of the League collective security system during the 1930s, those who started the war would have been deterred by the sure prospect of a crushing defeat. Isolationism was blamed both internationally and in the United States for the second global conflagration; its advocacy after the war became a very tough "sell" that drove its advocates underground, where they remained until the early twenty-first century.

It may seem—and be—chauvinistic to center this discussion on the United States, but the post-1945 situation justifies it. The United States emerged from the war as the overwhelmingly most powerful, physically capable state, rivaled only by a Soviet Union in overall nonmilitary power. America was supreme, and g3 rs

most world states needed American economic assistance to rebuild and military power to protect them from communist predators. The Americans in the U.S. State Department and their counterparts in the British Foreign Office and elsewhere were committed internationalists who believed, in Gideon Rose's words, in a liberal order conceptualized as a "positive sum game" based on "the potential for mutual gain from voluntary, rules-based international cooperation." They created an international order based on that premise that is now under some siege.

The basic premise of collective, international efforts is that aggregating the voice and resources of multiple countries increases the breadth and thus the effectiveness of those actions. It presumes that the multiple states that agree to cooperate have sufficiently similar interests and will support collective actions enough to convince those whom they oppose that their noncompliance is futile and that conformance with the collective demands is thus necessary. For a united front to arise and be effective, those banding together must agree on the values to be enforced (including the desirability of collective action) and on the greater effectiveness and personal and systemic virtue of collective action. Most importantly, they must be willing to accept and enforce collective judgments. The latter criterion is most problematic, since such proposals are likely to run afoul of strictly nationalist, sovereignty-based objections.

The Rise of Internationalism

The isolationists "won" the interwar debate over whether collective responses to international threats were preferable to individual responses. This "triumph" notably was most pronounced in the United States; the Americans retreated to "splendid isolationism," cutting off as much political interaction with the rest of the world as they could. During the 1930s, the battle cry for this movement, especially associated with Charles Lindbergh, the first person to fly an airplane solo across the Atlantic Ocean, was "America First," a slogan reprised by Trump when he was in office. The answer to going it together or alone was that the United States would go it alone.

World War II discredited that position—at awful costs (an estimated eighty million people died because of the war, roughly equally divided among civilian and combatant deaths). The internationalists had lost the 1930s, but they reemerged within the leadership of the major powers opposing fascism and went about fashioning and institutionalizing the liberal internationalist vision they brought to the postwar world.

The new order emphasized the underlying values and observations of the liberal internationalist argument and created an institutionalized system reflecting those beliefs. Proponents argued that the postwar geopolitical order was in such disarray that only the United States could take the effective lead in repairing it, and that the principles of liberal internationalism were the only basis on which this reconstruction could occur. Remaining advocates of exclusionary nationalism disagreed with this assessment and the implications of its implementation, especially possible incursions on sovereign prerogatives. The outcomes of the war, including the looming Soviet threat, rendered them mute, although it did not convert them.

The heart of the liberal internationalist position is the need for and benefit of cooperation across state lines to strengthen and redefine international relations. This cooperation includes a belief that collective action between member states is more effective than unilateral action, and that universality of membership and commitment are necessary conditions for effective action (a legacy of the League). The movement was, as Haass points out, dominated by the democratic states, which sought to use Wilsonian principles of diplomacy to "strengthen ties and foster respect for the rule of law within and between countries."

The liberal order was implemented through a series of elements that included, according to Rose, "international public goods such as global and regional security, freedom of the commons, and a liberal trading system." In other words, purpose of the order was to produce safety and access to economic opportunity through access to public goods (the "commons") and a trading system that promoted closer interaction.

The postwar 1940s provided a fertile geopolitical setting in which to create a series of institutional efforts to implement the liberal order. It began with the negotiation of the UN Charter in 1945 to create a successor to the failed League of Nations. Notably, it entreated all the world's countries to join and notably succeeded in getting the American commitment (the Charter was negotiated in San Francisco and the headquarters were to be located in New York to help ensure that outcome). Stronger collective security provisions than those of the League were also included but put in abeyance given the building Cold War confrontation. Economic well-being was fostered at the Bretton Woods meetings in New Hampshire, which produced the International Bank for Reconstruction and Development (IBRD or World Bank) and the International Monetary Fund. The purposes of the World Bank included providing loans for rebuilding wartorn Europe and funds for the development of less prosperous areas. The International Monetary Fund was created to stabilize international financial matters. Both remain vital institutions with headquarters in downtown Washington, DC. Bretton Woods also contained a proposal to promote global trade, but politics prevented the implementation of the World Trade Organization until 1994. This same dynamic helped, with American assistance, to create the movement that eventuated in the European Union.

The United States took the leadership in forming major initiatives to foster the sense of goodwill and safety the new order required, focused on the rising Cold War threat. On March 12, 1947, President Truman gave a speech where he argued the world was effectively divided into free and subjugated countries and that only the United States was physically capable of protecting the weak states. The address became known as the Truman Doctrine, and it was initially applied to providing the rationale for aid to Greece and Turkey to resist Soviet expansion into the Balkans. The United States led the establishment of its first military alliance during peacetime, the North Atlantic Treaty Organization (NATO), which is the subject of the Applications section of the chapter.

The Return of Isolationism

The internationalist consensus has eroded in the twenty-first century. The explanations for this erosion reflect changes in the nature of international politics and relations caused by phenomena like the rise of terrorism, the slowing of the global economy and the subsequent diminution of the popularity of globalization, and global activism in the form of wars—especially in the Middle East—that have drawn in the major powers and created new and unwelcome conditions such as migrant flows from those fleeing the vagaries of war or seeking economic betterment.

Rightly or wrongly, the liberal internationalist order has been blamed by some for the changing events and circumstances within the changing order. In the United States, for instance, questionable military involvements in places like Iraq, Afghanistan, and even Syria have led some to the conclusion that pursuing the liberal internationalist dream of growing global cooperation has overextended the United States in ways that diminish the situations in which it can act. In Europe, the flood of refugees into the countries of the European Union, among which they can move freely, was a large part of the motivation for British withdrawal from the European Union (Brexit).

The result has been to allow the reemergence of isolationism and unilateralism both in the United States and Europe. As Rose puts it, "liberalism's project ended up getting hijacked by nationalism. Large segments of many Western populations came to think the order wasn't working for them." This resurgence has been gradual in the new century. Its initial manifestation was a reaction to American failure to prevail in either Iraq or Afghanistan. President Obama was a spokesman for dialing back American military activism, completing the withdrawal from Iraq, championing (but failing to accomplish) a withdrawal from Afghanistan, and placing strong constraints on involvement in Syria. He did not extend this drawback from overt activism to other areas like economic cooperation, but it represented a crack in the solidarity surrounding the liberal consensus and thus an opening for a broader assault. As Cohen argues, Trump "merely accelerated a trend—that of Washington's retreat from its global responsibilities."

The attack by Trump on liberal internationalism represented a broad philosophical and operational assault, and it unleashed a backlash from supporters of the liberal order. Some of the condemnation has been strong and direct. In a January 2019 online *Foreign Affairs* article, Wright summarizes the Trump effect in stark terms. Trump, he says, "is the only President ever elected on a platform that explicitly rejected all of the pillars of U.S. grand strategy." Eliot Cohen, normally a reliably conservative voice, concurs, arguing, "The President has outlined a deeply misguided foreign policy vision that is distrustful of U.S. allies, scornful of international institutions, and indifferent, if not downright scornful, of the liberal international order." President Biden, a longtime internationalist, has reversed many of these emphases.

Cohen's strong words of condemnation reflect the continuing adherence many in the foreign policy elite have for the liberal order. They reflect a reaction to the Trump view of international relations, which was at odds with accepted practice. Trump's disdain for permanent interests and lack of support for international institutions reflects his opinion that the relations among states is a fluid, transactional enterprise wherein constancy and loyalty to others is less valued than the outcomes of individual interactions. Rose summarizes: "Trumpism is about winning, which is something you do to others. The order requires leading, which is something you do with others." Trump's attitude reflected a more transitory, varying attitude than the liberal order promotes. According to Wright, this basic orientation is reflected in policy toward the world: "a transactional relationship with other nations, a preference for authoritarian governments over democracies, a mercantilist approach to international economic policy, a general disregard for human rights and the rule of law, and the promotion of nationalism and unilateralism at the expense of multilateralism." This list is harsh and clearly constructed by an opponent of unilateralism, and it should be viewed as such.

Trump viewed his emphasis in terms of the long-running debate between liberalism and isolationism. In a speech before the United Nations in September 2018, he emphasized his conviction that the United States should act independently of others—essentially on its own—when he envisioned "a future of patriotism, prosperity, and pride" for the United States, sentiments that would clearly resonate more positively before an American than an international audience. Implicit in his assessment is a rejection of the internationalist position.

The unilateralist position associated with Trump represented the policy of the United States during his tenure. It represents a different image of international politics than has been the norm for the past three-quarters of a century. Of practical significance in this reformulation was a contrasting image of American ongoing relations with other countries that is much more fluid than has been the case in the past. Wright summarizes that contemporary foreign policy as "one in which the Trump administration has no permanent friends and no permanent enemies."

Normally, when one thinks of the internationalist-unilateralist distinction, it is in the context of political (e.g., United Nations) or economic associations like the European Union promoting positive goals of political cooperation or widening prosperity. The distinction also applies to dealing with more negative potential phenomena like preventing or defeating military threats, and the prime example since 1949 has been the North Atlantic Treaty Organization (NATO). It is relevant in the current context because then president Trump questioned continuing American participation in it largely on unilateralist grounds.

Application: The Fate of NATO

The North Atlantic Treaty (NATO) of 1949 is, in many ways, the crowning achievement of the liberal internationalists, and especially those in the United States who adhere to multilateral approaches to solving international problems. It was a precedent-setting event by virtue of being the first military association/alliance between the United States and other countries during peacetime, and it has persisted for over seven decades even though the purpose for which it was created (containing the Soviet military threat) has not existed in that form for over three decades.

NATO succeeded because the circumstances in which it was negotiated were fortuitous. Isolationism and unilateralism were universally blamed for allowing World War II to occur, and even in the United States, most people agreed that the splendid isolationism of the 1930s had provided the encouragement the Axis powers needed to proceed and that if the United States had been a committed member of the League, war might never have occurred. By 1949, it was also clear that the hopeful UN worldview of a world of cooperative powers enforcing the peace was collapsing into the Cold War. In these circumstances, the calls of those who counseled a multilateral approach to international conflict had the decided upper hand, and those who desired a traditional American retreat from the world had little chance of succeeding. NATO was thus the triumph of internationalism.

The dynamics that led to NATO were centered in the United States, which was by far the most powerful country in the post–World War II system at the time. Its military might, symbolized by the atomic bomb, confronted a huge Soviet Red army, but its overall superiority was unchallenged. The Americans were also the only people whose economy escaped the ravages of the war (the war stimulated the economy and helped end the Great Depression in the country), and America possessed the world's only fully functioning, solvent economic system. Whether they wanted to or not, the world had to listen to the United States. After the war, the voice of the United States was internationalist and so strong and resolute that it endured into the current century. It also reflected the sentiments of most Europeans.

The structure of the postwar world, of which NATO was a centerpiece, was fashioned through allied cooperation during the war itself. The UN Charter was the first piece, designed to be an improved universal international organization that avoided some of the pitfalls of the League of Nations—notably in the binding nature of its collective security provisions and the universality of its membership. This was followed by the Bretton Woods process and the extension of American assistance to war-torn countries menaced by communism. NATO was the security crown jewel in the liberal internationalist crown.

The North Atlantic Treaty was important from both an American and international vantage point for several reasons. It was indeed the first peacetime military alliance in American history. The United States had allied itself formally with other states during wartime to prosecute mutual efforts against common foes (the world wars being examples), but it was the first time it had done so during peacetime, and NATO created a military command to coordinate cooperative military preparation and war plans against its enemies. Additionally, NATO was endowed with a political arm, the NATO Council, the job of which was to reach common political judgments and to serve as a forum for consultation and cooperation among the members. Both arms of NATO remain vital parts of transatlantic cooperation, which was part of the intent of the formation of the alliance.

Because financial contributions became a point of contention under Trump, the initial funding of the enterprise should be mentioned. When NATO was negotiated and implemented, the economies of the European members were in shambles, and they simply could not afford the costs of NATO participation without sacrificing their economic recovery, which was deemed necessary to their resistance to communism. Thus, the Americans, the only people who *could* afford NATO, paid a disproportionate part of the bills. Some of that disproportion still exists and was part of the Trump assault on NATO's members not paying their fair share of costs.

The looming Soviet threat was, of course, the major operative challenge that allowed for broad support for the treaty and its implementation. Particularly after the national failure to recognize and blunt the fascist threat of the 1930s, the stage was set for international cooperation and even bipartisan cooperation within the United States. Democratic president Harry S. Truman was the leading American proponent of NATO, and he was joined in the effort by the powerful Republican chairman of the Senate foreign relations committee, Arthur Vandenburg, in leading ratification of the treaty through the U.S. Senate. The catchphrase of that cooperation was the idea that "politics ends at the water's edge"—the ideal that domestic affairs was a political battle but that when facing the rest of the world, the United States should maintain a united front with its friends and allies.

The result was the ultimate victory for the liberal internationalists, tying the United States both politically and militarily to Europe and setting the precedent for broader cooperation in the future. Of the greatest symbolic importance, the United States forfeited some sovereign control over its affairs—the protection of which is at the core of unilateralism—in the process. It was a wrenching experience, and one that illustrates the dynamic tension between the two preferences to this day. The clearest example was the nature and extent of commitment, a matter of some contemporary—if arguably disingenuous—concern largely on the part of the isolationists.

The operative and most controversial provision of the NATO Treaty was Article 5, known as the collective security article and the basis on which the American physical commitment to come to the aid of its allies is based. In one sense, it augmented the collective security provisions found in chapter VII of the UN Charter. The Charter provides for a collective security response to breaches of the peace, but it also grants permanent members of the Security Council (France, Great Britain, China, the United States, and Russia/Soviet Union) a veto over any actions. Because the Soviet Union was both a permanent member and the most likely violator, the provision disabled the council from action, which was the framers' intent in such a situation.

To deal with this problem, chapter VII of the UN Charter also contains Article 51, which provides for the formation of collective security alliances. NATO and Article 5 exemplified implementation of that provision. It also recognized a political reality in the United States reflecting its isolationist past and rigid adherence to protecting U.S. sovereignty.

The chief political objection to Article 5, expressed most strongly by American unilateralists in the Congress, was that a provision containing an automatic requirement to come to the military aid of an attacked ally violated Article 1, Section 8 of the U.S. Constitution, which reserves the exclusive right to Congress to make war. Thus, an automatic commitment would effectively transfer the war declaration power to whoever attacked a NATO country. American participation was so crucial to a successful NATO guarantee that the treaty's framers were forced to accommodate the Americans by removing automaticity of military action from the article. The result was a pledge with a politically necessary hedge.

To paraphrase the formal language of the NATO Treaty, Article 5 states that an attack against any member state is to be considered an attack against all members. In that event, the article entreats that "each and every member will consider this as an attack against all members and will take *such actions as it deems necessary, including the use of armed force, to restore and maintain the security of the North Atlantic area*" (emphasis added). The pledge commits the members to respond to such a provocation; the hedge is what the members pledge (and do not pledge) to do if such an attack occurs. As a literal, technical matter, they are not required to do anything but to talk the matter over. There is no obligation to use force. A pledge of automatic commitment would have torpedoed ratification of the treaty in the U.S. Senate and thus American participation in NATO. Instead, Article 5 creates the ability to prepare for the possibility of aggression and how to go about responding to it, but not any obligation to respond with military action. Since the war declaration is the quintessential expression of sovereign control, it was a unilateralist shibboleth that was too fundamental to challenge.

The commitment was less than the liberal internationalists wanted, because some analysts felt that it left the likelihood of a military response ambiguous. In the event the Soviets were contemplating an invasion of Western Europe (the contingency for which NATO was designed to avoid or defeat), they would have to ask themselves what the NATO, and especially the American, response would be. Would the United States commit armed forces and stop them, possibly starting World War III, if they acted? Or would they just debate the situation and decide not to act militarily?

Once nuclear weapons were introduced into the equation, the calculation became even more complicated. The French in particular believed that the United States would not honor a commitment to respond if doing so might risk their own nuclear annihilation and thus developed their own independent capacity to mount a nuclear defense regardless of what others wanted (the *force frappe*). Israel, which was tutored by the French, has a similar policy for their nuclear program.

The liberal internationalist/unilateralist divide thus resulted in a compromise where the price of acceptance of the treaty was an arguably diminished physical commitment. During the Cold War, the United States sought to make the prospects less ambiguous by stationing U.S. troops along the Iron Curtain frontier. This "tripwire," as it was known, meant American troops would be among the first killed in a Soviet thrust westward, making it more difficult to conclude a congressional postinvasion debate with inaction. It was the best they could do.

In the over seventy years since NATO came into existence in 1949, the provisions of Article 5 have been invoked only once. Ironically, the occasion was in response to the terrorist attack against New York and Washington on September 11, 2001, and it was the European allies who invoked the provision as a symbolic act of solidarity with their North American allies. The act further suggested a united effort and front against terrorist activity and called for cooperation among NATO members in pursuing the perpetrators and in subsequent activities against the common foe. The action raises some questions about the remarks by President Trump questioning whether continued American participation in the alliance was worth the effort and cost in 2018. During his June 2021 European trip, President Biden made a point of emphasizing the ongoing American commitment to the alliance.

Conclusion

Montenegro is a small country in the Balkans that was part of Yugoslavia until that country dissolved in 1992. It formed a union with Serbia that lasted until 2006, when Montenegro ended that merger and formed a union of its population of not quite 650,000 people with borders on Serbia, Bosnia, and Herzegovina, and Albania and the Adriatic Sea. Tiny Montenegro is hardly a geopolitical powerhouse and has no particular illusions of becoming one.

Montenegro became the twenty-ninth member of NATO on June 5, 2017, as part of its policy of integrating itself more fully with the rest of Europe. A year later, this created the basis for a conversation between President Trump and Fox News host Tucker Carlson on the latter's talk show. Carlson asked if Montenegro's membership meant his son might be forced into military service to defend Montenegro in the event it became involved in a war. Trump replied, "They have very aggressive people. They may get aggressive and congratulations, you're in World War III . . . That's the way it (NATO) is set up." In addition to the implausibility of such an act by tiny Montenegro (with an area slightly smaller than Connecticut), the president misrepresented Article 5, which is activated only when a member is menaced, not when it attacks someone else; it is a defensive, not an offensive commitment. The point, however, is what the exchange says about the liberal interventionist/unilateralist debate.

As noted, NATO is the crown jewel of the liberal interventionists' attempt to fashion international relations on a cooperative, multilateral base rather than on a unilateralist base. Without the alliance and the NATO Council, transatlantic cooperation would be more difficult in an institutional sense, and the Trump administration sought to loosen those bonds, reflecting its American nationalist philosophy that puts primary emphasis on the preservation of maximum sovereign control.

This is the current articulation of the answer to the desirability of going it together or alone. The consensus surrounding the liberal preference for collective cooperation and action has been challenged in this century by a retreat to a more exclusionary, nationalist view in various parts of the world. The question is what has caused this. The important questions are how permanent or transient this debate will be and what its short- and long-term effects on international relations will be. In terms of NATO, is international peace better served by a strong commitment to its provisions centered around Article 5? Or would a world in which those bonds were weakened or eliminated be a better, preferable place? NATO is about keeping the peace in an era when general war seems unlikely but could be catastrophic, as when NATO and the Warsaw Pact forces eyed one another across the barbed wire of the Iron Curtain. Cooperation no longer seems as crucial to world survival as it did, but does that make internationalism any less desirable and unilateralism any more acceptable?

Study/Discussion Questions

1. What are the liberal internationalist and unilateralist approaches to international relations? Compare and contrast them and their historic role in the United States.

2. The liberal internationalist philosophy has been dominant for a century. Discuss its genesis and evolution in both the United States and more widely from the League of Nations forward.

3. What are the premises of the two approaches? How did the interwar (1919–1939) experience affect the debate and shape of the post–World War II world?

4. Why is the American debate over internationalism and unilateralism so important? How has that debate evolved in the United States? What has the "Trump effect" been on contemporary discussions?

5. What is NATO? How and why has it been the centerpiece of the liberal internationalist approach to international relations since 1945?

6. The most controversial aspect of NATO is Article 5. What is the substance of that provision? What does it commit the United States and other members to do? How many times has it been invoked? When, by whom, and for what reason?

7. The United States has been one of the strongest proponents of unilateralism in the contemporary system. How do the provisions of the NATO Charter reflect how the NATO membership has dealt with that problem? If you were a member of a European delegation at NATO headquarters in Brussels, Belgium, how would you feel about the change of regime in Washington from Trump to Biden?

8. Recognizing any opinion will be a hybrid of pure positions, does internationalism or unilateralism make more sense to you? Defend your position.

Bibliography

Alcaro, Riccardo, ed. *The Liberal Order and Its Contestations: Great Powers and Regions Transiting in a Multipolar Era.* London: Routledge, 2018.

Beate, Jahn. *Liberal Internationalism: Theory, History, Practice.* London: Palgrave, 2013.

Blake, Aaron. "Trump's Montenegro Remarks Make It Abundantly Clear He Doesn't Understand NATO." *Washington Post* (online), July 18, 2018.

Carr, E. H. *The Twenty-Year Crisis, 1919–1939.* New York: Macmillan, 1939.

Chua, Amy. "Tribal World: Identity Is All." *Foreign Affairs* 97, no. 4 (July/August 2018): 25–33.

Cohen, Eliot A. "America's Long Goodbye: The Real Crisis of the Trump Era." *Foreign Affairs* 89, no. 1 (January/February 2019): 138–46.

Colgan, Jeff D., and Robert O. Keohane. "The Liberal Order Is Rigged: Fix It Now or Watch It Wither." *Foreign Affairs* 96, no. 3 (May/June 2017): 36–44.

Committee on Armed Services, U.S. Senate. *The North Atlantic Treaty Organization, Russia, and European Security.* Washington, DC: U.S. Senate, 2015.

Deudney, Daniel, and G. John Ikenberry. "The Liberal World: The Resilient Order." *Foreign Affairs* 97, no. 4 (July/August 2018): 16–25.

Gaddis, John Lewis. *Strategies of Containment: A Critical Appraisal of American National Security Policy during the Cold War* (revised and expanded edition). New York: Oxford University Press, 2005.

Haass, Richard. "How a World Order Ends and What Comes in Its Wake." *Foreign Affairs* 98, no. 1 (January/February 2019): 22–30.

Hazony, Yoram. *The Virtue of Nationalism.* New York: Basic Books, 2018.

Ikenberry, G. John. "The Plot against American Foreign Policy. Can the Liberal Order Survive?" *Foreign Affairs* 96, no. 3 (May/June 2017): 2–9.

Jervis, Robert, et al., eds. *Chaos in the Liberal Order: The Trump Presidency and International Politics in the Twenty-First Century.* New York: Columbia University Press, 2018.

Johnston, Seth A. *How NATO Adapts: Strategy and Organization in the Atlantic Alliance since 1950.* Baltimore, MD: Johns Hopkins University Press, 2017.

Kagan, Robert. *The Jungle Grows Back: America and Our Imperiled World.* New York: Knopf, 2018.

Kaplan, Lawrence. *N.A.T.O. 1948: The Birth of the Transatlantic Alliance.* Lanham, MD: Rowman & Littlefield, 2007.

———. *NATO Divided, NATO United: The Evolution of the Alliance.* Westport, CT: Praeger, 2004.

Kirshner, Jonathan. "Gone but Not Forgotten: Trump's Long Shadow and the End of American Credibility." *Foreign Affairs* 101, no. 2 (March/April 2021).

Kotkin, Stephen. "The Realist World: The Players Changed but the Game Remains." *Foreign Affairs* 97, no. 4 (July/August 2018): 10–15.

Lindley-French, Julian. *The North Atlantic Treaty Organization.* New York and London: Routledge, 2015.

Mearsheimer, John. *The Great Delusion: Liberal Dreams and International Realities.* New Haven, CT: Yale University Press, 2018.

Miller, Paul D. *American Power and the Liberal Order: A Conservative Internationalist Grand Strategy.* Washington, DC: Georgetown University Press, 2016.

Nye, Joseph S. Jr. *The Paradox of American Power: Why the World's Superpower Can't Go It Alone.* New York: Oxford University Press, 2003.

Rose, Gideon. "The Fourth Founding: The United States and the Liberal Order." *Foreign Affairs* 98, no. 1 (January/February 2019): 10–21.

Sexton, Jay. *A Nation Forged by Crisis: A New American History.* New York: Basic Books, 2018.

Sloan, Stanley. *Defense of the West: NATO, the European Union, and the Transatlantic Bargain.* Manchester, UK: Manchester University Press, 2016.

Smith, Tony. *Why Wilson Matters: The Origin of American Liberal Internationalism and the Crisis Today.* Princeton, NJ: Princeton University Press, 2017.

U.S. Army War College. *The Relevance of the European Union and the North Atlantic Treaty Organization for the United States in the Twenty-First Century.* Carlisle Barracks, PA: Strategic Studies Institute, 2017.

Walt, Stephen. *The Hell of Good Intentions: America's Foreign Policy Elite and the Demise of U.S. Primacy.* New York: Farrar, Straus, and Giroux, 2018.

Wright, Thomas. "Trump's Foreign Policy Is No Longer Unpredictable: Gone Are the Days of a Divided Administration." *Foreign Affairs Snapshot* (online), January 18, 2019.

8

Asymmetrical Warfare
The Forever War in Afghanistan

The physical evolution of warfare has been enormous over the past two hundred years or so. When the Napoleonic Wars were fought, soldiers marched into battle carrying muskets that fired a single bullet before they had to be reloaded. In battle, soldiers marched in close ranks that made them ready fodder for enemy musket fusillades and artillery. It was a brutal, and even by modern standards, bloody form of killing. The first half of the twentieth century was characterized by the ultimate applications of this Western-style warfare in two world wars.

That means of warfare has largely disappeared, replaced by another dominant form, asymmetrical warfare, a methodology and way of fighting more fitting and applicable where fighting mostly now occurs—in the internal affairs of the developing states. The purposes of asymmetrical warfare—enforcing or imposing the "national" interests of various groups within or between states and nonstate actors—has not changed the purposes of war so much as the ways it is conducted.

What is now called asymmetrical warfare is by no means new. Its roots are in antiquity and its tactics and strategies traceable at least back as far as Sun Tzu, the ancient Chinese military philosopher. In important ways, it is Eastern-style warfare that represents the application of principles allowing a militarily inferior force to compete with a larger, conventionally superior force. As such, it shares commonalities with the other major form of contemporary violence today, terrorism. Asymmetrical warfare is so pervasive that outside powers seeking to influence events in developing world situations find themselves drawn into developing world internal conflicts (DWICs) that they do not understand and are unprepared to fight, and they often lack enough interests to sustain the effort. That outcome is the essence of why warring groups may choose asymmetrical methods: those methods can make weaker groups (by conventional standards) more competitive and successful against otherwise stronger military opponents, and especially outside intervening powers.

The recently concluded (at least for Americans) war in Afghanistan illustrates this phenomenon. Variants of asymmetrical warfare are a long-standing part of the pattern of endemic Afghan instability. At the time of the September 11, 2001, terrorist attacks against the United States, one of the periodic Afghan civil wars was raging. The Taliban government, under attack by a coalition of rival tribal groups, was providing sanctuary to the Al Qaeda terrorists who committed these attacks and thus created an American interest where virtually no other interest had previously existed. When the Taliban refused to remand the Al Qaeda terrorists to American custody, the United States intervened to try to capture them. The attempt failed, and the United States had become involved in an asymmetrical war against the Taliban that lasted for over two decades before the United States left and the Taliban returned to power.

This chapter examines the challenge of asymmetrical warfare to thinking about war—its purposes, its conduct, and its outcomes. It will proceed in two sequential parts. It will examine the evolving nature of asymmetrical warfare. The discussion will move from a definition and examination of the dynamics to a brief comparison with terrorism and the difficulties that an outside conventionally armed state has when it intervenes in these wars. Second, it will apply those observations to the war in Afghanistan.

Principle: Asymmetrical Warfare

Asymmetrical warfare is ancient, but its modern prevalence combines perennial and contemporary influences, causes, and conditions. The pattern of warfare has changed enormously since the end of the Cold War. Remaining violent conflicts in the world are mostly internal wars in which the major powers may have limited interest. These wars have become the form of warfare for which all countries must prepare to some degree.

The result is the rising conceptual dominance of asymmetrical warfare. Two rejoinders need to be raised. First, the "new" way of war is neither new nor all that innovative. Asymmetrical warfare features the adaptations an inferior force makes when it is faced with a more powerful force with which it cannot compete successfully on the terms preferred by the superior opponent. The tactics and means may change, but the core rationales remain the same. Asymmetrical warfare thus is an approach to warfare, not a defined, set form of war or combat. It is a methodology, a way to organize the problem, not a method or set of battlefield or theater instructions. No two asymmetrical wars are the same, although their purposes may be. Thinking about and planning either to conduct or to counter asymmetrical situations requires considerable adaptability and openness to change. The lessons of one asymmetrical war may or may not apply directly to the next one.

The result is a changed contemporary global conflict environment. First, the imbalance in conventional capability between the United States and the rest of the world means no one is likely to confront the United States in large-scale conventional warfare, making necessary the adoption of different or asymmetrical approaches to negate that advantage. As Bruce Berkowitz puts it, "Our adversaries know they cannot match the United States in tanks, planes, and warships. They know they will most likely lose any war with us if they play according to the traditional rules." This innovation leads to the second new characteristic of the environment: the widespread adoption of asymmetrical ways to negate the problem of overwhelming military disadvantage and thus to reduce the military leverage greater power seems to convey. Asymmetrical approaches are intended, in Berkowitz's terms, "to change the rules to strategies and tactics that avoid our strength head-on and instead hit us where we are weak." This problem is progressive, because the core of asymmetrical warfare is constant adaptation, whereas conventional war is incremental, seeking better doctrinal solutions to problems.

The Context and Meaning of Asymmetrical War

Asymmetrical warfare is physically and conceptually distinct from Western-style warfare. It differs in terms of the reasons for which it is conducted, how those who employ it think and act, and in terms of the motives of the asymmetrical warrior. Asymmetrical warfare is not only militarily but also intellectually unconventional, both for those who practice and oppose its application. It is a methodology, not an ideology.

The heart of asymmetrical warfare is a mindset. The potential asymmetrical warrior always begins from a position of conventional military inferiority, and the problem is how to negate that disadvantage. Adaptability is at the heart of asymmetrical approaches to warfare. The asymmetrical warrior learns from what works and discards what does not. Since each asymmetrical campaign learns from experience, this means that each campaign will be different from others.

An example will help illustrate the point. Iraq attempted to confront the United States conventionally in Kuwait in 1990/1991 and was crushed. It learned from this experience that a future conflict with the United States could not be conducted the same way without equally devastating results. What to do? The answer in 2003 when the Americans invaded Iraq was to offer only enough resistance to American symmetrical force application to make the Americans think they were prevailing decisively, while regrouping to resist an occupation that they were powerless to prevent symmetrically. Thus, the limited use of irregular warfare (ambushes, car bombings, and suicide terror attacks) became the primary method of resisting the occupation—aimed to convince the Americans that the benefits of occupation were not worth the number of lives lost and treasure expended. Ultimately, it worked.

The Iraq experience introduced an important aspect about how the asymmetrical warrior can achieve his or her goals against an opponent it has no chance of defeating by conventional means. The contrast between asymmetrical objectives in entirely internal wars and those in which outsiders interject themselves illustrates the point. Asymmetrical warfare works in some situations, but not in all. The secret lies in understanding what the problem is and how to approach it.

Most asymmetrical wars occur in developing world situations. One group or another is displeased with its status and believes the situation can be rectified only by recourse to force. Normally, the insurgents begin their campaign less well armed and facing a government with much larger, usually conventionally armed forces. It cannot confront these opponents on their terms, and so it resorts to strategy and tactics that will allow it to shift the balance of power in its direction.

The problem is fundamentally different when an outsider intervenes to influence the outcome. The intervening party (often the United States) is likely to be so militarily superior that defeating it on the conventional battlefield is unthinkable. At the same time, its Achilles' heel is likely to be that it has lesser interests in the outcome and will, if engaged in protracted conflict including significant casualties, tire of the contest and leave. This problem is known as exceeding cost-tolerance (the amount of suffering an opponent is willing to endure to accomplish its objective).

The Lure of Asymmetrical Warfare

Asymmetrical warfare is attractive to participants in developing world situations because it often succeeds when the recourse to more conventional approaches almost always fails. The Iraqi experience with the United States provides one instructive allegory, and Vietnam another. The Vietnamese who opposed the United States could not match American firepower, a lesson they learned in their first direct encounter with the Americans at a place called the Ia Drang Valley. After that defeat, they retreated to a strategy of attrition, inflicting more casualties on the Americans than the United States would eventually tolerate while absorbing enormous losses of their own. Their cause, however, was much more important to them than the American mission was to the United States. American cost-tolerance was eventually exceeded, and the Americans left. The Vietnamese example suggests one variant of applying asymmetrical means, but all are different to some degree. Each situation is different and presents different problems. With no pretense of being exhaustive, at least two differences stand out.

First, political and military aspects of these conflicts will continue to merge, and distinctions between military and civilian targets and assets will continue to dissolve. The asymmetrical warrior will continue to muddy the distinction for two reasons. One is that he or she is likely to see conflicts as pitting societies against societies, so there is no meaningful distinction between combatants and noncombatants. Traditional symmetrical warfare draws sharp distinctions between the two. The other reason is that imbedding conflict within the fabric of society removes some of the advantage of the symmetrical warrior. Urban warfare, for instance, can be waged symmetrically only by concentrating firepower on areas where civilians and opponents are intermingled, where traditional rules of war prohibit actions targeting civilians, thereby inhibiting some actions, and where the problem of collateral damage (killing noncombatants) is a concern under conventional laws of war. The asymmetrical warrior often rejects these distinctions.

Second, the opposition in these kinds of conflicts often consists of nonstate actors acting out of nonstate motivations and without state bases of operation. International terrorist organizations, for instance, often carry out operations that cannot be tied to any state, and they are not clearly based in any state. This creates a problem of response for the symmetrical warrior. Whom does he or she go after? Whom does he or she attack and punish? This is a major problem the United States faced in dealing with Al Qaeda and the Taliban in Afghanistan and Pakistan: one cannot attack the enemy without attacking the sovereign territory of an ally.

The Asymmetrical Warfare-Terrorism Nexus

There is a dynamic, reciprocal relationship between asymmetrical warfare and terrorism. Recourse to terrorism is, in some ways, a form of asymmetrical warfare, and asymmetrical warriors (as well as some of their symmetrical counterparts) use terror as part of their operational tactics and strategy. As a tactical tool, terrorizing an enemy or a hostile target population may weaken the resolve or strength of that opponent. A terrorist attack in a major city may soften the resolve of the target population to continue resistance, as an example. It may also increase the target's resolve—bolstering rather than overcoming cost-tolerance.

The strategic relationship is complicated and reflects the strength of individual asymmetrical warriors. Terrorism is generally a method of the very weak, who can mount no serious conventional campaign to overcome an opponent but can hope to gain limited objectives by frightening that opponent to the point that it acquiesces to some terrorist demand. Purely terrorist attacks are generally not intended to achieve larger political goals, and their commission may be no more than a reminder to those attacked that the organization is capable of mayhem. Asymmetrical warfare, on the other hand, is the tool of a more robust insurgent movement which may not have the military strength to stand toe-to-toe with a conventional force, but whose strength is adequate to engage in military campaigns of attrition to wear down or discourage the opposition. The choice between the two techniques reflects levels of strength.

One can draw too fine a distinction between the two kinds of organization. A terrorist organization can grow into an asymmetrical warfare force, as former Al Qaeda in Iraq did when it became the Islamic State in 2014. At the same time, if an asymmetrical force suffers enough setbacks and is visibly weakened to the point it can no longer compete in an unconventional warfare role, it may revert to terrorism. The retreat of the Islamic State Caliphate suggests that happened to it. This ability to change shape and mission is nothing new. The writings of strategists like China's Mao Zedung and North Vietnam's Vo Nguyen Giap suggest that guerrilla and conventional forces could alternate roles and methods depending on their relative situations.

Terrorism and asymmetrical warfare are part of a continuum of forms of warfare with the common purpose of trying to prevail against a materially superior opponent. Terrorists operate at the lower end of the scale both in terms of ambition and capability, and asymmetrical warriors aim to transform a position of inferiority into a situation where they can prevail. Ironically, terrorism is often "showier" in that its results are often more spectacular and visually horrific, even if they have less effect on the final outcomes of conflicts. Asymmetrical warfare approaches, on the other hand, have more serious and long-term consequences that include the overthrow and replacement of governments and territories where outsiders may have perceived interests. This latter dynamic is why outsiders—including the United States—sometimes feel the need to intervene in these situations.

The Perils of Outside Involvement

Involvement in asymmetrical conflicts is the most likely form that major power engagement in military conflict will take for the foreseeable future. Such conflicts are almost always problematic and, as I have argued most extensively in *The Case against Military Intervention*, are likely to be unsuccessful, very frustrating, and expensive, as the long Afghanistan case experience volubly demonstrates. Committing forces to these wars is often like following Alice down the rabbit's hole.

The problem of involvement is that it tends to be open-ended, as these internally based conflicts drag on in a protracted manner that is extended when outsiders become involved. The rise of asymmetrical warfare and most of the longest wars in American history have coincided: the eight-year involvement in Vietnam between 1965 and 1973, followed by the eight-years-plus invasion and occupation of Iraq (2003 to 2011) and culminated by the recently ended twenty-plus-year involvement in Afghanistan (2001 to 2021).

The peril of outside involvement arises from the attempt to insert military might into a situation for which it is unsuited. The whole point of asymmetrical warfare is to foil the intrusion of superior conventional forces. The situations where involvement may be contemplated tend to be difficult, convoluted, and opaque in terms of the motives of the contestants, and outsiders have not shown great talent in identifying the political and military "side of the angels" in these encounters. In the American case in Afghanistan and other parts of the Middle East, moreover, those who have counseled involvement may not fully understand the situation and dynamics they are about to encounter, a point made forcefully by Gordon is his 2020 book.

The Military Dimension

Any military force contemplating deployment in an asymmetrical war must face certain uncomfortable and unfamiliar realities. The first is the nature of the opponent, its methods, and its goals. Developing world internal conflicts occur in locales very physically and socially unlike North America and Europe, for which most major power armed forces are designed to fight. The "natives" in asymmetrical conflicts know they cannot fight major power militaries head-on, and that they can compete only by changing the rules and methods of engagement. Asymmetrical forces avoid the kinds of confrontation at which they know they will lose, preferring instead more indirect forms of warfare. They consciously change the rules of engagement to make them uncomfortable for conventional forces. They declare there are no noncombatants, imbedding themselves in civilian populations, forcing the enemy to avoid attacking them or causing collateral damage that violates the intervener's rules of engagement. The asymmetrical warrior's goal is to overcome the intervener's cost-tolerance.

That goal is achieved by frustrating the opponent to the point that it tires of the contest and leaves. The yardstick of success for symmetrical warriors is the military defeat of its enemy as preface to imposing a settlement on it. It wins by winning. By contrast, the asymmetrical warrior's strategy of attrition seeks to frustrate the opponent and to get it to leave on its own. The asymmetrical warrior's goal is to keep on the pressure until the enemy leaves: it wins by not losing.

The Political Dimension

Two major political dilemmas face the potential intruder into these conflicts. The first is understanding them and thus what and who to support. In most of these situations, outsiders do not fully understand the nuances of the situations and who—if anyone—is worth supporting. Internal wars tend to be about loyalty to the sides fighting, and it is often difficult trying to determine which side (if any) represents the aspirations of the population. Failing to choose the side likely to prevail is a crucial problem that often befuddles outsiders.

The other problem surrounds the lack of intense and compelling outsider interest in the conflict. Was there, for instance, anything about any outcome that justified an eight-year commitment and the loss of over 58,000 American lives in Vietnam? Or eight years of combat and commitment in Iraq? Or the twenty-year military commitment to Afghanistan? Cases can be made on either side on all these involvements, but none are so overwhelmingly compelling as to gather universal, sustained agreement. The lack of intervener vital interests and thus popular support within its own population is the culprit.

Application: The Never-Ending Afghanistan War

The American military effort in Afghanistan was America's longest war, having surpassed the U.S. Marines' two-decades-long occupation of Haiti from 1915 to 1934, and it ended without American achievement of the goals for which it was engaged. Those who committed the first American forces to Afghanistan did not envision an endless war when they dispatched the first Americans there in October 2001. Their overt purpose was to attack, capture, and destroy Al Qaeda and its leader, Osama bin Laden. That failed mission, however, enmeshed the United States in a conventional civil war between the Taliban and insurgents under the banner of the Northern Alliance that became a civil war between the North Alliance–based government and the displaced Taliban that has lasted at least since 2003. The United States removed its last combat forces in July 2021. The civil war continues.

The campaign against bin Laden and Al Qaeda, of course, failed, as the terrorist leader and his followers slipped across the border into Pakistan. Despite this inability to accomplish this primary—and universally supported—goal, the United States stayed. When the Taliban returned to reassert their domain in 2003, the United States became part of the Afghan civil war, a role that was not envisioned in the original mission.

Afghanistan has been a classic asymmetrical war. On one side was the Afghan government, aided by a North Atlantic Treaty Organization (NATO)–based coalition and the United States. Thanks to outside assistance, the Afghan government has possessed a numerically superior conventional force. On the other side has been the insurgent Taliban, whose forces were inferior to those of the United States and its allies in conventional terms. In these circumstances, the Taliban had no choice but to adopt the methodology of asymmetrical force, a role it is still playing even after the Americans left.

The Afghan Labyrinth

Afghanistan is one of the most forbidding, unforgiving, and difficult countries in the world with which to make war. It is an ancient land with a discernible history dating back three to four millennia. It has always been a harsh and contentious place the history of which is punctuated by occasions in which it unites to repel foreign invaders and then falls back into tribal disunity and violent rivalry. Afghans always seem to be fighting, either against hated outsiders or among themselves. Since 2001, it has been both.

Historic interest in Afghanistan has largely geographic bases. The country has few natural resources to exploit or physical bases for development, and it is one of the poorest countries in the world. In 2016, for instance, the *CIA World Factbook* listed its three largest exports (in order) as opium, fruits, and nuts. It does have a strategic location in the heart of Asia that has made it a junction point, what the U.S. government has called a "land bridge," for travelers and traders throughout history.

That location has placed Afghanistan on the transit route of some of history's greatest conquerors. Alexander the Great passed through in both directions as he sought to subdue India, and Genghis Khan's Golden Hordes swept through and for a time occupied this rugged land. More recently, sovereign Afghanistan (it originally achieved its independence in 1747) was occupied and partially subdued by Great Britain, which fought three wars there. The Soviet Union invaded Afghanistan in December 1979 in a feckless attempt to shore up a communist regime in Kabul. Like virtually all the conquerors that had come before them, the Soviets retreated ignominiously.

For most of its history, Afghanistan has been a deeply divided society, with basic loyalty to tribal affiliations rather than the state. Afghanistan never evolved a strong, stable central government, and its attempts to create one have been fleeting and ultimately unsuccessful. This misery has been compounded by epidemic corruption over the sparse national wealth. As a March 10, 2017, *New York Times* editorial summarized the situation: "Afghanistan remains in the grip of a resolute insurgency and a kleptocratic, dysfunctional governing elite."

What passes for unity and peacefulness normally has occurred when geographically based ethnic tribal groups have had substantial autonomy and where such central regulation as existed was the result of tribal *loya jirgas* meetings between tribal leaders, the most recent of which convened in mid-2019. Whenever a central government in Kabul has attempted to assert its authority outside the tribal council system, it has been actively resisted, often violently.

The result is an Afghan society dominated by its tribal parts with a xenophobic dislike for and suspicion of outsiders. One tribal group has traditionally been most prominent. The Pashtuns are the largest ethnic group in the country. They are further divided into competing subunits, the most prominent of which are the Durrani and the Gilzai Pashtuns. Throughout most of Afghan history, Pashtuns were in the majority in the country, and for a time the terms "Afghan" and "Pashtun" were used interchangeably. Forced migration—largely to Pakistan—has cost the Pashtuns their majority status, but they retain a plurality (recently estimated as about 42 percent). Traditional Pashtun lands are concentrated in the southern and eastern parts of the country adjacent to and overlapping the Durand Line (the legal boundary between Afghanistan and Pakistan that is rejected as invalid by many Pashtuns). A sovereign state of Pashtunistan remains the goal of some tribal members. By some measures, the Pashtuns are a stateless nation (see chapter 16).

The Pashtuns are important for two reasons. First, virtually all Afghan governments have been headed by a Pashtun and have had the active support of the Pashtuns. Hamid Karzai, the president until 2014, is an urban Durrani Pashtun, and his support among the rural Gilzais who form the core supporters of the Taliban was always suspect. He was succeeded by Dr. Ashraf Ghani, a former chancellor of Kabul University and an urban Pashtun. Second, the Gilzai support base of the Taliban comes almost exclusively from rural-based Pashtuns, and most of the hotbeds of Taliban activity and control are in traditional Gilzai Pashtun lands. All Pashtuns are by no means Taliban, but virtually all the Taliban are Pashtuns.

The War and U.S. Involvement

The dynamics of the war are the direct legacy of the Afghan resistance to the Soviet occupation and its aftermath. That Soviet aggression produced a fierce resistance by the various Afghan tribes, aided by, among others, the Americans. The mujahidin, as the anti-Soviet Afghan resisters were collectively known, had two distinct elements: native Afghan tribesmen who, in typical Afghan fashion, formed a loose coalition to repel the Soviets that dissolved when the Soviets departed; and foreign fighters, mostly from other Islamic countries. Native Afghans formed the basis for both sides in the later civil war between the Taliban and the Northern Alliance. Many foreign fighters, some of whom had been recruited by a then-obscure Saudi activist named Osama bin Laden, became members of Al Qaeda.

The expulsion of the Soviets began the end of communist rule in Afghanistan. Successor governments came and went, but all were equally inept, corrupt, and unpopular. In reaction, a new movement primarily comprising students (talibs) from religious schools (madrassas) largely located in Pakistan formed and swept across Afghanistan. In 1996, the Taliban became the government of the country. That same year, Al Qaeda was expelled from Sudan. The new Afghan government welcomed them and provided them with protection.

The Taliban government's rule—or misrule—is well documented and inevitably spawned its own opposition. Gradually, a coalition of primarily non-Pashtun tribes formed under the banner of the Northern Alliance. By 9/11, the Northern Alliance and the Taliban were locked in a full-scale civil war, the outcome of which was very much in doubt. Meanwhile, Al Qaeda continued to operate training facilities in Afghanistan, planning, among other things, the 9/11 attacks.

The United States stayed on the sidelines of this conflict before 9/11, and it only intervened as part of the "war on terror." The U.S. entry in effect created a second conflict with its own objectives and conduct separate from and independent of the ongoing civil war. Although bin Laden's flight from the country effectively ended the military effort against Al Qaeda in Afghanistan (because the terrorists were now in Pakistan), it did not end NATO and American involvement. Rather, the result was the formation of the new Karzai government as the representative of the victorious Northern Alliance, with American blessing. When the Taliban left, the United States and NATO remained to help mop up residual Al Qaeda and Taliban resistance and to ensure they did not return. The effect was to bifurcate the fighting into a limited and failed effort to capture Al Qaeda, a goal in the highest American interest, and a continuing civil war in which the only American interest was to maintain in power a regime that would oppose Al Qaeda's return. That interest formed the basic rationale for the U.S. role.

The Taliban began to infiltrate back into the country in 2003 to launch a new phase of the civil war with the pre-9/11 roles reversed: the Karzai-led Northern Alliance formed the core of the government and the Taliban were the insurgents. Now reconfigured as the Afghan National Army, the renamed Northern Alliance force was no more capable of defeating the Taliban than they had been before.

It has become a classic asymmetrical war. The Taliban were a formidable match for the Afghan National Army without foreign help, but they were less powerful than and incapable of defeating the NATO/American forces in symmetrical warfare. The Taliban thus adopted an unconventional, asymmetrical approach to the war, aiming most clearly at overcoming American cost-tolerance by prolonging the conflict sufficiently to turn American public opinion against the effort and to force a withdrawal. The Taliban needed to overcome American cost-tolerance entirely, and in the end they succeeded. American public opinion overwhelmingly came to favor withdrawal, and it has occurred.

Never-Ending Conflict

The civil war in Afghanistan between the central government of Ghani and the Taliban is over, and the Taliban have won. The protraction and lack of visible success of either side is not unusual for an asymmetrical war where neither side can vanquish the opponent and impose the kind of peace that marks conventional wars. It is even more a war of attrition than most asymmetrical wars, as its inconclusive length is a testament.

The war would hardly be of interest to the West, and specifically the United States, were it not for 9/11. American interests in Afghanistan before the terrorist attacks were decidedly marginal, and without the Al Qaeda connection, it is almost impossible to imagine that the United States would have cared enough about the outcome to insert itself to affect the outcome. The clear American interest was in capturing bin Laden and his cohorts, and it failed. What was left was the internal war, in which the only discernible American interest was in victory for the side that would most oppose Al Qaeda's return.

Opposing the Taliban insurgency was in many ways a familiar problem. The Taliban conducted an asymmetrical campaign using largely guerrilla tactics and insurgent goals, and the Americans responded with counterinsurgency strategy. The effort, however, was plagued by at least three difficulties. One is that the Taliban proved to be tough, adept, and adaptive fighters defending harsh territory with which they are more familiar and comfortable than their opponents: the going was very difficult. The second problem is that the outsiders found themselves aligned with what many Afghans view as an anti-Pashtun coalition: the leadership from Karzai to Ghani are Durrani Pashtuns who have aligned themselves with other ethnic minorities like the Tajiks, who were the historic enemies of the rural Afghans who support the Taliban. Afghan history has been remarkably consistent in the sense that no government that is opposed by the Pashtuns has much chance of succeeding, and when a government is perceived to be an adjunct of urbanites in Kabul, it is doubly suspicious to Afghans from remote parts of the country. Third, the outsiders are exactly that—outsiders— and their presence is resented because they are unwelcome guests. Resistance to foreign military occupation is a universal human instinct, and it is especially strong among the Afghans.

The war in Afghanistan became asymmetrical and continued to be because of the outside intervention of the United States and its NATO allies. Prior to their involvement, the conventional civil war would likely have continued toward some internal resolution at some point. Interfering in that internal affair was not a prominent part of the rationale for intervention in the first place, but it became the de facto reason for staying. Destroying Al Qaeda was the real goal, and the Taliban were in the way. Operationally, the anti–Al Qaeda mission in Afghanistan ended when Al Qaeda fled.

With the Americans withdrawn, how the Afghanistan war will end depends largely on two factors. The first, of course, is the Al Qaeda factor. If Al Qaeda is otherwise destroyed or its return to Afghanistan successfully precluded, there is little reason for the outside world to worry about the civil war. The other is the outside, and especially the American, role, which is continuing but effectively nonmilitary. The war has not been cheap. The monetary costs have been enormous. Most unofficial estimates fall in the trillion-dollar range for outcomes that are hardly discernible, and over 2,500 American lives have been lost. President Obama announced early in his presidency the intention to get the United States out of Afghanistan by 2014, and he failed. The Trump administration did not do any better. The Biden administration has succeeded in removing the last American combat forces and thus essentially leaving the Afghans to fend for themselves.

Where does the effort stand? Analysts disagree, but none are wildly optimistic. The *New York Times* March 10, 2017, editorial argued, "The challenges that have stymied American generals in Afghanistan for years—including havens for insurgents in Pakistan, endemic corruption and poor leadership in the Afghan military—remain unsolved." That situation has not changed dramatically. The United States continues to try to induce the Taliban to reach a peace agreement with the government for a peaceful settlement including power sharing. With American power removed from the scene, the Taliban's incentives to stop short of a total victory are very slender. As Fair puts it, "The reason for this is simple: Pakistan and its proxy, the Taliban, are winning." The situation is unlikely to change nationally.

Conclusion

Warfare is both an ever-changing and never-changing human endeavor. The opponents change, the purposes for which wars are fought change, and the methods and tools of war change. At the same time, the fact that groups of humans find reasons to fight and kill other groups of humans remains one of history's true constants.

What is now called asymmetrical warfare is part of this march of history. The basic ideas and methods underlying this kind of war are as old as warfare itself and have been a recurring part of the historic pattern. What is arguably different is that differential fighting capabilities between countries and groups have widened to the point that asymmetrical warfare has become much more necessary for weaker participants than it was in the past. The war in Afghanistan is only the latest example of this form of warfare. In a world where major powers have not directly clashed in earnest since 1945 largely due to the fear of nuclear escalation, the prospects of involvement in deadly conflicts are more internally based in the developing world that will sometimes interest major powers like the United States and place them in asymmetrical warfare situations, at which they have not proven to be conspicuously adept.

Study/Discussion Questions

1. What is asymmetrical warfare? Contrast it with symmetrical warfare. Why has it arisen as the major military problem of the twenty-first century? Why is it likely to continue to be the dominant problem?

2. Where do asymmetrical wars tend to occur? What is a DWIC, why are those conflicts likely to be asymmetrical, and why is this important to the United States?

3. Discuss the problem posed by asymmetrical warfare. In what kinds of conflicts and by what kind of groups is it practiced?

4. Why has participation in asymmetrical warfare become such a large enterprise for the United States? What has the experience been? What political and military problems does it create?

5. Discuss the background and evolution of the Afghanistan war, beginning with its roots in the Afghan resistance to the Soviet occupation and leading to the 9/11 attacks. Why does the war have two distinct facets? What are they? Explain.

6. Building on the dual nature of the conflict, describe Afghanistan as an asymmetrical war. Put your discussion in the context of the Afghan historical experience.

7. How did the United States get involved in Afghanistan? What changes have occurred since the initial involvement that could or should have changed the nature of that involvement?

8. What do you think the lessons of Afghanistan should be for the United States in the future? Discuss.

Bibliography

Ansary, Tamim. *Game without Rules: The Often-Interrupted History of Afghanistan*. New York: PublicAffairs, 2012.

Barfield, Thomas. *Afghanistan: A Cultural and Political History*. Princeton, NJ: Princeton University Press, 2010.

Barnett, Roger W. *Asymmetrical Warfare: Today's Challenge to U.S. Military Power* (Issues in Twenty-First-Century Warfare). Washington, DC: Potomac Books, 2013.

Belasco, Amy. *The Cost of Iraq, Afghanistan and Other Global Terrorist Operations since 9/11*. Washington, DC: Congressional Research Service, December 8, 2014.

Berkowitz, Bruce. *The New Face of War: How War Will Be Fought in the 21st Century*. New York: Free Press, 2003.

Brodie, Bernard, and Fawn M. Brodie. *From Crossbow to H-Bomb: The Evolution of Weapons and Tactics of Warfare*. Bloomington: Indiana University Press, 1973.

Central Intelligence Agency. *CIA World Factbook, 2016*. Washington, DC: Central Intelligence Agency, 2016.

Coll, Steve. *Ghost Wars: The Secret History of the CIA, Afghanistan, and bin Laden from the Soviet Invasion to September 10, 2001*. New York: Penguin Books, 2004.

Ewans, Martin. *Afghanistan: A Short History of Its People and Politics*. New York: HarperCollins Perennial, 2002.

Fair, C. Christine. "Pakistan's Deadly Grip on Afghanistan." *Current History* 116, no. 789 (April 2017): 136–41.

Galula, David. *Counterinsurgency Warfare: Theory and Practice* (Praeger Classics of the Counterinsurgency Era). Westport, CT: Praeger Publishers, 2006.

Giap, Vo Nhuyen. *People's War, People's Army*. New York: Praeger, 1962.

Gordon, Philip H. *Losing the Long Game: The False Promise of Regime Change in the Middle East*. New York: St. Martin's Press, 2020.

Haass, Richard N. *War of Necessity, War of Choice: A Memoir of Two Iraq Wars*. New York: Simon and Schuster, 2009.

Jones, Seth G. "How Trump Should Manage Afghanistan: A Realistic Set of Goals for the New Administration." *Foreign Affairs* (online), March 21, 2017.

———. *In the Graveyard of Empires: America's War in Afghanistan*. New York: W. W. Norton, 2009.

Kaplan, Robert D. "Man versus Afghanistan." *The Atlantic* 305, no. 3 (April 2010): 60–71.

Kaurin, Pauline M. *The Warrior, Military Ethics and Contemporary Warfare: Achilles Goes Asymmetrical*. New York and London: Routledge, 2016.

Lowther, Adam B. *Americans and Asymmetrical Warfare: Lebanon, Somalia, and Afghanistan*. Westport, CT: Praeger Security International, 2007.

Malkasian, Carter. *The American War in Afghanistan: A History*. Oxford, UK: Oxford University Press, 2021.

Mao Ze Dung. *The Collected Works of Mao Ze Dung*. Volumes 1–4. Beijing, China: Foreign Languages Press, 1967.

New York Times Editorial Board. "Afghanistan Is Now Trump's War." *New York Times*, March 10, 2017.

Rashid, Ahmed. *Taliban: Militant Islam, Oil, and Fundamentalism in Central Asia* (second edition). New Haven, CT: Yale University Press, 2010.

Snow, Donald M. *The Case against Military Intervention: Why We Do It and Why It Fails*. New York and London: Routledge, 2016.

———. *The Middle East and American National Security: Ending Forever Wars*. Lanham, MD: Rowman & Littlefield, 2021.

————, and Dennis M. Drew. *From Lexington to Baghdad and Beyond: War and Politics in the American Experience* (third edition). Armonk, NY: M. E. Sharpe, 2010.

Sun Tzu. *The Art of War* (translated by Samuel B. Griffith). Oxford, UK: Oxford University Press, 1963.

Tomsen, Peter. *The Wars of Afghanistan: Messianic Terrorism, Tribal Conflicts, and the Failure of Great Powers.* New York: PublicAffairs, 2013.

U.S. Army and U.S. Marine Corps. *Counterinsurgency Field Manual* (U.S. Army Field Manual No. 3-24, Marine Corps Warfighting Publication No. 3-33.5). Chicago, IL: University of Chicago Press, 2007.

U.S. Marine Corps. *Afghanistan: Operational Culture for Deploying Personnel.* Quantico, VA: Center for Operational Cultural Learning, 2009.

Weston, J. Kael. *The Mirror Test: America at War in Iraq and Afghanistan.* New York: Vintage Books, 2016.

9

International Meddling and Interference

Russia in U.S. Elections, the United States in Guatemala

This volume began with an examination of sovereignty as the first, bed-rock principle of international relations. The core of sovereignty is that jurisdiction over territory, people, and other assets of states resides with whoever possesses sovereign authority, and no outsider has the right to claim or operate within other states without their permission. States, in other words, have total jurisdiction over what goes on in their sovereign territory. All states vehemently espouse this principle, because to deny it would undermine the basis of the sovereign international order. Those same states that trumpet the inviola-bility of sovereignty also violate other states' sovereignty regularly for a variety of reasons and by an array of means.

If the principle of sovereignty was in fact inviolable and universally enforced and enforceable, there would be no reason for a chapter examining "interna-tional meddling and interference." States do interfere with one another with some regularity and always have, using a broad variety of techniques to accom-plish different policy goals. Sovereignty is not a fiction as the foundation of the state system; neither is it a condition and principle all states obey. Although it may sound cynical, the position of states is roughly that their own sovereignty is sacred and must be enforced, but the sovereignty of others with which they interact, while rhetorically sacred, is fair game for interference by a wide variety of means should they feel the need to do so. To paraphrase an old homily, in the area of interference in the affairs of other states, what is good for the goose is not always good for the gander.

Why is this the case? Like so much of international relations, the answer is complex, and different motives and explanations are invoked by different coun-tries and officials. Generically, however, the anomaly begins with the clash of national interests and sovereignty. Protecting and promoting the interests that states hold is the primary source of international interactions with other states. Maintaining the sacrosanct nature of *their own* interests includes protecting their sovereignty, but occasionally the two values come into conflict. The most obvi-ous case in point occurs when actions taken by another state threaten a state's most important (i.e., vital) interests and where the only way to protect that inter-est is to intrude on the sovereignty of the offending state. The most dramatic case occurs when another state threatens action—military invasion, for instance—which directly threatens one's own sovereignty. In such situations, honoring sovereignty as an international principle threatens the most basic of national interests—one's own sovereignty, even survival. In these situations, the sanctity of honoring the sovereignty of others may be sacrificed to the well-being of the state defined in terms of national interests.

The result is a quandary that may appear to be a violation of principles, even more or less blatant hypocrisy. No state will admit that its sovereignty can be legitimately breached by others, because to do so would suggest that it is all right for another state to violate that sovereignty, and no state will admit to that. State interests, on the other hand, may be unobtainable unless some direct action is taken that may require violating the sovereignty (as well as breaking the laws) of the state against which it is directed. If illegal action is undertaken and that illegality is uncovered and publicized, its explanations will ring hollow and may prejudice it in future dealings with others. This has historically been a problem for countries like Russia, which has been identified as a violator of other's sovereignty regularly, making its protestations that it does not do these things less than convincing and making others reluctant to trust it.

International Meddling and Interference: An Overview

The terms "meddling" and "interference" are innocuous descriptors of the things states are willing to do to further or protect their national interests. A representative dictionary definition of interference refers to "unwanted or unnecessary" actions. Meddling, on the other hand, is variously described as intrusion "into other people's affairs or business" or to "busy oneself unduly with something that is not one's concern." A key element in meddling is that it involves "oneself in a matter without right or invitation." Sounds innocent, even civilized enough, but if that were the case, states would do so openly and would readily admit—in some cases with pride—that they meddle, but they do not. The reason is simple enough and is parallel to the diplomatic principle of reciprocity introduced in chapter 1: if limits are placed on how you deal with instances of meddling against someone, then you can expect some of the same restraint when you engage and are caught meddling in the affairs of others. Meddling and interference encompass a broad range of activities. Some of these are not terribly severe or objectionable, and the terms themselves imply a certain level of civility and restraint that is not always present.

Take an example elaborated in the next chapter: actions regarding the Iranian nuclear program. Israel and, to a lesser extent, the United States volubly oppose the nuclear research program sponsored by the Iranian government, and they have sought to "interfere" in its conduct. They have done so by what is arguably "meddling" in Iranian affairs. Instances in 2020, for instance, include the assassination of Iranian general Qasem Soleimani in January by the Americans and the murder of Iranian nuclear physicist Mohsen Fakhrizadeh by an apparent Israeli Mossad assassin in November. The latter "meddling" with the Iranian scientific community is particularly interesting because Mossad has never confirmed or denied its involvement and because the physicist was a civilian, raising the prospect of a retaliation in kind by Iran, a kind of retribution for the Israeli violation on the principle of reciprocity.

The locus of what is now classified as meddling and interference is in fact an updating and renaming of the kinds of clandestine activities states have always undertaken against one another. Generally, the sponsor for most of these kinds of actions was the clandestine services of various countries. In the United States, for instance, the Central Intelligence Agency (CIA) has always been divided into several divisions. In addition to science and technology and administration, the main distinction has always been between those activities devoted to the collection and analysis of information (some of which is obtained by interfering with the efforts of foreign governments to hide or protect information sources) and operations, which is generally charged with active measures to meddle and interfere. Other major states have similar organizational divisions.

Because interference and meddling generally require illegal activities against the countries at which they are directed, their existence and content is normally carefully guarded by those who devise and implement them. In practice, this generally means consigning these government functions to the secret, clandestine arms of national governments. The guiding operational principle of these attempts is the idea of *plausible deniability*. This phrase means that a successful intrusion or other form of clandestine activity only fully succeeds if the country conducting it leaves no evidence behind that can definitively tie it to whatever interference was undertaken and thus can deny involvement in any illegal forms of meddling. The qualification of "plausible" means that a country's intrusions may be widely suspected, but that there is not definitive proof of the action that preclude denying whatever was done. The involvement of the United States (along with the British) in overthrowing the Mossadegh regime in Iran in 1953 and helping to install the Shah of Iran as his successor is an example. The American participation was, according to Kinzer and others, orchestrated by Secretary of State John Foster Dulles, but no definitive evidence at the time could "prove" his and thus American complicity. Plausible deniability was also present in the two case applications in this chapter: the American role in engineering and executing the coup against Guatemalan president Jacobo Arbenz and his replacement by General Carlos Castillo Armas in 1954 and consistent Russian denial of any interference in the American presidential elections in 2016 and 2020 and other forms of cyberattack in 2021.

Forms of Intrusion

Interference and meddling are carried out by a broad array of clandestine or open means. Historic examples include (but are not necessarily limited to) both violent and nonviolent forms of intrusion. Some are methods that are long-standing enough to be thought of as venerable. Others have joined the repertoire of interference thanks to innovation in technologies that make them possible.

The methods have evolved across time. Some change has been the result of environmental advances. Thanks to modern electronics, for instance, it is much easier to engage in some forms of influence than it once was and harder to engage in others. Assassinations of troublesome personnel (i.e., officials who oppose whatever interests the meddlesome outsider seeks to create or protect) in a clandestine manner is increasingly difficult given global media coverage. The assassination of naturalized American journalist Jamal Khashoggi at the Saudi embassy in Turkey was undoubtedly conceptualized as a covert operation that would remove this critic of the Saudi regime. In past times, it might have been possible to make him simply disappear so that the regime could deny knowing what happened to him, but modern media investigation by his fellow journalists uncovered what had happened, made certain it was widely disseminated world-wide, and by doing so caused considerable embarrassment for Crown Prince Muhammad bin Salman (MbS) and the Saudi regime. The electronic media made plausible deniability impossible in this instance, and its example shows the limits of false explanations of embarrassing behavior in the media age.

The motivations to intrude and to influence other governments have not disappeared and are unlikely to do so. This is an increasing problem for aggressive regimes that have historically achieved many of their policy goals by employing threatening meddling behavior like the use or threat of violence.

Traditional means of interference and meddling may be more difficult than they once were, but that does not mean the traditional practices are disappearing. Although any list will likely be incomplete and omit the inventiveness of some meddlers, one can suggest some of the methods that have historically been employed and are still currently in use, separating them into categories of non-violent and violent interference and hybrids of the two but recognizing that the list is exemplary and not inclusive.

Nonviolent means tend to focus on the ability to influence actors in foreign countries by appealing to any latent tendencies toward corruption they may exhibit. Examples include the use of propaganda toward the country one is seeking to influence, including the generous use of lies against the target group within the government. This technique is usually employed clandestinely and denied by whatever group or country is using it. A common form of this influence peddling includes bribery of vulnerable persons in the target country, with common targets being people or groups sympathetic to the cause of the influence being promoted or corrupt, even venal, individuals in the target land. A common form often historically used by the United States is the financing of political movements to promote those ends. Vladimir Putin, for instance, cites American support for his rival Boris Yeltsin in the 1990s as an example of this form of meddling.

A more problematical form of meddling involves the use of violence against elements in a target country who oppose the interests of the intruder. Many of these actions fall within what is known as "wet operations" in the intelligence community and are the most extreme and criminal forms of interference; they are, in some places, also among the most common. Assassinations are the most obvious and conceptually problematic because they directly violate the diplomatic principle of reciprocity and raise the question about whether retribution in kind will follow. What is, for instance, the consequence of Israeli assassination of an Iranian physicist? Is an equivalent Israeli scientist now fair game? The ability to make such calculations and the physical consequences of killing normally prominent people make this a very emotional form of meddling, and one with at least some escalatory potential.

There are other violent forms of interference that may be carried out from time to time. Acts of destruction of another country's covert penetration amount to physical invasion (an aspect of the Guatemalan case in the next section) and the sponsorship or physical commission of acts of terror (see chapter 14). Some forms feature aspects of violence and nonviolence, such as corrupting officials to influence elections, acts of vandalism against political forces, or even acts of espionage, all ways in which different states seek to influence policies and actions that affect them. Successful actions must meet the core requirement of plausible deniability: no state openly admits it meddles or interferes, but most do and engage in considerable efforts to devise and implement new methods. The most difficult current manifestation of these efforts is the use of cyberwarfare.

Cyber Meddling: The New Frontier

In an increasing technologically obsessed world where developments in that environment seem ubiquitous, and where access to the "laboratory" of electronic technology is available to countless private "hackers" and national governments alike, it is not at all surprising that the cyberworld would also be a subject of great interest to those who engage in interference and meddling in other countries. So much of what governments do is devised, stored, and transmitted via the computers that form the heart of the electronic revolution that it is an obviously tempting target for those who would do mischief with the affairs of others. This temptation is particularly true because the means of protecting so much of the fruits of the cyberworld are much less well developed and effective than the means to intrude upon and steal or manipulate that output.

The root concept that is a prefix to describe various activities is "cyber," an ancient Greek word that means "space." Because of the nature of electronic activities (messages and data transmitted through space rather than transmission lines), the prefix is used to describe numerous nefarious activities, including those associated with interference and meddling. These activities include cybercrime, cyberwarfare, cybersecurity, and cyberattacks. Their common element is that they all involve interruption with computers and computer networks, including stealing information and manipulating/distorting information stored in computer networks. As increasing proportions of governmental and nongovernmental activities are developed, stored, and shared via cyberspace, the cyber realm has become prime ground for those entities interfering in the affairs of others.

The broad range of uses and abuses associated with cyber activity is explored in chapter 12, and it is introduced here for several reasons. First, it has become a primary medium that those interfering in the affairs of others employ. This is partly true because of the increasingly ubiquitous nature of cyber activity: it is spreading to most spheres of human activity. Second, it is activity that can be difficult to identify when a cyberattack on some computer-based information source occurs. The simple fact is that the development of new ways to collect and analyze cyber-transmitted activity outstrips more modest attempts to identify and protect that flow. Third, a good deal of the hacking that is the source of interference can be and is accomplished by private individuals whose sheer numbers make comprehensive surveillance virtually impossible. Fourth, governments have gotten into the business of cyber meddling and interference in major, concerted ways that includes making monitoring of those efforts difficult. Finally, and in some ways most importantly for present purposes, much cyber activity is very transparent, even ethereal, meaning it is more difficult, and in some ways impossible, to monitor and identify than other forms of meddling that leave a more concrete "trail." Cyberspace, in other words, is the natural habitat for people trying to build a case for the plausible deniability of their nefarious activities.

Application: Russian Election Interference and American Meddling in the 1954 Guatemalan Coup

Discussions of meddling and interference do not bring out conspicuous torrents of admissions of guilt by states, and especially those political entities that meddle and interfere the most. The public face of reactions to accusations against others that they have engaged in these acts tends to be sanctimonious horror against those accused of interfering with one's country and equally fervent but disingenuous denials when your country is accused of the same kinds of deeds. Most states engage in meddling and interference, and limits on the extent of that activity is motivated not by some sense of moral high-mindedness so much as the presence or absence of major national interests and the ability or inability to realize those interests clandestinely.

The two case examples in this section were chosen to illustrate this basic truth and the changing methods by which states act against one another. The first example surrounds the alleged meddling of Russia in the American elections of 2016 and 2020. States seek to influence one another's elections regularly, especially if a particular contest is between a candidate sympathetic to your interests and one who is not. Russia is alleged to have sought to use cyberattacks to influence American voters to vote for selected candidates, allegedly including Donald Trump. Confronted with this accusation, the Russians counter the United States did the same thing in Russia in the 1990s, promoting Boris Yeltsin to oppose the election of Vladimir Putin.

The other case is less well known but represents the same dynamics. In 1954, the U.S. government executed a coup d'etat against Guatemalan president Jacobo Arbenz, allegedly because of sympathies and ties to communism, but unofficially because the Guatemalan leader was opposed to many of the practices of the United Fruit Company, which controlled most of the banana trade coming out of that country. The methods employed were much more primitive than contemporary Russian efforts, but they did succeed in accomplishing their goal of overthrowing a democratically elected government.

Russian Election Meddling

It is not a great surprise that Russia would be one of the first countries to exploit cyber activity to meddle in the affairs of other governments or that the United States would be one of the first states against which they would apply those techniques. The Russians/Soviets were always adept at science and technology, even if governmental policies downplayed computer technologies and eventually left the country deficient in that area. The resulting gap in computing was one of the reasons then leader Mikhail Gorbachev concluded the Cold War needed to end so Russia could gain access to computing know-how. (See Snow, *The Shape of the Future*.) After the Soviet Union collapsed, there was, however, a reservoir of former Soviet scientists and their students both interested and knowledgeable in computing who could form the core of "hackers" who would engage in cyber mischief against the United States. As Putin pushed for Russian resurgence during the 2010s, some of this residue turned to means to hack into American (and other) databases in an international system where governmental secrets increasingly became imbedded in cyberspace.

The exploitation of cyberspace for political meddling and interference is a seamless marriage of intent and technique. The purpose of the meddler is to infiltrate a target society to manipulate its operation, to disrupt what it does, or to undermine its ability to perform its functions. In the modern international system, this means clandestine penetration of the systems that perform those functions, and most of them are performed on or by computers, which is the forum where cybercriminals engage in hacking, defined as "the unauthorized intrusion into a computer or network" for the purpose of altering "the system or its security features."

Cybercrime perpetrators have advantages worth mentioning. One is that the hacking of computer activities does not require the thief to be physically present at the scene, thereby making it more difficult to identify him or her in advance or to prove the thief's identity after the fact. The only incriminating evidence may be indirect and only detectable in retrospect. Most traditional policing techniques simply do not apply to the problem of cybercrime. Second, there is no single agreed definition of cybercrimes, which also means there is no accepted framework of law that covers the range of cybercriminal behavior. Third, cybercrime is also generally nonviolent; the cybercriminal steals material from computer networks for gain or to allow others to undermine some activity that the captured material performs. Fourth, although the results of cyber hacking may be profound, this may not be obvious at the time the crime occurs, with great repercussions. Hacking the programs that control missile defenses designed to destroy an incoming attack can have the highest impact, but that activity may not be obvious at the time the crime appears. Criminal laws and law enforcement techniques covering cyberattacks are underdeveloped areas and vary considerably from country to country. In large part because of the revelation of massive hacking into the database of SolarWinds, a major IT data collector and provider in late 2020, the Biden administration has proposed a 30 percent increase in the budget of the federal agency in charge of monitoring cybercrime, the U.S.

Cybersecurity and Infrastructure Agency (CISA). Whether this effort will materially improve the situation remains to be seen.

These characteristics help frame how difficult it is to deal with international cybercrime. Like so much of the electronic revolution generally, much more effort has been expended in the development of information gathering and analyzing techniques than in capability for detecting and regulating the results of those inquiries. Given the atomized nature of an enterprise in which individuals produce much of the problem, detection and apprehension are difficult, especially when hacking crosses national boundaries, which it regularly does.

Russian interference in the American elections of 2016 and 2020 reflects these characteristics. The interference in 2016 was directed mostly at the campaign of Democratic presidential candidate Hillary Clinton through intrusion into the files of the Democratic National Committee and the private files of Democratic officials, notably Clinton's. After the fact, the U.S. intelligence community investigated these breaches and concluded that the hacking was indeed traceable to the Russian government and to Putin, who was known to dislike candidate Clinton. The highly publicized Mueller Report basically accepted these conclusions. In 2020, Russian activity was apparently directed at meddling in the formal election process by attempting to hack into and presumably to alter the results of vote totals. In both cases, of course, Putin and his government totally, and with some expression of righteous indignation, rejected these conclusions and have continued to proclaim their innocence. During his single term, President Trump refused to lend credence to the essentially unanimous conclusion of experts in government of Russian guilt in either election. The SolarWinds precedent that became evident in 2021 demonstrates the effective "privatization" of these activities and caused Biden to warn Putin in their June 2021 meeting to curb cyber thieves operating in Russia.

First, the experiences highlight the problem that cyber dynamics do not leave a "hard" evidence trail definitively linking the Russians to the intrusions into the American electoral or other processes. The files hacked in 2016 were obviously not theft proof and apparently did not produce a definitive evidence trail that could be accessed after the fact. In 2020, Russian efforts were not successful in altering election outcomes, presumably because better barriers were in place to prevent or filter out the efforts of hackers (at this writing, no definitive report had appeared publicly on this subject). Further analysis of these cases and failures like the SolarWinds episode have stimulated a more concerted effort by U.S. government agencies like CISA.

A central problem facing the suppression of cybercrime is the anonymity of hackers, and this characteristic complicates national security efforts far beyond what transpired in 2016 and 2020. Parker, for instance, points out a hack "can be the work of almost anyone" and this complication makes more difficult national security efforts for the "larger problem of cyberwarfare. How does a government respond to an invisible attacker? How can a state prevent cyberattacks without attribution?" In the Russian cases, their complicity/guilt is widely accepted within the United States, but it is categorically denied by the Russians, and the Americans either do not have proof or, for a variety of reasons, may not want to reveal their sources. If the United States is to reduce or eliminate cyber-attacks on their secrets, it must find better ways to provide impenetrable barriers to unauthorized access, something like what Ramo calls "hard gatekeeping."

Some of the more polemic criticism of Russian intrusion into American political activities using cutting-edge technology to violate American sovereignty are disingenuous, even hypocritical. The Russians invested heavily in technologies designed to steal secrets from the United States during the Cold War and have sought to interfere in American politics before. Revelations of the blatant nature of the 2016 interference with the Democratic Party was chastening for them, although they denied their meddling. Their efforts in 2020 were apparently more restrained, but as far as is known publicly, they were also less effective. Will these experiences cause the Russians to cease interference in the affairs of other countries? Of course not, but it will probably redouble their efforts to perfect their cyber intrusions to reduce detection. The Chinese are doing the same thing.

Americans should not get sanctimonious about being the victims of meddling behavior, because the United States has interfered in the affairs of others as well. The most highly publicized cases have been in the Western Hemisphere, historically recognized as the American sphere of influence. The United States interfered in places where they feared communist interference or power grabs during the Cold War in places like Chile and Nicaragua, and in pre–World War II situations, usually where American economic interests were at stake. One of the more egregious, if less well publicized instances that combines anti-communism and economic interests was American involvement in the 1954 Guatemalan coup, to which the discussion now turns.

The United States and Guatemala, 1954

For major powers, meddling tends to be most intense and extensive in areas near their borders. The Russians interfere extensively in former republics of the Soviet Union like Ukraine (including Crimea) and the states of the Caucasus, and the Chinese tend to interfere in remote Asian parts of their country. The suppression of the Uighurs in the eastern part of the country is exemplary. For the United States, Latin America, and especially Central America and the Caribbean, is equivalent. Guatemala has been a good example.

For the United States, interference has had both geopolitical and economic roots and motivations, often in combination. Since the end of World War II, Latin America has been a more peripheral battleground of that competition. Most of South America has avoided direct, major involvement in American interference—with the exceptions Venezuela, Colombia, and Chile, but the shadow of the Americans has hung heavily over Central America and the island states of the Caribbean. American concern peaked during the 1950s under the direction of the Dulles brothers—Secretary of State John Foster and CIA director Allen (see Kinzer)—who tended to combine anti-communism and American economic interests. The concern with communism radiated from Cuba and was expressed both as a threat to control of the access routes to the Panama Canal and the danger that other regional states might follow the Cuban precedent and "go communist." The economic concerns centered on the expropriation of large, lucrative land holdings in some countries, which reformist governments sought to expropriate and return to the control of indigenous elements. The two concerns intermingled since some of the advocates of reform had Marxist ties and because Cuba acted as cheerleader and provocateur in many of the cases. American interference was thus to squelch communism and to protect the lucrative land holdings of companies like the United Fruit Company. Stopping communism was the normal rallying cry in public defenses of meddling, although defending "Chiquita Banana" (the advertising face of United Fruit) was arguably the underlying motivation of the intruders.

The situation in Guatemala was a textbook example of these dynamics. The country had been in a state of instability often referred to as revolution since 1944 that continued in one form or another until the American-organized and -assisted overthrow of the government of President Jacobo Arbenz in 1954 and the installation of General Carlos Castillo Armas in his place. Plotting for this overthrow was first authorized by President Truman as Operation PBFortune (the PB was the CIA's acronym for Guatemala) in 1952 and was an initiative embraced by President Eisenhower when he succeeded Truman. The motivation for Eisenhower was, according to archival documents released by the George Washington University National Security Archive in 1997, "cold war concerns" that "convinced President Eisenhower to order the removal of the democratically-elected leader by force." The Central Intelligence Agency was given the task of organizing and leading the coup.

The American interests that underlay this operation combined the related problems of communist penetration into Central America and economic interest of the United States in support of the United Fruit Company (UFC, in which the Dulles brothers had financial interests, according to Kinzer). Arbenz' political sins included land reforms expropriating lands to aid Guatemalan peasants and formally legalizing the communist Guatemalan Party of Labor. Part of the land expropriated for this purpose was either claimed or coveted by the UFC, thereby uniting the two rationales for involvement in overthrowing a democratically elected government. Eisenhower authorized Operation PBSUCCESS in August 1953. According to released CIA documents in the George Washington report, it "carried a $2.7 million budget for 'psychological warfare and political action' and 'subversion,'" classic tools of interference and meddling.

To carry out this intent, the CIA organized and funded a small force (about 480 men) under Armas. It invaded Guatemala on June 18, 1954, complete with CIA-provided air cover and propaganda provided by the CIA greatly exaggerating its size and effectiveness. The "invading force" did not perform well, but growing propaganda of their prowess spread to the capital of Guatemala City, and many officials panicked and fled. President Arbenz attempted to arm civilians to resist the invasion force, but his effort failed, and the president resigned and joined the exodus on June 27, 1954. Ten days later Castillo Armas became president. American participation in the operation was widely known despite trying to create deceptions permitting plausible deniability, and it worsened anti-American sentiment in the region.

An operation as brazen as PBSUCCESS would be difficult, if not impossible, to mount in the contemporary international system, even if similar motives remain. The year 1954 was, after all, when the greatest fear of the spread of communism gripped Americans, making actions that would be deemed reprehensible today more acceptable. Moreover, there was virtually no critical reportage of the action, which was decidedly amateurish by more modern standards. The "invading force" that led to the overthrow of Arbenz hardly existed and was inept, but these characteristics were barely noted at the time. The Eisenhower administration neither confirmed nor denied their interference in the affairs of a sovereign neighbor because nobody made them do so when it was happening. Contrast that experience with the Russian example, where alleged Russian interference has been scrutinized in detail and emphatically denied. The United States could get away with its nefarious meddling in 1954 because nobody was watching and criticizing. In 2016 and 2020, the Russians had the opacity of cyber transmission to provide a veil of secrecy and deniability of their nefarious actions. The environment in which interference occurs has changed, if not necessarily the intent.

Conclusions

Political interference and meddling represent activities that are less than ideal expressions of political idealism and honor, but they are activities that are regularly pursued in the relations among countries. They also represent a conceptual enigma in an international system based on the territorial sovereignty of its members. Sovereignty suggests that no outside actor, and especially not another state, can legitimately interfere in the affairs of other states. All states agree to this value in principle, and most states violate that principle in practice.

The conceptual incongruity lies in the relationship between sovereignty and interests and their intersection with the relations between states. States are dedicated to the sanctity of *their* sovereignty and, in the abstract, with the sovereignty of other states. The exception is when the actions or circumstances of other states impinge on the state's interests (and especially their vital interests) and only can be remediated by taking actions that impinge on the other state's sovereignty. In both the cases examined, that was the perceived case. American comparative strength impedes Russian reassertion of its Cold War status in the world, and one way to address this problem is by taking actions against the United States that weakens it. Purported actions by the Guatemalan government to nationalize land smacked of communist infiltration and attacked American business interests. Interpreting those actions with the spread of communism to the Western Hemisphere threatened basic American geopolitical interests, and so the American government meddled in Guatemalan politics and orchestrated overthrowing the government of Arbenz. Vital interests trumped fealty to the general principle of sovereignty. It is a dilemma that has always been present and is unlikely to go away. The actors and their methods may change, but interference is a constant.

Study/Discussion Questions

1. What are interference and meddling as they are used in international relations? What is plausible deniability, and why do states place so much emphasis on being able to claim it?

2. Sovereignty and interference and meddling are contradictory ideas and dynamics. Define each, how they are incompatible and how states reconcile the incongruity.

3. What forms of interference are common? How do cyber dynamics impact the practice of interference and meddling?

4. Compare and contrast the concepts of interference and meddling, sovereignty, and national interests. How do they interact in formulating state actions?

5. Discuss Russian interference in the 2016 and 2020 U.S. national elections. Why is cyber activity such an attractive method for the cybercriminal?

6. Speculate on the future of Russian interference and meddling against the United States and how the United States can react to it.

7. Outline the American interference in Guatemala during the Arbenz presidency. How was that interference justified? How were the two elements of justification related?

8. Why did the United States carry out the campaign that overthrew Arbenz? Was it legally or morally justifiable? Contrast Russian behavior in 2016 with American actions in 1954. Were the dynamics basically the same? Are either or both acceptable? Why or why not?

Bibliography

Arutunyan, Anna. "Russia Will Never See the United States the Same Way Again. After Trump, Washington Must Work Through Allies to Influence Moscow." *Foreign Affairs* (online), February 17, 2021.

Brose, Christian. "The New Revolution in Military Affairs." *Foreign Affairs* 98, no. 3 (May/ June 2019): 122–34.

Cullather, Nick. *Secret History: The CIA's Classified Account of Its Operations in Guatemala, 1952–1954* (second edition). Palo Alto, CA: Stanford University Press, 2006.

Doyle, Kate, and Peter Kornbluh, eds. *CIA and Assassinations: The Guatemala 1954 Documents* (The National Security Archive Electronic Briefing Book No. 4). Washington, DC: The George Washington University National Security Archive, 1997.

Fairfield, Joshua A. T. *Runaway Technology: Can Law Keep Up?* Cambridge, UK: Cambridge University Press, 2021.

Gleijeses, Piero. *Shattered Hope: The Guatemalan Revolution and the United States, 1944–1954*. Princeton, NJ: Princeton University Press, 1992.

Grow, Michael. *U.S. Presidents and Latin American Interventions: Pursuing Regime Change in the Cold War*. Lawrence: University of Kansas Press, 2008.

Hennessey, Susan. "Deterring Cyberattacks: How to Reduce Vulnerability." *Foreign Affairs* 96, no. 6 (November/December 2017): 39–46.

Immerman, Richard H. *The CIA in Guatemala: The Foreign Policy of Intervention*. Austin: University of Texas Press, 1982.

Intelligence Committee, United States Senate. *Russian Active Measures Campaigns and Interference in the 2016 US Election*. Vol. 5, no. 11. Washington: Senate Intelligence Committee.

Isikoff, Michael, and David Korn. *Russian Roulette: The Inside Story of Putin's War on America and the Election of Donald Trump*. New York: Twelve Books, 2018.

Jankowicz, Nina. *How to Lose the Information War: Russia, Fake News and the Future of Conflict*. London: I. B. Tauris, 2020.

Jarmon, Jack A., and Pano Yannogerogos. *The Cyber Threat and Globalization: The Impact on U.S. National and International Security*. Lanham, MD: Rowman & Littlefield, 2018.

Kaplan, Fred. *Dark Territory: The Secret History of Cyber War*. New York: Simon and Schuster, 2017.

Kinzer, Stephen. *The Brothers: John Foster Dulles, Allen Dulles, and Their Secret World War*. New York: Times Books, 2013.

McPherson, Alan. *A Short History of U.S. Intervention in Latin America and the Caribbean*. New York: Wiley, 2016.

Mueller, Robert S. III. *The Mueller Report: The Final Report of the Special Counsel into Donald Trump, Russia, and Collusion*. New York: Skyhorse, 2019.

Parker, Emily. "Hack Job: How the United States Invented Cyberwar." *Foreign Affairs* 96, no. 4 (May/June 2017): 133–38.

Pastor, Robert A. *Exiting the Whirlpool: U.S. Foreign Policy toward Latin America and the Caribbean*. Tufts, MA: Perseus, 2006.

Rabe, Stephen G. *The United States Wager: Cold War in Latin America* (second edition). Oxford, UK: Oxford University Press, 2015.

Ramo, Joshua. *The Seventh Sense: Power, Fortune, and Survival in the Age of Networks*. Boston, MA: Little Brown, 2016.

Rid, Thomas. *Active Measures: The Secret History of Disinformation and Political Warfare*. New York: Farrar, Straus, and Giroux, 2020.

Schlesinger, Stephen, Stephen Kinzer, et al. *Bitter Fruit: The Story of the American Coup in Guatemala*. Cambridge, MA: Harvard University Press, 2005.

Segal, Adam. *The Hacked World Order: How Nations Fight, Trade, Maneuver, and Manipulate in the Digital Age*. New York: PublicAffairs, 2016.

Shimer, David. *Rigged: America, Russia, and One Hundred Years of Covert Electoral Interference*. New York: Knopf, 2020.

Snow, Donald M. *The Shape of the Future: The Post–Cold War World* (three volumes). Armonk, NY: M. E. Sharpe, 1991, 1995, 1999.

Springer, Paul. *Cyber Warfare: A Reference Handbook* (Contemporary World Issues). New York: ABC/CLIO, 2015.

United States Department of Justice. *The Mueller Report: Report on the Investigation into Russian Interference in the 2016 Presidential Election*. Washington, DC: U.S. Department of Justice, August 18, 2019.

United States Department of State. *Intervention of International Communism in Guatemala*. Westport, CT: Greenwood Press, 1954.

United States Senate. *Report of the Select Committee on Intelligence, United States Senate on Russian Active Measures Campaign in the 2016 U.S. Election*. Washington, DC: United States Senate, August 19, 2020.

Weeks, Gregory B. *U.S. and Latin American Relations*. New York: Wiley Blackwell, 2015.

Zegart, Amy, and Michael Morrell. "Spies, Lies, and Algorithms: Why U.S. Intelligence Agencies Must Adapt or Fail." *Foreign Affairs* 98, no. 3 (May/June 2019): 85–96.

PART III
Systemic Problems

10

Nuclear Proliferation

Israel, North Korea, and Iran

In the pre-dawn hours of July 16, 1945, the skies over White Sands, New Mexico, were set ablaze by the blinding light of the world's first atomic explosion. It was so vivid that the sky was illuminated as far away as Albuquerque, nearly one hundred miles distant. Radiation could still be felt by visitors to the Trinity Site fifty years later. The nuclear age was born over the New Mexican desert that day.

Robert Oppenheimer, the "father" of the bomb, captured the awe of the occasion as the first bomb exploded. He later recalled saying at the time, "There floated through my mind a line from Bhagavad-Gita (a venerable Indian text), 'I am become death, the shatterer of worlds.'" General Lesley Grove, the military commander of the Manhattan Project, added as he watched the explosion, "This is the end of traditional warfare." Nuclear weapons and hope to avoid their use in anger has been a central concern of international relations ever since. On the positive side, no country has used these weapons in anger in war since August 6 and 9, 1945, when the United States attacked Hiroshima and Nagasaki with them to force the Japanese surrender that ended World War II. If anything, the possession of those weapons may have leavened conflict between possessors who realize that a nuclear war could end human civilization. For as long as nuclear weapons exist and especially are possessed by multiple states, civilization-ending nuclear war can occur. The core concept for avoiding that event is nuclear proliferation.

In the ensuing years since 1945, the number of countries who possess the weapons has increased. In order of attainment, the official list now stands at eight members: in order of their joining the nuclear "club," they are the United States, the Soviet Union/Russia, Great Britain, France, China, India, Pakistan, and the Democratic People's Republic of Korea (DPRK or North Korea). Israel is also a possessor but neither acknowledges nor denies that it has the weapons, and South Africa is the only state to deploy the weapons and subsequently dismantle their arsenal as white rule was ending in the country. Several other states, notably Iran, are considered potential proliferators. Possible and likely proliferators are the focus of nonproliferation efforts.

The concern arises from the enormous destructive power of the weapons and the fear that *someone else* in possession of these weapons might use them against you. Proliferation first occurred when the Soviet Union exploded an atomic bomb in 1949. The increase has continued to the present. The argument for nonproliferation is that those states seeking the capability are less stable than current possessors and thus more likely to start a nuclear war.

The focus in this chapter is three states that are or may become nuclear pos-sessors: Israel, North Korea, and Iran. Each case is different. Israel has possessed the weapons since 1968 but has never admitted to or denied it. North Korea (the Democratic People's Republic of Korea or DPRK) is the world's newest weap-ons state. Iran is a potential nuclear state that has not yet developed or deployed nuclear weapons but could on short notice. Each has followed different paths to their particular status, presenting comparisons that help us understand why some states "go nuclear" and others do not.

Dealing with the spread of nuclear weapons has been a complex concern for over three-quarters of century. It reached a crescendo with the negotiation of the nuclear Non-Proliferation Treaty (NPT) of 1968. The NPT prohibited addi-tional states that did not already have nuclear weapons from acquiring (or trying to acquire) them. It also required current possessors not to aid in the spread of nuclear weapons and made them promise to reduce and eliminate their own arse-nals. It has been a mixed success.

Principle: Nuclear Proliferation

Proliferation is a delicate problem, largely because its underlying aim is both dis-criminatory and condescending to those at whom it is aimed. The desire to limit possession of nuclear weapons largely comes from countries that already possess them and is aimed at those who do not. The implicit assumption is that it is all right for possessors to have and keep nuclear weapons, but not for others to do so. The possessors' implication is clear: we are responsible enough to have these weapons; you may not be. The assertions and arguments underlying the dis-tinction are inherently discriminatory and condescending, and the question that must be answered is, why some but not others? Invariably, the distinction comes back to assumptions regarding responsibility. The problem is structurally com-plex. To understand it, one can look at three questions: What is the nature of the problem? Why is it a problem? And what can be done about it?

The Nature of the Proliferation Problem

The roots of the contemporary proliferation problem lie in the Cold War fear of nuclear war. Its major purpose was to prevent the spread of nuclear weapons to states that did not have them and to limit the size and destructiveness of the arsenals of possessing states. Underlying this effort, there was concern about the destabilizing impact of burgeoning nuclear possession, which in turn spawned two additional complications. One was about the kind of capability proliferators were attempting to obtain. The other was the mechanics of how proliferation could occur and how to prevent it from happening.

There are two basic forms of proliferation: vertical and horizontal. *Vertical proliferation* refers to the impact of additional weapons an already nuclear-armed state may gain. It is a concern both because more weapons add to the potential deadliness of confrontations and because those increments can spawn arms races in which additions by one side cause the other to build more, resulting in a potentially destabilizing arms spiral. Efforts to control vertical proliferation are the traditional object of arms control. Most of the nuclear arms treaties negotiated by the United States and the Soviet Union during the Cold War (such as the Strategic Arms Limitations Talks and the Strategic Arms Reduction Talks) were attempts to limit vertical proliferation. Contemporary proliferation efforts center on *horizontal proliferation*: the spread of nuclear weapons to states that currently do not possess them; generally, when the term *proliferation* is used now, it is in reference to horizontal proliferation.

Proliferation concerns have centered on obtaining nuclear warheads (bombs) and ways to get them to target (delivery systems). The problem of nuclear weapons production has two components. The first is the knowledge of how to fabricate a nuclear device. Nuclear physics has been taught openly for over sixty years now in the world's (and notably American) universities, so that knowledge is widely available both to most governments and undoubtedly to many private groups. The knowledge genie is clearly out of the bottle. The other requirement for building nuclear weapons is possession of adequate supplies of weapons-grade (i.e., highly enriched) isotopes of uranium/plutonium, which generally are byproducts of nuclear reactions in certain types of power generators. Access to such materials is highly guarded and restricted, and aspirants to nuclear weapons must either possess nuclear reactors that can produce weapons-grade materials or be able to purchase or steal such material from those who possess it.

The Problem Proliferation Poses

The short answer to why proliferation is a problem is that one has much less to fear from a weapons capability that one's actual or potential adversaries do not possess than from a capability that they do possess. In classic Cold War thinking about nuclear proliferation, the more additional countries obtained the weapons, the more "fingers" there would be on the nuclear "button." That problem has been augmented by the fear that some of the potential proliferating states are more politically unstable than others and thus might be more likely to use them than current possessors are.

In classic terms, the problem of the spread of nuclear weapons to nonpossessors is known as the $N+1$ problem. The idea is straightforward. In the formulation, N stands for the number of states that currently possess nuclear weapons and refers to the dynamics among them. $+1$, on the other hand, refers to the added problems that are created for the international system (notably the states that form N) by the addition of new $(+1)$ states to the nuclear club.

Current members (N) and potential proliferators $(+1)$ see the problem essentially from opposite ends of the conceptual spectrum. Current members generally believe that the current "club" membership is acceptable and stable; their evidence is the absence of nuclear war. Viewed this way, the emphasis is on the problems created by new members, and the criterion for concern is the likelihood of increased destabilization. Members of N tend to look for and find sources of destabilization that should be opposed and want to restrict membership. Members of $+1$ see the problem differently. They do not see their own acquisition of nuclear weapons as destabilizing and are righteously indignant at the notion that their acquisition would destabilize the system.

In the current context, nonpossessors are more likely to make the argument that their membership in the nuclear club will stabilize their situations and even global politics generally, because it is a fact that no state that possesses nuclear weapons has ever been the victim of a nuclear aggression against it or has initiated nuclear hostilities. Indeed, one argument that some analysts have made in recent years is that gaining nuclear weapons capability is a useful—even necessary—means to avoid being attacked by an aggressive United States. Would, for instance, the United States have invaded Iraq had that state possessed nuclear weapons? Some argue the American attack would have been less likely and that Saddam Hussein's major error was in not getting a nuclear capability to deter the United States from invading the country. Some even argue that had he not abandoned his nuclear weapons program, he might still be alive and in power.

There is a further $N+1$ problem irony—it is generally viewed as a problem only by the current nuclear club. Ironically, a country that aspires to become a member (a $+1$ country) may be viewed as a problem before it gets the capability, but once it has done so and has demonstrated its "responsible possession" of the capability by not starting a nuclear war, it becomes part of the club and views other aspirants as part of the problem.

The nuclear problem may be qualitatively worse when there are more nuclear powers, but one obstacle to sustaining international momentum behind nonproliferation has been that it has not occurred at the pace envisioned by those who most feared the prospects. The nuclear club was largely established by 1964, when China obtained nuclear weapons and pushed the number to five. Since then, only three states have publicly become ongoing members (India, Pakistan, and North Korea).

The problem changed with the end of the Cold War system. Previously, nuclear deterrence was between states with large arsenals of nuclear weapons—notably the United States and the Soviet Union. The dynamic of deterrence, captured in the idea of assured destruction, was that any nuclear attack against a nuclear-armed superpower would be suicidal, because the attacked state would retain such devastating capabilities even after absorbing an attack it would be able to retaliate against the attacker and destroy it, making any "victory" decidedly Pyrrhic (costing far more than it was worth). Because potential attackers were presumably rational (or at least not suicidal), the prospects of a counterattack that would certainly immolate them was enough to dissuade (or deter) an attack in the first place.

The Contemporary Problem of Proliferation

The proliferation problem has changed in two important respects. First, nuclear arsenals and policies have changed. All the major weapons states still maintain nuclear arsenals, but they are smaller than they used to be. The primary Cold War antagonists, the United States and the Soviet Union/Russia, had arsenals of weapons capable of reaching the other's territory of 10,000 to 12,000 warheads; the number today is closer to 7,000. China, the rising nuclear power, is moving toward a similar arsenal size. Second, and more important in the current context, the threats in the contemporary environment come from states that will, at best, have a small number of nuclear weapons at their disposal but may not be dissuaded by Cold War threats. Thus, as Joseph Pilat puts it, "There are real questions about whether old, Cold War–vintage concepts . . . really address the needs of today." The question is what replaces those concepts.

In a text published originally in 1996, Eugene Brown and I laid out a framework for categorizing mechanisms that could be used to deter unwanted nuclear behavior. Within this framework, arms proliferation can be dealt with in two ways, acquisition (or front-end) and employment (or back-end) deterrence. Acquisition deterrence consists of efforts to keep states from obtaining nuclear weapons in the first place. The effort consists of related activities. Persuasion, or convincing states that gaining nuclear weapons is not in their best interests, seeks to convince possible proliferating states not to do so. Successful multilateral efforts through the United Nations and under the NPT to dissuade Iran from making a positive nuclear weapons decision fall into this category. If persuasion does not work, then coercion (threatening or taking punitive—including military—action to prevent proliferation) may occur. In isolated situations like Israel, anti-proliferators have simply ignored the situation.

The current proliferation focus is the spread of nuclear weapons to countries—and especially unstable countries—in the developing world. The stalking horses were Israel and South Africa, both of which conducted highly clandestine weapons development programs that led to their acquisition of nuclear capability. Both countries developed their programs outside the Cold War context: Israel because of its fear its Islamic neighbors might destroy it; South Africa because of the alleged threat posed by neighboring black states (the so-called frontline states). When South Africa dismantled its apartheid system, it also destroyed its nuclear weapons. Israel continues to maintain, and even to expand, its nuclear arsenal.

The other form of dissuasion is employment deterrence. If efforts to keep states from gaining nuclear weapons fail, then one must turn to efforts to keep possessors from using the weapons they do acquire. Once again, there are two mechanisms for doing so. One is the conventional nuclear threat of retaliation. The threat is to retaliate with such devastating—including assured destruction—force that it would be suicidal. Thus, the horror scenario of a possible future North Korean attack against the United States might consist of lobbing a handful of weapons against American targets and inflicting severe but not societally fatal damage; North Korea would be destroyed in the U.S. retaliation. The other form of employment deterrence threat is denial, the promise that if an attack is launched, it will fail because the potential attacked state has the capability to defend itself from an attack.

The major mechanism by which nonproliferation has been enforced is the NPT. It went into effect in 1970. Most countries of the world are or have been members of the regime, and the question is whether the treaty will remain a viable means to avoid more proliferation in the future.

The Iranian and DPRK cases illustrate both strategies. Iran remains a case of successful acquisition deterrence, whereas the failure to dissuade North Korea into abstaining makes dealing with the DPRK an employment deterrence exercise. The two are related in that the reasons for failing to dissuade the North Koreans may be instructive in how to deal with Iran. Israel operated outside nonproliferation efforts and was unaffected by them (they gained weapons status in 1968, the same year the NPT was negotiated). Each of these different situations and outcomes can be examined by comparing them to one another.

Application: Israel, the DPRK, and Iran

Israel, North Korea, and Iran, especially in combination, may seem an odd set of countries for comparing problems created by proliferation. Israel is rarely used as an example, despite having become a clandestine proliferator over fifty years ago, and it is part of the arguably most dangerous and unstable geopolitical region of the world. It represents a colossal failure of anti-proliferation efforts. The DPRK was part of the NPT but left it and built nuclear weapons without dire international consequences. Iran may seem a more likely candidate for inclusion because of the animosities between that country and the United States and Israel, as well as its rivalry with the Sunni Arab states of the Gulf. Israel clandestinely obtained the weapons through efforts that began shortly after its independence and managed to hide their development until they fabricated their first atomic bomb in 1968. Western, and especially American, support for the beleaguered Israelis in their confrontation with the Arab states created such empathy for Israel that the Americans neither condemned the effort nor publicized it as a proliferation failure. Efforts to stop the North Korean program were ongoing for some time, but they rejected the efforts and built an arsenal without apparent international consequences. The Iranians were not so lucky. Their research in atomic matters has always been much more public, thus more scrutinized, and more controversial given their conflict with the United States and Israel.

Israel is an exceptional case. Its arsenal is sizable and capable of obliterating much of the Middle East if employed in anger. That arsenal serves as its "hole card" in its security relationship with other Middle Eastern states. Should Islamic states attack Israel (as they historically have done) and threaten to defeat Israel, the Israelis could respond by attacking and annihilating the invaders. The threat that might be carried out, the "Samson Option," might also destroy Israel, but the Arab states recognize the possibility Israel might carry out the threat, and that it is the core of Israeli security policy. Israel armed its then small arsenal when they were in danger of losing the Yom Kippur War in 1973; they have not been seriously threatened since.

North Korean nuclear aspirations date back to the 1950s and were an obsession of Kim il-Sung, the country's founder. The DPRK has been the most backward and generally friendless state in the region and felt humiliated by the outcome of the Korean War in 1953. They wanted power and recognition from other east Asian states. Nuclear weapons acquisition was the answer.

The other state mentioned prominently in Middle Eastern proliferation concerns is Iran. Its situation is also distinct. First, it has significant foreign policy differences with the United States. Second, Iran denies any interest or desire to build, and especially to use, nuclear weapons. These claims are widely disbelieved in some policy circles, especially in the United States and Israel since the Israeli election results of 2021. Third, Iran is a member of the NPT, but it has been deemed to be an untrustworthy, rogue regime whose word cannot be taken at face value. Iran is a potential proliferator.

Israeli Nuclear Weapons

According to Hersh, whose *The Samson Option* is the most complete popular examination of the Israeli nuclear program, the effort formally began in 1954 when Israel announced a cooperative program with France as part of "Atoms for Peace." Others place the dynamics much further back in Jewish history to the siege at Masada in 73 AD, and its ensuing mass suicide of Jews in the fortress. That event has reverberated through the Jewish experiment, culminating in the Holocaust and the cryptic lesson of a long and tortured history: "Never again." Beres states the lesson more elaborately: "Israel must understand that it can never be just another state . . . Israel, more than any other state, must not count on others ultimately to protect it, but must be prepared to do so alone." That sentiment is the basis for Israeli nuclear weapons.

That Israeli contemporary sentiment goes back to the Israeli state's emergence. In 1948, Prime Minister David Ben Gurion, as quoted in a 2015 *National Interest* study, "made it clear it was his mission to ensure that the one homeland for the Jewish people would be protected from an ever-present threat of Arab attack." Although the United States had promised to guarantee Israeli survival, the Israelis, joined and probably influenced by the French, were not certain how far the Americans would go to honor their commitment, and the Israeli nuclear program emulated the French *force frappe* as a nuclear strike force that could be activated and employed with or without American blessing. The United States has never wavered in its commitment to Israel but never had to face the prospect of having to honor it if Israel was being decimated in a war that might escalate to the nuclear level and engulf the United States as well. Possibly as an indirect recognition of this trepidation, the United States has never publicly addressed the Israeli arsenal's existence or commented on the fact that it was an act of proliferation that the United States has consistently condemned other states for contemplating or implementing.

The Israeli Nuclear Arsenal and Policy

Israel is the only nuclear power in the Middle East, and this status provides it with a disproportionate regional military and geopolitical strength well beyond its population base of roughly eight million citizens. All the potential and historical regional enemies of the Israelis are aware of the Israeli ability and stated willingness to use it against an enemy that threatens to overrun them, that the response would be nuclear if Israel felt physically imperiled, and that they would be destroyed in the process. Van Creveld (quoted by Hirst) states the effect nuclear weapons have on the military equation: "Our armed forces are not the thirtieth strongest in the world, but the second or third. We have the capability to take the world down with us. And I assure you that will happen before Israel goes under." Beres reinforces this determination: "Israel's nuclear force would never be used except in retaliation for massive first strikes. It is *almost* inconceivable that Israel would ever decide to preempt an enemy aggression with a nuclear strike." (Emphasis in original)

This Israeli nuclear policy is based on two major principles that both defines why the country has nuclear weapons and when it might use them. The first is "the bomb in the basement," a euphemism for the fact that Israel has never explicitly acknowledged their possession of nuclear capability. This position allows the Israelis to portray themselves as nonproliferators and leaves their enemies to wonder if Israel really does have nuclear bombs in their "basement." The second and more fundamental principle arises from the reason Israel felt the need to obtain the weapons in the first place. Based in terms of the Jewish state's history, the Samson Option states why and under what circumstances Israel might use nuclear weapons. It emphasizes Israeli resolve and puts its potential enemies on notice that it would be willing to use those weapons against an enemy if it seems necessary. The Samson Option analogy tells an enemy that if another Masada occurs, the besiegers would die too. This is an extraordinary position. It is implicit in all nuclear deterrence theorizing, since the basis of deterrence has operated under the principle of retaliation as the deterrent: the doctrine of mutual assured destruction (MAD), for instance, warns a potential aggressor that an attack would be followed by a devastating retaliation that would destroy the aggressor. The Israeli doctrine goes a step further and explains why Israel would take an action that might result in its own (and the rest of the world's) destruction.

International Impacts

The assumptions and implications of Israeli nuclear policy are more explicit and grislier than those of most other countries who have gone through the nuclear weapons proliferation process. While Israel's nuclear capability was being developed, almost all the world was unaware either of the program or the doctrine by which it would be governed. This silence has always been most deafening in the United States, from which many of the principles of nuclear science were derived and, in some cases, purloined. The Samson Option and its implications do not represent a position that any other state—and certainly not the United States—could state or embrace publicly, and this may explain why the Israeli policy is not widely disseminated or known. Anticipating world reaction to a policy that potentially involves decimating the world (which the Samson Option implies) may have been part of why the Israelis kept the program and its strategy secret (along with avoiding attempts by outsiders to destroy the program in its infancy, which Israel did to Syria and Iraq). Could any other country have gotten away with Israeli nuclearization?

Regional nuclear hegemony has been useful for Israel, but it has potential costs in proliferation terms. There are two clear benefits. One has already been raised: having a regional nuclear monopoly makes Israel the military hegemon of the Middle East, a position it could not possibly obtain in any other manner. Iran is its current main rival, for instance, with a population base ten times the size of Israel, but it does not directly confront the Israelis because of Israel's nuclear hole card. This advantage allows, even facilitates a major Israeli foreign policy priority, the expansion of Israeli sovereignty over areas like the West Bank and Golan (see Snow, *The Middle East and American National Security*). With Israeli nuclear weapons in place, nobody dares challenge Israeli expansionism; if Israel either did not possess or was not the sole possessor of nuclear weapons in the region, its ability to do so would be far more difficult.

This latter realization creates a regional proliferation problem. Of all the other Middle Eastern countries, the most prominent rival of Israel for regional power is Iran (see chapter 11). That country has a large population and believes it should be viewed as the major power among regional countries west of Pakistan and east of Egypt. Iran also has an active nuclear program and could physically develop a nuclear weapons capability in a year or less. The result could be a nuclear confrontation between Israel and Iran in which Israel might be disadvantaged. Israel has attacked potential nuclear rivals in the region before. Would it do so again against Iran (possibly with nuclear weapons) if it felt besieged? Would such an action be consistent with the Samson Option? No one really wants to know the answer to that question.

The Case of the Hermit Kingdom (North Korea)

The North Korean case is different. The Democratic Republic of Korea (DPRK) is the most recent country to acquire nuclear weapons, and, unlike Israel, it has done so quite publicly. Its decision and implementation came at the end of a long period of negotiation between the North Koreans and the other countries part of the six-party talks (the United States, Russia, China, Japan, and North and South Korea) that began in 2003 and which vacillated between U.S. administrations. The formal talks ended with the ascension of President Trump, who transformed formal proceedings into a personal dialogue with North Korean leader Kim Jong-un that eventuated in the North Korean ascension to nuclear status in 2018.

DPRK recalcitrance about its nuclear weapons program is motivated partly by American military presence on the Korean peninsula, the fear of absorption into the Republic of Korea, and their relationship with China, which sees the DPRK as a buffer against having a hostile unified Korea on its borders. The DPRK is one of the most destitute countries in the world, relies on China to help maintain its meager standard of living, and is almost totally ignorable and inconsequential except for its nuclear status. Lankov summarizes their importance: "Pyongyang cannot do away with these programs. That would mean losing a powerful military deterrent and a time-tested tool of extortion. It would relegate North Korea to being a third-rate country on a par with Mozambique or Uganda." This factor cannot be overestimated.

The history of the nuclear program and concerns about it is long-standing. The United States and the DPRK have been antagonists since the 1950s, and post–Korean War hatred may have provided the impetus for the North Korean programs. As Norris put it in 2003, "The fact that North Korea was threatened with nuclear weapons during the Korean War, and that for decades thereafter U.S. weapons were deployed in the South, may have helped motivate former President Kim Il Sung to launch a nuclear program of his own." When the six-party talks dissolved in 2006, the DPRK clandestinely ramped up its program, which became operational in 2018 when, despite ongoing summit meetings between Trump and Kim Jong-il, the North Koreans began fielding warheads and delivery systems, actions which drew objections but not retaliation from the Americans.

In this light, one is left with what to make of the North Korean nuclear weapons decision and its implementation. Since the DPRK is now nuclear-capable, the question is what would keep them from using these weapons (the employment deterrence question)? It is difficult to conjure reasons why they would launch a preemptive strike against anyone, given that the certain response would be its own utter and certain destruction. Despite this reality, the leadership does not rule out doing exactly that in what they view as necessary circumstances. The threat is less nonsensical if they truly believe their threat helps them deter the United States from attacking them. The idea that the United States needs to be deterred may seem outlandish to Americans, but not to North Koreans who are well aware of Saddam Hussein's "mistake" in abandoning his program. DPRK proliferation occurred without serious consequence for the proliferator. The acquisition deterrence effort is now an employment deterrence problem.

The Iranian Contrast

Israel is the only Middle Eastern nuclear weapons state, but it is not the only regional state that has or may have nuclear ambitions. Given the general instability of the region, the prospects of more than one weapon state is chilling to many analysts. If there is any one area where conflict could lead to nuclear war, it may be the Middle East, where states might use nuclear weapons against Israel or one another. As well, proliferation by one state could easily lead to more regional nuclear-armed countries. It is a sobering prospect.

Concern with Iran is currently the focus of regional proliferation concerns. Iran is engaged in military competitions both with Israel and with its Sunni brethren in several places. Its abstinence from nuclear acquisition has relegated it to second place in regional power calculations, a status that eschewing proliferation prohibitions would reverse. Doing so would probably trigger Saudi acquisition (e.g., buying weapons from Pakistan), which could trigger further spread. Israeli weapons started this dynamic; Iranian acquisition could activate a spiral. Maintaining a weapons-free Iran (proliferation control) is the crucial variable.

Whether Iran has (or has had) proliferation ambitions is a matter of disagreement. The Iranians have consistently denied that their nuclear activities are anything but peaceful, but other countries, led by the United States and Israel, have voiced great skepticism about those assertions. The American suspicion is part of the aftermath of the Iranian Revolution of 1979, which overthrew the American-backed Shah, captured the U.S. embassy in Tehran and held its personnel hostage for 444 days, and declared a fundamentalist Islamic Republic of Iran, and their chief enemy has been the "Great Satan" (the United States), with whom conflict is possible. The two countries have not had formal relations since.

The main contrast with the other cases is that Iran signed an agreement in 2015 with the 5+1 powers (the permanent members of the UN Security Council plus Germany) in which it abjured any right to build nuclear weapons and agreed to international inspection of its nuclear facilities (the Joint Comprehensive Plan of Action or JCPOA). This agreement has been denounced by Israel and some Americans, led by former President Trump, who did not trust the Iranians and did not believe they have honored or will honor their bargain, and so he rescinded American participation in it in 2018. One of the chief architects of the JCPOA was Biden secretary of state Antony (Tony) Blinken, and the United States is likely to resume negotiations to reinstate the agreement in modified form. That dynamic aside, the JCPOA remains in force, and there have been no major demonstrated instances of Iran violating its provisions. Even when the United States dropped out of the agreement, it remained in force due to the continued participation of the other non-American parties. If nothing else, the agreement demonstrates it is possible successfully to engage in proliferation control efforts: keeping that condition is the major proliferation challenge.

Iran is thus still an acquisition deterrence problem, in contrast to Israel and the DPRK. The Iranians have not reneged on their nonproliferation agreement despite the withdrawal of the Americans from the JCPOA and strangling American sanctions against them. The Iranian government has never wavered on its commitment to nonproliferation, American concerns about Tehran's sincerity and honesty notwithstanding. What would make them change their minds?

Proliferation has often occurred when a country feels threatened by a nuclear-armed rival and develops nuclear weapons to deter that rival. This dynamic was evident in the Cold War and in Indian and Pakistani proliferation. The same condition affects Iran, which faces an antagonistic nuclear-armed Israel and is part of the bloody advocacy of a Palestinian state, thereby confronting it with the Israelis. If the United States (and others) wants to "disincentivize" any change in Iranian commitment not to "go nuclear," a Palestinian accord may be a priority they should pursue more publicly. The key to the Iranian case may well be whether Israel remains an unrequited opponent or active, positive participant in the process.

Conclusion

Especially for Americans, the three proliferation problems in this chapter represent distinctly different situations and problems. The first two cases, Israel and the DPRK, have progressed beyond acquisition to employment deterrence problems. What distinguishes them is their relationship to the United States and the rest of the world. The dynamics of employment deterrence are not publicly applied to the Israelis because of the official non-recognition of the existence of the Israeli arsenal. The Israelis hint at the bomb in the basement; the Americans unofficially deny there is a bomb or a basement. Given the Israeli reference to the "Never Again" lesson of Masada and the "Samson Option," there are clearly deterrence issues that have not been raised due to the unique Jewish experience and U.S. self-guilt about the Holocaust. How that dynamic translates into an employment strategy is not clear. The Israelis might, under special circumstances at which some of them have hinted, become an employment deterrence problem.

The DPRK has also become an employment deterrence problem. It is physically the result of the failure of acquisition deterrence efforts that tried unsuccessfully to keep the North Koreans non–weapons possessing. That failure, combined with earlier similar decisions by countries like India and Pakistan, raises questions about the efficacy and effectiveness of current efforts and is particularly troublesome given the supposedly unpredictable, rogue behavior of Kim Jong-un. Collectively, however, the Israeli and DPRK nuclear status does raise significant questions about whether the current NPT-based regime can deter a future dedicated proliferator.

The only successful case of dealing with the acquisition deterrence dynamic is Iran. The Iranians have consistently denied any intent or desire to become a nuclear weapons state, although their scientific ability to do so in less than a year is well established. The Iranians have some incentive to threaten to "go nuclear," notably in the form of the Israeli arsenal and the desire to put pressure on the United States to release impounded Iranian funds held by the Americans. What deters them? Is it the fear that the discovery by Israel that they were arming would trigger an Israeli nuclear attack on them? The Israelis may well be psychologically capable of doing so if the Iranian program is not so advanced that they could respond and trigger the full Samson process. Meanwhile, the Iranians remain committed to the JCPOA, a position the Biden administration supports. Keeping Iran an acquisition problem is the current most important nonproliferation problem; its continuation under a new, hardline regime in Tehran is a major challenge for the Biden administration.

Study/Discussion Questions

1. What is proliferation? What forms does it take? How do these relate to types of nonproliferation effort? Explain.

2. What is the $N+1$ problem? Define it and explain why it illustrates the delicacy of the proliferation problem. Why is it so difficult to resolve?

3. What means are available to deal with proliferation? Distinguish between acquisition and employment deterrence. How does each work?

4. Compare and contrast Israel, the DPRK, and Iran as proliferation problems. How are they similar and different from one another? How are they connected in the continuum of proliferation dynamics? Elaborate.

5. Why did Israel reject nonproliferation? Why is being a nuclear weapons state important to them? What is the likelihood they will ever "denuclearize"? Under what

circumstances might they change their minds?

6. Why did the DPRK break from the NPT? What does their experience suggest for other states that might want to "go nuclear"?

7. What is the Iranian position and physical commitment on nuclear weapons possession? Why could Israel provide an incentive for them to change their posture, and if so, in what direction?

8. If you were representing a country contemplating getting nuclear weapons but in an adversarial relationship with the United States as Iran is, would that fact affect your decision? Compare the Iranian precedent and the American posture regarding the Israel nuclear arsenal, and discuss the debate about whether Iraq made a mistake abandoning their nuclear program.

Bibliography

Amanat, Abbas. *Iran: A Modern History*. New Haven, CT: Yale University Press, 2017.

Axelworthy, Michael. *A History of Iran: Empire of the Mind*. New York: Basic Books, 2016.

Beres, Louis Rene. *Surviving Amid Chaos: Israel's Nuclear Strategy*. Lanham, MD: Rowman & Littlefield, 2016.

Cha, Victor D., and David C. Kang. *Nuclear North Korea: A Debate on Engagement*. New York: Columbia University Press, 2008.

Cohen, Avner. *Israel and the Bomb*. New York: Columbia University Press, 1998.

———. *The Worst-Kept Secret: Israel's Bargain with the Bomb*. New York: Columbia University Press, 2010.

Cohen, Michael D. *When Proliferation Causes Peace: The Psychology of Nuclear Crises*. Washington, DC: Georgetown University Press, 2017.

Debs, Alexandre, and Numo P. Mantiero. *Nuclear Politics: The Strategic Causes of Proliferation* (Cambridge Studies in International Relations). Cambridge, UK: Cambridge University Press, 2017.

Delury, John. "Trump and North Korea: Reviving the Art of the Deal." *Foreign Affairs* 96, no. 2 (March/April 2017): 46–51.

Feldman, Shai. *Israeli Nuclear Deterrence: A Strategy for the 1980s*. New York: Columbia University Press, 1983.

Hersh, Seymour M. *The Samson Option: Israel's Nuclear Arsenal and American Foreign Policy* (with a new afterword). New York: Vintage, 1992.

Hirst, David. *The Gun and the Olive Branch: The Roots of Violence in the Middle East*. New York: Harcourt Brace, 1977.

Karpin, Michael. *The Bomb in the Basement: How Israel Went Nuclear and What That Means for the World*. New York: Simon and Schuster Reprints, 2006.

Katz, Yaakov, and Yoaz Hendel. *Israel versus Iran: The Shadow War*. Washington, DC: Potomac Books, 2012.

Kim, Sung Chull, and Michael D. Cohen. *North Korea and Nuclear Weapons: Entering the New Era of Deterrence*. Washington, DC: Georgetown University Press, 2017.

Lankov, Andrei. "Changing North Korea." *Foreign Affairs* 88, no. 6 (November/December 2009): 95–105.

Mattson, Roger. *Stealing the Atom Bomb: How Denial and Deception Armed Israel* (second edition). Woodbury, NJ: Roger J. Mattson, 2016.

Mendelsohn, Jack. "The New Threats: Nuclear Amnesia, Nuclear Legitimacy." *Current History* 105, no. 694 (November 2006): 385–90.

Nasr, Vali. "Biden's Narrow Window of Opportunity on Iran: Washington Must Quickly Resurrect the Nuclear Deal—Or Risk a Full-Blown Crisis in the Middle East." *Foreign Affairs* (online), March 2, 2021.

The National Security Strategy of the United States of America. Washington, DC: The White House, March 2006.

Norris, Robert S. "North Korea's Nuclear Program, 2003." *Bulletin of the Atomic Scientists* 59, no. 2 (March/April 2003): 74–77.

O'Reilly, Kelly P. *Nuclear Weapons and the Psychology of Political Leadership: Beliefs, Motivations, and Perceptions.* New York and London: Routledge, 2016.

Oberdorfer, Don, and Robert Carlin. *The Two Koreas: A Contemporary History.* New York: Basic Books, 2014.

Pilat, Joseph F., Nathan E. Busch, et al. *Routledge Handbook of Nuclear Proliferation Policy.* New York and London: Routledge, 2015.

Ratcliff, Jonathan E. B. *Nuclear Proliferation: Overview, History, and Reference Guide.* New York: CreateSpace Independent Publishing Platform, 2016.

Sagan, Scott, and Kenneth N. Waltz. *The Spread of Nuclear Weapons: An Enduring Debate.* New York: W. W. Norton, 2012.

Seth, Michael J. *North Korea: A History.* London: Red Globe Press, 2018.

Shavit, Ari. *Does This Mean War? Top Israeli Strategists Debate the Iranian Bomb.* Tel Aviv: Haaretz, 2012.

Simon, Steven. *Iran and Israel: The Iran Primer.* Washington, DC: United States Institute for Peace Press, 2019.

Snow, Donald M. *The Middle East and American National Security: Ending Forever Wars.* Lanham, MD: Rowman & Littlefield, 2021.

———. *Regional Cases in Foreign Policy* (second edition). Lanham, MD: Rowman & Littlefield, 2018.

———. *The Shadow of the Mushroom-Shaped Cloud.* Columbus, OH: Consortium for International Studies Education, 1978.

———, and Eugene Brown. *The Contours of Power: An Introduction to Contemporary International Relations.* New York: St. Martin's Press, 1996.

Solingen, Etel, ed. *Sanctions, Statecraft, and Nuclear Proliferation.* Cambridge, UK: Cambridge University Press, 2012.

"Welcome to Israeli Nuclear Weapons 101." *The National Interest* (online), September 20, 2015.

Wit, Joel S., David Poneman, and Robert Gallucci. *Going Critical: The First North Korean Nuclear Crisis.* Washington, DC: Brookings Institution Press, 2004.

11

Power Changes and Status

Superpowers, Pivotal States, and the Middle East Conflict

Power is the ubiquitous underlying factor in much of international relations. It has been the central concept of most of the concerns in the preceding chapters, culminating in the analysis of controlling the development and plans for using the penultimate expression of the most dramatic form of physical power, nuclear weapons. Sovereignty may be the underlying principle and value of those who operate the mechanisms of international relations; power in its myriad forms is a primary means used by international actors.

States covet, nurture, and attempt to increase their power in the belief that greater power provides the state with more ability to protect and promote its pursuit of interest. To facilitate being able to achieve their goals, states seek to maximize their relative power statuses. Barring a condition of stasis in which all states are equally powerful or all states have as much power as they felt they needed to achieve their goals, the process of trying to increase national power—often at the expense of other states—is an apparently inevitable part of the relations among states.

This dynamic is at the heart of international relations and it structures many of the interactions among states. It is a pervasive but illusive pursuit, for at least two reasons already raised. First, there is not universal agreement about what constitutes power generally and in specific circumstances. Different instruments of power are available in different situations, but measuring those instruments and their effects is difficult, making estimates of effectiveness difficult in discreet situations. The use of economic power is exemplary. The United States, as noted in chapter 10, used economic coercion against Iran (principally the impounding of funds and coercing other countries not to do business with them) to keep the Iranians from going nuclear (which they maintain they do not want to do anyway). Has it worked? It has made life more difficult for Iranians and probably made some of them more anti-American than they otherwise would be. Has it inhibited their nuclear weapons decision? Nobody knows for sure.

Second, power balances change, partly because of conscious policy actions and partly due to unrelated circumstances. The economic relationship between China and the United Sates is an example. In the early twenty-first century, the gross size of the Chinese economy surpassed that of the United Sates in GDP (gross domestic product), making China's economy the largest in the world. Much geopolitical debate since has focused on what that change means and what, if anything, the United States can do to reverse it. Some critics argue the change has affected the relationship in fundamental ways; others disagree. Both countries say and act as if the changes are highly consequential. Neither side specifies what the consequences are.

Power calculations also change in at least two ways. One way is to distinguish between physical levels on a regional or global basis. Some analysts hold that important regional powers can be described as pivotal states, because their status and actions are pivotal to how the region operates. The most important states at the global level are accorded superpower status. The historical primary indicator of superpowers has been the possession of sizable nuclear arsenals. The end of the Cold War has moderated the simplicity of these distinctions. It is probably adequate to distinguish pivotal status as a characteristic of countries with interests defined regionally and superpowers as countries whose interests and capabilities are global.

How useful is it to think of countries as superpowers or as pivotal states? The designations are imprecise and to some degree arbitrary. Superpower status has been most often associated with countries possessing nuclear arsenals, but not all globally prominent states earned the designation. A 2000 study of pivotal states included several weapons possessors it considered pivotal to their regions but did not qualify as superpowers. India and Pakistan, Brazil, Indonesia, Egypt, Algeria, Turkey, South Africa, and Mexico all have the characteristics of pivotal states: the "capacity to affect regional and international stability." Superpowers can also meet this criterion, but they can largely destroy much of world civilization.

Principle: The Existence and Rise of the Pivotal States

The locus and dynamics of state power has evolved. The Cold War often extended to and had a large influence on regional power interactions. The developing world was a particular ground of the Cold War and of the competition of the Cold Warriors for worldwide influence. Superpower interests tended to mute more natural regional dynamics and impeded the development of regional interactions that could have yielded pivotal state prominence to countries that were the most powerful in their areas of the world. The end of the Cold War reduced that outside interference and control over regional politics. A major artifact of that reduction of East-West conflict within regions has been to untether regional conflicts from Cold War bounds. Who is the more or less dominant state in regional competitions has taken on greater importance within different geographic and geopolitical regions; these distinctions have taken on greater significance in the post–Cold War world.

The emergence of conflict among what are described here as pivotal states has become a salient concern. The removal of the communist–anti-communist framework has largely upended the structure of regional politics and reduced (the United States) or removed (Russia) superpower considerations as an ongoing guideline for regional politics. One result has been to reduce constraints imposed by outsiders on the competition within regions. An effect of that change has been to raise the impact the most important regional states have on the relations within the region and between the regions and the rest of the world. Largely because of this dynamic, the identity and role of the pivotal states has taken on added salience in the post–Cold War world.

Although it is not a universally acknowledged designation, the term employed here for these newly more important states is pivotal state. It is a term that is not widely used in comparative rankings of states. The image that it conjures is a category of states that occupy or seek to establish a position within a geographic region parallel to the role played by the superpowers worldwide during the Cold War. As Chase, Hill, and Kennedy described it in a 2000 book, the defining characteristic of pivotal states is "their capacity to affect regional and international stability." The pivotal states are the countries whose interactions most affect the geopolitics of various regions and whose positions and power must be considered in outside interaction with a particular region.

Each geographical region has pivotal states, and they generally serve as positive forces depending on the region and how divisive its geopolitics may be. The most important regional pivots in Latin America are Brazil and Argentina in South America and Mexico in Central America, for instance. All three are well established Catholic majority states which have been independent for well over a century and who have, over time, worked out their differences. The South American states had different colonial masters and speak different languages, but they evolved a peaceful modus vivendi. Mexico, of course, must coexist with and accommodate a difficult superpower on its border and restiveness among its Central American neighbors to the south. Most of Africa and Southeast Asia lack a pivotal state, and this may contribute to regional disorder. The most intense competition for the mantel of pivotal state is in the Middle East, a situation described in the next section.

Pivotal states are the most consequential states in the region in which they are located. They are a stabilizing influence in those regions where their status is recognized or where their primacy is accepted as inevitable. There will always be some resistance to their status from pretenders or when the pivotal state is "different" enough that it accentuates animosities based on ethnic, religious, political, or other grounds. The result can be a situation where there is more than one pretender to pivotal status in a region. In that case, the competition for acceptance of the designation may be a source of conflict and even intra-regional violence. In such unsettled areas, stability is the captive of the success or failure of regional efforts to resolve differences about regional ordering and priorities. The Middle East is the most prominent case of all these problems and their consequences.

Understanding and working with pivotal states is an important and often an underappreciated problem for outside powers, including superpowers, in their relations with regional pivotal states. During the Cold War, the superpowers actively pursued close relations with the most important regional states and sought to overlay an extension of the East-West struggle to those regions. The effect was to extend the Cold War geopolitical struggle to areas where its basic feature, communism versus anti-communism, was not a crucial or even relevant consideration before their arrival. In the Middle East, for instance, the superpowers were primarily interested in securing access to Gulf petroleum reserves, and the pivotal states were those countries that either possessed large reserves or influenced states that had such reserves. Saudi Arabia, arguably not a pivotal state by any measure other than oil reserves, is a case in point.

The concept and existence of pivotal states is thus an important, integral part of the practice of international relations for two basic reasons. First, if a power from outside the region seeks geopolitical entrance or access in a particular region, it must identify who the pivotal actor or actors are, with which actor the outsider can best work to mutual advantage, and what rivalries the analysis may uncover that can impede the actions of the outsider. Second, the pivotal state is a gatekeeper of sorts whose interests must be identified and accommodated if the outsider is to succeed in the region. When there is conflict over which state is pivotal or can wield the most influence, the outsider may have to choose sides among pretenders in what are often complex and difficult situations.

Application: The Pivotal State(s) in the Middle East

The Middle East is an excellent area for examining this process. It is the most volatile part of the world and arguably the most likely source of a violent clash that could spread to and engulf other parts of the world. It is disorderly, at least in part because it has no widely accepted pivotal state to quell its cacophony and to impose or negotiate a semblance of order. Instead, it has three de facto pretenders to pivotal state status: Iran, Israel, and Saudi Arabia. By normal standards of ascendancy to that role, Iran would be the leading candidate for leadership status, and Iran acts as if it wants recognition and acceptance of its pivotal status. It is the oldest continuous civilization in the region east of Suez, has a population nearly double that of its nearest rival (Saudi Arabia), and would be among the region's most prosperous states should American sanctions be lifted. Saudi Arabia is larger in area, and it is home to Mecca and Medina, the holiest sites of Islam. Its absolutist theocratic monarchy is an anachronism, and oil wealth is its major claim to pivotal status. Israel, thanks to its nuclear weapons, is the military hegemon, but it is hard to think of a Jewish state as the pivot in an otherwise exclusively Muslim region.

The physical region is ambiguously defined in geographic terms, and how one categorizes the region geographically critically affects the conferral of pivotal status. For present purposes, the region can be thought of as bounded by the Mediterranean Sea on the west, the Suez Canal south to the Indian Ocean, east to both banks of the Persian Gulf, and north to the southern Turkish border. The definition includes the major contenders for pivotal status in the Middle East in the contemporary geopolitical mix but excludes Muslim-majority powers such as Turkey, Egypt, Pakistan, and Afghanistan for different reasons. These countries are all large and historically powerful enough to think of themselves as major regional powers but do not currently compete fully in regional power politics. The return of any of these states to active engagement in regional competitions could change the pivotal state conversation.

The Competitors

The competition for recognition for Middle Eastern pivotal status emerges from this background and set of geopolitical circumstances. There are three major candidates, two of which seek recognition as the region's most important Muslim state (as well as symbol of their Islamic sect), and one non-Muslim state that seeks to protect itself from the Muslim majority, many of which have historically considered it an enemy they seek to destroy. The two Islamic countries, of course, are Iran and Saudi Arabia, and each has a contrasting case for recognition of its primacy. Iran is the larger and more powerful of the two by measures such as geography, population, and military force size and experience. The main advantage of the Saudis is religious: their size, stature, and wealth make them the titular head of Sunni Islam in the region, and Sunnis constitute an estimated 80 to 90 percent of all Muslims. Moreover, the Saudis are true Arabs (descended from natives of the Arabian Peninsula).

Shia, on the other hand, constitute the other 10 to 20 percent of Muslims. In addition to being non-Sunni, many (including the Iranians) are also non-Arab, making them suspect among many Sunni Arabs. Iran is the major stronghold of the Shia faith; other countries with Shia majorities or large concentrations include Iraq, Bahrain, and Lebanon. The ruling regime of war-torn Syria belongs to a variant of Shiism, and war-ravaged Yemen is roughly evenly split between adherents of Shiism and Sunnism.

In geopolitical terms, Iran is the leading claimant to pivotal status, but its claim is contested in three ways. The first barrier, prominent since the 1979 revolution and the resulting animosity between Tehran and Washington, is the United States. Since the protracted hostage crisis at the American embassy in the Iranian capital, the two countries have not had direct diplomatic relations, instead communicating through intermediaries for over forty years. The United States was one of the participants in the 5+1 talks that produced the Iranian nonproliferation agreement, and the Americans were signatories of the 2015 JCPOA accord. The Trump administration removed the United States from that agreement in 2018, ironically arguing that Tehran had lied about its compliance. The Biden administration reinstituted negotiations to rejoin the JCPOA in April 2021, spearheaded by Secretary of State Antony Blinken, one of the American negotiators of the original 2015 agreement.

The second problem has been the emergence of cooperative relations between the Saudi-led Sunni states and Israel. The arrangement has stopped short of any kind of formal alliance, but it serves as a demarcation line between the Iranian-influenced Shia Crescent (mainly Iran, Iraq, Syria, and Lebanon) and the Arabs. How this relationship between Jewish Israel and the Sunni Arab states, especially over contentious disagreements about Palestine, will evolve in this arrangement is an open question. The third barrier, then, is Israel. At the most obvious level, the shadow of Israel's nuclear arsenal hangs over Iran as well as the rest of the region, both providing the basis of Israeli military dominance and as a none-too-subtle warning of the possible consequences of an Iranian attempt to break away from its nuclear celibacy.

The claim of Israel and Saudi Arabia is compromised in different ways. It is hard to imagine any part of the Muslim world acceding to the idea of a Jewish-led region (a goal that Israel denies). Beyond flaunting petro-dollars, the Saudis lack the moral and physical support in the region to gain major support as the pivotal state. The Saudis face a fundamental dilemma in trying to assert leadership. In order to gain support for any claim to leadership, the Saudis must change, which means becoming a more normal member of the international system. The keys to doing so are political modernization and secularization. Both of these changes are absolute anathema to the Wahhabi religious support base on which rule by the House of Saud is dependent for its wealth and its legitimacy. Changing to become internationally respectable probably means alienating, even losing, the support base on which the regime is premised.

The contest for status is difficult but consequential. To assess who "wins" and what that means for the region and potentially for the rest of the world, the discussion first turns to a review of change in the region and how that process translates into outcomes in the competition for pivotal state status in the region.

The Sources of Change

The winds of change are clearly blowing across Middle East sands, and the structure of interests and policies with which the rest of the world has treated the Middle East over the past century or more require examination and assessment as a result. Understanding where those relations are headed, however, requires looking briefly at the factors that elevated the Middle East and its oil to the place it now occupies.

The first agents of change are historical, starting with World War I. The major impact surrounded the war's conclusion, notably the defeat and dismemberment of the Ottoman Empire and its replacement by League of Nations mandates in parts of the region. As chronicled by authors like Anderson in *Lawrence in Arabia*, the impact was to subdivide responsibility for the region, by dividing it into sovereign jurisdictions (most of which were geographically flawed and resulted in current problems), and to allow the emergence of states like Saudi Arabia (which gained independence in 1933) and the reemergence of powers like Iran under the rule of the Shahs. This rearranging was done, of course, in the name of access to oil and the wealth it could create.

The impact of World War II was also dramatic. A major theater of the war centered on access and control of Middle Eastern oil, and the war settled that issue, especially after the United States blocked Soviet attempts to impose themselves in Iran. Two other war-related outcomes may have been more important. Largely at American insistence, the prewar European energy system was replaced with one based on cheap, accessible, and secure Middle Eastern oil as the primary energy source. The result was to cement the importance of the oil-rich regions in Western, and later Cold War, terms. The other impact was the inexorable exodus of Jewish survivors of the Holocaust into Palestine. With world public support and embarrassment as pillars, the creation of an independent state of Israel was inevitable, and with it one of the pillars of conflict that frames change today.

The Cold War had an impact as well. Particularly before Russia began the furtive exploitation of its own reserves, access to Persian Gulf oil was a major Soviet priority, as was any action that would complicate Western access to the reserves. These priorities in turn required a Russian presence in the region. The incompatibility of atheistic communism with highly sectarian Islam made the spread of Soviet influence difficult to achieve, and they used the arming of willing Islamic states like Egypt and Syria as their entrée into the region. Russian "mischief" made minimizing the Soviet presence one of the pillars of American Cold War policy in the region.

The Challenge of Change

During the Cold War, the Middle East was, by current standards, relatively stable. The major source of instability and violence was the ongoing battle regarding the existence and status of Israel that resulted in wars between the Israelis and their surrounding Muslim states in 1948, 1956, 1967, and 1973, all of which resulted in victories for Israel. Two of these wars' outcomes still influence regional geopolitics. The most consequential was in 1967, when Israel occupied and informally annexed former territories of Islamic states, notably on the West Bank and the Syrian Golan Heights. The other was 1973, when Israel came the closest than it ever had to defeat and threatened nuclear retaliation in the event of imminent defeat. The effect was to centralize nuclearization in the region, a prospect that remains not far from the present surface of regional concerns.

The fall of Shah Reza Pahlavi, the rise of militant Shiism in his place, and the Iranian seizure of the American embassy in Tehran effectively imploded the thirty-year tranquility for the United States. The American arrangement with Iran had been a pillar of U.S. regional policy in the region, and it dissolved with the 1979 crises that resulted in both sides treating the other as the "great Satan." That aphorism still persists. America remains the major external guarantor of Israeli security, and the problem of Soviet penetration of the region took care of itself in 1991. The result has been change-driven new dynamics to which the system and its members are still adapting.

The New Manifestations of Change

The Arab Spring fizzled in its implicit promise of intellectually liberalizing and modernizing the politics of the Middle East, but it has had residual effects that help form the parameters in which the sands of change are shifting regional politics. Egypt is a prime example. Along with Iran, it is the largest and most populous among regional states, and the Persian and Egyptian empires have historically been the physical and intellectual bulwarks of the region. Having just experienced its own revolutionary experience in 1979, Iran was largely exempt from the Arab Spring, but it had major disruptive effects on Egypt, which has been quiescent and inactive throughout most of the recent turmoil in the region.

For now, at least, Egypt is not a "player" in the regional politics of the area. The power struggle for supremacy as the regional power is now located in the Persian Gulf and has Iran and Saudi Arabia as its major contestants.

The Syrian Civil War has been one major artifact of the Arab Spring, which in turn spawned the most upsetting regional phenomenon of the 2010s, the rise and then decline of the Islamic State (IS). The descendant of the Al Qaeda in Iraq organization, IS emerged as the most effective opponent of the Syrian government and used that role as a springboard to declare and launch its quest to become a sovereign territorial entity, the Caliphate. The reign of IS was, however, as unexpectedly short as its ascent. The large credit for stopping and defeating IS goes to Kurdish territorial militias (the *pesh merga*) motivated to evict the IS invaders from territories the Kurds believed were part of their destiny within their own sovereign state, Kurdistan. The Kurds join the Palestinians as the world's two largest and most vocal stateless nations (nationalities that desire but do not have their own sovereign state), and their causes constitute one of the most difficult problems of the region (see chapter 16).

All these dynamics swirl in the current Middle Eastern mix and suggest the desirability of reassessing the interests that states both within and outside the region have. Increasingly, the changes that are accumulating raise questions about how outside countries should assess Middle East dynamics and the politics of the region. The long-standing conflict between Israel and Palestine illustrates this dilemma, of which the issue of Palestinian statelessness discussed in chapter 16 is a prominent part.

The Contest: What Is the Pivotal State?

The winds of political change are blowing in the Middle East, and one of the many areas in which change will likely manifest itself is in the relative power of regional states, including the relative if subtle change in which state or states will have their comparative claims to pivotal state status burnished or tarnished. The United States will have a not insignificant role in changes in orientation and substance. The resulting changes could help influence and even reshape the competition for pivotal state, but they probably will not resolve it. The status of each of the aspirants for pivotal state recognition will likely be affected.

The areas where change could be most dramatic center on the Israeli-Iranian conflict and competition. Israel was the centerpiece of regional interest and supportive activity for the Trump administration, manifested in two obvious ways. Most directly, the Trump administration supported Israeli expansionist claims in the region that were opposed by virtually all other regional actors and many other powers. The most dramatic in a symbolic manner was the recognition of Jerusalem as the true capital of the country and the relocation of the U.S. Embassy from Tel Aviv (the capital recognized by virtually all other countries) to Jerusalem. The recognition extended to parts of East Jerusalem claimed by the Palestinians as *their* capital. The United States also recognized the annexation of parts of the Syrian Golan Heights to the Israelis. A major effect of these actions was to align the United States more closely with the Israeli right (symbolized by

Prime Minister Benjamin Netanyahu) and thus in opposition to the traditional "two-state solution" for Israel and a fully sovereign Palestine. These actions were compatible with the expansionist "Greater Israel" propounded by Netanyahu but at odds with traditional American policy regarding Palestine.

Given changes in U.S. and Israeli leadership, two major changes are likely to influence Israel's status. First, the Biden administration will almost certainly reorient policy toward both the Palestinian state and other Israeli territorial expansion. Biden and Blinken have supported the two-state solution and are also likely to push for a reorientation of U.S. policy that seeks to contract Israeli expansionism in places like Syrian Golan, a change in status on which the post-revolutionary government of Syria is likely to insist. As the Israelis seek to improve relations with the Persian Gulf oil kingdoms to isolate and effectively encircle Iran, the Arabs have begun reminding Israel that they support a sovereign Palestine, opposition to which has been a bedrock of the Netanyahu incumbency. The end of Netanyahu's rule is likely to soften Israeli policy in the region, a change that will be welcome in Washington and European capitals.

Israel has had two major responses to this problem, which has become more acute since Trump left the White House. The showiest manifestation has been the Israeli diplomatic initiative toward the Gulf oil states. It is and will continue to be an "odd couple" relationship. On the positive side, cooperation between the Jewish Israelis and the conservative, Wahhabist Arabs offers the prospect of marrying Israeli technological and educational preeminence to Gulf oil money, a prospect that could greatly energize both countries. On the other, negative side, the Arabs and the Israelis have been sometimes mortal enemies since Israel was established in 1948. There is virtually nothing the Israelis and the Saudis and their allies have in common other than their opposition to the expansion of Shiite Iran's ambitions and the animosities the Sunni Arab states have toward non-Arab Iran.

The second state with a claim to pivotal state status is Iran. If the discussion is limited to the demographic and physical status, the case for designating Iran as the pivotal state is strong. If one views Jewish Israel as the primary rival to that status, one immediately confronts a conundrum. On the one hand, the Israelis represent a small proportion of regional population, virtually all of which is Muslim and as such opposed to having a Jewish "island" in a Muslim "sea." The conundrum, of course, is that the relationship is based on Israeli nuclear weapons possession, which serves both as a threat to those states and to their Shiite rivals, the Iranians. Israeli-Iranian rivalry and active animosity both allows relations between the Israelis and the Arabs and diverts Iranian efforts at establishing its claim as the state that matters most.

The Iranian claim is thus frustrated in two ways. The first is the impact of Israeli nuclear weapons both on the military component of pivotal state claims and the realities of military activities in the region. For as long as Israel remains the only nuclear weapons state in the region, no one can challenge Israeli policy with any threats that have a major military component. The Samson Option means fighting the Israelis effectively can have only two military outcomes: losing to Israeli conventional forces or prevailing and facing the possibility of nuclear destruction by Israel. These options are particularly unattractive to Iran. Israel is aware of this dynamic and the fact that it holds only if Israel is the sole regional nuclear power. Iran's only military recourse is indirect, as in the campaign it helps sponsor of unconventional warfare against Israel. This will not resolve the Israeli nuclear hegemony problem, and it insures there will not be regional tranquility. Moreover, Israel clearly finds the current situation desirable. From their vantage point, maintaining nuclear hegemony is vital and worth enforcing with military and paramilitary force. The April 2021 attack apparently carried out by Mossad on an Iranian nuclear facility in Natanz is evidence. Some agreement that removes or lessens the nuclear imbalance but assures Israel's sense of ultimate security is the likely key to resolving this source of regional tension.

The second source of Iranian frustration is its rivalry with the Arab states. The Iranians *are* different than their neighbors on the peninsula and elsewhere. The differences are ethno-linguistic and sectarian. The Iranians are Shia, non-Arab, and do not employ Arabic as their written or spoken language. They are Caucasians ethnically, Shia by sectarian choice, and they speak Persian. They do not look like, speak like, or pray in the same way as the Arabs. In recent years, they have sought to consolidate their influence in the Shia Crescent countries wedged between Arabia and Turkey to assert their influence.

Saudi Arabia is the third pretender to pivotal status in the region, and it is the least likely to gain recognition as the pivotal state. Saudi Arabia has some of the physical wherewithal for the status, such as a large physical territory, a reasonably large population (a little less than half that of Iran), and most importantly one of the world's largest reserves of petroleum. Moreover, the two holiest places in Islam (Mecca and Medina) are in Saudi territory, all Muslims are required to make a pilgrimage to these places at least once in their lifetimes (the *hajj*), and the Saudis control access to these sites. Because of its manifest drawbacks—notably a medieval political and social system—these assets hardly translate into a strong argument for regional leadership.

If one were to lay out the geopolitical cases for the three pretenders, Iran would be the most likely designee by virtually any geopolitical criteria. It is a large country with the region's largest population, which is well educated and skilled. Israel's population has both these characteristics, but there are only about 10 percent as many Israelis as Iranians. Iran's major drawbacks are its religiously militant government (reinforced by the outcome of their 2021 presidential election) and its non-Arab, non-Sunni religious basis. Iran's rise to prominence has also been opposed by the United States.

Conclusion

The Middle East contest for pivotal status was chosen for three reasons. First, the area is the most unstable and conflictual area in the world, and a major aspect of the conflict comes from the conflict among regional states for maximum prestige and influence—who is the pivotal state? Second, the United States has been heavily involved—arguably overinvolved—in the area, at different times strongly supporting all three aspirants for pivotal status. Third, the area is arguably the most violence-prone part of the world, and the Israeli nuclear arsenal means any conflict in which the Israelis might become involved is a potential nuclear conflict the escalatory potential of which is unknown. Creating a more tranquil Middle East is thus a major world—and thus American—priority.

Creating a consensual regional order could add to the stability of the situation, so identifying the pivotal state could reduce the volatility of an already contentious region. It is no easy task given the divisions among the contenders and the issues (especially nuclear weapons) that divide them. Stabilization is the most important international issue affecting the area.

The American position has been ambivalent. American support for Israel has been constant, but policy regarding the disposition of Palestine has vacillated. Iran was a major American ally for the quarter-century rule of the Shah, but his replacement by the Shiite government and conflicts arising from that change has made the two former allies into implacable opponents ever since that 1979 event. The Americans have always tolerated the Saudis because of the need for their oil. That dependence has largely disappeared. The result is not coherent policy, and who the United States considers its major negotiating partner can make a big difference in how the region evolves. More specifically, promoting, recognizing, and working with a pivotal state arguably is the most important priority for the United States.

What can or should the United States do? Under Trump, the American government tilted heavily toward support for Israel while demonizing Iran. The Biden administration promises a more evenhanded approach toward the two rivals. Which way do you think the United States should tilt in its treatment of the two major states? Most specifically, how can the United States positively influence the relations between Israel and Iran on the two major issues that divide them and threaten the world, Palestine and especially nuclear weapons?

Study/Discussion Questions

1. Define power. Why is it so important in international relations? How do calculations of power change? Discuss.

2. What are superpowers and pivotal states? Compare and contrast them. Which countries are considered pivotal? Why are pivotal states particularly important in the developing world?

3. Why are pivotal states an important part of international geopolitics? Discuss.

4. Why is the competition for pivotal state status so important in the contemporary Middle East?

5. Who are the major competitors for pivotal state status in the Middle East today? Discuss the claims and status of each and how they have contributed to the current competition.

6. What have the principal sources of change in the Middle East been since the end of World War II? Discuss each and how they have contributed to the current competition.

7. Discuss the Israeli-Iranian competition for pivotal state status. What is the significance of Israeli nuclear weapons on the contest? Why is

the resolution important to the competition and its resolution?

8. How has U.S. policy on the Middle East pivotal state question vacillated over time? Why is a resolution important to the United States and the world? How do you think it should be resolved?

Bibliography

Abhyanker, Rajenda. *Syria: The Tragedy of a Pivotal State*. London: Palgrave Macmillan, 2020.

Anderson, Scott. *Lawrence in Arabia: War, Deceit, Imperial Folly and the Making of the Modern Middle East*. New York: Anchor Books, 2013.

Bellin, Eva. "Democratization and Its Discontents: Should America Push Political Reform in the Middle East?" *Foreign Affairs* 87, no. 4 (July/August 2008): 112–19.

Betts, Richard K. "Pick Your Battle: Ending America's Era of Permanent War." *Foreign Affairs* 93, no. 6 (November/December 2014): 15–24.

Bregman, Ahron. *Cursed Victory: A History of Israel and the Occupied Territories, 1967 to the Present*. Trenton, TX: Pegasus, 2015.

Brown, Nathan J. "The Occupation at Fifty: A Permanent State of Ambiguity." *Current History* 116, no. 704 (December 2017): 331–36.

———. "The Palestinians' Receding Dream of Statehood." *Current History* 110, no. 740 (December 2011): 345–51.

Carter, Jimmy. *Palestine: Peace Not Apartheid*. New York: Simon and Schuster, 2006.

Chase, Robert S., Emily B. Hill, and Paul Kennedy, eds. *The Pivotal Sates: A New Framework for U.S. Policy in the Developing World*. New York: W. W. Norton, 2000.

Clark, Ronald W. *The Greatest Power on Earth: The International Race for Nuclear Supremacy from Earliest Theory to Three Mile Island*. New York: Harper and Row, 1980.

———. "Pivotal States and U.S. Strategy." *Foreign Affairs* 75, no. 1 (January/February 1996): 33–51.

Della Pergola, Sergio. "Israel's Existential Predicament: Population, Territory, and Identity." *Current History* 109, no. 731 (December 2010): 383–89.

———, and Rebhun Uzi, eds. *Jewish Population Identity: Concept and Reality*. New York: Springer, 2018.

Dowty, Alan. *Israel/Palestine* (fourth edition). London: Polity Press, 2017.

Eland, Ivan. *No War for Oil: U.S. Dependency and the Middle East*. Oakland, CA: Independent Institute, 2011.

Freedman, Robert, ed. *Israel and the United States: Six Decades of U.S.-Israeli Relations*. New York and London: Routledge, 2018.

Haass, Richard N. "The Unraveling: How to Respond to a Disordered World." *Foreign Affairs* 93, no. 6 (November/December 2014): 70–79.

Hammond, Jeremy R. *Obstacle to Peace: The U.S. Role in the Israeli-Palestinian Conflict*. New York: Worldview, 2016.

Harms, Gregory, and Todd M. Ferry. *The Palestinian-Israeli Conflict: A Basic Introduction* (fourth edition). London: Pluto Press, 2017.

Held, Colbert C., and John Thomas Cummings. *Middle East Patterns: Places, People, and Politics* (sixth edition). Boulder, CO: Westview Press, 2013.

Hummel, Daniel R. *Covenant Brothers: Evangelicals, Jews, and U.S.-Israeli Relations*. Philadelphia, PA: University of Pennsylvania Press, 2018.

Jewish Virtual Library. *Vital Statistics: Latest Population Statistics for Israel*. May 11, 2018.

Maloney, Suzanne. *Long Reach: Iran as a Pivotal State in the Muslim World*. Washington, DC: U.S. Institute for Peace, 2008.

Mandelbaum, Michael. "The New Containment: Handling Russia, China, and Iran." *Foreign Affairs* 98, no. 2 (March/April 2019): 123–31.

Muravchik, Joshua. *Making David into Goliath: How the World Turned against Israel*. New York: Encounter, 2016.

Owen, John M. "From Calvin to the Caliphate: What Europe's Religious Wars Tell Us about the Modern Middle East." *Foreign Affairs* 94, no. 3 (May/June 2015): 77–89.

Petras, James. *The Politics of Empire: The U.S., Israel, and the Middle East*. Atlanta, GA: Clarity Press, 2014.

Ross, Dennis. *Doomed to Succeed: The U.S.-Israeli Relationship from Truman to Obama*. New York: Farrar, Straus, and Giroux, 2015.

Salehi-Isfahani, Djavad. "The Dilemma of Iran's Resistance Economy: Imperviousness to Sanctions Will Require Growth." *Foreign Affairs* (online), March 29, 2021.

Scheindlin, Dahlia. "Netanyahu's Foreign Policy Is Bad for Israel." *Foreign Affairs Snapshot* (online), February 8, 2019.

Shavit, Ari. *My Promised Land: The Triumphs and Tragedy of Israel*. New York: Spiegel and Grau, 2015.

Snow, Donald M. *Cases in U.S. National Security: Concepts and Processes*. Lanham, MD: Rowman & Littlefield, 2019.

———. *The Middle East, Oil, and the U.S. National Security Policy: Intractable Conflicts, Impossible Solutions*. Lanham, MD: Rowman & Littlefield, 2016.

U.S. Department of Defense. *Assessing the Impact of U.S.-Israeli Relations on the Arab World*. Washington, DC: U.S. Department of Defense, 2015.

Van Creveld, Martin L. *The Land of Blood and Honey: The Rise of Modern Israel*. New York: Thomas Dunne, 2010.

12

Cyberwar and Cybersecurity
May the Force Be with Whom?

The 1960s movie and television versions of *Star Trek* opened with a pan-orama of space and intoned, "Space, the final frontier" as the starship *Enterprise* appeared and streaked across the screen. The narrator intoned that the five-year mission of the spaceship was "to boldly go where no man has gone before." The adventure, presumably set in the 2260s, was made into a series of movies and a weekly television program that ran from 1966 to 1969. It is still in syndication, fascinating new generations with the prospect of exploring, meeting, and possibly interacting with other life-forms.

This fascination has also been an obsession of scientists and people generally who have wondered how space might be utilized and exploited, and that curiosity has inevitably included the prospect of militarizing space or otherwise using it for earthly political advantage, sometimes nefarious. The prospects received major notoriety in the 1980s when President Reagan proposed a nuclear missile defense in space—the Strategic Defense Initiative (SDI)—to protect against a Soviet missile attack (Gary Guertner and I coauthored a book on SDI symbolically titled *The Last Frontier: An Analysis of the Strategic Defense Initiative* in 1986). SDI was quietly shelved when Reagan left office as unworkable. Russian cyberattacks on the 2016 U.S. presidential election process and beyond, including the 2020 election and broad-scale hacking into business and private citizen accounts, provide a more recent example of the fascination—and mischief—potentially involved.

The problem of cybersecurity is widely recognized as a national security problem. As Zegart and Morrell argue, "Today, an assortment of malign actors perpetrate millions of cyberattacks around the world every day." Cumulatively, Brose concludes, "A revolution is unfolding today." In partial (and arguably largely symbolic) response, the Trump administration consolidated cyber elements of U.S. government activity in cyberspace into a separate U.S. Space Force in 2019 to organize military responses better.

In fact and fiction, a concern with information, its uses, its protection, and its exploitation for national security and other purposes is thus nothing new, even if the term "cyber" and some of the techniques associated with it are. Adding the prefix cyber changes how these tasks are done, not what is done. The national security question is how it should be handled in the contemporary scene. What difference does *cyber* make?

An example from World War II illustrates the role of cybersecurity concern without the computer-generated and -stored information component that frames the contemporary debate. During the American island-hopping campaign in the Pacific, a major problem was how to deprive Japanese defenders of information about American military actions. The Japanese routinely intercepted walkie-talkie communications between American units, allowing them to discern U.S. troop movements. It was a cyber protection problem, and the Americans solved it by "encrypting" their communications. The medium was 420 Navajo Marine "code talkers," who communicated exclusively in Navajo, a language with which the Japanese had no familiarity. The Japanese were never able to discover that the "code" was an American Indian language and break it. Some of the cyber problem of today is finding a new Navajo-like language to protect against the challenges presented by the cyber age.

The problem of protecting information, which is the core of cyber concerns at all levels, was both created and made more difficult by the very processes it created. It is pervasive. Once information enters electronic systems that are the habitat of cyberspace, it becomes part of the vast cyber territory where, unless aggressive actions are taken at protection, it becomes prey vulnerable to exposure or theft unintended by the source of the information. Cybersecurity is the dynamic enterprise that attempts to secure computer-generated or -processed information from those whom the original producer did not authorize that access. The information can be individual data like social security or credit card numbers or corporate proprietary science which, if exposed, would undercut product comparative advantage in the marketplace. In the public realm, the information could be voter preferences in elections or private communications between political figures. In national security, it may involve protecting secrets that can reinforce or compromise the country's safety as well as the activation and use of weaponry dependent on cyber direction.

It also extends into the private sector where, in May 2021, the Russian ransomware criminal group DarkSide apparently hacked into the Colonial Pipeline's computer system and demanded a large ransom to release the company's systems. The precedent was important because the pipeline transports about 45 percent of the East Coast's gasoline from Texas to market. The incident was the first in a series of attacks on the private sector. They have continued, the Russians keep denying any complicity with cyber hackers who operate from Russian soil, and the issue remains a matter of contention and tension between Presidents Biden and Putin.

Ever since the highly publicized and debated intrusion in the 2016 election process in the United States by Russian hackers apparently commissioned and directed by the Russian government, the problem of cybersecurity and even the possibility of cyber*war* has intruded into the American political debate, and the allegations of interference in the 2020 election have kept this problem in the public eye. The war analogy, generally vaguely drawn and unfocused on any specific set of events or prospects, has extended the rapidly evolving technology of things "cyber" into the national security debate. The subject does not focus on traditional national security problems and solutions, is difficult to conceptualize in familiar national security constructs, and has a slightly ethereal aura that makes it difficult to grasp.

Principle: The Cyber Challenge

The problem begins conceptually. National security emphasizes maintaining the physical safety of countries (or groups within them) from harm or extinction. Cyber formulations may involve threats to the state and its people, but those threats arise from different bases, notably electronic networks and virtual reality and the application of those capabilities to military or other national security problems. The core concentration is thus on the technologies that compose the computer revolution and actions that hostile others may take to interrupt, steal, or subvert that information and formulations. Given the ubiquity of electronic, computer-based, or -extended activities within society, this encompasses a very wide range of activities and operators. As one considers all the actions that can fall under the label of "cyber," the list is almost infinite, and when it is combined with the subjective nature of what threatens different people, it becomes almost unwieldy, leading the authors of a RAND Corporation study on cybersecurity to conclude the "term is applied too inclusively." Many of the challenges to which cyber technology is applied are traditional forms of hostile statecraft like espionage, sabotage, and propaganda. The goals are not new; the "packaging" is.

The medium in which cyber activity takes place, cyberspace, only adds to the confusion. The heart of cyber concern is information technology, which is a pervasive part of modern social interaction. The breadth of concerns that attach to the information revolution provides fertile ground for speculation and the building of a virtually infinite array of potential threats, some of which frighten some people more than others but also diffuses any systematic, focused delineation of the threat and thus the priority that should attach to solving it. "In cyberspace," Zegart and Morrell explain, "the targets are machines or systems that change constantly."

It was probably inevitable that the complex of activities and ideas that share the cyber moniker would find their way into the national security conversation. The electronic revolution, including the information accumulation and transmission that is at its heart, represents the kind of magnet toward which the national security community is drawn: a new technological, scientific endeavor the prospects of which are not known but that could include applications producing military advantage. That motivation is normally double-edged, meaning scientists must ask themselves both how these technologies could be applied for military advantage and how they could ensure that those applications could not successfully be used against their countries. This endeavor exists in an environment of considerable uncertainty because, by definition, one cannot know what one will discover and how it might be applied until the discovery is made and its implications explored. This is as true for non-defense applications of cyber technology with which the reader may be more familiar as it is for national security applications. In either the national security or civilian sectors, the process is ongoing, dynamic, and changing.

Understanding the cyber phenomenon begins by trying to come to grips with its unique vocabulary and concepts. These involve using familiar national security terms with somewhat different meanings than are attached to those terms in more conventional analyses. This exercise in turn makes it possible to describe the kinds of cyber threats that exist and to place them in the traditional national security framework.

Cyber Terms and Definitions

The root term in the discussion is "cyber." It is the adaptation of an old Greek word referring to space, and it has been adapted to the electronic cyber revolution. Universal agreement about what exactly is encompassed by the term does not exist, although the Oxford Dictionary offers this definition: "relating to electronic communications networks and virtual reality." The heart of cyber phenomena is thus computers and their major "products," information technology and virtual reality. As it has been adapted to the national security debate, cyber refers to attempts to manipulate the processes and products of information technology to intrude on the cyberspace of either individuals or national security systems that use information technology as part of their operating base.

It is a slippery term, since it depicts an evolving phenomenon in the national security environment. Is, for instance, cyberspace intrusion a distinct form of activity, or is it a component of other forms of activity? Klimburg, for one, suggests that it is both. "It is difficult to take the measure of cyberconflict," he argues, "because it is now a part of every other form of conflict; it affects everything while deciding little on its own, at least so far." It is also not the exclusive province of any group.

National security concerns and actions usually involve foreign actors, especially national governments or subnational groups, but also includes private groups and individuals. Cyber activity as often as not is conducted by individual "hackers" either acting on their own or with some mysterious, hidden relationship to a sponsor, most problematically a hostile foreign government or movement. The practical effect is to muddy even more the identification and priority one assigns to cyber actions. Parker argues: "a larger problem with cyberwarfare is uncertainty. How does a government respond to an invisible attacker?" This ephemeral quality of intrusion into hyperspace leads to some colorful evocations. Slaughter, for instance, refers to anonymous hackers as "the invading hordes of the twenty-first century." This description may be hyperbolic, but it creates a dilemma that Parker points out, "A cyberattack could be the work of almost anyone."

Much of the discussion of cyber phenomena is directed at how the United States can protect itself from hostile cyber actions, and this is certainly the primary concern of American national security planners. It implicitly suggests a kind of victimization that probably leaves too much of an impression of American innocence in this area. A great deal of the computer revolution at the heart of cyber actions is, after all, American, and a significant part of the networks and manifestations of information technology were products of American science and technology. This means the United States has significant capabilities both to create and counter cyber developments, and focusing that effort is one of the purposes of the U.S. Space Force.

The basic term to describe what former director of the National Security Agency general Michael Hayden has called the largest unregulated and uncontrolled domain in the history of mankind is the idea of *cyberspace*. The heart of the idea is that cyberspace is the internet environment through which ideas flow and the domain of information technology structures. The U.S. national security information collection, control, and dissemination effort is part of this environment and has designated it a part of the country's "critical infrastructure." This network has developed in a basically unplanned, random, and chaotic manner to a size and complexity that is difficult to understand and even more difficult to regulate.

Cybersecurity and Cyberwar

The most common term used in national security discussions is *cybersecurity*. Like other cyber concepts, it is a compound word with a compound meaning. Its heart is the security of its domain, which in the case of cybersecurity is largely the protection of computer-based information and applications in cyberspace that harm the entity that needs protecting. In traditional national security calculations, the safety sought is normally physical and expressed in terms of safety from physical harm and, at worst, extinction.

Definitions of cybersecurity abound, but they all emphasize actions and methods designed to protect electronic information from being stolen, compromised, or successfully attacked. These distinctions are usually attached to notions of computer security, because that is the medium in which most of the information is stored and transmitted. The security aspects of cybersecurity relate to stealing or distorting information in cyberspace for personal, commercial, or national advantage. The aspects of cybersecurity most interesting to national security are those with direct political or geopolitical applications, from the theft of government military secrets, the compromise of military technologies by interrupting private or public cyber bases, the discovery and weaponization of new cyber-based possibilities, to more traditional geopolitical activities like interference in the internal politics of target countries or regions within countries.

Cybersecurity can be both an offensive and a defensive tool. Most discussions of the problem tend to focus on the defensive aspect: what can be done to deny access to information, its manipulation, and uses to which it can be put. Vulnerability exists for any entity with information stored or transmitted on computer networks, which is a network of potential targets. Efforts to engage in the development and application of technologies designed to thwart cybersecurity breaches, of course, tend to vary depending on the degree of threat different entities pose and on resources to engage in counter-technology efforts.

Eff.... reinforce cybersecurity are compromised by a conundrum familtific phenomena. Knowledge with applications to controlling or use of scientific advances is not abstract but is dependent on the oblems that can be remediated. Countermeasures presume meauntered, and this means that those who want to engage in scienmischief are always a step ahead of those who seek to rein in those efforts. For better or worse, the development of countermeasures has generally received less priority than the burgeoning discovery of new applications in the cyberworld, and this makes it more difficult to devise technologies that enhance security of the systems themselves and how they can be used, as recent ransomware attacks demonstrate.

The concept of *cyberwar* presents a particularly dramatic and potentially traumatic example of this problem. Like cybersecurity, the term "war" is used in a different way than in the traditional military context. The traditional core of definitions of war is that they involve armed conflict between hostile political units, with their key element being physical fighting to subdue or destroy the other side's will or ability to resist the imposition of politically defined terms, up to and including physical subjugation. War in the cyber context normally lacks the employment of organized forces in combat, unless one stretches the meaning of combat to include electronic means and counter-means to protect or subvert the computers, control systems, and networks of one side (which may or may not be engaged in traditional war at the same time). Rather than being direct instruments of war, cyberwar capabilities are generally conceptualized in supportive roles to aid the pursuit of goals by adversaries.

Libicki offers a useful distinction of types of cyberwar, what he calls strategic and operational cyberwar. In his view, strategic use consists of "a campaign of cyberattacks one entity carries out on another," whereas operational cyberwar "involves the use of cyberattacks on the other side's military in the context of a physical war." Operational cyberwar is closer to traditional notions and conduct of military actions, because it can involve actions like interrupting communications between weapons systems being aimed at enemy targets and those who control the attack. Directing drones to targets is an area where this activity could apply, just as cyberwar capabilities can have responsibility for aiming the weapons in the first place. The 2016 Russian election campaign is an example of the strategic application of cyberwar concepts in a non-lethal sense.

The use of the term war suggests the furtiveness, level of effort, and seriousness with which cyber activities in the national effort are viewed, but it is not a literal description that can be translated from one domain to the other. Cyberwar is a part of an increasing number of military purposes and capabilities, but it is in a supportive, capabilities-enhancing role, not a physical war-fighting role. Computers and their operators may clash on virtual battlefields where the object is to make one electronic device outperform the other, but they do not literally fight and kill one another. But things change in the cyberworld, and one cannot discount the prospects of what will be possible in the future. When the classic 1940s movie *1984* was filmed, the technology only allowed depiction of intrusions on personal and private behavior through crude cardboard "eyes" watching the population. Its author, George Orwell, would have been shocked by the extent of the ability to monitor and intrude today that is a routine part of the physical capacity of governments and others.

The Cyber Problem

The ubiquity of the cyber phenomenon makes it difficult to grasp and solve. It is all part of the domain of cyberspace, which is conceptually limitless. It is not the exclusive, "sovereign" province of any political jurisdiction in the way that the physical atmosphere above national territory is. No country or body has exclusive or effective power to regulate cyberspace or to enforce violations of norms and regulations which, by and large, do not exist beyond those included in the 1967 Outer Space Treaty. Much cyber activity is private in nature, conducted by individuals who may be violating some domestic laws for which they can be prosecuted if they are caught, but the ephemeral nature of cyberspace makes apprehension more difficult than catching someone who holds up a convenience store. When nefarious activity is conducted by governments trying to conceal their role, it is often difficult as well to determine the locus of activity that travels through cyberspace. It is not impossible to do so, but the "forensics" of cyber-crime are far less developed than those covering domestic criminal actions.

The task is made even more difficult because cyberspace is used to conduct some of the hidden business that governments have historically conducted against one another. The most famous act of cyber aggression for Americans is Russian interference in the 2016 presidential election discussed in the next section. The manipulation of cyberspace to hack into the election process is the unique characteristic of that intrusion, but the idea of interfering in the electoral processes of other countries is a long practiced but officially illegal violation of sovereign states. The United States, principally in the Western Hemisphere but also in more remote locations like Iran, has long interfered to promote or defeat candidates. What was unique about the 2016 and 2020 elections is that the United States was or will be the victim rather than the perpetrator and that the intrusions were committed in cyberspace rather than by Central Intelligence Agency personnel on the ground. The ethereal nature of cyberattacks makes them both more difficult to observe and harder to account.

Application: Responding to Cybersecurity

Cyber problems can manifest themselves at an increasing number of levels and in different ways. The first is the political level, where the major security issue is the sanctity of national efforts and entities. Russian interference cases are a very public manifestation of that problem. The Russians were engaged in sabotaging the American electoral process through a propaganda campaign involving both cyber penetration and conventional espionage efforts. The use of cyberspace to disseminate misinformation was an obvious intrusion that was difficult to discover, monitor, and interfere with, and the opacity of the effort has made it difficult to assign and prove cupidity against a Russian leadership that denies the entire effort. It did not possess an overtly military component, but it did compromise the integrity and security of the American political system by clandestinely seeking to influence voters and even to subvert efforts to count votes accurately.

The second level is the more overtly military threats to security that cyber activities may pose, and this can happen in at least two distinct ways. One is that space is the medium in which cyber activities take place, and efforts to protect or interfere with the medium can convey potential military advantage for opponents. Second, that same space may provide a platform from which future capabilities will find an increasingly attractive, and menacing, venue. These kinds of concerns were part of the impetus for consolidating efforts in the United States around the U.S. Space Force.

The potential ability of cyberwarriors to obscure their nefarious behaviors is a prime objective of those who must thwart national security–based attacks. This problem can be handled most effectively using the resources of the U.S. federal government, and more specifically by specialized cyber agencies within the government in an increasingly internationally competitive environment. As cyber efforts have spread into the private sector largely in the form of ransomware attacks, jurisdictional line and remedies have become more complicated.

The problems created by the cyber revolution are not so much unique additions to the things that countries do to one another as they are about new ways that states attempt to accomplish traditional political actions against one another. The challenges are consequential because of the extent to which the operation of society has become based in information generation, exchange, and protection. The cyber revolution has not yet produced a game-changing military technology and capability like nuclear weapons did seventy years ago. The cyber phenomenon is, however, a driving part of the scientific revolution that is changing life generally, and so even that limit on the impact of cybercapability may change as well.

The 2016 Russian Election Interference Controversy and Beyond

The Russian electronic interference in the 2016 presidential election in the United States was both a unique and simultaneously thoroughly traditional event in the ways in which states intrude on one another's sovereignty. It was unique in the sense that it was conducted by manipulating cyberspace by so-called cyberwarriors and that it represented a large-scale effort to interfere with an *American* election. It was a thoroughly traditional, if extra-legal, event in that states (including the United States) interfere with the politics of other countries all the time.

The unique aspect is that the election intrusion was conducted by hackers who found ways into files of the Democratic National Committee and the private files of certain Democratic politicians, notably presidential candidate Hillary Clinton. The American intelligence community investigated these claims, and their unanimous conclusion was that the hackers were Russian and were probably employed in some manner by the government of Vladimir Putin. The Russian president, of course, has consistently denied the perpetrators were Russian or that his regime was in any way linked to them. Complicating the investigation of the hacking was President Trump's apparent acceptance of Putin's denial and thus his rejection of the accumulated evidence of the U.S. intelligence community. The special commission headed by Robert Mueller tried to reach a definitive conclusion on whether or how the Russians acted to protect against a repeat performance from Moscow in 2020. There were similar suspicions that the Russians had in fact mounted operations in 2020 to assist in the reelection of Trump, an accusation that Biden has taken more seriously.

The problem posed by cyber dynamics comes from the difficulty of finding a "hard" evidence trail that could definitively link the Russians to the intrusion. The files that were stolen were obviously not theft proof. The intrusions that occurred required some sophistication, but they were actions that dedicated hackers—from paid Russian operatives to President Trump's 400-pound lone wolf—could have carried out. This process left no literal "paper trail," making it difficult to prove cupidity and easy to deny legal responsibility. The certainty of the American intelligence community about who committed these acts, however, suggests there are classified methods available to allow conclusive detection of these kinds of action if they are utilized, which they were not at the time of the intrusions.

The anonymity of hacking creates a dilemma with national security implications that goes far beyond the substantive case. A cyberattack, Parker points out, "can be the work of almost anyone," and this creates a "larger problem of cyberwarfare. How does a government respond to an invisible attacker? How can a state prevent cyberattacks without attribution?" This difficulty extrapolates into the problem of how can you punish an intruder whose guilt you know about but cannot prove? This has been a problem of American attempts to deal with Russian actions, and the answers are not clear, because foreign hackers and propagandists are not afraid to launch attacks against the United States in and through cyberspace, according to some analysts. RAND analysts translate this into a Department of Defense mandate to "figure how to deter foreign actors in cyberspace as effectively as in nuclear and conventional war." Ramo suggests a strategy of "hard gatekeeping" to make penetration of hardened networks impossible.

This question of penetrability is the unique national security contribution of this episode. It has gained continuing traction because of its connection in time to the 2016 presidential election, the possibility that the Russians sought to undermine the election prospects of the Democratic candidate by their actions, and that the Trump campaign may have had some involvement in the plot, a point of partisan disagreement. The fact that the Russians felt they could carry out these attacks against the United States adds to the outrage that surrounds the episode. Worse still, it is not entirely clear that capabilities and protocols in place to prevent a recurrence in 2020 by the Russians or some other cyberspace opponent like China worked to avoid interference.

Some of the concerns about Russian violations of American sovereignty are disingenuous, if not openly hypocritical. The United States has been a consistent historical intruder in other politics, including those of Russia (the United States was an open champion of Boris Yeltsin against Putin). In his May 8, 2018, announcement removing the United States from the Joint Comprehensive Plan of Action with Iran, President Trump openly suggested the Iranians replace their government, a recurrent theme in reference to Tehran. The Russians interfered clandestinely; the American president did so on global television. Americans may (and do) dislike others turning the tables on them, but their indignation is tainted by historic U.S. practices. The real challenge of the 2016 incident (beyond possible internal political ramifications) lies in the future: finding ways to detect and thwart cyberattacks and unambiguously identifying perpetrators and punishing them.

The Space Force (USSF)

The idea of war in space has been a staple theme of science fiction for centuries. Much of this speculation has featured alien attacks and invasions of the Earth and its inhabitants. In the twentieth century, sightings of alien "flying saucers" in the skies over the American West created a whole tourist industry in Roswell, New Mexico. Almost all this emphasis occurred in a milieu of questionable scientific knowledge.

The situation has changed. Military activity in space is a serious area of inquiry, and development not by alien intruders but by earthbound humans seeking to gain advantage over their rivals is occurring there. The use of space is regulated internationally by the Outer Space Treaty of 1967, which remains in force and has 108 states as members. The original signatories were the United States, the United Kingdom, and the then Soviet Union, and the only state mentioned in speculation about space but not a member is Iran, which acceded to the document in 1967 but never ratified it.

Two aspects of the treaty are notable here. First, it accepts the conventional definition of outer space as "the physical universe beyond earth's atmosphere." All activity in space is justified by this parameter. Second, the treaty is permissive regarding the military use of space. Its only military restriction is against "placement of weapons of mass destruction (e.g., nuclear weapons) in space." All other activity, notably most uses related to cyberwar, is permitted.

The militarization of cyberspace has become a major area of global military competition that was formally recognized by the Trump administration. On June 18, 2018, Trump announced a proposal to create a sixth independent branch of the U.S. military, the U.S. Space Force (USSF). This "new combatant command," according to Roulo, would include U.S. Space Command (formerly part of the U.S. Air Force) and a Space Development Agency staffed by personnel from existing agencies.

The new Space Force came into formal existence as an independent military force on December 20, 2019. It is the smallest independent armed force with less than 5,000 members, mostly U.S. Air Force personnel who were part of the Air Force Space Command established on September 1, 1982. Secretary of the Air Force Heather Wilson is quoted by Roulo as estimating the additional cost of the new force at $15 billion over its first five years. The new force is controversial, but the point is that it is an institutional response to cybersecurity in addition to U.S. Air Force activity in this area.

Conclusion

Cyber activity has a strong link to national security. The exploitation of the potential of computers and computer networks has been influenced greatly by defensive concerns: how cyberspace can be made more secure and what military and other national security potential capabilities can be created to protect that security. One unique characteristic of the information technology revolution, especially from a security vantage point, has been effectively to "democratize" the exploitation of cyberspace for good and not-so-good ends. Individuals and small groups of people can manipulate access to the information and processes of cyberspace, and this creates a thriving enterprise both among those who wish to breach sources of information and those who try to protect those sources.

The problem in the national security area is particularly critical. Government national security–related organizations like the National Security Agency spend great effort and resources both learning how to deny access to vital information by those who would use it for nefarious purposes and devising methods to penetrate the equivalent kinds of efforts by others. For the government, the emphasis is on the protection of privileged or secret information with potential value for enhancing or undermining the security of the country.

At this point in time, cyberspace use in the national security environment has been derivative, not basic. Clearly, the information process has both the discovery of new information with scientific—and by extension—military applications and protection as mandates. The prototype of the internet, after all, was the product of a Defense Advanced Research Projects Agency (DARPA) grant, the purpose of which was to allow university research laboratories to communicate scientific findings among themselves more efficiently, thereby enhancing the speed of scientific discovery. Some of those findings inevitably had military and other dramatic applications, which was part of the rationale for the effort. The same dynamic applies to cyberspace.

In the publicly available contemporary environment, cyberspace and its problems are difficult to isolate and to solve. Cyber capabilities provided the context in which Russian 2016 hacking occurred and presumably was repeated in 2020. The motivation came from nefarious Russian political motivations. Cyber activity itself, like all scientific endeavors, is value neutral about how it is used. Billionaire Warren Buffett, addressing Berkshire Hathaway's annual shareholder's meeting in May 2018 (he owns the insurance company), warned that "cyber is uncharted territory and it's going to get worse, not better," adding it "will get more intense as time goes by." He was talking specifically about the insurance business, but his comments surely apply to national security and international concerns. Is what we see of cyber potential the tip of the iceberg of the international and national security future? What does all this say about the cyber phenomenon and how it should be handled?

Study/Discussion Questions

1. What does it mean to talk about cyber phenomena? What are its core concepts? How does its use alter the ways information is collected, stored, protected, and attacked?

2. Are the various cyber concepts basic national security problems per se, or are they examples of the application of cybercapabilities to traditional national security concerns? What are the national security purposes?

3. What is the cyber "problem"? Is it something new or the latest way in which traditional problems are manifested? Cite examples of how problems like protecting intelligence and interfering with other countries have been accomplished in the past.

4. How does cyberwar affect the way calculations of national security are made both about major rivals like China and Russia and others like North Korea and Iran?

5. What are the basic terms used to describe and discuss cyber ideas? What does "cyber" mean? Apply the basic concepts to national security.

6. Discuss the 2016 case of Russian interference in the American presidential election. Is it primarily an example of the basic problem or an illustration of how cyber phenomena can be applied to more traditional national security concerns?

7. What is the U.S. Space Force? Discuss the roots of the concept, why it has come about, what its status is, and whether you think it is a good idea.

8. Can or should the United States have a discrete cyber strategy, or is cyber a part of other aspects of strategy? How does this distinction affect how we think about cybersecurity in the broader context of national security?

Bibliography

Acuff, Jonathan M., Lamesha Craft, et al. *Introduction to Intelligence: Institutions, Operations, and Analysis.* Washington, DC: CQ Press, 2021.

Brodie, Bernard, and Fawn M. Brodie. *From Crossbow to H-Bomb: The Evolution of Weapons and Tactics of Warfare.* Bloomington: Indiana University Press, 1973.

Brose, Christian. "The New Revolution in Military Affairs." *Foreign Affairs* 98, no. 3 (May/June 2019): 122–34.

Buchanan, Ben. *The Cybersecurity Dilemma: Hacking, Trust, and Fear between Nations.* Oxford, UK: Oxford University Press, 2017.

Buffett, Warren. "Cyber Is Uncharted Territory." *Yahoo Online,* May 5, 2018.

Clarke, Richard A., and Robert Knake. *Cyber War: The Next Threat to National Security and What to Do about It.* New York: ECCO Books, 2011.

Futter, Andrew. *Hacking the Bomb: Cyber Threats and Nuclear Weapons.* Washington, DC: Georgetown University Press, 2018.

Guertner, Gary L., and Donald M. Snow. *The Last Frontier: An Analysis of the Strategic Defense Initiative.* Lexington, MA: Lexington Books, 1986.

Harris, Shane. *@ War: The Rise of the Military-Internet Complex.* New York: Mariner Books, 2014.

Hennessey, Susan. "Deterring Cyberattacks: How to Reduce Vulnerability." *Foreign Affairs* 96, no. 6 (November/December 2017): 39–46.

Isikoff, Michael, and David Korn. *Russian Roulette: The Inside Story of Putin's War on America and the Election of Donald Trump.* New York: Twelve Books, 2018.

Jamieson, Kathleen Hall. *Cyberwar: How Russian Hackers and Trolls Helped Elect a President: What We Don't, Can't and Do Know* (revised edition). Oxford, UK: Oxford University Press, 2020.

Jarmon, Jack A., and Pano Yannakogeorgos. *The Cyber Threat and Globalization: The Impact on U.S. National and International Security.* Lanham, MD: Rowman & Littlefield, 2018.

Kaplan, Fred. *Dark Territory: The Secret History of Cyber War.* New York: Simon and Schuster, 2017.

Kinzer, Stephen. *The Brothers: John Foster Dulles, Allan Dulles, and Their Secret World War.* New York: Times Books, 2013.

Klimburg, Alexander. *The Darkening Web: The War for Cyberspace.* New York: Penguin, 2017.

Kramer, Franklin, Stuart H. Starr, and Larry Wentz, eds. *Cyberpower and National Security.* Washington, DC: Potomac Books, 2009.

Libicki, Martin C. *Cyberspace in Peace and War.* Annapolis, MD: Naval Institute Press, 2016.

Nez, Chester, and Judith Schleiss Avila. *Code Talkers: The First and Only Memoir by One of the Original Navajo Code Talkers of WWII.* New York: Penguin Group, 2011.

Parker, Emily. "Hack Job: How America Invented Cyberwar." *Foreign Affairs* 96, no. 3 (May/June 2017): 133–38.

Perkovich, George, and Ariel E. Levite, eds. *Understanding Cyber Conflict: Fourteen Analogies.* Washington, DC: Georgetown University Press, 2017.

Ramo, Joshua. *The Seventh Sense: Power, Fortune, and Survival in the Age of Networks.* New York: Little Brown, 2016.

Reveron, Derek S., ed. *Cyberspace and National Security: Threats, Opportunities, and Power in a Virtual World.* Washington, DC: Georgetown University Press, 2012.

Rid, Thomas. *Cyber War Will Not Take Place.* Oxford, UK: Oxford University Press, 2017.

Romaniuk, Scott N., and Mary Manjikian. *Routledge Companion to Global Cyber-Security Strategy.* New York and London: Routledge, 2021.

Rosenzweig, Paul. *Cyber Warfare: How Conflicts in Cyberspace Are Challenging America and Changing the World.* Westport, CT: Praeger Security International, 2013.

Roulo, Claudette. "Space Force to Become Sixth Branch of Armed Forces." *Department of Defense News* (online), August 9, 2018.

Scharre, Paul. *Army of None: Autonomous Weapons and the Future of War.* New York: W. W. Norton, 2018.

———. "Killer Apps: The Real Danger of an AI Arms Race." *Foreign Affairs* 98, no. 3 (May/June 2019): 135–44.

Segal, Adam. *The Hacked World Order: How Nations Fight, Trade, Maneuver, and Manipulate in the Digital Age.* New York: PublicAffairs, 2016.

Singer, P. W., and Allan Friedman. *Cybersecurity and Cyberwar: What Everyone Needs to Know.* New York: Cambridge University Press, 2014.

Slaughter, Ann-Marie. "How to Succeed in the Networked World: A Grand Strategy for the Digital Age." *Foreign Affairs* 95, no. 6 (November/December 2016): 76–89.

Springer, Paul. *Cyber Warfare: A Reference Handbook* (Contemporary World Issues). New York: ABC-CLIO, 2015.

————. *Encyclopedia of Cyber Warfare.* New York: ABC-CLIO, 2017.

Steinnon, Richard. *There Will Be Cyberwar: How the Move to Network-Centric War Fighting Has Set the Stage for Cyberwar.* London: IT-Harvest Press, 2015.

U.S. Senate, Select Committee on Intelligence. *Russian Interference in the 2016 Election.* New York: CreateSpace Independent Publishing Platform, Volume 1–2, 2018 and 2020.

Yannakogeorgos, Panayotis, and Adam M. Lowther. *Conflict and Cooperation in Cyberspace: The Challenge to National Security.* Boca Raton, FL: CRC Press, 2016.

Zegart, Amy, and Michael Morrell. "Spies, Lies, and Algorithms: Why U.S. Intelligence Agencies Must Adapt or Fail." *Foreign Affairs* 98, no. 3 (May/June 2019): 85–96.

13

Maritime Chokepoints, Global Trade, and International Competition
The *Ever Given* Reminder

Naval chokepoints used to be a core concern in geopolitical calculations of the economic and military competitiveness of numerous states, particularly those for whom seaborne trade was a major source of prosperity or, in extreme cases, national existence. Before the transition to airborne travel for much international business, no analysis of the stature of states could be complete without reference to the ability to conduct or deny to others unfettered water-based travel and commerce. Chokepoints have been downgraded as a central concern in contemporary international calculations, but the *Ever Given* crisis of March 2021 demonstrates they remain part of the conversation.

Chokepoints have clearly faded into the geopolitical background. In part, this recession of concern reflects world conflict and international interactions more generally since 1945. Although the Cold War competition was very intense and dangerous, it was not primarily a contest over who controlled the seas. Naval concerns focused on surveilling enemy missile-bearing submarines and the menace they posed. Concern over the movement of goods and services through junction points in and between significant bodies of water was not so important; international commerce in petroleum was the exception.

Political concern with obstructions to the free movement of shipping on the world's seas could become a geopolitical concern again in this century. There has not been a major interstate naval battle since the United States moved by sea island hopping toward the Japanese home islands in 1945. The physical setting for future non-ground warfare has moved from the seas to space, including cyberspace (see chapter 12). At the same time, the emphasis of maritime activity has shifted to burgeoning world trade, where getting international goods and raw materials to market can often most efficiently be carried out by seaborne means. The world's oceans and seas are now the medium of much commerce, not war. Much of the traditional publicly expressed concern over interrupting or limiting access to the "sea-lanes of communication" (SLOCs) has faded.

The 2021 *Ever Given* crisis reminded us that some of the problems of interruption and control of the SLOCs have simply gone dormant but can still have potentially major consequences. The giant container ship grounding on the bank of the Suez Canal was, of course, an accident caused by high winds that grounded the giant vessel (at 1,312 feet in length, it is longer than the Empire State Building at over 1,100 feet is tall) in the bank of the canal at a narrow place, where it was wedged across the canal, effectively blocking the channel until it could be freed by an international effort; economic losses because of the problem have been estimated at nearly $10 billion a day for the six days of the crisis. It was an accident, but one cannot help but wonder what would have happened had it been done on purpose.

The incident brought into sharp relief the world economy's dependence on shipborne traffic and trade. A United Nations Conference on Trade and Development (UNCTAD) 2020 study, for instance, stated that 80 percent of global merchandise by volume is carried by shipping, which translates into 70 percent of trade by value. Not all of that total transits one or more of the world's chokepoints, but enough does that the destruction or interruption of transits (choking off chokepoints) could have enormously dilatory effects on the international system.

The problem of chokepoints does not affect all countries and regions in the same way or to the same extent. The United States, for instance, is a major maritime power with significant seaborne trade entering and leaving American ports on both the Atlantic (e.g., Savannah, Georgia) and Pacific (e.g., Long Beach, California) Oceans. A shrinking amount of that trade, especially since its dependence on Middle East oil has declined, traverses anything but the open Atlantic and Pacific sea-lanes, where there are essentially no natural or manmade barriers. The only real exception is the Panama Canal. Control of access to the canal is a major military priority of the U.S. military and serves as the best example of how chokepoints are relevant to the United States.

Contrast that level of vulnerability with China's. A good deal of Chinese commerce is with the Western Hemisphere—notably the United States—and it is unaffected by chokepoints. An increasing percentage of Chinese international dealings, however, are with two destinations where they must pass through chokepoints. These destinations are the Middle East and the European Union (EU). Shipping to either destination must pass through the Strait of Malacca. China has become a major consumer of imported oil from the Middle East, meaning its ships must pass through the narrow Strait of Hormuz to gain access to that resource. Its other destination, primarily to sell manufactured goods, is Western Europe. To get there, it must pass through the Bab el-Mandab separating Yemen and Djibouti and must transit from the Red Sea to the Mediterranean through Suez (making the *Ever Given* crisis personal for them). Cargo headed for northern Europe must also pass through the Strait of Gibraltar.

Most of these places and problems are personally alien to Americans. Oil passing through the Strait of Hormuz is an historical exception. This exemption from the geopolitical reality of maritime chokepoints may be dissolving, however, due to economic and geopolitical forces that are particularly relevant in evolving Sino-American relations. China, as noted in chapter 2, has mounted a significant economic challenge to American economic leadership in the world, and a great deal of that challenge is based in trade, much of which gets to market via maritime shipping. A sizable proportion of that trade must travel through significant chokepoints. Unfettered transit through these chokepoints is thus crucial to the Chinese economic "miracle." At the same time, China is an energy deficient state that relies greatly on imported petroleum from the Persian Gulf. Many contemporary analysts prophesy that a confrontation between the two countries is the major geopolitical challenge facing the international system. If that happens, the problem of chokepoints could greatly influence the trajectory and outcome of that competition.

Principle: The Idea and Impact of Chokepoints

What exactly is a chokepoint? The term is associated with military strategy and especially (but not exclusively) naval strategies and locations. *Wikipedia* offers a comprehensive definition: "a geographic feature on land such as a valley, defile, or bridge, or a maritime passage through a critical waterway." The need to pass through a chokepoint requires that a traveler seeking to traverse one must concentrate its assets and thus leave them more vulnerable to attack. The concept has largely receded—but not disappeared from the center of most military discussions. This change partially reflects the decline of naval warfare generally. Hardly anyone expects that situation to change anytime soon.

Why has this been the case? First, the nature and relative emphasis on naval warfare has decreased as the medium of fighting and control has moved to the arena of airspace and even cyberspace. Airplanes can attack merchant and naval warfare vessels, often with devastating effect (a prospect first demonstrated by the American Billy Mitchell in the 1920s), and they also allow surveillance of naval activity that removes the surprise element for vessels other than submarines. The Japanese sneak attack on Pearl Harbor in December 1941 would have been impossible to conceal in the air age, since the attack force (ironically dominated by aircraft carriers and bomber aircraft) would have been surveilled from the time it left its home ports in Japan. In World War II, control of the air supplanted control of the seas as the critical non-ground dimension of warfare. One of the geographic locales where airplanes supplanted ships was in the protection or menacing of chokepoints.

A second major factor was economic and geopolitical. Naval dominance is expensive, and only large and very wealthy countries can afford to field and maintain large navies. Most of the countries that do so are "natural" maritime states—countries with sizable maritime exposures and hence traditions—that possess both sizable maritime and trading histories that have required powerful navies to protect. Great Britain and the United States are prime examples.

In the post–World War II environment, the only country that clearly met the criteria for naval supremacy was the United States. The United States is a natural naval power with long coastlines on the Atlantic and Pacific Oceans, a long tradition of interaction with Europe, and a shorter but still significant attachment to East Asia. It also has a long experience as both a fishing and trading country. The two major protagonists since 1945 were the Soviets and the Chinese. Neither was in an economic or geopolitical position to challenge American naval power. The chief debility facing the Soviets/Russians was (and is) the problem of the

absence of warm water ports: they can venture to sea year-round only by travers-
ing the Dardanelles and Bosporus chokepoint. China simply lacked the resources
during the Cold War to become a naval power and has only recently shown signs
of aspiring to be one.

Dealing with naval chokepoints has always been a not especially glamorous
part of the naval tradition for both commercial and military reasons. The commercial aspect is of greatest importance to trading nations, who want to transport goods to and from markets in the cheapest and most expeditious manner.
When the *Ever Given* was stuck in the Suez Canal, for instance, a virtual flotilla of
other merchant ships from around the world were either in the canal or waiting
in line to enter it, and during the six days when the ship was aground, their only
alternatives were to wait in line or to seek an alternative shipping route. The only
feasible alternative route was to turn around ships near the southern end of the
canal zone and send them southward around the Cape of Good Hope (South
Africa) and northward up the coastline of western Africa. Ships at the northern
end would have been forced to follow the same route in reverse, with the added
burden of having to sail the length of the Mediterranean Sea and through the
Straits of Gibraltar (another chokepoint) to reach the Atlantic. Estimates of the
costs of such diversions were in the billions of dollars.

Chokepoints are also militarily significant, because they can be used either
to facilitate or impede the ability of affected states to reach military destinations.
The problem is different for countries like the United States and Great Britain,
who have direct access to the world's great oceans without passing through any
major manmade or natural barriers, making them "natural" maritime powers for
whom chokepoints are a more natural asset to exploit than a barrier to overcome. This is indirect contrast to a country like Russia, which has most of its
ports ice-blocked and must rely on its ability to transit one of the world's most
formidable chokepoints.

Major Chokepoints

Chokepoints can be either on land or on the seas, as noted earlier. On land, they
are generally narrow areas in rugged terrain through which a force must pass
but is vulnerable to defensive efforts by an opponent. A narrow canyon where
defenders can occupy the high ground is a prototypical example. In contemporary considerations, the emphasis is on naval chokepoints, which is why the discussion has centered on barriers to passage involving the movement of cargo or
naval combat forces. Chokepoints may be natural bodies of water with adjacent
land areas at least on two sides or manmade barriers such as intercoastal canals.
For illustrative purposes, we will identify and discuss several of these that have
particular interest to naval strategists in the contemporary world. The list distinguishes between natural and artificial barriers. In the contemporary international setting, the designations of most concern have been chokepoints through
which petroleum from the Middle East has been transported. That weighting
may lessen as global dependence on fossil fuel energy declines.

Manmade Chokepoints

Important bodies of water like oceans allow those who use them to cut substantially the length of voyages in time and cost, and thus travel on and between them is a major value for seafaring countries. In addition, they are likely to have substantial military value to whoever controls them and to be the target of whoever oppose the country that does control them. Two major interoceanic canals, each over a century old, dominate this form of chokepoint. They are the Panama and Suez Canals.

Panama Canal: The Panama Canal is the maritime bridge between the Atlantic and Pacific Oceans, and as such is a major commercial and military form of transit and control. Using the canal cuts a trip that takes literally thousands of miles by any other water route to a fifty-one-mile journey. The alternatives are longer and less attractive alternatives: sailing around the Cape Horn routes of the Drake Passages or the Straits of Magellan at the Antarctic tip of South America or going through the Arctic Archipelago and the Bering Strait.

Work on what became the Panama Canal began in 1881 under the direction of Ferdinand de Lesseps, who had led construction of the Suez Canal a decade earlier. The French eventually abandoned the Panama project, and it was taken over by the Americans in 1904, who completed and opened the waterway in 1914. The United States operated the canal until 1977, when the Torrijos-Carter Agreement ceded the canal and surrounding canal zone to the Panamanians, who have operated it ever since.

Control over who uses the canal and for what purposes is and has been a major driver of American national security policy in both Central America and the Caribbean region of islands that guard its eastern approaches. Because it allows the U.S. Navy to move its fleet between two oceans, it is of special importance as a military asset that creates great naval flexibility by facilitating moving assets from one ocean to the other. The sanctity of control of the canal and approaches to it dominate American concern regarding influence on governments of countries whose territory and locations "guard" the canal and approaches to it and have been primary drivers of American policy and actions in Central American countries like Nicaragua and Caribbean locations such as Cuba. Part of the reason for maintaining control over the American naval base at Guantanamo Bay, for instance, is that the base is part of the defense perimeter guarding the Panama Canal.

The Panama Canal is at heart an American-made chokepoint to protect American interests from hostile others who might seek to control it to their advantage and the disadvantage of American primacy in the Western Hemisphere. With numerous deep-water ports on both coasts, the canal serves less of an economic function than other shortcuts around the world, but it is a clear centerpiece of U.S. national security calculations.

The Suez Canal. Although they are the two most important manmade maritime chokepoints, the Panama and Suez Canals offer points of commonality and contrast. They are, for instance, built differently. The Panama Canal has an elaborate and expensive system of locks and dams that raises and lowers ships into the canal from the oceans, whereas Suez is essentially a single stream that does not have to change the altitude of the ships passing through it. Suez is also lon-ger. It connects the Mediterranean Sea at its northern terminus at Port Said to its southern terminus at the city of Suez 120 miles away. Major shipping then moves into the Gulf of Suez to the Red Sea and southward to the Bab el-Mandab (another chokepoint linking the Arabian Sea and Indian Ocean). Suez is thus the major midway point for trade between East Asia, the Middle East, and Europe. In 2020, slightly over fifty ships a day sailed through it, almost all carrying petro-leum or goods in one direction or the other. Notably, most of that traffic must ultimately traverse through another, natural chokepoint or points before reach-ing its destination.

An important point of contrast between the Panama and Suez Canals is that their primary uses and emphases are different. The Panama Canal's primary importance to the United States has always had a more significant national secu-rity emphasis as a matter of oceanic control and in inter-American affairs. The Panama Canal is normally thought of as an *American* construct to which other countries have access if they pose little or no threat to the United States.

The Suez Canal is different. Its status affects many Eurasian states, and no country as powerful as the United States has clear claim to it. Ownership and control have passed among different countries and entities. The canal has always been technically the property of Egypt, with effective operational control of operation by British and French private operators. In 1956, a crisis arose when Egyptian president Gamal Abdul Nasser nationalized it, precipitating the Suez Crisis of October–November 1956 featuring Egypt and Israel.

An interesting distinction between the two canals is that the Suez Canal is supposed to be politically neutral in armed conflicts in which its use may play a part. On October 29, 1889, the eight major European powers and the Ottoman Empire signed the Convention of Constantinople neutralizing the partisan use of the canal during war. Under its provisions, the canal can be used "in times of war as in times of peace, by every vessel of commerce or of war, without distinc-tion of flag." The canal was part of the conflict between Israel and Egypt before they completed their peace treaty in 1982, but it has otherwise played a neutral military role.

Natural Chokepoints

Chokepoints that are natural physical features and in strategically important places are more numerous than those constructed by man. They are, in almost all cases, natural impediments to seaborne transit. In general, they are natural barriers like strings of islands through which shipping must pass to make voy-ages shorter, thus cheaper, than they might otherwise be. Chokepoints are not inherently controversial; it is, for instance, entirely possible to navigate through the Straits of Malacca, a transit point from the Indian Ocean to the South China Sea and ultimately into the Pacific Ocean or north to East Asia, without inter-ruption. The "guardians" are Malaysia and the island of Sumatra, a part of Indo-nesia. If uninterrupted by one of these countries, the straits do not provide any impediment to transit. If one or the two states decide to interrupt movement through the strait, however, its structure and location may force the user to have to consider or make unhappy decisions. One is simply to abandon the route, thereby avoiding the choke hold, but doing so is unfortunate, because chokepoints are important both because they are shortcuts between destinations and because employing an alternate route is likely to be longer and more expensive than using the chokepoint.

Application: The *Ever Given* and the Revival of Chokepoint Concerns

The March 23, 2021, grounding of one of the world's largest container ships in the Suez Canal caused a loud, possibly transient sensation in the global media that lasted until the ship was finally freed from the sandy bank on which it had gotten stuck. Once extricated from its captivity, it was refloated northward toward Port Suez and into the Mediterranean Sea to complete its voyage to Rotterdam, the Netherlands, to deliver its containerized cargo to market.

The story of the grounding and freeing of the ship was treated as a discreet story of a maritime accident and would hardly have attracted any attention had the *Ever Given* not been, at over 1,300 feet in length, one of the world's largest seaborne transporters of cargo. To most people who do not inhabit or frequent ports where these enormous ships enter and from which they depart, the visual impact of the mega-sized ship lodged in one of the canal's banks and stretching across its width was the major impact of the story. When it was freed and made its way north, their interest rapidly evaporated. For shippers, of course, the impact was greater, because it caused a major delay of other ships in or preparing to enter the Suez Canal Zone. The delays cost to those who transport their goods to market on ships was upwards of $10 billion. The trauma of the event was more frightening because it occurred in a body of water through which roughly 10 percent of global commerce flows. Since the ship was freed in six days and shipping then resumed, the losses for shippers were attenuated and those who were the customers to whom the shipping was going were probably hardly affected.

If the discrete event could be viewed as an isolated occurrence with confined impact, the greater lesson may have been that it revived some awareness of the historic problem of the potential impact of manipulating chokepoints for geopolitical reasons. A question that is raised but seldom emphasized is the prospect of manipulating access and transit through the world's chokepoints as a matter for geopolitical purposes by major states in the international maritime trade, either as shippers or as parties who might exploit manipulation of both manmade and artificial chokepoints to their advantage. This potential problem is probably especially important along the oceanic trade routes between East Asia and the Middle East and Europe. At the center of this potential problem is China, which is in a global economic and potentially national security competition with the United States that many observers believe has the potential to intensify, even to the military level. One potential venue of that competition is maritime, and it may help explain some of the Chinese expansion of their naval assets in recent years.

The Asian Chokepoint "Chain"

Commerce between eastern Asia and the West has been a longtime source of exploration and conflict, generally with China at one end of the transit and Europe and more recently the Western Hemisphere at the other. Overland routes have always been limited by the size and volume of goods that could be transported by caravan across the great Eurasian expanse plagued by geographic and human barriers that impeded traffic and limited the flow. Numerous conquerors have attempted to conquer the lands along these routes. The massive invasion by the Mongols orchestrated by Genghis Khan and his successors was the most successful and managed to create some order, but it lasted for only about a century. The alternative is maritime trade.

The historical emphasis of maritime interchange has been on the links between the Orient and Europe. Western Europe has been at one end of that dynamic, which was augmented by the Middle East and its petroleum beginning in the twentieth century; the other end of the chain has been Eastern Asia, with China at its anchor. Since China has emerged as a world power emphasizing economic and trade as its core, it has become a contested route to travel, but an increasingly important one. The *Ever Given*, after all, was travelling from Tanjung Pelepas in Malaysia to Rotterdam when it ran aground in the Suez Canal.

The problem with the Asia-Europe shipping routes is that there are chokepoints impeding travel by the most direct, fastest, and thus safe and profitable means of transit. Different sources provide different lists of these impediments, often based on the national origin of the classifier and thus how and what they emphasize. To illustrate the importance and problems that chokepoints create, there are three from the east-west transit route that skirts the southern extremity of Asia and are vital to commerce and potentially vulnerable to naval maneuver and engagement. All have the Indian Ocean as part of their journey. They encompass major traffic in goods and services between East Asia and Europe and include chokepoints affecting the flow of oil either westward or eastward to the Far East. They individually and collectively represent both the actuality and potential of the chokepoint for conflict. The three are the Strait of Malacca, the Strait of Hormuz, and the Bab el-Mandab.

The Strait of Malacca is the most critical. Security for its traffic is shared by the two littoral states, Malaysia and Indonesia, but the narrowness of the body of water makes security difficult, because those who might want to interrupt ship traffic or purloin goods can utilize both naval and land-based launching points on either side of the waterway. The strait has been a particular habitat for pirates, and it is one of the world's most congested chokepoints at the Phillip Channel near Singapore, where the channel is only 1.5 nautical miles wide.

The Strait of Malacca is geographically and geopolitically of the greatest importance to China, and secure access through it is thus a primary concern of a Chinese government seeking to expand both its economic posture, access to petroleum, and geopolitical position. Concern with the prospects of interruptions of seaborne transport of energy are a reason for Chinese attempts to gain support for building a very costly overland oil pipeline from the Persian Gulf to

China and may be linked to China's attempt to transform transit through the South China Sea into an effective manmade chokepoint under their control.

Particularly since the traumatic events in 1979 in the Middle East, the Strait of Hormuz has been the most highly publicized chokepoint in the world. The reason is simple: one-third of the world's liquified natural gas and almost a quarter of its oil must pass through this relatively narrow (twenty-one to fifty-two nautical miles) ninety-nautical-mile-long waterway connecting the Persian Gulf with the Gulf of Oman and the Arabian Sea. The area is contentious and occasionally confrontational because Hormuz washes Middle East rivals Iran and Saudi Arabia and several of the Gulf oil monarchies, notably the United Arab Emirates (UAE) and Oman. The protection of oil tankers is a major geopolitical priority of the Saudis and their allies and is periodically threatened by Iranian warships both in the Persian Gulf and the straits and from Iranian territory that defines the northern shores of the strait.

When the Shah of Iran ruled, his government effectively maintained order and free passage of oil tankers in and out of the Persian Gulf through the strait. This arrangement was effectively the result of an agreement with the United States by which Iran was effectively "deputized" to maintain freedom of navigation through the strait in return for preferential treatment from the Americans assisting the Shah's White Revolution aimed at Westernizing and modernizing the country. When the Shah fell in 1979 and was replaced by the Islamic Republic of Iran, that condominium evaporated, and the United States had to assume the role of patrolling the route, often with Iranian harassment.

The Strait of Hormuz's centrality may change. Global efforts to attenuate climate change hinge significantly on reducing carbon emissions into the atmosphere, and burning oil is a leading contributor to that problem. If the world needs less gasoline and other oil products, the geopolitics of the Strait of Hormuz will diminish for countries like the United States, but that is not true of its European allies, and it is particularly not true of China.

The other major chokepoint affecting the voyage westward and eastward between the Far East and Europe is the Bab el-Mandab. It sits at the south end of the water route from the Indian Ocean to the Suez Canal Zone. Its southern extremity is the Gulf of Aden and its junction with the Red Sea. The passage is bordered by the east African state of Djibouti on the west and Yemen on the east, and the two countries collectively form the barriers through which shipping must transit into the Red Sea and toward the Suez Canal at the northern end of the Red Sea. Aside from its importance as a chokepoint, the Djibouti-Yemeni region is primarily known as the first place that coffee was cultured. The Yemeni side of the Bab el-Mandab also explains part of the reason for the fierce fighting between Yemeni elements for control of that country.

The Chinese Dilemma

China has a quandary as it faces the problem of Asian chokepoints. China has portrayed itself as a prime champion of alternatives to a carbon-based system, but it has an energy problem. Energy consumption is the single strongest correlate of economic productivity. If the Chinese economy is to maintain or surpass the United States as the world's largest and strongest economy, it must have access to adequate energy resources to fuel its productivity. Until the technology provides an adequate substitute, that means it must buy oil, because China is a petroleum-poor country. Its attention thus has turned to the Persian Gulf, meaning it has a vested interest in assuring that the chokepoints between that area and China—particularly the Strait of Malacca and the Strait of Hormuz—are open to them. Europe, with its own addiction to Arab oil, has similar concerns over the Bab el-Mandab and Suez. Since China also exports manufactured goods to northern European destinations, it also has an interest in chokepoints like the Strait of Gibraltar.

China recognizes this situation. The Chinese Navy has expanded greatly since the turn of the century, a development that has had some analysts scratching their heads: surface navies are generally viewed as a shrinking priority, even an anachronism. The expanding navy, by contrast, has a role in ensuring the integrity of Chinese use of the sea-lanes of communication (SLOCs) between East Asia and points west like the Persian Gulf and Suez. At the same time, the Chinese have taken provocative actions trying to close or strictly limit international maritime traffic through the South China Sea, thereby attempting to create a longer journey for other Asian countries to the Strait of Malacca and farther west. Other countries, and notably the United States, have ignored these policies that effectively would make a manmade chokepoint out of that body of water (which also has significant petroleum reserves beneath its waters).

Conclusion: The *Ever Given* as Harbinger or Anomaly?

The *Ever Given* incident faded rapidly into obscurity after the giant container ship was freed from the side of the Suez Canal by an ad hoc coalition of international participants in the rescue mission, allowing the ship to continue its journey through the remainder of the canal and into open waters. Once the extraction was effectuated, ships stuck in the canal in either direction could complete their journey, and ships backed up in the Mediterranean and Red Seas could enter and pass through the canal, thereby ending the physical crisis in the shipping industry. The incident has quietly faded into obscurity, the subject of a trivia question. But could it be more?

The incident did remind the strategic community of the existence and possible consequences of chokepoints and their interruption, a problem that has received little public scrutiny in a world militarily dominated by flying machines and other uses of the atmosphere and beyond like cyberspace. Such attention as the problem has gotten has tended to be attached to the Strait of Hormuz and harassing of oil shipping by the Iranians and periodic skirmishes between Iranian naval units and American naval ships trying to keep the oil flowing freely (except, of course, Iranian oil). That activity has been essentially localized and ritualized, and it is not a major part of the fabric of world conflict.

The *Ever Given* incident is a reminder of just how much havoc that plugging a chokepoint can create. In this case it was an accident, and one that could be remedied without hostile outside action. It was, however, a reminder that chokepoints continue to exist, that they are vital to the world commercial system, and that their interruption can cause at least a low level of international consternation. It also reminds us that the competition between the United States and China for economic supremacy utilizes travel through the major Asian chokepoints significantly, and that the dependency on untrammeled passage through the world's major chokepoints is a particular priority for an economically ambitious but energy-deficient China, a fact the Chinese clearly recognize.

Chokepoints are not the most pressing problem facing the international system, but they can and occasionally do raise nettlesome difficulties if exploited for partisan purposes in times of tension, and they can create or exacerbate difficulties in the relations among the world's states. The discussion in these pages has highlighted the most globally important but not all the world's significant geopolitical situations in which chokepoints do or could come into play. For northern Europeans, for instance, egress into and out of the Baltic is potentially choked by the Danish and Dover Straits, and Russian geopoliticians must worry about their ability to round the northern tip of Norway with their missile-bearing submarines and to traverse through the Dardanelles and Bosporus from the Black Sea to the Mediterranean Sea and beyond. Most of the time, these are potential and not actual pressing problems, but like the general problem of chokepoints, they are matters of concern for geopoliticians and others concerned with national security matters in international relations.

Study/Discussion Questions

1. What is a naval chokepoint? Why are they important parts of maritime transit and trade? Why have they become a less prominent topic in modern geopolitical calculations?

2. Why are chokepoints more important to some countries than to others? Contrast the American experience with chokepoints to that of China's experience.

3. What is the *Ever Given* incident? What happened? Describe the experience and how it served as a reminder of the problem and potential importance of chokepoints.

4. Why is the problem of chokepoints so important in international commerce and trade? Discuss why this problem is especially important to China and its ambitions as a world power.

5. What are the major categories of chokepoints. Why are the two major important manmade chokepoints critical as geopolitical and economic factors? Briefly describe each.

6. Discuss the series of chokepoints through which ships travelling from East Asia to the Middle East oil fields or northward into Europe must pass. Briefly describe each.

7. What is the quandary that China faces as it contemplates the gantlet of chokepoints through which it must travel from China westward,

emphasizing energy purchase to fuel its economic productivity. Discuss.

8. To what extent does the *Ever Given* episode revive the naval problem caused by chokepoints? Why is this a particular problem for China and a potential source of friction between the United States and China? Is the *Ever Given* episode simply an anomaly, or could it indeed be a harbinger of geopolitical frictions to come?

Bibliography

American Defense Council. *China's Global Maritime Projection: Its Domination of Seven of the Ten Global Shipping Chokepoints.* Washington, DC: American Defense Council, 2003.

Brown, Kerry. *CEO China: The Rise of Xi Jinping.* London: I. B. Tauris, 2016.

Campbell, Kurt M., and Ely Ratner. "The China Reckoning: How Beijing Defied American Expectations." *Foreign Affairs* 97, no. 2 (March/April 2018): 60–70.

Charles Rivers Editors. *The Suez Canal and the Panama Canal: The Turbulent Histories of the Globe's Two Most Important Canals.* New York: Vintage Reprints, 2009.

Christensen, Thomas J. *The China Challenge: Shaping the Choices of a Rising Power.* New York: Norton, 2016.

Congressional Research Service. *Naval Modernization and Implications for U.S. Navy Capabilities: A Report of the Congressional Research Service.* St. Petersburg, FL: Red and Black Publications (Dorrance), 2020.

Corr, Anders, ed. *Great Powers, Grand Strategies: The New Game in the South China Sea.* Annapolis, MD: Naval Institute Press, 2018.

Ellerman, Bruce A. *A History of the Modern Chinese Navy: 1840–2020.* New York and London: Routledge, 2021.

———. *The Making of the Modern Chinese Navy: Special Historical Characteristics* (Anthem Impact). London: Anthem Press, 2019.

French, Howard W. *Everything under the Heavens: How the Past Helped Shape Push for Global Power* (reprint edition). New York: Vintage, 2018.

Harvey, Neil. *The Modern Chinese Navy* (second edition). Brunswick, OH: Neil Harvey, 2018.

Hayton, Bill. *The South China Sea: The Struggle for Power in Asia.* New Haven, CT: Yale University Press, 2015.

Konabell, Zachary. *Parting the Desert: The Creation of the Suez Canal* (reprint edition). New York: Vintage, 2009.

Love, Kenneth. *Suez: The Twice-Fought War.* New York: McGraw-Hill, 1969.

McCauley, Melissa. *Distant Shores: Colonial Encounters on China's Maritime Frontier.* Princeton, NJ: Princeton University Press, 2021.

McCullough, David. *The Path between the Seas: The Creation of the Panama Canal, 1870–1914.* New York: Simon and Schuster, 2001.

Noer, John Halvard, and David Gregory. *Chokepoints: Maritime Economic Concerns in Southeast Asia.* Darby, PA: Diane Publishing Company, 1996.

Office of Naval Intelligence. *The PLA Navy: New Capabilities and Mission for the Twenty-first Century.* Washington, DC: Office of Naval Intelligence, 2020.

Parker, Matthew. *Panama Fever: The Epic Story of the Building of the Panama Canal.* New York: Anchor Books, 2009.

Paulson, Henry M. *Dealing with China: An Insider Unmasks the New Economic Superpower.* New York: Twelve Books, 2015.

Ray, Natanda. *The South China Sea Dispute: Past, Present, and Future.* Lanham, MD: Lexington Books, 2016.

Rudd, Kevin. "How Xi Jinping Views the World: The Core Interests That Shape China's Behavior." *Foreign Affairs Snapshot* (online), May 10, 2018.

Sabahuddin, Hangar. *Important Naval Chokepoints.* Ottawa: NATO Association of Canada, 2013.

Saunders, Phillip C., Christopher D. Jung, et al. *The Chinese Navy: Expanding Capabilities, Evolving Roles.* New York: Create Space Independent Publishing Platform, 2012.

Shambaugh, David. *China's Future.* Cambridge, UK: Polity Books, 2016.

Snow, Donald M. *Cases in U.S. National Security: Concepts and Processes.* Lanham, MD: Rowman and Littlefield, 2019.

United Nations Conference on Trade and Development (UNCTAD). *Review of Maritime Transport 2020. UN Publication.* Geneva, Switzerland: UNCTAD, 2020.

PART IV
Global Crises

14

The Evolving Nature and Problem of Terror

The Perpetual Threat

The actuality or threat of terrorism has been a security problem for at least two millennia. Those who study it for a living generally place the first instances of organized terrorism back to Biblical times in the form of Jewish resistance to the Roman occupation of Palestine, and it has been an episodic problem ever since. Periodically, some group decides that it cannot achieve its political goals in any other way but by recourse to what is, in some ways of thinking about, the ultimate form of asymmetrical warfare. The latest rearing of the ugly head of terrorism began to surface in the latter part of the twentieth century as international religiously based terror, and it has dominated warlike behavior since. With the defeat of the Islamic State (IS), it has apparently receded as the major challenge to world peace and stability. The question is whether, or more probably when, it will return to the international center stage, or whether other forms like domestic terror will become dominant.

The terrorist attacks of September 11, 2001, occurred two decades ago, and they punctuated a growing problem that had been building for at least two decades but had not yet achieved global notoriety. Since then, new groups have spread terror to other places. After 2014, the focus was on the Islamic State (IS), but that group's ascendance has clearly passed. If history is any guide, it will recur: it may have, at least indirectly, been reprised on January 6, 2021, at the U.S. Capitol in the arguable form of domestic terror.

The answer requires investigating the nature of the terrorist problem, how it is changing, and what can be done about it. It begins by examining briefly the dynamics of and problems created by terrorism and terrorists. It then moves to how terrorism has evolved structurally as a problem since September 11 and what efforts have been mounted against it. It concludes by examining the evolving nature of the threat and how to attack it.

The tragic terrorist attack by the Islamic terrorist group Al Qaeda (AQ) against the World Trade Center on September 11, 2001, was a seminal international and national event. Internationally, 9/11 signaled a new and frightening escalation of a problem that had troubled other parts of the world for a long time. Nationally, the attacks traumatized an American population suddenly aware of its vulnerability to terrorist violence and spawned a major national mandate for dealing with it. The antiterrorist movement worldwide has had successes and failures against elements of the old AQ network, most notably the assassination of AQ founder and leader Osama bin Laden in 2011. AQ has also faded but remains a diffused threat in parts of the Middle East and elsewhere. IS became the most prominent successor, but it has receded as a threat to global politics. The evolution from AQ to IS to some other threat is a central dynamic of the future and illustrates a basic characteristic of the phenomenon: terrorists and their movements come and go, but terrorism survives.

Terrorist activity has moved geographically. The United States has not experienced a major coordinated attack by a foreign terrorist organization since 2001, although it has endured "lone wolf" attacks by individuals inspired by ideological groups like IS. Instead, much organized terrorism has been against foreign targets, principally in Europe but also in Asia. If it has changed venues for now, terrorism nonetheless remains a major force that poses threats to greater parts of the world. Domestic terrorism may be the new face of the problem in the United States and elsewhere.

Principle: The Nature and Problem of Terrorism

The first step in coming to grips with terrorism is defining the term. This is an important consideration, because so many phenomena in the contemporary political arena are labeled terrorist. Without a definition and a set of criteria, it is hard to tell whether a specific movement, or act, constitutes terrorism.

A comprehensive, universally accepted definition of terrorism does not exist. Rather, there are many different definitions people and organizations in the field employ. Some commonalities recur and will allow the adoption of a definition for present purposes. The U.S. government offers the official definition in its 2003 *National Strategy for Combating Terrorism*: "premeditated, politically motivated violence perpetrated against noncombatant targets by subnational groups or clandestine agents," a definition formalized in title 22, chapter 38 of the U.S. Code. In *Attacking Terrorism*, coauthor Audrey Kurth Cronin says terrorism is distinguished by its political nature, its nonstate base, the targeting of innocent noncombatants, and the illegality of its acts. Jessica Stern, in *Terrorism in the Name of God*, defines terrorism as "an act or threat of violence against noncombatants with the objective of exacting revenge, intimidating, or otherwise influencing an audience." Alan Dershowitz (in *Why Terrorism Works*) notes that definitions typically include reference to terrorist targets, perpetrators, and terrorist acts.

These definitions share three common points of reference: terrorist acts, terrorist targets, and terrorist purposes. The main difference among them is whether they specify the nature of terrorists and their political bases. The State Department, Cronin, and Dershowitz all identify terrorist organizations as nonstate-based actors. Cronin emphasizes that "although states can terrorize, by definition they cannot be terrorists." In the rest of this case study, terrorism will be defined as "the commission of atrocious acts against a target population normally to gain compliance with some demands the terrorists insist upon." It does not specify that terrorism must be committed by nonstate actors. Terrorism is terrorism, regardless of who carries it out.

Terrorist Acts

Terrorist acts are the most visible and recognizable manifestations of terrorism. For most people, these acts are synonymous with the broader phenomenon of terrorism. They share several characteristics. First, terrorist acts are uniformly illegal. Terrorist acts upset the normalcy of life by either injuring or killing people or destroying things. Regardless of the professed motives they espouse, these actions break laws wherever they are committed and are subject to criminal prosecution. Terrorists attempt to raise the legitimacy of their actions by proclaiming them "acts of war" (currently holy war or *jihad*), but the simple fact remains that terrorist acts are against the law. Whether terrorism is crime or war (or both) has consequences for how it is treated and how it is countered.

Second, the general purpose of terrorist acts has been to frighten the target audience. The word *terrorism* is derived from the Latin root *terrere*, which means "to frighten." The method of inducing fright is through the commission of acts of violence that induce fear in those who witness or experience the acts or believe they could be the objects of similar future attacks. Terrorists hope the targets conclude that compliance with their demands is preferable to living with people's fear of being victims themselves. Fright is accomplished by disrupting the predictability and safety of life within society, one of whose principal functions is public safety. Thus, a major purpose of terrorist mayhem is also to undermine this vital fiber of society. A third and related purpose of terrorist acts is to cause widespread disorder that demoralizes society and breaks down the social order in a country.

A more tactical use of terrorism is to provoke overreaction by a government in the form of repressive action, reprisals, and overly brutal counterterrorism that may lead to the overthrow of the reactive government. This has been a favorite tactic of Boko Haram, the Nigerian-based terrorist group that has attempted to lure the government in Lagos to attack regions that will alienate the inhabitants and help recruit support for the terrorists.

A fourth purpose of terrorist action is punishment. Terrorists often argue that an action they take is aimed at a specific person or place because that person or institution is somehow guilty of a transgression and is thus being meted out appropriate punishment for what the terrorists consider a crime. Although the Israeli government would be appalled at the prospects of designating their actions after Palestinian bombing attacks by bulldozing the homes of the families of suicide terrorists (or bombing the homes of dissident leaders) as acts of terror, from the vantage point of the Palestinian targets of the attacks, they certainly must have seemed so, most recently in 2021.

Stern (in *Terrorism in the Name of God*) adds another motivation that is internal to the terrorist organization: morale. Like any other organization, and especially terrorist groups in which the "operatives" are generally young and immature, occasional attacks may be necessary simply to demonstrate to the membership the continuing potency of the group to keep the membership focused and their morale high. As Stern puts it, "Attacks sometimes have more to do with rousing the troops than terrorizing the victims."

Terrorist Targets

Terrorist targets can be divided into two related categories. The first is people, and the objective is to kill, maim, or otherwise cause some members of the target population to suffer as an example for the rest of that population. The second is physical targets, attacks against which are designed to disrupt and destroy societal capabilities and to demonstrate the vulnerability of the target society. The two categories are related in that most physical targets contain people who will be killed or injured in the process. Attacking targets in either category demonstrates that the target government cannot protect its members and valued artifacts.

There are subtle differences and problems associated with concentrating on one category or the other. Attacks intended to kill or injure people are the most personal and evoke the greatest emotion in the target population, including anger and the will to resist and seek vengeance. From the terrorist vantage point, the reason to attack people is to undercut their will to resist the demands that terrorists make. Dennis Drew and I have referred to this as *cost-tolerance*, the level of suffering one is willing to endure in the face of some undesirable situation. The terrorist seeks to exceed the target's cost-tolerance by making the target audience conclude that it is physically or mentally less painful to accede to the terrorist's demands than it is to continue to resist those demands.

Overcoming cost-tolerance is not easy, and it usually fails. For one thing, terrorist organizations are generally small and have limited resources, meaning that they usually lack the wherewithal to terrorize enough of the target population to make members become individually fearful enough to tip the scales. Should terrorist groups obtain and use weapons of mass destruction, such a turn of events would be a game changer. Attacking and killing innocent members of a target group may and usually does infuriate its members and increase, rather than decrease, their will to resist.

When the targets are physical things rather than people per se, the problems and calculations change. The range of potential physical targets is virtually boundless. In attacking places, the terrorist seeks to deprive the target population of whatever pleasure or value the object may provide for them. The list of what are called *countervalue* targets covers a broad range of objects, from hydroelectric plants to athletic stadiums, from nuclear power generators to military facilities, from highways to research facilities, and so on. The ransomware attack on the Colonial Pipeline in May 2021 by Russian hackers combines a terrorist attack with cyberwar techniques and could be a bellwether for a new variant.

Terrorist Objectives

The ultimate goals of terrorist groups are political. To paraphrase the Clausewitzian dictum that war is politics by other means, so too is terrorism politics by other, more extreme means. Likewise, the objectives are pursued by means that color perceptions of the objectives. Sometimes, the objectives are clearly articulated, and at other times they are not. Historically, the more grandiose the goals, the less likely they have been achieved.

Terrorism is the method of the militarily weak and conceptually unacceptable. The extremely unorthodox nature of terrorist actions arises from the fact that terrorists cannot compete successfully using the accepted methods of the target society for creating change. Terrorists lack the military resources to engage in open warfare, at which they would be easily defeated, or in the forum of public discourse and decision, because their objectives are likely unacceptable, distasteful, or even bizarre to the target population.

The fact that terrorist objectives are politically objectionable to the target sets up the confrontation between the terrorists and the target. Normally, terrorist goals are stated in terms of changing policies or laws repressing them. Because the terrorists are in a small minority, they cannot bring about the changes they demand by normal electoral or legislative means, and their demands are likely to be viewed as so basically lunatic and unrealistic that they are not taken seriously by the target. The demands make perfect sense to the terrorists, and they are frustrated and angered by the dismissal they receive.

Determining whether terrorists achieve their goals or fail is complicated by the contrast between the short- and long-term levels of objectives. Modern terrorists have rarely been successful at the strategic level of attaining long-range objectives. AQ did not force the United States from the Arabian Peninsula (Osama bin Laden's stated goal), and IS failed to institute a sectarian caliphate. At the same time, the terrorist record at achieving tactical objectives (carrying out terrorist attacks) is not a total failure. If terrorists continue to exist and to achieve some tactical goals, they remain a force against the targets of their activities.

Evolving Terrorism since September 11, 2001

The peril posed by terrorism is changing. The events of September 11 reintroduced the world to a 2,000-year-old phenomenon largely forgotten during a century of world wars and a Cold War that could have turned into a nuclear Armageddon. Understanding the new threat introduced by the 9/11 attacks and lone-wolf assaults like the Murrah Building bombing in Oklahoma City in 1995 was different for at least two reasons. First, the new form of terrorism was physically and conceptually different from anything encountered before, and it continues to change. It was nonstate-based terrorism arising not from specific political communities or jurisdictions but instead flowing across national boundaries like oil slipping under doors. It has been religious, demonstrating degrees of fanaticism and intolerance that, while present in many religious communities, are alien to most people's ability to conceptualize. It is also usually fanatically anti-American and anti-Western in ways and for reasons most Westerners have difficulty comprehending. That stereotype may not be permanent. Any group with a grievance can become terrorist if it cannot achieve its end in any other way. Terrorism is a strategy to achieve ends; it is not an ideology.

Second, understanding contemporary terrorism is made more difficult by its changeable nature and practitioners. The AQ of 2001 was hard enough to understand, but it has evolved and morphed greatly since. Modern terrorism is truly a hydra-headed monster both in terms of who employs it and for what reasons.

Stern, in *Terrorism in the Name of God*, usefully articulates the requirements for a successful terrorist organization: resiliency (the ability to withstand the loss of parts of its membership or workforce) and capacity (the ability to optimize the scale and impact of terrorist attacks). The larger the scale of operations the terrorist organization can carry out without large losses to its members, the more effective the organization is. Conversely, an organization carrying out small, relatively insignificant acts while having large portions of its membership captured or killed is less effective.

Resiliency and capacity are related. To carry out large operations like 9/11 or the IS campaign, an organization must have a sophisticated, coordinated plan involving multiple people or cells who must communicate with one another both to plan and to execute the attack. The Achilles' heel in terrorist activity is penetration by outsiders, and the key element in doing so is to interrupt communications and destroy its ability to operate (in other words, to reduce its resiliency). The most effective way for the terrorist groups to avoid penetration is to minimize communications that can be intercepted, but doing so comes at the expense of the sophistication and extent of its actions (reduction in capacity).

The result is a dilemma that contemporary terrorist organizations face. Historically, according to Stern and others, most terrorist groups have followed an organizational form known as the *commander-cadre* (or *hierarchical*) model. This form of group is not dissimilar to the way virtually all complex enterprises are structured everywhere: executives (commanders) organize and plan activities (terrorist attacks) and pass instructions downward through the structure for implementation by employees (cadres).

Commander-cadre arrangements have advantages associated with any large, complex organization: they can coordinate activities maximizing capacity; can organize recruitment efforts and absorb, indoctrinate, and train recruits; and can carry out ancillary activities such as fundraising. The disadvantage of these organizations is that they become more permeable by outside agencies because of their need to communicate among units. Modern electronics become a double-edged sword for the terrorist: they facilitate communications in executing attacks, but those communications can be intercepted and lead to resiliency-threatening penetration.

One result of antiterrorist efforts has been to cause these organizations to become what Stern refers to as the "protean enemy." AQ still exists but is no longer a hierarchically organized entity that plans and carries out terrorist missions as it did before. Instead, it has adopted elements of the alternate form of terrorist organization, the *virtual network* or *leaderless resistance* model, and has dispersed itself into a series of smaller, loosely affiliated terrorist organizations that draw inspiration from the center.

Particularly since the assassination of bin Laden, these mutations, sometimes called "franchises," have increasingly become the public face of terrorism both for AQ and other terrorist entities. AQ activities, for instance, are usually carried out by spin-offs like AQ in the Arabian Peninsula in places like Yemen or by AQ in the Maghreb in places like Mali. Al-Shabab, also an AQ affiliate, is a major actor in Somalia. What distinguishes the actions of such groups is a relatively modest size and geographical reach. Since the collapse of the caliphate, IS has followed a similar strategy.

The effect of changes has been to make the competition between terrorist organizations and their suppressors more sophisticated, difficult, deadly, and expensive. The change has organizationally been in both directions. At the more expansive level, IS emerged in 2014 as a much larger, ambitious entity than previous contemporary organizations, none of which had professed an ambition as large as establishing a territorial state. At the other extreme, much operational terror—especially in the United States—has been transferred to publicly leaderless resistance practitioners acting essentially as lone wolves or as transient coalitions with specific, if generally illegal, means. Each end of the spectrum represents an evolutionary permutation that creates new horrors and problems for target societies. They are also almost certainly not the last forms terrorism will take in the years ahead.

Application: Dealing with Contemporary Terrorism

What kind of threat does terrorism pose today? What kind of threat will it pose in the future? What will that threat look like? Terrorism has been venerable, and its persistent, if episodic, recurrence suggests that it has enough appeal to desperate groups who feel they have no other way to achieve their goals that they are likely to continue to turn to terrorism as a blueprint. Groups with deeply held grievances of all political persuasions have from time to time employed terrorism. There is no convincing evidence that is changing.

Understanding efforts to deal with terrorism is a two-step process. It begins by looking at the categories of terrorist suppression, the overarching concept under which the various efforts can be grouped. The other perspective is looking at the terrorism problem in organizational terms, from the discontented individual lone wolf to larger terrorist organizations like IS and beyond. In both cases, the distinctions often blend in practice. Individual terrorists are often recruited by virtual networks, for instance, and successful virtual networks may broaden their purview.

Suppressing Terrorism: Antiterrorism and Counterterrorism

Conventional terrorism suppression is divided into two methods: antiterrorism and counterterrorism. The two terms are sometimes used interchangeably, but each refers to a distinct form of action with a specific and different contribution to the overall goal. Any program of terrorist suppression will necessarily contain elements of both, but not specifying which is which only confuses the issue.

Antiterrorism refers to defensive efforts to reduce the vulnerability of targets to terrorist attacks and to lessen the effects of terrorist attacks that do occur. Antiterrorism efforts begin from the implicit premise that some terrorist attacks will be attempted and some will succeed tactically, and that two forms of suppression effort are necessary. First, antiterrorists seek to make it more difficult to mount terrorist attacks. Airport security to prevent potential terrorists from boarding airliners or the interception and detention of suspected terrorists by border guards are examples. Second, antiterrorists try to mitigate the effects of terrorist attacks that might or do occur. Blocking off streets in front of public buildings like the White House so that terrorists cannot get close enough to destroy them is one approach, and civil defense measures (e.g., hazmat operations) to mitigate the effects of an attack is another way to deal with the problem. The assault on the U.S. Capitol on January 6, 2021, reminds us these efforts do not always succeed and how difficult it is to anticipate and protect all possible targets.

There are three related difficulties with conducting an effective antiterrorist campaign. One is that it is necessarily reactive; terrorists choose where attacks will occur and against what kinds of targets, and antiterrorists must try to anticipate or respond to the terrorist initiative, and sometimes they guess wrong. A second problem is the sheer variety and number of potential targets. The list is almost infinite, and terrorists seek to randomize what they attack so that potential victims are always off guard and antiterrorists will have trouble anticipating where attacks may occur. The third problem is *target substitution*: If antiterrorist efforts are sufficiently successful that terrorists determine their likelihood of success against a specific target (or class of targets) is significantly diminished, they simply go on to other, less well-defended targets.

The other form of terrorist suppression is *counterterrorism*, offensive and military measures against terrorists or sponsoring agencies to prevent, deter, or respond to terrorist acts. Counterterrorism thus consists of both preventive and retaliatory actions. Preventive acts can include actions such as penetrating terrorist organizations or apprehending and using physical violence against terrorists before they carry out their operations. Retaliation is often military and paramilitary and includes attacks on terrorist camps or other facilities in response to terrorist attacks or disruption or elimination of concentrations of terrorists. The purposes of retaliation include punishment, reducing terrorist capacity for future acts, and hopefully deterrence of future actions by instilling fear of the consequences.

Counterterrorism is inherently and intuitively attractive. Preventive actions are proactive, and in their purest form, preventive counterterrorist actions reverse the tables in the relationship, effectively "terrorizing the terrorists." Pounding a terrorist facility as punishment after enduring a terrorist attack at least provides the satisfaction of knowing the enemy has suffered as well as the victim.

Ideally, antiterrorism and counterterrorist efforts act in tandem. Counterterrorists reduce the number and quality of possible attacks through preventive actions, making the task of antiterrorist efforts to ameliorate the effects of attacks that do succeed less difficult. Further counterterrorist action then can hopefully reduce the terrorists' capacity for future mayhem. The result is a more manageable threat confronting the antiterrorists. In practice, however, these efforts sometimes come into operational conflict.

The Contemporary Threats

The shape of the terrorist threat has undergone a major transformation. AQ still exists, and despite losing physical control of the caliphate, IS continues to inspire some Muslims. The growing phenomenon in North America and Europe is random attacks inspired and sometimes carried out by IS or AQ operatives or home-grown persons or groups. A growing problem is acts by random, often deranged, individuals who may (or may not) be inspired by major terrorist groups or who may be acting out of perceived mandates from such groups. Lone-wolf attacks in the United States and elsewhere and international attacks for which recognizable groups take credit after the fact are examples. The future remains murky, but it seems likely that this pattern will continue as a prominent part of the international environment. Attacks by individuals or ad hoc groups have been most likely to continue to be the norm in developed countries, mostly because more formal groups are usually identified and suppressed before they can act. The attackers of January 6 may be the harbinger of anti-state terror of the future.

Lone-Wolf Terrorists

The phenomenon of terrorism by individuals apparently unconnected to any organized terrorist group has been a recurring part of the terrorism problem for a long time. Because their actions are idiosyncratic, isolated, and often erratic, they have not individually received the level of attention that more systematic, organized movements do. Cumulatively, however, the rise in their prominence, especially in the United States, parallels a decline in activities by larger, more monolithic organizations. For Americans, lone wolves have been the living face of terror in their lives. January 6 may have added to or altered that face.

Awareness of lone wolves in the United States emerged in the 1990s with the unrelated cases of Unabomber Theodore Kaczynski (the deranged university professor who killed three and wounded over twenty others with letter bombs between 1978 and 1995) and Timothy McVeigh, who killed 159 people in the truck bombing of the Murrah Federal Building in Oklahoma City in 1995. Since these highly publicized cases, there have been an increasing number of episodic instances of domestic lone wolves in various unrelated locations from San Bernardino, California (where a disgruntled and radicalized employee attacked fellow workers at a social service agency), to Orlando, Florida, site of an attack on a packed nightclub that left forty-nine dead. These atrocious events followed other well-publicized attacks such as the massacre of over thirty fellow soldiers by Major Nidal Hasan at Fort Hood, Texas, in fall 2009 and the 2013 bombing at the Boston Marathon by two brothers. It is often difficult to distinguish between "honest" terrorist activity and the actions of simply deranged killers.

What are the characteristics of the lone-wolf terrorist? The European Union Instituut voor Veiligheids- en Crisismanagement offered a useful set of interrelated characteristics in a 2007 study. First and foremost, lone wolves act individually rather than as parts of organized and directed groups. Second, lone wolves do not belong to any organized terrorist group or network. Third, they act without the direct influence of a leader or hierarchy. Fourth, the tactics and methods they employ are conceived and conducted by the individual without "any direct outside command or direction." Lone-wolf terrorist activities are conceived by individuals who act autonomously in designing and carrying out their acts. The extent of their autonomy compounds the difficulty of identifying and suppressing them in advance. Their lack of affiliation means they likely do not appear on terrorist watch lists, and unless they engage in aberrant behavior that causes citizens to report them to authorities, they present no preattack footprint.

The autonomy of lone wolves and the ad hoc nature of groups of which they may be a part makes them extremely difficult to identify in advance, because, by definition, these individuals are usually antisocial loners. Belonging to no formal terrorist groups, they have no communications that can be intercepted and traced back to them, and they may be able to evade detection for a long time after they commit their acts, unless they make some crucial mistake that leads to their apprehension. Many are not consciously terrorist and deny that what they do is terrorism, even when their behavior meets the criteria of terrorist acts.

Two other factors make the isolation and categorization of lone-wolf terrorism problematic. One is whether an individual act meets the criteria for terrorism laid out earlier, whether it is an instance of pure depravity, or when the overt acts are not considered terrorist by perpetrators or supporters. This difficulty is particularly relevant when trying to determine the objective of a lone-wolf attack. McVeigh, in his twisted way, had the apparent objective of avenging the Branch Davidians who had died at Waco, Texas.

The other factor is the degree of autonomy and independence of the apparent lone wolf. Groups with diverse messages of hate increasingly publicize their causes and exhort their followers on the internet, and it is often unclear whether apparently independent acts have been influenced by such appeals. There is evidence, for instance, that Major Hasan was "inspired" by extreme antiabortion appeals on the internet, and he was influenced by the violent sermons of American-born, Yemen-based Muslim cleric Anwar al-Awlaki, an AQ supporter who exhorted American Muslims and others to rise and attack infidels.

Domestic Terror? The January 6, 2021, Insurrection

On January 6, 2021, a group of Americans numbering in the hundreds invaded the U.S. Capitol, overwhelmed the U.S. Capitol police guarding the building and its inhabitants (principally members of Congress and their staffs), and went on a destructive rampage of the building as members and their staffs fled or attempted to find shelter from the attacking throng. The entire spectacle was captured and broadcast globally for the world to see.

As it was unfolding, it was not entirely clear why the invasion was occurring. The "rioters" had no clear leaders articulating the reasons for the action. January 6 was the day the Electoral College was formally to convene and declare President Biden the victor in the 2020 election and to authorize his inauguration as the country's forty-sixth president, a ceremonial action the attack seems to have been intended to block. This inference led critics to speculate on the possible role of outgoing incumbent Donald Trump, who had regularly accused that the election process had been rigged against him and should have been voided. The event has been frequently labeled an insurrection. FBI director Christopher Wray has called it an act of domestic terrorism. What was it? If it was terror, it represents a new domestic variant beyond the actions of lone wolves.

A definitive public depiction of what happened has not yet been reached in the hyper-partisan atmosphere of contemporary American politics, and it may never be. Our interest here is in determining whether the movement was a new form of domestic terrorism, how enduring the phenomenon will be, how it may evolve or mutate, and what can or should be done about it. The answers are necessarily tentative.

The first problem is definitional: how do we categorize what occurred. Was it *domestic terror* or something more noble and acceptable? Two conceptualizations have dominated early discussions, and both seem to apply. The first is domestic terrorism. *Wikipedia* blends definitions in the literature, defining it as "the committing of terrorist acts in the perpetrator's own country against their fellow citizens." These acts are intended to coerce or intimidate a government or the civilian population "in furtherance of political or social objectives." The US Code (2331, 5) states clearly the illegality of "acts dangerous to human life that are a violation of criminal laws of the United States or any state." These definitions are clearly compatible with descriptions of terror.

The other concept is *insurrection*. This term is used to describe why the attack occurred. There is basic agreement on the definition of the term. Stripped of detail, it is "a violent act against an authority or government." The *Cambridge Dictionary* elaborates the definition as "an organized attempt by a group of people to defeat their government or ruler and take control of the country." This definition is broader and more expansive than the core definition of domestic terror and suggests, somewhat contradictorily, a more ambitious and less fully developed ideology and action plan than is associated with terrorist organizations.

The extent to which this variant of domestic terror represents a serious problem depends largely on the continuing support it receives from the American citizenry. Lone-wolf terrorism is a limited—though deadly—problem because it is generally limited to a single or small group of supporters, and their suppression generally causes them to disappear. In the case of January 6, there have been no expressions or accusations of an ongoing movement beyond rumblings from fringe groups, although that judgment could change. Perpetrators have been arrested and will be tried, and that could be the end of the episode. Terrorist movements do come and go, and unless the January 6 "movement" is reignited, it may suffer a similar fate. The history of terrorism has been so resilient across time to make prediction of its permanent disappearance problematical.

The level of attention to the intellectual underpinnings among those who organized and led the January 6 attack on the Capitol (whatever they may turn out to be) has been less extensive and its results less coherent than that of many historical movements, and it may well prove to be a "one off" phenomenon. Historically, domestic terrorist forays have experienced limited success and less sustained support than elsewhere. Whether the actions of January 6 turn out to be different will help determine whether these "insurrectionists" are more than a small historical footnote in the history of domestic terror in the United States.

Conclusion

The terrorism problem continues to evolve. Before the 9/11 attacks, acts of terror were considered a horrible aberration, not an integral part of international existence. The single most deadly terrorist act in history changed that perception. The threat of terrorism is now considered ubiquitous, and efforts to suppress it are now a pervasive part of everyday life. The war on terrorism is now an accepted, institutionalized part of the political environment nationally and internationally.

The terrorism phenomenon is dynamic. It has become more diffuse and atomized as the efforts of terrorism suppressors have forced terrorists to adopt different, more clandestine forms and approaches to attaining their lethal goals. Lone wolves epitomize this diffusion. At the same time, the emergence of IS from the Syrian Civil War showed large-scale terrorism continues to exist, if precariously. Moreover, history suggests there will be other, newer permutations.

The organized terrorism represented by AQ and IS now share international attention with the actions of individual lone wolves whose motives are difficult to catalog and difficult to discover in advance. "Organized" terror associated with formal organizations like AQ and IS is more concentrated in the developing world, where governments have fewer resources to engage in effective counterterrorism than do the developed countries. Domestic terror has been added to the violence of individual terrorists in the most developed countries.

The terrorism future is hard to predict in terms of where and by whom terror may occur. It may become more diffuse and closer to home, as it did in Washington, DC. Some perpetrators, like Timothy McVeigh, may be homegrown and either true lone operators or members of loosely organized coalitions that come together for a specific cause. January 6 may be a prototype. These kinds of phenomena can arguably be classified as terrorist, and what they do is compatible with definitions of terrorist acts described here. They may be the face of contemporary terror, but like all groups that have preceded them, they will fade away. Unfortunately, history suggests they will be replaced by some successor groups and causes. In the end, we may be left with Pogo's reminder: "We have met the enemy, and he is us."

Study/Discussion Questions

1. Define terrorism. What are its three common elements? Can states be terrorists?
2. What do terrorist acts seek to accomplish? In what circumstances do they succeed or fail? Include in your answer a discus-sion of cost-tolerance. Why is the strategic-tactical distinction important in assessing terrorist activity?
3. What kinds of targets do terrorists attack? Why are some more difficult to protect than others?

4. How has international terrorism changed since 9/11, notably in terms of terrorist organizations?
5. What are the standard distinctions among forms of terrorism suppression described in the text? Describe each as an element in lessening or eliminating the problem of terrorism.
6. How did the emergence of IS represent a major change in the terrorism threat? How was IS different than the others?
7. The text argues that the IS threat is on the wane, because it has attempted to be much more than a terrorist organization. Discuss this argument. How does the IS failure affect the future evolution of terrorist activity?
8. Terrorism changes and evolves. Based on what you have read, what do you think the terrorism pattern will look like a decade from now? Will domestic terror become a larger problem? Was January 6 a harbinger of things to come? What do you think?

Bibliography

Art, Robert J., and Kenneth N. Waltz. *The Use of Force: Military Power and International Politics* (seventh edition). London: Rowman & Littlefield, 2008.

Atran, Scott. "The Moral Logic and Growth of Suicide Terrorism." *Washington Quarterly* 29, no. 2 (Spring 2006): 127–47.

Benard, Cheryl. "Toy Soldiers: The Youth Factor in the War on Terror." *Current History* 106, no. 696 (January 2007): 27–30.

Berger, J. M. *Extremism* (MIT Press Essential Knowledge Series). Cambridge, MA: MIT Press, 2018.

Chenoweth, Erica, Richard English, et al. *The Oxford Handbook of Terrorism.* Oxford, UK: Oxford University Press, 2019.

Clarke, Richard A., ed. "Terrorism: What the Next President Will Face." *Annals of the American Academy of Political and Social Science* 618 (July 2008), 4–6.

Cockburn, Patrick. *The Rise of the Islamic State: IS and the New Sunni Revolution.* London: Verso, 2015.

Cole, Juan. "Think Again: 9/11." *Foreign Policy* (September/October 2006): 26–32.

Cronin, Audrey Kurth. "IS Is Not a Terrorist Group: Why Counterterrorism Won't Stop the Latest Jihadi Group." *Foreign Affairs* 94, no. 2 (March/April 2015): 87–98.

———. "Sources of Contemporary Terrorism," in Audrey Kurth Cronin and James M. Ludes, eds. *Attacking Terrorism: Elements of a Grand Strategy.* Washington, DC: Georgetown University Press, 2004.

Dershowitz, Alan M. *Why Terrorism Works: Understanding the Threat, Responding to the Challenge.* New Haven, CT: Yale University Press, 2002.

Fleishman, Charlotte. *The Business of Terror: Conceptualizing Terrorist Organizations as Cellular Businesses.* Washington, DC: Center for Defense Information, 2014.

Gerges, Fawaz A. *ISIS: A History.* Princeton, NJ: Princeton University Press, 2017.

Hoffman, Bruce. "From the War on Terror to Global Insurgency." *Current History* 105, no. 695 (December 2006): 423–29.

———. *Inside Terrorism* (second edition). New York: Columbia University Press, 2006.

Instituut voor Veiligheids- en Crisismanagement. "Lone Wolf Terrorism." June 2007. http://www.transnationalterrorism.eu/tekst/publications/Lone-Wolf.%20Terrorism.pdf.

Jenkins, Brian. "International Terrorism," in Robert J. Art and Kenneth N. Waltz, eds. *The Use of Force: Military Power and International Politics*, 77–84. New York: Rowman & Littlefield, 2004.

Johnson, Daryl. *Hateland: A Long, Hard Look at America's Extremist Heart*. Amhurst, NY: Prometheus Books, 2019.

Laqueur, Walter, and Christopher Wall. *The Future of Terrorism: ISIS, Al-Qaeda, and the Alt-Right*. New York: Thomas Dunne Books, 2018.

Law, Randal D. *Terrorism: A History* (second edition). Boston: Polity, 2016.

Maher, Shiraz. *Salafi-Jihadism: The History of an Idea*. Oxford, UK: Oxford University Press, 2016.

Martin, Gus. *Understanding Terrorism: Challenges, Perspectives, and Issues* (fifth edition). Thousand Oaks, CA: Sage, 2015.

McCants, William. *The ISIS Apocalypse: The History, Strategy and Doomsday Vision of the Islamic State*. New York: St. Martin's Press, 2015.

Nacos, Brigette. *Terrorism and Counterterrorism* (sixth edition). New York and London: Routledge, 2019.

Perliger, Aria. *American Zealots: Right-Wing Domestic Terrorism* (Columbia Studies in Terrorism and Irregular Warfare). New York: Columbia University Press, 2020.

Rapaport, David C. "The Four Waves of Terrorism," in Audrey Kurth Cronin and James M. Ludes, eds. *Attacking Terrorism: Elements of a Grand Strategy*, 46–73. Washington, DC: Georgetown University Press, 2004.

Silke, Rapaport. *Routledge Handbook of Terrorism and Counterterrorism*. New York and London: Routledge, 2020.

Simon, Jeffrey D., and Brian Michael Jennings. *Lone-Wolf Terrorism: Understanding the Growing Threat*. Buffalo, NY: Prometheus Books, 2016.

Snow, Donald M. *The Middle East, Oil, and the United States National Security Policy*. Lanham, MD: Rowman & Littlefield, 2016.

———. *Regional Cases in Foreign Policy* (second edition). Lanham, MD: Rowman & Littlefield, 2018, especially chapter 1.

———, and Dennis M. Drew. *From Lexington to Baghdad and Beyond: War and Politics in the American Experience* (third edition). Armonk, NY: M. E. Sharpe, 2009.

Stern, Jessica. "Mind over Martyr: How to Deradicalize Islamic Extremists." *Foreign Affairs* 89, no. 1 (January/February 2010): 95–108.

———. *Terrorism in the Name of God: Why Religious Militants Kill*. New York: ECCO, 2003.

———. "The Protean Enemy." *Foreign Affairs* 82, no. 4 (July/August 2003): 27–40.

———, and J. M. Berger. *ISIS: The State of Terror*. New York: ECCO, 2015.

Warraq, Ibn. *The Islam in Islamic Terrorism: The Importance of Beliefs, Ideas, and Ideology*. London: New English Review Press, 2017.

Weiss, Michael, and Hassan Hassan. *ISIS: Inside the Army of Terror* (updated edition). New York: Regan Arts, 2016.

White, Jonathan R. *Terrorism and Homeland Security* (ninth edition). East Windsor, CT: Wadsworth, 2016.

Wood, Graeme. "What ISIS Really Wants." *The Atlantic* 321, no. 2 (March 2015): 78–90.

15

International Population Movement

Restricting or Increasing Immigration in the United States, Europe, and China

The migration of people from one place to another precedes recorded human history. People have moved for many reasons, most frequently seeking a better life, but also to avoid distress, suppression, and even extinction. Immigrants, refugees, and asylum seekers are a constant that has been increasing in this century and has reached critical proportions in some places. The problem is exacerbated by a burgeoning world population growth rate, mostly in the developing world, in contrast to relatively stagnant or shrinking growth in the developed world.

There are competing, contradictory forces at work in this equation. There are two basic stimuli for migration. One directly involves immigration of people from the developing to the developed world. The motive is both economic and political: seeking prosperity and freedom. For receiving countries, immigrants do provide necessary augmentation of shrinking labor forces and thus stimulate productivity. The result can be positive for both sides, but its synergism is partially upset by the prospects that undesirables—especially terrorists and criminals—will infiltrate the immigrants. The other stimulus is largely internal to the developing world in terms of privation and atrocity associated with internal conflicts that produce massive refugee and asylum-seeking populations.

The result is a demographic conundrum that most developed countries have avoided confronting or resolving, especially in an era when anti-immigrant sentiments have increased. Many politically influential people advocate economic growth and expansion and restrictions on immigration, positions that are at least partially contradictory in practice. Economic growth requires an expanding workforce, but developed countries are experiencing a stagnating or even declining workforce size. There are only two ways to change the equation: enlarging the indigenous workforce by increasing the birth rate or by importing workers. The first solution takes time and collides with values about family size. Importing workers is a much faster method for swelling the workforce.

Human migration is a two-way proposition. On one hand are those who seek to relocate for one reason or another, including economic benefits and fear for their lives. On the other are those in the sovereign jurisdictions to which the migrants seek to relocate who must decide whether to accept them. It is rarely a seamless, smooth process. It can also be a difficult, often traumatic, and even dangerous experience.

Migration is one of the most enduring aspects of the human experience. At some level of remove, essentially everyone is an immigrant or the descendant of immigrants; the only humans who can rightfully claim nonimmigrant status are direct descendants of the earliest humans from the Great Rift Valley in Africa whose descendants still live there.

Human migration in its various forms is a large, important, and controversial contemporary phenomenon. In 2005, the UN Department of Economic and Social Affairs reported that there were 191 million international immigrants (people residing in countries other than that of their birth). That figure fluctuates from year to year, as some immigrants are repatriated and others leave voluntarily or flee their native lands. The reasons they move are various and complicated, but the net result is a constant flow of people across borders.

The immigrant question has always been important for the United States. As the admonition to "bring me your tired, your huddled masses" on the Statue of Liberty heralds, the United States is a quintessential immigrant state, with waves of immigrants from various places arriving at different times in the country's history to constitute one of the world's most nationally and ethnically diverse populations. Sometimes the process of new immigrant waves has been orderly, open, and noncontentious, but it has also been surrounded by considerable disagreement and rancor.

In quantitative terms, the American example is not extreme, but its dynamics may be a harbinger of a future where migration is likely to increase, possibly greatly. Europe joins the United States in this concern. It is host to a considerably larger comparative immigrant population than the United States, especially in a few select countries like Germany. In recent years, a surge of political conservatism has made immigration controversial and slowed its pace. One result is a collision between restrictive immigration policies and expansive economic pressures.

Principle: Human Population Movement

Population movement is a normal occurrence in much of the world. Some countries are more permissive than others about letting citizens leave (emigrate) or enter from other countries (immigrate), but some population movement is a regular part of international activity, and one that is arguably increasing in a globalizing world in which international population and interaction of all kinds is increasing. Employing an accepted definition used by Koser that an international immigrant is "a person who stays outside his usual country of residence for at least one year," the global total of immigrants today is over 200 million people. Immigration is, however, only one, if the largest, form of human movement. Understanding the problem in a contemporary context requires beginning by classifying different categories of those who traverse borders.

Forms of Movement

There are various categories of people who leave their homes for other locations. Immigration is the historically largest and most generic category, but there are others. Two that stand out are refugees and asylum seekers, both because of their prominence in contemporary international relations and because they are often the result (or even the cause) of great human suffering. Labor requirements associated with declining birth rates in many developed countries may be creating a new class of demographic immigrants.

Immigrants are often subdivided into various categories. Legal immigrants are those individuals who have migrated to a country through prescribed channels, meaning their immigration is recognized and accepted by the host government. Countries allow immigrants into the country for a variety of reasons and in different numbers depending on the needs or uses they perceive for such populations. Parts of Europe—notably Germany—have long admitted workers from places like Turkey to augment shrinking workforces as their population ages, and the United States has historically given priority status to people with particularly needed education and technical skills, such as scientists and engineers from developing countries like India.

There are, however, other, more controversial categories of immigrants. In the contemporary debate, the most controversial are so-called *irregular immigrants*. The UN Department of Economic and Social Affairs defines this class of people as "those who enter a country without proper authorization or who have violated the terms of stay of the authorization they hold, including by overstaying." Other terms for irregular status include illegal, undocumented, and unauthorized immigrants. As Koser points out, "there are around 40 million irregular immigrants worldwide, of whom perhaps one-third are in the United States." The most publicized and largest part of that total are irregular by virtue of illegal entry into the country; some of the most problematical, however, are individuals who have entered the country legally but have overstayed the conditions of their residence, as in not leaving after student or temporary work or study visas have expired.

A special category of immigrants is refugees. Broadly speaking, refugees are the most prominent example of what the UN Commission on Human Rights (UNCHR) calls "forcibly displaced people," who, according to 2017 UNCHR figures, numbered about 65 million worldwide. The largest numbers of people within this category are refugees (displaced people living outside their native countries) at about 21.3 million, internally displaced persons (refugees within their own countries) at about 43 million, and asylum seekers (people who have sought international protection but whose applications have not been acted upon by the host country). Those who seek refugee status often come from developing countries where human misery is both economic and political, meaning that it is sometimes difficult to determine why a refugee or group of refugees seeks to migrate. As Koser points out, "though an important legal distinction can be made between people who move for work purposes and those who flee conflict and persecution, in reality the two can be difficult to distinguish."

The dynamics of immigration as a global issue requires looking at the phenomenon from at least three vantage points. The first is the motivation for immigration: why do people emigrate from one place to another, and what roles do they fulfill when they become immigrants? The second is where the phenomenon of immigration is the most and least evident on a global scale. The third concern is immigration as a problem, both globally and locally.

Immigration Motivations and Functions

Why do people migrate? One way to think about the reasons for immigration is in terms of "push" and "pull" factors. Push factors are motives to leave a political jurisdiction—conditions that make people want to leave or that push them out. Pull factors, on the other hand, refer to perceived positive attributes to attract immigrants to different destinations—or serve to pull people to different locations. When push and pull factors are both present, the immigration pipeline is particularly strong.

The most obvious push factor is to improve one's living conditions by relocation. People decide to leave for both political and economic reasons: politically to avoid conflict or discrimination in their homeland, and economically in the hope or promise of a materially better life. This basic statement of motivation has numerous variations, as Choucri and Mistree enumerate:

> the most obvious patterns of international migration today include the following: migration for employment; seasonal mobility for employment; permanent settlements; refugees who are forced to migrate; resettlement; state-sponsored movements; tourism and ecotourism; brain drains and "reversals" of brain drains; smuggled and trafficked people; people returning to their country of origin; environmental migration and refugees from natural shortages or crises; nonlegal migration; and religious pilgrimage.

The economic motivation, to move somewhere where economic opportunities are better than those where one lives, is growing. As Choucri and Mistree summarize, "during good times people migrate to find better opportunities; during bad times people migrate to escape more difficult circumstances." In either situation, the motivating factor is opportunity, which is manifested in the availability of jobs because, as they add, "To the extent that population growth exceeds a society's employment potential, the probability is very high that people will move to other countries in search of jobs."

Demographics also enter the picture. Population growth rates are highest in developing countries, and that means the rising number of job seekers is greatest in these countries relative to the number of jobs available. In the developed world, on the other hand, where population growth rates are often below levels to maintain current population sizes, the overall population is aging, and thus the percentage of citizens in the active workforce is diminishing. Goldstone explains the consequence: "the developed countries' labor forces will substantially age and decline, constraining economic growth in the developed world and raising demands for immigrant workers." Indeed, there are estimates that the developed countries that will be most successful in the future are those that are best able to augment their shrinking workforces with immigrant labor. This dynamic creates pressure for population migration from developing to developed countries globally.

The Demographic Imperative

Demographics and politics affect this dynamic. As Bloom points out in an International Monetary Fund publication, two factors help define the impact. One is the "demographic dividend," the process through which a country's aging structure can spur economic growth. This trend is partially vitiated by the "dependency ration," the economic pressures working-age individuals feel "to support those who are not of working age." As people live longer but have fewer children, the result is a lower percentage of workers supporting a larger percentage of older, retired citizens (what Bloom calls "global graying").

Bloom calls population aging "the dominant demographic trend of the twenty-first century." It has immigration implications. Bloom concludes that "relaxing the institutional and economic barriers to international migration from regions with relatively large working-age populations could alleviate those labor shortages." Anti-immigrant political sentiments are the major obstacle to this solution.

The kinds of talents that immigrants can contribute to different areas make their acceptance either more or less positive. The smallest and most welcome category of immigrants is what the United Nations refers to as "highly skilled workers." Far more problematic are the economic immigrants who have comparatively low skill levels. Unskilled immigrants—especially irregular immigrants—pose a distinct moral and practical dilemma for receiving states. These immigrants do jobs that the citizens are either unwilling to do or that they will not do at the lower wages that migrants will accept (especially irregular migrants). Thus, without a pool of such laborers, some vital services either would not get done or only would be done at higher costs.

Refugees present a separate problem. They can also be divided into skilled and unskilled groups, with the skilled often constituting professionals from the country from which they flee, and the unskilled composed mainly of subsistence farmers and the like. The skilled parts of the population are more likely to be absorbed into the country to which they flee, whereas the unskilled generally cannot be absorbed and become a burden on the country or on international relief or philanthropic bodies. Moreover, most refugees are from developing countries and flee to adjacent countries, which are also poor and thus lacking the resources to tend for their new citizens. Most of the Syrian refugees, for instance, have fled to nearby countries like Turkey, Lebanon, Jordan, and Iraq.

The World Situation: The Human Tragedy Factor

There are two overlapping continuing trends in worldwide immigration. The first is demographic: most of this population movement is from the developing to the developed world, and especially to Europe and North America. In addition, this immigration is increasing numerically: there are more immigrants worldwide now than there have been. A significant element, however, is demographic, based in aging populations in the developed world and the consequent need to import younger workers both to sustain economic activity and to support an aging and unproductive population.

The other trend is political. Some fragile developing world countries are disintegrating into violence with a multinational basis along ethnic and religious lines, and the result is the furtive, extremely bloody and gut-wrenching violence against populations segments including innocent and often defenseless civilians of which Syria and South Sudan are currently the most publicized examples. The worst cases are currently concentrated in the Middle East.

These demographic and political trends are likely to increase in the future. As Goldstone points out, "the developed countries' labor forces will substantially age and decline, constraining economic growth in the developed world and raising the demand for immigrant workers." The rate at which populations are aging, and how governments respond to this problem, varies greatly, with different consequences. Japan, for instance, has one of the world's most rapidly aging populations and has, for cultural reasons, resisted allowing non-Japanese immigrants into the country. China also faces the same problem, because it is reluctant to import non-Han Chinese into the country. This is already having two effects. First, it means a shrinking portion of the population is part of the productive workforce that produces, among other things, the wealth needed to support older, retired citizens. Second, it means a contraction in productivity and population. The cumulative effect of these dynamics is the projection of a smaller and less economically prominent Japan and China in the future.

The scale of immigration from the developing to the developed world is not going to go away. If anything, it will increase in the future. As Goldstone suggests, "Current levels of immigration from developing to developed countries are paltry compared to those that the forces of supply and demand might soon create across the world." The degree to which this likely trend is a concern depends on whether or to what degree one views immigration as a problem.

Application: The Continuing U.S., European, and Asian Experiences

Those on the receiving end of population migration have various, sometimes contradictory reasons for accepting or rejecting the influx of new peoples into their countries. The largest current incentive to encourage immigration is the need for additional sources of labor in developed countries. Humanitarian concerns over the plight of beleaguered people sometimes enter the calculus. On the negative side in the present system, there is the danger that in admitting desirable new individuals and groups, one will also allow undesirable, even dangerous people into the country in the process. The result is a dynamic tension about immigration.

This concern exists in the United States, Europe, and parts of Asia. All are concerned about the quantity and quality of outsiders who seek entry and especially the quality of immigrants. The United States has a smaller (but not nonexistent) need for immigrant labor. Europe, on the other hand, has a large need for additional labor, which has made it a much larger recipient of that immigration. Because much of that movement comes from the Middle East and North Africa, it has a real concern with terrorists entering the EU area. Asian problems also include racism. The political challenge in the United States has been over how to restrict immigrants and has been symbolized by the debate over building a wall along the U.S.-Mexican border. In the European Union, the debate is over the loss of sovereign control of borders due to EU actions to take over the boundary regulation function. The most dramatic example of the role of that dispute is the Brexit decision. In Asia, the need for workers is a growing problem.

The U.S.-Mexican Border Problem

The migration of large numbers of people from Mexico and Central America has become a major American political issue since the 1990s, when the population of irregular immigrants increased from around four million to twelve million or more coming across the long, porous frontier between the United States and its Southern neighbors. There has always been partisan disagreement about how much of a problem this migration creates and what should be done about it. During the Trump administration, the question and its solution focused on building a wall along the border, a priority abandoned by the Biden administration.

The U.S.-Mexico border case is intensified by the nature of the border. At 1,933 miles of mostly desolate, rural topography, it is a very long and difficult frontier to "seal," as its proponents advocate. At the same time, the U.S.-Mexico boundary is the world's only direct land border between the developed and developing worlds.

The U.S.-Mexico case is also distinguished by its sheer volume and the accompanying complexity of the problem. No one, of course, knows exactly how many irregular immigrants are in the United States. The total is a larger number than for any other country, although there are several countries such as Germany that have a higher percentage of immigrants in the population than the United States, with the largest numbers in highly populated states like California, Texas, and Florida. The issue is also complex. The concern about the U.S.-Mexico border not only involves immigration, but the integrity of the frontier also has strong implications for the trafficking of illicit drugs into the United States and potentially for terrorists seeking to penetrate American soil. For present purposes, the immigration problem is most relevant.

Immigration is, and always has been, an integral part of the human, including American, experience. Although for most times and purposes, it has been one of the proud elements of the American heritage, it has had its dark side in the form of negative reactions to the migration of some people to the United States at different times. Throughout American history, what is now referred to as illegal immigration has always been a part of the pattern, and the history of immigration politics is largely an attempt to regulate both the quantity and quality (measured both in point of origin and skill levels) of immigration to the country. For Americans, the immigration problem along the U.S.-Mexico border is the most dramatic current manifestation of a worldwide pattern of international immigration.

The sheer volume of irregular immigrants in the United States is the heart of the perceived problem in the American political debate. More specifically, it is about irregular immigration by Mexicans and Central Americans into the country in larger numbers than many prefer. Efforts to secure the border are aimed at reducing or eliminating the flow of irregulars into the country; efforts to apprehend and deport irregular immigrants already in the country are aimed at reducing those numbers.

There are essentially two groups that make up that community. By far the most numerous are *economic immigrants*. There is no systematic indication that their participation in or contribution to crime is any greater than that of the population at large; indeed, it is probably lower. The other group is comprised of *criminal immigrants*, individuals who enter the country to engage in criminal behavior, most notably people engaged in narcotics trafficking in one way or another. This group brings with it the violent crime that has ravaged Mexico in particular and is the source of virtually all the concern over the impact of immigration on crime.

Dividing the irregular immigrant community into these two categories helps in understanding the problem and what to do about it. One must begin by asking the question, why do immigrants come illegally to the country? In the case of the economic immigrants, the answer is economic opportunity: jobs. This should not be surprising, given the disparity of wealth between the United States and Mexico and Central America, and it is why economic immigrants migrate worldwide.

This leads to the second question of whether this immigration is good or bad for the United States. Positively, the influx has the demographic of enlarging the available workforce in a U.S. labor market challenged by low birth rates. Negatively, most of these immigrants are not well enough educated or skilled for cutting-edge jobs, and recruitment of these kinds of workers must be aimed at other parts of the world, notably in Asia.

Most irregular economic migrants have been displaced Mexicans and Central Americans who have come to the United States in the pursuit of economic advancement, including the accumulation of enough money to send remittances back to their local communities and families in their former homes. Their migration is like economic migration everywhere, moving from where there is no economic opportunity (jobs) to where such opportunities exist.

The immigration problem and its solution take on a different complexion put in these terms. If there are jobs available that irregular immigrants fill, then there must be a labor need that these immigrants fulfill. Generally, this means low-skill, low-paying jobs, often with one or more of the so-called 3-D characteristics of being dirty, dangerous, or difficult. If there were Americans willing to do these jobs at wages that employers were willing to pay and that produced services at prices consumers could afford, there would not be jobs, and there would be no incentive for migrants to immigrate. That they have done so and continue to do so indicates not only that such opportunities exist, but that they have not been sated. That is simple supply and demand.

A distinction is also made qualitatively about immigrants. Advocates of permitting only documented workers into the country are often implicitly expressing a preference for highly skilled "legal" immigrants like scientists and engineers, about whom there are few objections on other than social grounds. Skilled immigrants are clearly favored and are less controversial, but they quantitatively do not fulfill all the functions that less skilled, "illegal" economic immigrants provide.

The European and Asian Problems

The immigration problem elsewhere in the world is different. The most current concern has been specifically related to the problem of terror that has periodically consumed much of northern North Atlantic Treaty Organization–related Europe, but immigration pressures are also spreading to Asia, and notably China. Also, the reasons for migration more often involve refugees and asylum seekers than it does irregular immigrants. Terrorism containment is more pressing and difficult because of the existence of enclaves of people from terrorist-vulnerable societies and the difficulty of monitoring new terrorists. At the same time, the continuing influx and EU attempts to take over functions that ultimately affect control of borders has become a highly divisive issue.

As events in recent years clearly demonstrate, Europe has been in the throes of an "epidemic" of limited, but often spectacular, terrorist attacks that have caused some divisions both within and between European countries. Europe is more proximate to the Middle East crucible of terrorist activity than is North America, and it has welcomed and accepted people from these countries for generations. Given European demographics and geography, it has a difficult time excluding all those who want to enter the EU area from the Middle East or North Africa. Europe is proximate to the problem, vulnerable to it, and in a difficult position trying to stanch terrorist penetration.

The mix between immigrants and refugees is different in the American and European situations. Due to violent instability in the Muslim world, UNCHR statistics for June 2017 show that the three countries with the most refugees are all in the region close to Europe: Syria with 4.9 million, Afghanistan with 2.7 million, and Somalia with 1.5 million. Of these, the victims of the Syrian Civil War represent the largest and most compelling problem. The nearly 5 million refugees are part of a larger internal displaced persons problem that more than doubles that number.

This juxtaposition creates a unique construction of the problem for Europeans. Countries like Germany both need and already have sizable migrant populations whom they have recruited because of endemic labor shortages. In several European countries, these populations have not been well assimilated, and the isolated ghetto environments in which they reside may be prime recruiting grounds for groups like the Islamic State. Alienating or turning away refugees who might become immigrants is not a good way to build the loyalties that will dampen radicalization of parts of the population.

A special circumstance surrounds how immigrants and refugees enter Europe and the ability of individual countries to regulate their movement and especially their ability to enter the sovereign territory of countries without obtaining permission from the governments of those countries. This problem bears some resemblance to the border issue in the United States. It is probably not a coincidence that this issue is of salience in both the United States and the United Kingdom.

The migration dilemma pits population movement versus the enduring question of sovereignty. Economic immigration needs create the incentive for much of Europe to make it relatively easy to let people into the EU area and to facilitate their movement. Part of the economic union's structure is free movement of people across sovereign boundaries without restriction or even routine monitoring of who comes and goes, which facilitates the greater integration of the union. That means, however, that anyone who can get by whatever barriers there are to entry into the EU territory cannot be excluded from any part of the union. That, in turn, means that individual states lose control over the gatekeeping function of those borders, a loss of sovereign control. This potential loss has been a rallying cry of those promoting stronger border measures in the United States. The events of 2015 and 2016 in the European Union, depicted in the discussion of Brexit, enlivened that same concern in Great Britain as well, and one reason the United Kingdom voted to leave the European Union was to plug the pipeline of immigrants from the continent to the British Isles—to reassert British sovereign control over who enters the country.

The Asian problem is different and centers most dramatically around China. Largely as the result of population control measures undertaken in the last century like the law that limited couples to having no more than one child, the Chinese birth rate has dropped to below replacement levels that will result in a shrinking population in a few years. Demographically, the working-age population is also shrinking, placing great pressures on China to care for its aging population and threatening to slow China's economic miracle. There is a large pool of replacement workers in China's outlying areas like that inhabited by the Uyghurs or in Tibet, but the Han Chinese who rule the country do not trust these nationalities, whom they consider inferiors. The result is a demographically based dilemma that China must solve if it wants to continue being a premier world power.

Conclusion

Human migration is one of humankind's oldest and often most difficult phenomena. Most individuals prefer to live where they have always lived, and being uprooted is often a very traumatic and unpleasant experience. The inducement and trauma were probably less severe when there were far less people and migration was less encumbered by contact with other peoples who viewed the migrating population with fear, suspicion, even hatred. With a world population of over eight billion people, commodious places to migrate are shrinking. Moreover, the entire land surface of the world—other than Antarctica—is now under the sovereign control of some political authority, and those migrating must gain the permission of the occupying authority to take up residence.

The different forms of movement create varying problems and emotions, depending on circumstances. Normally immigration, the most generic description of movement, has been the least traumatic unless the migration of people from one locale to another is so massive as to activate nativist reactions in the receiving country. This has been the pattern in the United States, where people from an earlier generation of immigration have objected when people from somewhere else seek to settle in their sovereign space. The migration of Mexicans and other Central Americans across the southern border is just the most recent example.

Controversy and emotion increase when the migration consists solely or in large measure of refugees seeking safety or asylum from disastrous conditions in their countries of origin. The causes of refugee flows are normally disputed by the government of the originating country, even when the mistreatment of the people who become immigrants is obvious. The decision to accept or reject refugees is difficult for the receiving country, because it likely strains relations with the government of the country of origin and may entangle it in the dynamics of what caused the refugee problem in the first place. The situation is amplified if there are sizable numbers of political asylum seekers among the fleeing refugees. These factors are counterbalanced by humanitarian suffering and deprivation, especially when those seeking refuge are part of an even larger population of internally displaced people in the country of origin. These concerns all swirl around the ongoing tragedy in Syria.

The contemporary situation adds two contradictory factors to the issue: demographic needs and political motives and impacts. The demographic imperative is the need for additional young members of the labor force in developed countries where declining birth rates do not produce adequate numbers of entrants into the job market and where outside augmentation is necessary to keep the economy operating at peak levels. The "pull" involved is especially great for highly skilled, educated immigrants, but it means that people from economically disadvantaged developing world countries are attractive, needed commodities pulled toward the more prosperous but labor deficient developed world.

Immigration has become a partisan political issue in some receiving countries, generally on one or both of two grounds. One is a nativist reaction to the influx of people who are different than the "natives," whether the differences are ethnic, religious, linguistic, cultural, or political. Immigrant differences may be threatening to some people in the receiving countries. This phenomenon is present in European reactions to Middle Eastern immigrants and refugees and in Chinese reactions to and treatment of the Uyghurs and others who live outside the Han core and are somehow different than the Han. It is also true of the objections of some of the America Firsters in the United States.

Finally, the immigration/population movement phenomenon impinges on politics and geopolitics. One of the suspicions within American objections to increased quotas of Central Americans to immigration with a track to citizenship is that the purpose is partisan politics motivated by increasing potential citizens who will vote Democratic when they achieve citizenship. Geopolitically, the need for workforce augmentation drives countries to seek out healthy working-aged immigrants to provide fuel for the fire of economic competitiveness. Altruism and humanitarianism may be pushed aside or relegated to window dressing status in the process, but the result may be to allow people to go from a worse to a better situation, which ideally is what population movement is all about.

Study/Discussion Questions

1. What is immigration? Into what categories are immigrants normally placed? Define, discuss, and compare each to the others.
2. Why do people migrate? Use the "push-pull" analogy to help describe reasons for the differences. Apply this analysis to migration across the U.S.-Mexican frontier.
3. What are the current demographic and political factors affecting migration trends worldwide? Describe each factor in detail. What basic trends arise from these observations?
4. What basic forces cause and impede people from migrating and for receiving countries to resist these migrants? Are the two forces reconcilable? How?
5. Describe the U.S.-Mexico border problem in terms of the threats and positive effects of irregular immigrants crossing that line.
How did Trump's wall affect the situation?
6. What is the nature of the European immigration problem? Discuss this problem in geographic, demographic, and jurisdictional terms, as well as links to terrorism. How did this problem affect Britain's Brexit decision?
7. Why does China face a particularly difficult demographic challenge? Describe the problem in both population distribution and economic terms. Why does it pose a particular problem for the Chinese?
8. Why is the immigration problem likely to increase in the future? How does exclusionary immigration sentiment relate to demographic trends and needs in the developed world? Are anti-immigration and economic/geopolitical pressures more important? Can they be reconciled?

Bibliography

Alden, Edward. *The Closing of the American Border*. New York: HarperCollins, 2009.
Betts, Alexander, and Paul Collier. *Rethinking Refugee Policy in a Changed World*. Oxford, UK: Oxford University Press, 2017.
Bloom, David E. "Population 2020." *Finance and Development* 57, 1 (March 2020). Online Publication of the International Monetary Fund.
Borjas, George J. *Heaven's Door: Immigration Policy and the American Economy*. Princeton, NJ: Princeton University Press, 2016.

———. *We Wanted Workers: Unravelling the Immigration Narrative*. New York: W. W. Norton, 2016.

Chomsky, Avia. *Undocumented: How Immigrants Become Illegal*. Boston: Beacon Press, 2014.

Choucri, Nazli, and Dinsha Mistree. "Globalization, Migration, and New Challenges to Governance." *Current History* 108, no. 717 (April 2009): 173–79.

Collett, Elizabeth. "Destination: Europe: Managing the Migrant Crisis." *Foreign Affairs* 92, no. 2 (March/April 2017): 150–56.

Corr, Anders, ed. *Great Powers, Grand Strategies: The New Game in the South China Sea*. Annapolis, MD: Naval Institute Press, 2018.

Daniels, Roger. *Coming to America: A History of Immigration and Ethnicity in American Life*. New York: Harper Perennials, 2019.

Fiddean-Qasmiyeh, Elena, Gil Loescher, et al. *The Oxford Handbook of Refugee and Forced Migration Studies*. Oxford, UK: Oxford University Press, 2014.

Gest, Justin. *The New Minority: White Working Class Politics in an Age of Inequality*. Oxford, UK: Oxford University Press, 2016.

Goldstone, Jack A. "The New Population Bomb: The Four Megatrends That Will Change the World." *Foreign Affairs* 89, no. 1 (January/February 2010): 31–43.

Haynes, Chris, S. Karthick Ramakrishnan, and Jennifer Merolla. *Framing Immigrants: News Coverage, Public Opinion, and Policy*. Washington, DC: Russell Sage Foundation, 2016.

Hoskin, Marilyn. *Understanding Immigration: Issues and Challenges in the Era of Mass Population Movement*. Albany, NY: SUNY Press, 2017.

Jardina, Ashley. *White Identity Politics* (Cambridge Studies in Public Opinion and Political Psychology). Cambridge, UK: Cambridge University Press, 2019.

Jones, Reece. *Border Walls: Security and the War on Terror in the United States, India, and Israel*. New York: Zed Books, 2012.

Kingsley, Patrick. *The New Odyssey: The Story of the Twenty-First-Century Refugee Crisis*. London: Liveright, 2017.

Koser, Khalid. "Why Immigration Matters." *Current History* 108, no. 717 (April 2009): 147–53.

Maril, Robert Lee. *The Fence: National Security, Public Safety, and Illegal Immigration along the U.S.-Mexican Border*. Lubbock: Texas Tech University Press, 2012.

Martin, Susan F. "Waiting Games: The Politics of US Immigration Reform." *Current History* 108, no. 717 (April 2009): 160–65.

McDonald-Gibson, Charlotte. *Cast Away: True Stories of Survival from Europe's Refugee Crisis*. New York: New Press, 2016.

Money, Jeannette, and Sarah P. Lockhart, eds. *Introduction to International Migration: Population Movements in the 21st Century*. New York and London: Routledge, 2021.

Payan, Terry. *The Three U.S.-Mexico Border Wars: Drugs, Immigration, and Homeland Security*. Westport, CT: Greenwood, 2006.

Rabben, Linda. *Sanctuary Asylum: A Social and Political History*. Seattle: University of Washington Press, 2016.

Rozenthal, Andres. "The Other Side of Immigration." *Current History* 106, no. 697 (February 2007): 89–90.

Snow, Donald M. *Cases in International Relations* (seventh edition). Lanham, MD: Rowman & Littlefield, 2018.

———. *The Middle East, Oil, and the United States National Security Policy*. Lanham, MD: Rowman & Littlefield, 2016.

Van Hear, Nicholas. "The Rise of Refugee Diasporas." *Current History* 108, no. 717 (April 2009): 180–85.

Van Wolleghem, Pierre Georges. *The EU's Policy on the Integration of Migrants: A Case of Soft-Europeanization?* London: Palgrave, 2018.

Wong, Tom K. *The Politics of Immigration: Partnership, Demographic Change, and American National Identity.* Oxford, UK: Oxford University Press, 2016.

16

Stateless Nations
The Fate of the Palestinians and the Kurds

There are numerous sources of international differences that make world politics disorderly, conflicting, occasionally violent, and often unjust for some or all parties. A major category of those imperfections involves the question of rightful territorial possession both within and between states. The political map of the world does not always reflect the territorial jurisdictions that all people and groups feel represent their values. The result is disagreement that can be both very deeply felt and the cause of considerable division and conflict.

Two major manifestations of this form of disagreement dominate the contemporary division and disagreements. One occurs when state boundaries arbitrarily divide members of a group with national aspirations into more than one state. The other exists when a group with national aspirations is housed within a disputed territory where those who exercise power preclude that national group from forming a state. The dynamics of the two situations are different, but their effect is to create stateless nations where self-determination is denied to some who live there. These situations are uncommon, but they often roil more tranquil circumstances otherwise. They are most prevalent in the Middle East, where two stand out. The most publicized and violent is the conflict over a Palestinian state, made more horrific because of the status of Gaza. The other conflict is over Kurdish nationalism, which is less publicized but involves many more people.

The Israeli-Palestinian situation is fundamentally a question of who—Israelis or Palestinians—has a superior sovereign claim over the West Bank of the Jordan River. Israel has occupied this space since 1967 and has established and expanded Israeli settlements in many parts of the region, an arguable de facto claim of sovereign authority. The Palestinian Arab population, many of whom were displaced during the establishment of the Israeli state, claims the territory as the basis of the Palestinian state. Since 2006, when formally joined to the Palestinian claim of statehood, Gaza has become a confounding element in the Palestinian equation. If a Palestinian state comes into being, Hamas-dominated Gaza will expect to be part of the settlement. Gaza, however, does not physically border the West Bank area that presumably would form the core of such a state, and the only way for such a conjunction is a physical corridor across Israel which would effectively partition northern Israel from the rest of the country and is totally unacceptable to the Israelis.

The other example is the Kurds, a distinct and ancient ethnic, nationalist group who inhabit parts of four Middle Eastern states: Turkey, Iraq, Iran, and Syria. They form a majority in each of the areas of those states where they live, but they are in a minority in all four of the countries. Kurdish nationalism is high, and there is virtually unanimous sentiment to carve a state of Kurdistan from the Kurdish regions of each country. Their fate has become more widely known because of their role in defeating the Islamic State (IS).

Principle: Stateless Nations

In ideal world order, national identities and loyalties and political jurisdictions would coincide. All the people with a distinct self-identity would be able to live in a sovereign state with like individuals, and no national group would be denied a territorial state of their own or be forced to live in a state where their national identity was politically denied or the subject of discrimination. Unfortunately, that is not universally the case, and the results are territorial disputes—situations where multiple population groups claim rightful sovereign authority over the same territory. In the worst cases, the competing claims are very deeply held, mutually exclusive, zero-sum advocacies that are irreconcilable among the parties themselves and where outside parties either cannot or will not assert enough power to create and enforce outcomes that will be acceptable to some, and preferably all, of the affected parties.

These situations pose a fundamental challenge to the international order. Internal conflicts have become the most common form of organized violence (war) in the contemporary international system, eclipsing and virtually eliminating traditional wars between states as sources of violent turmoil. Many of these situations arise either from multinationalist or irredentist roots and have arisen at least in part from the efforts of peoples in decolonized locales to come to grips with questions about the physical boundaries and appropriate holders of sovereign legitimacy in different areas. The losers in these situations are members of stateless nations: groups with a national self-identity that lack a territorial home of their own.

Irredentism, Multinationalism, and Developing World Conflicts

The key element in understanding the maladies that plague stateless nations begins with the dichotomy between the anthropological term "nation" and the political and legal term "state." The international system is sometimes said to be composed of "nation-states," suggesting a conjunction of the two concepts that would produce stable sovereign entities and result in minimal instability and violence. The problem is that, in a literal sense, there are very few pure nation-states, and in the places where the connection breaks down, instability, often involving territorial boundaries, is most likely to occur.

The term "nation" refers to the identification people have with others. The nation is the primary point of loyalty many people have, and this identification extends to political loyalties to the state or some other entity. No list is comprehensive and not all nationally defined groups possess all the characteristics, but common indicators of national identification include race, ethnicity, language, religion, common territorial habitation, and shared historical experience. The national identity that groups adopt is often the basis for their loyalty to and support for or opposition to the state.

The most common form of discontinuity between the concepts of nation and state occurs where at least two nationally self-identified national groups live within a state, the basic definition of multinationalism. The terms multiethnic and multicultural nationalism, both of which convey much of the essence of nationality, are sometimes used to distinguish this political connotation of multinationalism in developing countries.

This situation is common to almost all the countries of the developing world and, to a lesser degree, in the developed world as well. Writing in 1993, for instance, Welsh surveyed the world's countries and concluded that 160 of the then 180 recognized sovereign states were multinational in one way or another. It becomes a destabilizing source of territorial dispute when one or more of the groups decide they want to change the physical or political balance by eliminating, suppressing, or displacing one or more other national groups who reside in the state. These motives can result in internal violence to overthrow the offending national group or even to secede.

Multinationalist-inspired instability is the most common form of disconnection that underlies territorial disputes, but it is neither the only one nor even, in some cases, the most difficult and intractable form that territorial disputes take. Another form, often associated with particularly difficult, intractable territorial situations, arises from instances of irredentism.

Irredentism is a term with an interesting genesis. It derives from the Italian word that means "unredeemed," and it was first used to describe aspirations about Italian lands during the process of unification of Italy in 1870. It is now used more generically to describe what the *Free Dictionary* calls a movement or sentiment the purpose of which is "the recovery of territory culturally or historically related to one's nation but now subject to a foreign government." If the broad purpose of multinationalist efforts is to alter the state to make it more congenial to some or all the national groups that reside in a given sovereign territory, irredentists challenge the rightful possession and exercise of sovereignty by groups in territories they consider rightfully theirs.

The fundamental purpose and impact of these groups is to attack the problem of stateless nations. Groups making irredentist claims are basically arguing one of two pernicious conditions prevent them from achieving what they regard as their rightful national endowment. One of these is territorial occupation that prevents their assertion of sovereign authority over territory that would allow them to serve as a sovereign state. The other is the situation where territory they view as rightfully theirs is within the unjust sovereign jurisdiction of several states and where their intent and purpose is to unite those areas into a single state. These two situations form the bases for the two applications in the next section.

Statelessness can be the basis for violence and instability when a stateless group asserts its determined intent to alter the boundaries of political jurisdictions so that they can refigure the map and create a state of their own. This determination will almost invariably be rejected and resisted by political authorities in the existing territory in which the new state is proposed, and the clash between contending parties will often result in internal violence. The alternative is frustration on the part of members of the stateless group or the group it proposes to replace. Both outcomes are destabilizing for the international system, because the result can be internal warfare that destabilizes the area involved and can result in an intractable conflict and violence.

Territorial disputes arising from statelessness are not common in contemporary international relations, but where they exist, they are particularly difficult, furtive, and violent. The question of what group has the legitimate claim to exercising sovereignty in a given territory has various roots and longer or shorter histories depending on the region and the conflict. All share a commonality: the forced cohabitation of antagonistic groups in the same territorial space and the desire of one group or another to break away and seek its own separate state. The disputes tend to be irresolvable in any acceptable political way, because the contesting groups of people dislike or distrust one another to the point they cannot amicably reach mutually acceptable outcomes. The longest lasting conflicts tend to be in the Middle East, where the roots of conflicts can be traced back over millennia and where the basis of disagreement and hatred can be traced to tribal differences, often influenced by religious factors that have defined and deepened the disagreements across time.

Application: Palestine and Kurdistan

Two conflicts exemplify statelessness especially well because of their unique characteristics, because they are both major irritants to regional and world peace, and because they each represent the territorial issue of being contests in which at least one aspirant is a stateless nation. They differ in the context in which the claim to statehood is based and in the structure of the problem and alternative solutions.

They also differ in important factual ways. The Palestinian quest for statehood has deep historical roots in the more or less constant struggle for possession of the various territories included in the Levant, but their current dilemma has its roots in post–World War II events, notably the establishment of the state of Israel and the Israeli occupation of territory in 1967 on the West Bank of the Jordan River that the Palestinians (and most of the international community) have long claimed as the site of Palestine. Structurally, it is primarily a dispute between Israel and the Palestinians, and it currently has a particularly complex and seemingly intractable interactive element in the status of Gaza. The Kurdish desire for statehood is more long-standing, and it is a condition in which the Kurds have consistently been denied the right to self-determination. The current problem has its roots in the settlement of World War I, where Kurdistan was made part of several other states. Structurally, it is a contest between the Kurds and those states, notably Turkey, Iraq, Iran, and Syria. In a sense, Kurdistan already exists, but it does as an area within those four states, none of which is willing to allow the Kurds to unite those areas into the sovereign state of Kurdistan. The international community, with the notable exception of the former Trump administration, accepts the Palestinian claim and advocates an end of the Israeli occupation of the West Bank. There is also considerable support for Kurdistan, but it is measured because of opposition of North Atlantic Treaty Organization member Turkey and non-Kurdish areas of other states the Kurds hope to incorporate.

The Case of Palestine

The plight of the Palestinians has been a major issue between Israel and the Palestinian Arabs at least since the end of World War II and even before. It is essentially a territorial dispute between the Jewish people of Israel and the mostly Sunni Muslim Arabs who think of themselves as Palestinians. Israel is an accepted sovereign state, but previously the Jews were a stateless nation with a difficult, often tragic history punctuated by Hitler's attempted extinction of the Jewish people in the 1930s and 1940s. Many surviving European Jews heeded the call for a Zionist exodus and ended up in what was then considered Palestine, part of the British mandated zone from the breakup of the Ottoman Empire. Already living in that area (largely in peace with the Jewish settlers already there) were the Palestinian Arabs, another classic stateless nation that sought a sovereign home in the same region. Historic Palestine was the area both wished to claim as their own.

The Arena and the Contestants

There is not universal agreement on exactly what territory conclusively defines Palestine, a common regional malady in the Middle East due to the many states and empires that have ruled all or parts of the region since antiquity. In a general sense, the area is thought of in contemporary times as being composed of Israel (pre-1967), the West Bank (including East Jerusalem), and the Gaza Strip. It is not a physically large area: internationally accepted (pre-1967) Israel is about the size of New Jersey, the West Bank is about the size of Delaware, and Gaza is a narrow peninsula along the eastern Mediterranean coast northward from the Sinai Peninsula of Egypt. Gaza is about twice the size of Washington, DC.

The largest physical part of the territorial dispute is the West Bank. Its continued possession by Israel was central to former prime minister Benjamin (Bibi) Netanyahu's dream of Greater Israel and the attraction of more of world Jewry to the Israeli state. Without the West Bank, Israel does not consider the country whole: it is not stateless, but neither is there a complete Israeli state that fully marries nation and state. Netanyahu, recently deposed leader of Israel, has been the leading proponent of this position. For Palestinians, the situation is stark. Without the West Bank, there is no sovereign Palestinian entity other than the Gaza Strip. Israelis may not enjoy an entirely fulfilled marriage of statehood and nationality without the West Bank. The Palestinians are a stateless nation without full sovereign control of the territory they think of as Palestine.

Pre-1967 Israel and the West Bank are distinct in terms of population. The population size of pre-1967 Israel is approximately six million, of whom about five million are Jewish and the rest are mostly Palestinian Arabs and a small number of Christians. The West Bank, on the other hand, has a Palestinian majority of about three million and, including East Jerusalem, a Jewish population of nearly a half million settlers. Gaza has a population of about two million, virtually all of whom are Palestinian Arabs. The detailed numbers are not precise, but when the three parts of historic Palestine are combined, there are slightly more Palestinian Arabs than Jews in that population. Demographic trends (the Arab population is growing at a faster rate than the Jewish population) are unfavorable to the Israelis, and this fact also affects the attractiveness of various solutions to the territorial dispute. Among other things, Jewish migration is the way to tilt the demographics in Israel's favor. That ties demographics to territorial claim, since essentially the only place to accommodate those immigrants is in the occupied territories.

Stripped of its historical and religious trappings, the dispute between the Israelis and Palestinians over the West Bank is thus conceptually relatively straightforward: who has the superior claim to sovereign domain over Palestine? Part of the question has been effectively decided. There is little controversy about Israeli sovereignty over territories ceded to the Jewish state in 1948 and as expanded up until the 1967 war. There are also many individual claims by former Palestinian land and homeowners over the rightful ownership of property in Israel that they abandoned when they fled and which were subsequently claimed by Israelis.

That leaves the West Bank, which is an ongoing problem for two basic reasons. The first is the general question of Israeli settlements on the West Bank. These settlements are enclaves (generally on the best land, which effectively means land with adequate water under it) and are residential areas reserved for Jews, often immigrants. They are not claimed as sovereign territory, but they have become such permanent-looking features that it is increasingly impossible to see Israel abandoning them to a Palestinian state. Arab control over the West Bank would likely entail displacement of the settlers. The other problem is the old city of East Jerusalem. Both Israel and the Palestinians claim it as their national capital. It rests along the border between Israel and the West Bank, and it has been the destination of much Jewish settlement outside the pre-1967 boundaries. The religious and political significance of Jerusalem make it possibly the most intractable part of the territorial dispute. The Gaza Strip is a particular problem, since it has no border with the West Bank and transit through Israel is necessary to get from Gaza to the West Bank.

Possible Solutions: One State, Two States, or Conflict without End?

The question of Palestinian statehood and where to locate a sovereign Palestinian state has been one of the most nettlesome international problems of the post–World War II period. Every American president since 1948 has become involved in its solution, and all have failed. In his first pronouncement on the subject, President Trump intoned that he could live with either a one-state or a two-state solution (the only viable alternatives), whichever the parties could agree to. His pronouncement was immediately dismissed as disingenuous: the heart of the problem is that the sides have never been able to agree on *any* solution.

The basic alternatives are easy to state but have proven impossibly difficult to achieve. The first is a one-state solution, where all three of the constituent parts of greater Palestine (Israel, West Bank, and Gaza) are incorporated into a single state. This solution is opposed by the Palestinians, who are convinced the Israelis would dominate such a state, and by some Israelis who fear that demographics ensure they will become a minority in that state. It does, however, solve the problem of Jewish immigration onto the West Bank and of the status of East Jerusalem, which would become the capital of the unified state. The two-state solution has had the backing of virtually all the international community, but it has faded as an attainable outcome for the Palestinian people. It calls for an independent Palestine on the West Bank and Gaza and an independent Israel consisting of the pre-1967 territory, some settlements along the border, and presumably some part of East Jerusalem. Most of the opposition comes from factions (including the Netanyahu regime) who favor a concept of Greater Israel and who fear that a sovereign Palestine would be a launching pad for terrorist activities against the Jewish state.

There are four pivotal considerations that affect disposition of the conflict. The first is Israel's demographic and geopolitical dilemma. Israel was established and prides itself as a state that is both democratic and Jewish. The problem is how to remain both under different territorial solutions. If there is a single-state solution, demographics work in their disfavor. If Israel remains democratic, the Arabs will soon outnumber the Jews in such a state, and the Jews will be in the minority, potentially leaving the outcome a democratic but non-Jewish state. If the Jews renounce one-man, one-vote democracy, the state can remain Jewish, but not fully democratic. The two-state solution may reduce Israel geographically to something like its pre-1967 size, but it will remain solidly Jewish (a five-to-one ratio of Jews in the population), allowing Israel to remain *both* Jewish and democratic.

The second is Israeli security, and it has two parts. The first, already discussed, is the vulnerability Israel faces of being cut in two by hostile forces attacking west from the West Bank. The second is the fear that a hostile West Bank and a sovereign Palestine will serve as a sanctuary for terrorists attacking Israel. This fear also motivated Israel to build a barrier fence along the West Bank frontier to regulate Palestinian movement in and out of Israel. Netanyahu proposed a semi-sovereign Palestine with occupying Israel Defense Forces contingents on the West Bank for security purposes. Militant factions controlled by the Hamas-dominated regime in Gaza have harassed and attacked Israel as well. Virtually all outsiders dismiss this proposal.

The third, and ultimately most vexing, problem is East Jerusalem. It cannot be the capital of two countries, and neither side is willing to accept their exclusion while it becomes the other's capital. Given the emotional ties both have to religious sites in parts of Jerusalem, neither can abandon it. That leaves two unhappy options. One is to partition the city so part is in Israel and part in Palestine. Conceivably, one zone could become the capital of Israel and the other the capital of Palestine. Virtually no one thinks such a solution could work. The other possibility is either to declare Jerusalem a neutral city-state, possibly under international jurisdiction (which has been tried unsuccessfully) or to declare that it will not be the capital of either country. Neither Israelis or Palestinians finds this outcome satisfactory.

Fourth, and possibly most intractable, is the problem of Gaza. The Gaza Strip is a narrow patch of land bordering on the Mediterranean Sea on the west, Egypt in the south, and north and east by Israel. With an estimated population of around two million Palestinian Arabs on a land mass roughly twice the size of the District of Columbia, it has been technically part of the territory of Palestine since 2016 (it was previously part of Egypt). It has been contentious, fighting with Israel in 2007, 2008, 2014, and most recently 2021.

The major problem is what to do with Gaza. The basic options are independence or union as a part of Palestine. Neither is ideal. Given its size and proximity to Israel, an independent Gaza would likely be nonviable economically and subject to what amounts to bullying by the Israelis. Integration in a West Bank Palestine is the obvious solution, but it has two drawbacks. One is whether the Palestinian state will ever come into being. The "two-state solution" that would create Palestine has become what Shikaki calls a dead letter: it is "over," he argues in a May 2021 *Foreign Affairs* online article, and many agree. The other is that Gaza and the West Bank are separated by part of Israel and can be reached only by driving across or flying above sovereign Israeli territory—in effect creating a corridor to allow such passage. Israel absolutely rejects any such notion, because they do not trust the Palestinians and because the corridor would dissect Israel into two parts, a prospect the avoidance of which has always been a vital interest since independence in 1948. The Gaza problem is thus intractable but must somehow be resolved if there is to be a Palestinian state.

I have called this problem "irresolvable" in previous editions of this text. The enmity and distrust between the two sides on virtually all issues makes an amicable division of a dispute over a parcel of land the size of Delaware a major international issue. Because the Palestinians lack the physical power to wrest control from Israel, they cannot assert their claim militarily. Thus, until the sides decide that resolution and the hopeful peace that will follow are more important than what divides them, the result will continue to be Palestinian statelessness.

The Case of Kurdistan

The Kurdish quest to end its long statelessness is physically more imposing than the Israeli-Palestinian conflict: it spans a longer period of time, it involves territory and people in four Middle Eastern states, and it has been and continues to be a major source of geopolitical struggle between the Kurds and all those countries where the Kurds live and in which they claim statehood for Kurdistan. Global awareness appears and then disappears. It arose in the early 1990s when Iraq's threats of genocidal retribution drove thousands of Iraqi Kurds into uneasy exile in Turkey. It has resurfaced with the prominent role that Kurdish *pesh merga* territory-protecting militias played in the campaign against the IS.

Table 16.1. Kurdish Population Distribution

Location	Designation	Estimated Population
Turkey	Northern Kurdistan	18 million
Iraq	Southern Kurdistan	5 million
Syria	Western Kurdistan (Rojava)	2 million
Iran	Eastern Kurdistan	8 million
All Other		2–3 million
Total		35–36 million

Source: The Kurdish Project, 2016.

The Kurds are concentrated principally in four countries. They are most numerous in Eastern and Southeastern Turkey (Northern Kurdistan), and their other major concentrations are in Northern Iraq (Southern or Iraqi Kurdistan), Northern Syria (Western Kurdistan or Rojava), and Western Iran (Eastern or Iranian Kurdistan). Census figures are not very precise, but the number of Kurds within territories claimed as part of a Kurdish state is in the range of thirty-five million, which means that were Kurdistan to come into being, its population would be roughly that of Saudi Arabia and greater than Iraq (after the Kurds currently counted as Iraqi were subtracted from the Iraqi population). Its distribution is summarized in table 16.1.

The Dream of and Demand for a Kurdistan

The concerted movement toward Kurdish statehood emerged in the early twentieth century, and its progress (or lack thereof) has been highlighted by three major events: the Versailles peace negotiations of 1919, the plight of the Iraqi Kurds after Saddam Hussein threatened their slaughter in 1991, and most recently, the prominent role of the Kurdish *pesh merga* (Kurdish for "those who face death") in defeating the IS Caliphate. These calendar highlights do not define the longer-standing desire of the Kurds for statehood so much as they provide road markers of international awareness of the Kurdish situation.

Each is significant for a different reason. A Kurdish delegation petitioned the peacemakers in Paris in 1919 to create a sovereign state of Kurdistan in the Kurdish area as part of carving up the Ottoman Empire. There were multiple claimants to the areas, including European powers like Britain and France, former regional powers like Persia, and the Turkish successor state to the Ottomans. Ultimately the claims of non-Kurds prevailed. The precedent of denying the Kurds what they viewed as their destiny was established, but at least a larger part of the world became aware of their fate.

In 1991, after his stunning eviction from Iraq and rebellions against him (in, among other places, the Kurdish region of Iraq), Saddam Hussein threatened to renew chemical warfare and other attacks against the Kurds in reprisal. Fearing their extinction at the hands of their own president, thousands fled to Turkey. Their plight was widely reported on global television, and the United States, in order to please the Turks, announced a no-fly zone in the Kurdish region from which Iraqi forces were excluded to entice the Kurds to go home. In 1992, the Kurdish area was deemed autonomous and the first Kurdish Regional Government (KRG) was elected.

The final element has been the Kurdish role in the fight against the Caliphate. Iraqi and Syrian Kurdistan were prominent parts of the land initially conquered by the IS as it spread eastward toward Baghdad, and especially in the early going, Iraqi *pesh merga* militia forces were the most effective (for a time virtually the *only* effective) barriers to the IS offensive. This experience called for much further Western reliance on the Kurds to push back the Caliphate. With the Caliphate effectively dissembled, the Kurds are bound to expect some territorial compensation for their efforts, and the international system will have difficulty denying it to them. If history is a guide, however, they will find some way to frustrate Kurdish aspirations.

The Geopolitical Resistance

Kurdish irredentism is opposed by all four of the existing states from which Kurdistan would be forged. Resistance to the idea is highest in the two states, Turkey and Iraq, where the Kurds are most prominent and where secession would be most harmful to the existing state. The geopolitics of the region plays into these considerations, and although there is considerable support for the Kurdish cause, it is difficult to find outsiders who can or will offer their wholehearted support for the Kurds.

Turkey. Opposition to Kurdish self-determination is strongest in Turkey for several reasons. Kurds constitute roughly 20 percent of the Turkish population, making them numerically close to half of the population of a future Kurdistan. Kurdish majority territories are concentrated in the eastern part of the country, including the Anatolia region that has been developed for its water resources and as a tourist destination. The Kurdish area is about the size of the state of Washington in a country that is slightly larger than Texas. In addition, the Kurds, principally under the leadership of the Kurdish Workers Party (PKK), have waged a civil war/terrorist campaign against the government in Ankara that was formally ended in 2013. The PKK, however, is Marxist and the Turks accuse them of collusion with Russia, also a Turkish rival. Turkey routinely accuses the Kurds of being terrorists. Fighting between the PKK and the government flares up occasionally.

The Turks oppose *any* Kurdistan more than any other regional country. Their motivation arises from the belief that a Kurdish state anywhere would be a platform for encouraging secession by the Turkish Kurds, which is almost certainly true. As a result, the Turks have not been particularly supportive of Iraqi *pesh merga* military efforts against IS, which they feel could be a launching pad to establish a fully independent Iraqi Kurdish state along their border. A similar rationale exists toward Syrian Kurdistan, and the Turks, who fundamentally oppose the Caliphate, find themselves in the anomalous situation of opposing (or not supporting) a primary opponent (Iraqi Kurds) of an enemy they would like to see destroyed (the Caliphate).

Iraq. Since Saddam Hussein's atrocities against the Kurds and especially since the American invasion and occupation, the epicenter of attention to Kurdistan has centered on the Kurdish Autonomous Region of Northern Iraq. The region is home to roughly five million Kurds, and since 2003, they have been increasingly self-reliant and independent of the central government in Baghdad. Their territory abuts the Kurdish regions of all the other candidate countries and contains significant petroleum reserves in the Zagros Mountain region that makes it valuable to Iraq. The Kurds are linguistically and ethnically distinct from the Sunni and Shiite Arabs of the rest of the country. Moreover, there have been predictions that Iraq, which is a country with no history or tradition of nationhood, could break apart into three countries, and there is little doubt that the Kurds would be the first to secede. The KRG has progressively acted like a sovereign government in all but name (its border with the rest of Iraq, for instance, is controlled by the *pesh merga*, who act as border guards). This situation would likely form the basis for a fully independent and unified Kurdistan.

Iran and Syria. Iran has the second-most Kurds (about eight million) and the second-most territory that is potentially part of any state. It contrasts with the others in that it is not Arab or Sunni. Its people are ethnically like the Kurds (whose language is akin to Persian), but they share different religious traditions. In popular discourse, there have been far fewer publicized separatist pronouncements coming from Eastern Kurdistan than from Turkey or Iraq, although the emergence of an independent Kurdistan in Iraq would certainly arouse demands among Iranian and Syrian Kurds to join the new state. The Kurds are least numerous in Syria (about two million), and they live in remote, lightly populated parts of Eastern Syria contiguous with Turkey about which the Syrians have shown little interest. Liberating territory in Syria occupied by the Caliphate benefits Syrian Kurds and will likely stimulate demands for an independent state with the expulsion of IS from the region.

Conclusion

Territorial disputes involving stateless nations are among the most difficult, vexing problems that confront the international system in a world of imperfectly drawn sovereign state boundaries that divide people who want to live together or aggregate people who do not. The problem of multinational states and their trials have been the cause of many ongoing and potential violent conflicts. The situations where a territory is coveted by more than one party (Palestine) and where sovereign boundaries keep nationalities in separate jurisdictions when they yearn for a common national home (Kurdistan) demonstrate the desperation and furtiveness of these difficulties.

Territorial disputes are truly zero-sum situations where one side "wins" at the expense of the other. Compromise is difficult because one side controls the territory at the other's expense. Turkish Anatolia cannot simultaneously be part of Turkey and Kurdistan, and the West Bank cannot be sovereign Palestine and part of Israel at the same time.

The situations are geopolitically distinct. The continued control of the Occupied Territories by Israel is opposed by virtually all countries except the United States, and actions by the Trump administration (Jerusalem, Golan, and sanctions against Iran) have undoubtedly emboldened the Netanyahu government but do not engender the same enthusiasm in President Biden, as evidenced by his pressure on Israel to cease its May 2021 bombardment of Gaza. It is problematic how Israeli policy might be affected by a return to a less supportive U.S. government. Moreover, volatile Israeli politics affect what can happen. Netanyahu lost the prime minister's position in June 2021, and this event, combined with the defeat of Trump in 2020, has a potentially significant impact on the Israeli position. The new Israeli government won by only a single vote in the Knesset, so things could change, and yet another consideration has been added to an already explosive situation.

The Kurds have more international advantages. The KRG has been functioning for over a quarter century and provides a governmental framework for a viable Kurdish state in the autonomous parts of Iraq and beyond, and Kurdish oil reserves could help underwrite its viability. It also faces a formidable array of states, led by Turkey, who vehemently oppose the Kurdish dream. The performance of the *pesh merga* in the defeat of the IS Caliphate, however, gives them useful international support. For both the Palestinians and the Kurds, however, modifying the terms of the zero-sum game is a difficult task.

Study/Discussion Questions

1. What is the heart of the problem of territorial disputes? Discuss the problem of why they exist and why they are so difficult to resolve.

2. What are multinationalism and irredentism? Discuss these as outcomes of the post–World War I and II worlds.

3. Why are territorial disputes important phenomena in contemporary international relations, especially given changes in the overall pattern of violence in the world?

4. Why are territorial disputes so difficult to resolve to the satisfaction of all claimants? How do the Israeli-Palestinian and Kurdish problems illustrate this difficulty?

5. Discuss the structure of the Israeli-Palestinian dispute. Include a discussion of Palestine and Gaza on the structure of this conflict.

6. What are the possible outcomes to the Israeli-Palestine dispute? Describe each. Why has it proven so difficult to reach an agreement?

7. Who are the Kurds? Where do they live? Why do they desire the creation of a Kurdistan, and from where would it be carved?

8. Who opposes the creation of a Kurdish state, and what is the basis of their objections? Given the resistance that exists, what are the prospects on an independent Kurdistan?

Bibliography

Agha, Hussein, and Ahmed Sami Khaladi. "A Palestinian Reckoning: Time for a New Beginning." *Foreign Affairs* 100, no. 2 (March/April 2021): 129–41.

Allsop, Harriet. *The Kurds of Syria: Political Parties and Identity in the Middle East.* London: I. B. Tauris, 2015.

Ambrosio, Thomas. *Irredentism: Ethnic Conflict and International Politics.* Westport, CT: Praeger, 2001.

Atef, Maged. "Sinai Suffering: The Peninsula Has Become a Breeding Ground for Terror." *Foreign Affairs Snapshot* (online), March 13, 2017.

Aziz, Mahir. *The Kurds of Iraq: Nationalism and Identity in Kurdish Iraq.* London: I. B. Tauris, 2014.

Benn, Auf. "The End of the Old Israel: How Netanyahu Has Transformed the Nation." *Foreign Affairs* 95, no. 4 (July/August 2016): 16–27.

Brown, Nathan J. "The Palestinians' Receding Dream of Statehood." *Current History* 110, no. 740 (December 2011): 345–51.

Carter, Jimmy. *Palestine: Peace Not Apartheid.* New York: Simon and Schuster, 2006.

Chaliland, Gerard, and Michael Pallis. *A People without a Country: The Kurds and Kurdistan.* Northampton, MA: Interlink Publishing Group, 1993.

Chazam, Naomi, ed. *Irredentism and International Politics.* Boulder, CO: Lynne Rienner, 1991.

Della Pergola, Sergio. "Israel's Existential Predicament: Population, Territory, and Identity." *Current History* 109, no. 731 (December 2010): 383–89.

Dowty, Alan. *Israel/Palestine* (Hot Spots in Global Politics) (fourth edition). London: Polity Press, 2017.

Eppel, Michael. *A People without a State: The Kurds from the Rise of Islam to the Dawn of Nationalism.* Austin: University of Texas Press, 2016.

Erakat, Noura. *Justice for Some: Law and the Question of Palestine.* Palo Alto, CA: Stanford University Press, 2019.

Gelvin, James L. *The Israeli-Palestinian Conflict: One Hundred Years of War* (third edition). Cambridge, UK: Cambridge University Press, 2014.

Gunter, M. Michael. *The Kurds: A Modern History.* Princeton, NJ: Markus Weiner Publishers, 2015.

Hammond, Jeremy R. *Obstacle to Peace: The U.S. Role in the Israeli-Palestine Conflict.* New York: Worldview Publications, 2016.

Izady, Mehrdad. *The Kurds: A Concise History and Fact Book.* London: Taylor and Francis, 2015.

Khalidi, Rashid. "The Palestinians Will Not—and Cannot—Be Ignored: A Revived Palestinian Nationalist Movement Could Upend the Status Quo." *Foreign Affairs* (online), June 30, 2021.

King, Diane E. *Kurdistan on the Global Stage: Kinship, Land, and Community in Iraq.* New Brunswick, NJ: Rutgers University Press, 2013.

Livni, Tzipi. "Anger and Hope: A Conversation with Tzipi Livni." *Foreign Affairs* 95, no. 4 (July/August 2016): 10–15.

Masalha, Nur. *Palestine: A Four Thousand Year History.* London: Zed Books, 2018.

Meiselas, Susan. *Kurdistan: In the Shadow of History.* Chicago, IL: University of Chicago Press, 2008.

Muravchik, Joshua. *Making David into Goliath: How the World Turned against Israel.* New York: Encounter Books, 2015.

Peleg, Ilan. *The Democratization of the Hegemonic State.* Cambridge, UK: Cambridge University Press, 2007.

Phillips. David L. *The Kurdish Spring: A New Map of the Middle East.* New York: Routledge, 2017.

Ross, Dennis. *Doomed to Succeed: The U.S.-Israeli Relationship from Truman to Obama.* New York: Farrar, Straus, Giroux, 2015.

Shaked, Ayelet. "Ministering Justice: A Conversation." *Foreign Affairs* 95, no. 4 (July/August 2016): 2–8.

Shavit, Ari. *My Promised Land: The Triumph and Tragedy of Israel.* New York: Spiegel and Grau, 2015.

Shikaki, Khalil. "Fighting in Gaza the Start of a More Violent Era: The Search for a Two-State Solution Is Over." *Foreign Affairs* (online), May 19, 2021.

Smith, Charles D. *Palestine and the Arab-Israeli Conflict. A History with Documents* (ninth edition). New York: St. Martin's Press, 2016.

Snow, Donald M. *The Case against Military Intervention: Why We Do It and Why It Fails.* New York and London: Routledge, 2016.

———. *The Middle East, Oil, and the U.S. National Security Policy: Intractable Conflicts, Impossible Solutions.* Lanham, MD: Rowman & Littlefield, 2016.

———. *National Security* (seventh edition). New York and London: Routledge, 2020.

Tal, Alon. *The Land Is Full: Addressing Overpopulation in Israel.* New Haven, CT: Yale University Press, 2016.

Van Creveld, Martin L. *The Land of Blood and Honey: The Rise of Modern Israel.* New York: Thomas Dunne Books, 2010.

Welsh, David. "Domestic Politics and Ethnic Politics," in Michael E. Brown, ed. *Ethnic Conflict and International Security.* Princeton, NJ: Princeton University Press, 1993.

17

Global Climate Change
Paris and Beyond

Global climate change represents one of the clearest, yet most controversial, truly international issues facing the world. It is a problem that cannot be solved by the individual efforts of states, but it must be done collectively if it is to be done successfully. It is controversial because there is substantial political, if not scientific, disagreement both about the nature and severity of the problem and over the structure and content of proposed solutions to climate change. President Trump was the most prominent of the skeptics when he was in office.

This chapter examines the problem from two related vantage points. The first is the nature and extent of global warming, what does and does not require controlling, who the most egregious offenders are, and how it might be solved. The second is the controversial process surrounding international efforts to deal with global climate change. The original lightning rod for this effort was the Kyoto Protocol of 1997, which expired in 2012. Attempts to implement and move beyond the actions prescribed in that treaty failed until the Paris Climate Agreement of 2015, from which the Trump administration withdrew in June 2017 and which the Biden administration rejoined as one of its first acts of the new president in 2021.

The issue of climate change—the extent to which the earth's climate is gradually warming due to human actions or natural processes—is one of the most controversial, divisive, and yet consequential problems facing international relations in the twenty-first century. No one, of course, favors a gradual or precipitous change in global climate because the consequences could be catastrophic. The issue contains a perceptual disconnect. Over 97 percent of all disinterested scientists agree the problem is real. Thus yet, as Helm points out, "the public gets more indifferent or even skeptical." Most of this skepticism is American and is politically motivated.

Regardless of how serious the problem is, global warming is clearly a classic, full-blown transnational issue. As Eileen Claussen and Lisa McNeilly put it, "Climate change is a global problem that demands a global solution because emissions from one country can impact the climate in all other countries." Global warming, in other words, will be curbed internationally or likely it will not be overcome at all.

The underlying dynamic, if not its seriousness, can be easily stated. Global warming, the major manifestation of climate change, is the direct result of the release of so-called greenhouse gases into the atmosphere in volumes that are beyond the capacity of the ecosystem to eliminate naturally. There are several greenhouse gases. The largest part of the problem comes from the burning of fossil fuels such as petroleum, natural gas, coal, and wood, which releases carbon dioxide, methane, and nitrous oxide into the air in large quantities. According to U.S. Environmental Protection Agency figures in 2017, emissions from fossil fuel burning and "forestry" account for 76 percent, methane for 16 percent, and nitrous oxides for 6 percent of emissions. The natural method of containing the amount of carbon dioxide and its ultimate damaging residue, carbon, in the atmosphere is the absorption and conversion of that gas in so-called carbon sinks, which separate the two elements (carbon and oxygen) and release them harmlessly back into the atmosphere. Both levels of emission and carbon dioxide elimination are parts of the problem.

The cumulative effect is that there is more carbon dioxide in the atmosphere than there used to be, and it acts as a greenhouse gas. What this means is that as heat from the sun radiates off the earth and attempts to return in an adequate amount into space to maintain current climate, carbon dioxide acts as a "trap" that retains the heat in the atmosphere rather than allowing it to escape. This blanketing effect keeps excess heat in the atmosphere.

The expired Kyoto Protocol of 1997 (named after the Japanese city where it was finalized) was the most visible symbol of reaction to global warming and has been the lightning rod of the procedural and substantive debate over it. The heart of the protocol was a series of guidelines for the reduction of emissions almost exclusively by the developed countries. The requirements of the agreement were controversial because of the differential levels of reduction they imposed, especially on the United States. The Kyoto Protocol expired in 2012, creating a sense of concern among supporters of international attempts to control climate change through international regulation and a sense of relief among skeptics. The emphasis eventually moved to Paris, where an agreement was reached in December 2015. Like its predecessors, the Paris Climate Agreement has been controversial, and its future effectiveness was clouded by the announcement of the U.S. withdrawal from the agreement in 2017 and reentry in 2021.

Principle: Global Climate Change

The urgency and importance of the Paris climate accord depends vitally on the dangerousness and consequences of the problem. The debate over climate change is contentious. At least three related factors make a calm, rational debate over the extent and consequences of global warming difficult to conduct. The first has been the absence of immediate consequences of whatever change is occurring. Over the past quarter century or more, global warming has indeed been occurring, but until recently the effects have been so gradual and generally small that either they have gone unnoticed by most people until very recently or have not been definitively attributable to the phenomenon. As the frequency of violent climatologically induced events like tornadoes and hurricanes and weather fluctuations have increased, the connection is becoming harder to ignore. Global warming is blamed for numerous contemporary events, from the melting of polar ice caps to recent patterns of violent weather, but there is lingering disagreement about whether manmade global warming is the underlying culprit.

Second, there are abundant scientific disagreements about the parameters of the problem and its solution. Some of the disagreement is honest, some possibly self-interested, but for every dire prediction about future consequences, there is a rebuttal from somewhere. This debate often becomes shrill and accusatory, leading to confusion in the public about what to believe.

Third, almost all the projections have until recently been sufficiently far in the future to allow considerable disagreement and to discourage resolution. The scientific evidence to date may be strong, but the actual consequences were distant enough that extrapolation was subject to adequate uncertainty that some scientists can take the same data and reach diametrically opposed conclusions. The window of consequences has narrowed. Many scientists now argue that actions in the current decade of the 2020s could be crucial if harmful change is to be avoided.

Parameters of Debate

That global climate is changing is not contested on any side of the debate over global warming. The Intergovernmental Panel on Climate Change (IPCC) has investigated the extent to which this has happened in the past and has concluded that the average surface temperature of the earth increased by about one degree Fahrenheit during the twentieth century and "that most of the warming observed over the past 50 years is attributable to human activities." (Much of the IPCC material in this section is from the 2001 report of Group I–III of the IPCC, cited in the bibliography.) Extrapolating from trends in the last century, the IPCC predicted additional warming between 2.2 to 10 degrees Fahrenheit (1.4 to 5.8 degrees Celsius) in this century. The primary culprits are the greenhouse gases cited in the Kyoto Protocol that result from deforestation (and its destruction of carbon sinks), energy production from the combustion of fossil fuels (natural gas, oil, and coal), transportation (primarily cars and trucks, but also trains and other modes), cattle production (methane gases), rice farming, and cement production.

The extent of these effects depends on the amount of change caused by global warming. IPCC II data project an average rise of between six and thirty-six inches in sea levels by 2100. Using the higher figure, the impact on some countries would be dramatic. A thirty-six-inch rise would inundate territory in which ten million people live in Bangladesh alone, forcing their relocation to scarce higher land. The same increase would cover 12 percent of the arable land of the Nile River delta in Egypt, which produces crops on which over seven million people are dependent. Some estimates suggest the island country of Vanuatu in the South Pacific would simply disappear under the rising waters. Many resort and retirement communities along the American Atlantic shoreline and the Florida peninsula could be catastrophically affected. Worldwide, it is estimated that forty-five million people would be displaced.

Warming ocean water could also have dramatic effects, for instance, by affecting ocean currents that now have an influence on climate in various parts of the world. The Atlantic Gulf Stream, for instance, could be affected by warmer water coming from polar areas, changing patterns for the coastal United States and Europe. As an example, Gulf Stream effects that tend to keep major hurricanes off parts of the American coast (e.g., the South Carolina Lowcountry) could and in some instances have been diverted, resulting in new patterns of hurricane, tornado, and storm impacts. Large-scale changes in patterns of ocean circulation are possible worldwide.

The debate has a strong political element, particularly in the United States, where it has become a partisan issue. Republicans, especially supporters of Trump, downplayed the threat, and even tried to portray it as a foreign policy plot to weaken the American economy, since much of the burden would fall on American efforts to ameliorate it, which will be expensive and could endanger American economic preeminence. Democrats accept the dire science of global warming, and Biden accepted that American leadership could provide a positive core for revitalizing American economic leadership as the world leader in investigating and producing solutions.

The Skeptics

The consensus on climate change is not shared universally. As weather patterns have become more volatile and the effects of climate-based events have become increasingly frequent and calamitous, it has become impossible to deny altogether that climate is not changing for the worse. The thrust of counter-arguments has drifted from denial of change to causation and the accuracy of apocalyptical projections if something is not done to arrest and reverse current trends. The newer thrust, most vociferously associated with the Trump administration, raises questions about whether fluctuations are natural historical anomalies or are "manmade," a euphemism for change resulting from human activity.

Some scientists—admittedly, a relative few—disagree with the accuracy of these projections and the direness of the consequences that they project. There is little disagreement about the historical record (e.g., the amount of climate change in the last century) because that is based on observed data that can be examined for accuracy. There is, however, some disagreement on the precise causes of change (e.g., scientists affiliated with the power industry tend to downplay the impact of energy production as part of denying manmade culpability).

There tend to be three criticisms of climate change scientists that can be phrased in terms of questions. The first is how much effect will global warming have? A second, corollary question is how much will those effects accumulate under different assumptions about natural and manmade adjustments to these effects? Third, how difficult are the solutions?

There is strenuous disagreement on all these matters. Consider, for instance, the projections on how much average surface temperatures will increase in this century if action is not taken. Estimates range from one to ten degrees Fahrenheit, and that is a considerable difference in terms of the physical consequences to the world and humankind. If the actual figure is at the upper end of that spectrum, the impact on things like snowpack, glacier, and polar ice cap melting will be considerable, with oceans rising at the upper limits of predictions (around three feet). Parts of Tampa Bay and New Orleans, among other places, will be underwater unless levees are constructed to keep the water out, and Vanuatu may become the next Lost City of Atlantis (an analogy often made by climate change scientists). The impacts could be more subtle but no less traumatic. Rising ocean levels and increasing saltwater intrusion into underground freshwater aquifers that supply drinking water could create another class of problems, for instance. The list goes on.

Who knows which part of the range is correct? The answer is that with any scientific certitude, no one does. The amount of warming is necessarily an extrapolation into a future that does not exist, after all, not an observation of something that does. Clearly, it is in the interests of those who either do not believe in the more severe projections or who would be most adversely affected by concerted efforts to reduce emissions to believe in the lower projections and to deny the more severe possibilities.

Because the effects are not all immediate and unambiguous, the average person has little way to answer the second question: What does all this mean? Is the world headed for an environmental catastrophe if something is not done to slow, stop, or reduce the phenomenon of global warming? Scientists on both sides of the issue are passionate and self-convinced, but they have not made a case to the world's public that is universally compelling, understandable, and convincing.

This leads to the third question: What should be done about global warming? The immediate answer, of course, is that it depends on what and how bad the problem is. Most of the world's scientific community has accepted the basic science of the problem, but largely economic forces in the United States have been prominent among major powers in denying or downplaying the problem and resisting international solutions. The major source of historic U.S. objection is not the veracity of climate change science, but it is instead directed at the differential obligations for solving it that efforts like the Paris agreement attempt to do: reductions with economic consequences that would make the American economy less competitive and the exclusion of developing world countries with large pollution potentials from regulation. This was the heart of the Trump objection.

There is, of course, a hedge in answering the third question that reflects a deep American belief that technology will somehow find a way to ameliorate the problem. That is the position often taken by the American energy and transportation industries, and it is an approach that has worked to solve other problems at other times.

Application: Kyoto to Paris and the Continuing Crisis and Controversy

Climate change is a classic *transnational issue*, meaning it transcends national boundaries and cannot be dealt with successfully by individual states. The underlying causes are essentially global, and they can be solved only by the efforts of all countries, acting individually or preferably cooperatively.

The process has been difficult for both scientific and political reasons. The scientific community, as already discussed, is virtually unanimous in assigning causation: the production of excess carbon dioxide and other gases injected into the atmosphere, catastrophic fires like the Amazon rain forest fire of August 2019, and the harvesting of trees that historically have served as "sinks" where photosynthesis breaks down carbon dioxide into harmless carbon and oxygen.

The problem is that fossil fuel burning, the chief source of greenhouse gases, is vital in a political and economic sense. Economically, fossil fuel burning creates energy that powers much economic activity. Energy production and use are the strongest correlates of economic activity, meaning the more energy a country uses, the more its economy is likely to thrive. The converse is also true. This means attempts to curb fossil fuel can differentially affect countries, which creates the possibility of geopolitical advantage and disadvantage. Science and commerce are at odds.

Different effects of compliance with climate-based guidelines are central dynamics in the international politics of climate change control. This differential has been prominently framed in developed–developing world terms. In the early days of the movement, almost all the pollution was caused by energy production in the developed world. Emission baseline figures for 1990 used in the Kyoto process showed the United States was responsible for 36 percent of global emissions, followed by the European Union (24.2 percent), the Russian Federation (17.4 percent), and Japan (8.5 percent). The next largest polluter was Australia with 2.1 percent.

Excluded from these baseline figures were the largest developing countries, China and India. The Chinese have taken advantage of disparities in becoming a global economic power. U.S. Environmental Protection Agency figures published in 2017 reflect the change: China now produces 30 percent of greenhouse gas emissions, followed by the United States (15 percent), the European Union (9 percent), India (7 percent), Russia (5 percent), and Japan (4 percent). The politico-economic dynamics help explain why the United States has been such a harsh critic and reluctant participant in the climate control process. The Trump administration's withdrawal from the Paris agreement was the most dramatic example of that reaction.

The Road to Paris

The chronology of global warming as a formal international concern was described by the UN Framework Convention for Climate Change (UNFCCC) secretariat in a 2000 publication, *Caring for Climate*. In 1979, the First World Climate Conference was the initial step. That meeting brought together international scientists concerned with the effects of human intervention in the climate process and the possible pernicious effects of trends that they observed. It also provided the first widespread recognition of the greenhouse gases phenomenon.

The process has evolved, with important points corresponding to the most important conferences and agreements it produced. The major signposts were the Kyoto Protocol of 1997 that produced the first major, comprehensive agreement on the subject, the Bali-Copenhagen process beginning in 2007 to produce a follow-on to Kyoto (which, by its own provisions, expired in 2012), and the Paris Climate Agreement of 2015.

The *Kyoto Protocol* was a complicated document, the details of which go beyond present purposes. Several elements can, however, be laid out that provide a summary of what the protocol attempted to do and, based on those purposes, the objections that have been raised to it.

The overarching goal of the protocol was reduction in the production and emission of greenhouse gases and thus the arrest and reversal of the adverse effects of climate changes. The protocol identifies six gases for control and emission reduction. Three of these gases are "most important" based on emission contribution. Carbon dioxide accounted for fully half of "the overall global warming effect arising from human activities" in the UNFCCC's language, followed by 18 percent for methane and 6 percent for nitrous oxide. The other three specified categories, the "long-lived industrial gases," are hydrofluorocarbons, perfluorocarbons, and sulfur hexafluoride. The goal of the protocol was a global reduction in the production of targeted gases of 5 percent below the baseline year for measuring emissions by the period 2008 to 2012.

The Kyoto accord created a complicated set of categories of states that included differential emissions reduction goals for each category. It placed the burden of reduction on the most developed countries, those members of the Organization for Economic Co-operation and Development with the largest economies, most productive industrial plants, and thus the greatest consumers of fossil-fuel-derived energy.

Most of the rest of the world was exempted from the reduction quotas or was required to make much smaller contributions. Most critically and controversially, some of the emerging developing states were excluded altogether because they had historically not contributed to the problem and it was assumed that they would learn from the pollution mistakes of the developed world and not follow in the polluting footsteps.

Kyoto grew into a source of contention between the United States and China that helped undermine the accord. Although the United States was an early supporter of the Kyoto process during the Clinton years, it never signed the protocol, and the George W. Bush administration was a leading global opponent. The heart of the Bush objection was that Kyoto discriminated unfairly against the United States, and much of this assertion was based on the advantage that China had as a non-emissions reducer under its provisions.

The American position changed almost immediately after Bush took office. On March 13, 2001, Bush announced that he no longer favored U.S. participation in the protocol. In the process, the administration stated publicly that it would not send the treaty signed by Clinton to the Senate for ratification. As a result, the United States remained the most important country in the world outside the protocol and thus did not consider itself subject to its requirements, a position it continued to maintain—a harbinger of things to come under Trump.

Bush administration objections to the protocol focused on two basic themes. The first was cost and burden to the United States. Although some other countries had higher percentage reduction quotas than the United States, treaty opponents argued that having to bear 7 percent of 36 percent of the total required reductions was an excessive burden. In addition, U.S. emissions were already 15 percent above the 1990 level by the end of the millennium and, according to Victor, rising at 1.3 percent per year, thereby demanding even further reductions. Thus, the administration argued the United States was being asked to do too much proportionately. Compliance was viewed as economically ruinous in terms of the additional expenses of doing business and the loss of comparative advantage to industries in other countries that are not regulated by these requirements, notably China. This objection recurred under Trump. The second objection was the exclusion of developing countries from the requirements of the protocol. In most cases, this exclusion was innocuous, as most of these countries did not and would not contribute meaningfully to greenhouse gas in the foreseeable future.

The Bush administration's criticism was principally aimed at China and India. China has since become the largest greenhouse gas emitter. India does not pose quite as urgent a threat, but with a population the size of China's and an emerging technological and industrial capacity, it could be. As of 2017, these two countries were responsible for about three-eighths of global emission figures. One of the few signals of progress at Copenhagen was a joint accord between China and the United States to address this problem.

The tenth anniversary of the Kyoto accords was marked by a major UNFCCC conference in Bali, Indonesia, in December 2007. Nearly 10,000 delegates attended the meeting to draft a follow-on agreement that would improve upon the results of the Kyoto Protocol. Gaining American participation and support was a major objective of the conferees. Major issues introduced at the Bali meeting included future targets for carbon dioxide emissions reductions and the participation of countries excluded under the annexes of the Kyoto agreement, notably China and India. The American delegation insisted that developing economies like those of China and India agree to participate in the reduction of emissions. These outcomes were sufficiently positive that the Bush administration endorsed the Bali outcome.

Turning the general agreement into a specific, binding, and effective accord proved to be the hard part—the "devil in the details." Among enthusiasts of global warming control (which included President Obama), there were high hopes for the December 2009 Copenhagen summit. The summit was attended by 115 heads of state and generated much anticipation prior to its beginning on December 8. The Copenhagen summit failed. It neither formally proposed nor enacted any binding, mandatory agreements to supersede Kyoto after its 2012 expiration, nor did it create a framework for a global treaty by the date of Kyoto's expiration. As the meeting wound down inconclusively, a group of major countries, including the United States, China, India, Brazil, and South Africa, convened an "Informal High Level Event" on December 18, the day before the summit was to adjourn. The result was something called the Copenhagen Accord calling for a goal of no more than a two-degree-Fahrenheit increase in global temperatures. This accord was noted but not adopted by the conference.

The Paris Climate Agreement

Climate change advocates hoped Paris would mark an important breakthrough in the process begun in the last century. There were hopeful signs. For one thing, President Obama had been an enthusiastic leader in the process from the beginning. When the United States deposited its accession to the accord on Earth Day in April 2016, the global climate control community believed it had taken a major step toward gaining the big power/big polluter support success required. China was also a signatory. The Paris agreement seemed off to a good beginning.

Then the United States acted like it has so often in the past regarding multinational agreements and announced in June 2017 its intention to remove itself from the arrangement. The action was, in a post–World War II context, not really all that unusual. There is a pattern. When an American administration (usually Democratic) leads the United States into international arrangements that may threaten some aspect of American sovereign control, a subsequent administration (often Republican) reverses the initiative and pulls the United States away. This pattern occurred in the 1992 Earth Summit, where the United States enthusiastically supported the Biodiversity Treaty and then subsequently rejected it. The Clinton administration was an enthusiastic supporter of Kyoto, and George Bush renounced it almost immediately upon assuming office. The United States has proposed or supported other initiatives from UN-sponsored human rights proclamations (e.g., the UN Declaration on Human Rights and Convention on Genocide), economic initiatives like the International Trade Organization, and the International Criminal Court, and then denounced them. In a real sense, President Trump was just carrying on an American tradition. In rejoining the Paris accord in 2021, President Biden was too.

At the core of the Rome process is the attempt to reduce global emissions by engaging the largest polluters as active participants—notably China and the United States but also rising polluters like India. These three countries currently account for over half the global carbon dioxide emissions. Including China and India in global efforts served the dual ends of maximizing participation in the effort *and* of placating American concerns. The Obama administration devoted special attention to orchestrating these conditions.

The agreement itself is notably non-coercive. The basic underlying dynamic is a series of emission reduction targets that the signatories agree to implement. These goals are not specified in the agreement itself; they are voluntarily agreed to, and progress is self-reported. These provisions are intended, among other things, to assuage political elements in the United States that react negatively to any appearance of intrusion on American sovereign control of its affairs.

Two major questions surround the Paris agreement. The first, and in terms of climate change most important, is whether it will succeed in achieving its stated purpose of helping arrest global warming. The prospects are mixed. On the positive side, almost all the world's countries are parties to the agreement, and the goals they have set for themselves could make a significant contribution to amelioration. There are possibly conflicting variables at play, however, including whether countries meet their goals (an assessment made difficult by the lack of strict reporting requirements), the continued participation by states that are major emitters, and the pace both of conservation efforts and the spread of alternative, and especially renewable, energy sources.

The second question is the American role in the process. The United States is only the third original participant to renounce its participation (Venezuela and Iraq are the others). Indeed, the withdrawal announcement of President Trump included the possibility the United States might negotiate reentry on terms it considered more favorable to American interests, an action the new Democratic administration has carried out.

The larger impact of American absence has been self-inflicted damage. The United States has been a global leader in researching, developing, and commercializing nonfossil energy sources like solar and wind power. These areas are compatible with and connected to the process, to the point that, as Deese points out, "rapid reductions in the price of renewable energy and increases in the efficiency of energy consumption have made fighting climate change easier, and often even profitable." The result had been to establish the United States on the inside track as the leader both in climate science and in the commercialization of the Paris-based movement. Withdrawing from Paris forfeited that advantage for the Trump years and opened the door for competitors, notably China and even Saudi Arabia, to take over that leadership. Deese, for instance, reports that China plans to invest $340 billion in this sector, and the Saudis planned to invest $50 billion by 2020 (both more than the U.S. government). Biden has signaled a major intention to reengage the United States in the competition.

China president Xi Jinping is, as Krupp points out, a chemical engineer by training, understands the potential and science of this endeavor, and has acted to assert Chinese leadership. Krupp points out that, "In 2015, China installed more than one wind turbine every hour on average and enough solar panels to cover two soccer fields every day." They also cancelled construction of one hundred coal-fired power plants, the most visual symbol of Chinese pollution, in 2017. China already leads the world in the production of solar panels, wind turbines, and lithium storage panels. Will their burgeoning efforts and their return to Paris reengage American clean energy efforts, which, according to Deese, currently employ "over three million Americans"?

Conclusion

Hardly anyone disputes that climate change is taking place or that its effects are not pernicious to some degree. No one is a pro–global warmer, but there is considerable reluctance to attack and eradicate the problem, and this has until recently been especially true in the United States, whose participation in the effort is critical to its solution.

The United States and China are both at the heart of the problem and its solution. American alienation from the international efforts rose from what some Americans viewed as two unfair aspects of the Kyoto process that carried over into subsequent international efforts up to and including the Paris agreement. They are the imposition of crippling emissions reduction requirements that disadvantaged the country in the global economy and the exclusion of China from emissions requirements. The two objections were, of course, interrelated, as Chinese exclusion and American inclusion added to Chinese comparative advantage in production costs, largely at the expense of American competitors. Both arguments have abated since Kyoto, but the Trump administration resuscitated them in withdrawing from the Paris accord.

The tables have turned decisively. China had become the world's greatest polluter, but under the leadership of President Xi Jinping, it has become a leader in emission reduction and in the development and marketing of alternative, non-polluting energy sources. Both efforts can eclipse American initiatives.

The United States is in a pivotal position to provide decisive global leadership in containing and reducing global warming if it chooses to do so. The Trump administration was suspicious of climate science and believed that participation in the global effort surrounding the Paris accords would disadvantage American economic competitiveness. Its response was to withdraw from the Paris process, effectively forfeiting America's ability to provide global leadership in the effort.

The Biden administration sought to reverse the Trump role by doing three things in its first months in office. First, it appointed John Kerry, former secretary of state, senator, and Democratic candidate for president, as special presidential envoy for climate, signaling a more visible U.S. effort. Second, Kerry's appointment was accompanied by a return of the United States to the Paris accords, reinforcing the effort to rejoin the global effort.

The third element of the Biden approach was potentially the most intriguing. Opponents like Trump consistently portrayed participation in the international climate effort as an economic liability that would undercut American competitiveness in the global economy. Biden turned that assertion on its head, arguing instead that U.S. leadership could be the engine that revitalized the American economy and reestablished American economic leadership worldwide. His basic thrust was to use federal resources to encourage and underwrite a major American effort on the climate problem that begins by tying American scientific and innovative resources to designing solutions to global warming and then reinvigorating the manufacturing sector to produce products that implement the global plans. It was billed as a win-win solution wherein American global leadership is reestablished and the American economy is reinvigorated.

This initiative had not been implemented as of mid-2021. Predictably, the swamp of American partisan politics has intruded, mostly in objections to the volume of federal dollars that might have to be dedicated to it. Biden and his supporters called for an investment of over a trillion dollars for the initiatives, and his opponents balked at the amount. The program may or may not materialize at such a grand level, but with forecasts that this decade may be critical toward reaching a "tipping point" where irreparable harm is done to the ecosystem, something needs to happen. But what?

At the beginning of this chapter, climate change was described as a true transnational issue. That uniqueness has at least four significant emphases. First, global warming is truly a global issue that affects the entire planet and can be solved only by essentially universal actions by the countries of the world. Special burdens fall on countries like the United States and China that contribute most to the problem and are the leaders in exploring solutions. It is arguably impossible to see how these problems can be remediated without the active participation of both countries. Second, responding to this problem will have direct impacts on two of the most important motors of the global economy: energy production and use, and transportation. Third, climate change is the only environmental problem that intensifies or is intensified by other major environmental problems. Rising water levels affect the ability of the earth to produce food, and desertification is increased by warming, to cite two examples. Fourth, climate change is a problem that is intimately related to other vital conditions of life. The climate change problem is largely the result of humankind's need for energy, but the process also creates additional natural resource problems. The quality of future human life depends on finding and implementing solutions.

Study/Discussion Questions

1. What is a transnational issue? Why is climate change considered a "classic" transnational issue? How does this dynamic affect how we think about the climate change issue?

2. Describe the nature of global warming. What causes it? How does it work? How and why are fossil fuel burning and deforestation the "villains" causing the problem? Who bears responsibility for creating and solving the problem?

3. What factors make a rational debate on climate change difficult? Discuss the positions both of climate change proponents and skeptics. What makes reconciliation of their positions intractable?

4. List and briefly discuss the major efforts on climate change control from 1979 to the present. What is the basis of the tension between environmental and political and economic factors that has been present throughout the process?

5. What has the historic treatment of developing countries like China and India been in climate change negotiations? Why has that position been a sticking point in international efforts to gain cooperation on agreements? Use the Chinese case to illustrate the point.

6. Discuss the Kyoto Protocol as the landmark agreement on climate change control. What did it propose? Why was it controversial? Why did attempts at a "follow on" agreement fail before it lapsed in 2012?

7. What is the Paris Climate Agreement? What does it try to do? How is it an improvement from previous agreements? For what stated reasons did American president Trump oppose it as grounds for U.S. withdrawal?

8. How has the American position on climate control changed since the 2020 election? What are the essential elements of the Biden approach to the problem? Do you think they are viable? Why or why not?

Bibliography

Ackerman, John T. *Global Climate Change: Catalyst for International Relations Disequilibria.* PhD Dissertation. Tuscaloosa: University of Alabama, 2004.

Black, Richard. "Copenhagen Climate Summit Undone by 'Arrogance.'" *BBC News* (online), March 16, 2010.

Blau, Judith. *The Paris Agreement: Climate Change, Solidarity, and Human Rights.* London: Palgrave Macmillan, 2017.

Browne, John. "Beyond Kyoto." *Foreign Affairs* 83, no. 4 (July/August 2004): 20–32.

Claussen, Eileen, and Lisa McNeilly. *Equity and Global Climate Change: The Complex Elements of Global Fairness.* Arlington, VA: Pew Center on Global Climate Change, 2000.

Crook, Clive. "The Sins of Emission." *The Atlantic* 301, no. 3 (April 2008): 32–34.

Deese, Brian. "Paris Isn't Burning: Why the Climate Agreement Will Survive Trump." *Foreign Affairs* 96, no. 4 (July/August 2017): 83–92.

Enwerem, Michael C. *The Paris Agreement on Climate Change: A Better Chance of Tackling Global Climate Change.* New York: CreateSpace Independent Publishing, 2016.

Gates, Bill. *How to Avoid a Climate Disaster: The Solutions We Have and the Breakthroughs We Need.* New York: Knopf, 2021.

Helm, Dieter. *The Carbon Crunch: How We're Getting Climate Change Wrong—and How to Fix It.* New Haven, CT: Yale University Press, 2012.

Henson, Robert. *The Thinking Person's Guide to Climate Change* (second edition). Washington, DC: American Meteorological Society, 2019.

Intergovernmental Panel on Climate Change. A Report of Working Groups I–III. *Summary for Policymakers—Climate Change 2001.* Cambridge, UK: Cambridge University Press, 2001.

Klein, Daniel, and Maria Pia Carazo. *The Paris Climate Agreement: Analysis and Commentary.* Oxford, UK: Oxford University Press, 2017.

Klein, Naomi. *This Changed Everything: Capitalism versus the Climate.* New York: Simon and Schuster, 2015.

Krauss, Lawrence M. *The Physics of Climate Change.* New York: Post Hill Press, 2021.

Krupp, Fred. "Trump and the Environment: What His Plans Would Do." *Foreign Affairs* 96, no. 4 (July/August 2017): 73–82.

Leggett, Jane. *Paris Agreement: United States, China Move to Become Parties to Climate Change Treaty.* Washington, DC: Congressional Research Service, September 12, 2016.

Luterbacher, Urs, and Detlef F. Sprinz, eds. *International Relations and Global Climate Change.* Cambridge, MA: MIT Press, 2001.

Mann, Charles C. "What If We Never Run Out of Oil?" *The Atlantic* 311, no. 4 (May 2013): 48–63.

McKibben, Bill. *Falter: How the Human Game Began to Play Itself Out.* New York: Henry Holt and Company, 2019.

Nersenian, Roy L. *Energy Economics: Markets, History, and Policy.* New York and London: Routledge, 2016.

Pirages, Dennis C., and Theresa Manley DeGeest. *Ecological Security: An Evolutionary Perspective on Globalization.* New York: Rowman & Littlefield, 2004.

Podesta, John, and Peter Ogden. "The Security Implications of Climate Change." *Washington Quarterly* 31, no. 1 (Winter 2007–2008): 115–38.

Romm, Joseph. *Climate Change: What Everyone Needs to Know* (second edition). Oxford, UK: Oxford University Press, 2018.

Schelling, Thomas C. "The Cost of Combating Global Warming: Facing the Tradeoffs." *Foreign Affairs* 75, no. 6 (November/December 1997): 8–14.

Schuetze, Christopher F. "Ignoring Planetary Peril, a Profound 'Disconnect' between Science and Doha." *International Herald Tribune* (online), December 6, 2012.

———. "Scientists Agree Overwhelmingly on Global Warming. Why Doesn't the Public Know That?" *International Herald Tribune* (online), May 16, 2013.

Schwartz, Peter M. *Energy Economics*. New York and London: Routledge, 2017.

Sivaram, Varun, and Sagatom Saha. "The Trouble with Ceding Climate Leadership to China: Risky for the World, Costly for the United States." *Foreign Affairs Snapshot* (online), December 10, 2016.

Stavins, Robert N. "Why Trump Pulled the U.S. Out of the Paris Accord: And What the Consequences Will Be." *Foreign Policy Snapshot* (online), June 5, 2017.

Stern, Todd, and William Antholis. "A Changing Climate: The Road Ahead for the United States." *Washington Quarterly* 31, no. 1 (Winter 2007–2008): 175–87.

Suzuki, David, and Ian Harrington. *Just Cool It: The Climate Crisis and What We Can Do*. London: Greystone Books, 2017.

UN Framework on Climate Change. *COP 21 Final Agreement: Paris 2015 United Nations Climate Change Conference*. New York: United Nations, 2015.

U.S. Environmental Protection Agency. *Global Greenhouse Gas Emissions Data*. Washington, DC: U.S. Environmental Protection Agency, April 13, 2017 (online).

Victor, David C. G. *Climate Change: Debating America's Options*. New York: Council on Foreign Relations Press, 2004.

Vidal, John, Allegra Stratton, and Suzanne Goldenberg. "Low Target, Goals Dropped: Copenhagen Ends in Failure." Guardian.co.uk (online), December 19, 2009.

Wallace-Wells, David. *The Uninhabitable Earth: Life after Warming*. New York: Tim Duggan Books, 2019.

Wirth, Timothy. "Hot Air over Kyoto: The United States and the Politics of Global Warming." *Harvard International Review* 23, no. 4 (2002): 72–77.

18

The COVID-19 Pandemic

"Disease Knows No Frontiers"?

Large-scale natural health crises, known generally as epidemics and pandemics, are a recurring part of the human experience that have periodically challenged the growing human population of the world. They have descended on different parts of human civilizations and have ravaged the populations wherever they have appeared. Most of them have apparently arisen from deadly strains passed along by various animal species to unprotected and unaware populations that did not recognize the unseen menace that was spreading among and killing them. The COVID-19 pandemic that was first observed in Wuhan, China, in late 2019 is the latest example of a recurrent cycle. As efforts to tame this pandemic proceed, major systemic questions include what, if anything, can be done to prevent a next, and possibly worse, recurrence and how better to contain those that do occur.

A common theme in the history of pandemics is that they have appeared unexpectedly, have spread through the affected population uncontrollably, killing countless parts of that population, and have eventually spent their deadly energy and disappeared. For most of human history, the state of medical science was sufficiently underdeveloped not to allow early prediction of impending disasters. The medical community (such as it was at different times) was unable to foresee the approach or onset of these diseases, to treat and save victims, or to minimize the human tragedy of the event.

The science of today is far more advanced in some areas, and it has been applied to eliminating forms of historic pestilence like infantile paralysis (polio) within the lifetime of many living world citizens. Decisive progress is not universal in identifying and treating all forms of communicable disease, most notably influenza-based diseases of which COVID-19 is an example. It is an intriguing question how the COVID pandemic will end and whether its end will stimulate a global effort to mitigate the kinds of causes of COVID and similar viruses in the future. The effort is especially important given the truly worldwide nature of this pandemic and thus the apparent need for global cooperation and effort to avoid its repeat. Part of the answer lies in the tension between epidemiology and the global political will to apply medical science to the problem.

Although the historical record is opaque due to the infancy of much human science in the past, the current problem can be put in historical context that at least allows some hypothetical comparison of the past and present. Comparison is difficult because the globe, and especially the number and distribution of humans on the planet, has changed greatly across time. Population sizes and number of deaths from various diseases were not collected systematically for much of human history, for instance, making entirely reliable comparisons regarding the losses and psychological and physical traumas of various outbreaks impossible and speculative.

Population demographics and communications were also vastly different when historical pandemics occurred. When the Plague of Athens occurred during the Peloponnesian War in 429 BC, there was no way to warn people it was coming, what it would be like, or what might be done to mitigate its impact. In these circumstances, the virus that bore the disease killed an estimated 75,000 to 100,000 Athenians (roughly one quarter of the population). The losses helped prevent an Athenian victory in the war, but the virus did not spread widely because the population outside the directly affected area was sparse. By contrast, COVID-19 has been more deadly, but not in strictly comparative terms. As of late May 2021, COVID had killed an estimated 3.5 million worldwide out of a world population of over 7.8 billion. In absolute terms of number of deaths, COVID has been deadly, but not in comparative terms. In some important ways, the scale of death and suffering has been as much of the result of contemporary population size as it has been the virility of the disease itself.

The years 439 BC and 2021 AD are, of course, hardly comparable by any measure. In early world history, what we now call pandemics were more infrequent and isolated. The most famous exception to that depiction was the Black Death/bubonic plague of the fourteenth century in Europe that killed an estimated 200 million people, roughly one-quarter of the population. In the process, there was an actual drop in estimated world population, the last time that has occurred.

These comparisons are presented not because they record with any reliability the comparative suffering and devastation that epidemics and pandemics have inflicted on humankind across time. Instead, they suggest that events like the COVID-19 pandemic can be placed in historic perspective. Many of these, as briefly discussed in the next section, have been notably more catastrophic and debilitating. Until at least the nineteenth century, medical science was insufficiently developed either to understand the nature of the various pestilences that caused horrific tragedies or of measures that might have been taken to mitigate or eradicate them.

Major disease-based catastrophes have been a recurrent, if generally unpredicted, aspect of the human condition. Historically, they were infrequent but generally catastrophic where they did occur. The historic cases bear at least two contradictory resemblances. First, they generally remained more isolated than contemporary outbreaks because there were less people in the world and they were more greatly dispersed. Human opportunities to spread diseases were thus less likely to occur, thereby limiting "opportunities" to spread contagious diseases. Second, when diseases did enter these dispersed human communities, they tended to be more devastating to the exposed populations than contemporary outbreaks—including COVID—because the state of medicine was such that little could be done to mitigate the accompanying spread and suffering. The pandemics simply had to run their courses.

The contemporary world offers some incomplete and contradictory parallels. Human populations passed 1 billion early in the twentieth century, currently stand at about 7.8 billion and is, by some estimates, expected to rise to 9 billion or more by the middle of the century. In terms of potential victims of new pandemics, there is thus a qualitatively and quantitatively much larger potential victim "pool" than there was during earlier times. Possible casualty figures are enormously larger than they were before, and they can overwhelm the ability of many societies to cope with the problem. The difficulty that highly populous countries like India have had with the COVID crisis offers a grisly preview about what the worst might be like.

Fortunately, medical science is far more advanced today than it was in earlier times, meaning that efforts at mitigation, and even more hopefully, early detection, offer the possibility of ameliorating future viral and other outbreaks. The impressive work of major pharmaceutical firms in developing and distributing vaccines to protect against COVID-19 has been one of the most hopeful developments of the current pandemic. Brilliant and his associates suggest that solutions may even be available. Epidemiology, they argue, "has the tools to return the world to a state of relative normalcy." Politically based resistance has been a new major factor in slowing recovery.

Much of the effort has been led by the United States, beginning with Operation Warp Speed in the Trump administration and stimulated by the Biden administration's massive efforts to get Americans vaccinated and to provide vaccines to other countries that lack the scientific and manufacturing base to produce them. The primary impediments to these efforts have included human resistance to being inoculated, international and domestic political objections, and lack of adequate supplies of vaccine worldwide.

The current pandemic has also included a significant political element that will almost certainly be present in future outbreaks. If efforts to mitigate and eliminate the existence and severity are medically possible, international and domestic politics complicate medical and humanitarian efforts. The most important impediments are probably international and involve questions about how to adopt and implement palliative measures. The World Health Organization (WHO) has been the major international vehicle for worldwide efforts, but its abilities have been limited by the powers and capabilities it has been granted. Much needs to be done to develop a better international effort to attack the next outbreak. At the same time, purely domestic concerns in some countries like the United States have limited and arguably hampered efforts to control and eliminate the disease. What must happen politically to make national efforts more effective as well?

Principle: The Problem of Pandemics

Medical emergencies like the spread of highly deadly pathogens such as viruses have indeed been a recurring theme of human history, arising episodically and ravaging the human populations exposed to them. Some have had profound effects on the evolution of mankind, and many have indeed been more consequential to the human story than the current emphasis on the unfolding COVID crisis. The disaster and suffering created by this latest pandemic should not be understated, even if casualties as a part of the existing population are considerably smaller than in earlier catastrophes. Two factors that began to emerge in the twentieth century and are maturing in the current century have affected both the nature and impact of these events. The first is the development of modern medical science and its ability both to identify and to moderate the impact. Second, there is a much higher awareness within publics worldwide of the extent of the disaster that is affecting them and the world. These changes become part of understanding the context of the current crisis.

The Nature of the COVID Pandemic

The outbreak of COVID-19 burst onto the world stage in late 2019, and it was declared a Public Health Emergency of International Concern by the World Health Organization (WHO) on January 30, 2020. It was upgraded to the status of a pandemic on March 11, 2020, a designation by which it has been universally known ever since. The term pandemic is the designation for the most widely spread infectious diseases, which begins when the outbreak and spread of some form of the disease occurs "in excess of what's normally expected," according to Howard. It becomes an epidemic when there is "more than a normal number of cases" of the illness, and a pandemic when there is a "worldwide spread" of the new disease. The derivation of the term pandemic comes from the Greek terms "pan" and "demos" combined to mean all people. What thus distinguishes a pandemic from a lesser outbreak of a disease is that all people are vulnerable to and can contract the disease.

The COVID-19 pandemic was the result of a virus known as SARS-CoV-2 (Severe Acute Respiratory Syndrome Coronavirus-2). An airborne coronavirus associated with transmission by contact with bats, the COVID virus was first encountered in Wuhan, China, in late 2019. Many early cases were linked to people who had visited a seafood warehouse and market in that city, although Chinese authorities have not confirmed the link in detail. There have also been unconfirmed reports of Chinese governmental mismanagement or complicity in the early failure to report or adequately contain the outbreak.

At the risk of some oversimplification, the COVID-19 pathogen is the result of a form of some strain of influenza that is transmitted in aerosol form from an infected animal to a human victim. A WHO publication offers a simplified explanation of the process by which such contact translates into something far more serious. "An influenza pandemic occurs when a new influenza emerges and spreads around the world, and most people do not have immunity. Many viruses that have caused past pandemics originated from animal influenza viruses."

Not all historical disastrous disease outbreaks can be ascribed to this description of origin or extent. The term pandemic has evolved to refer to airborne diseases that are mutations of existing viruses but are sufficiently distinct from preexisting strains that human immunity has not occurred and, in most cases, will not occur without some medical intervention that protects potential victims from the disease or can treat people infected by it. These viruses, in other words, will spread through unprotected human environments unless medical actions are taken to interrupt them. Further, outbreaks of pandemics cannot yet be definitively anticipated, or their characteristics identified in advance of disease appearing and likely spreading to human populations. Moreover, since most of them originate in multiple animal species that are not captives, trying to identify an outbreak in advance by monitoring possible carriers has not been feasible.

The COVID-19 experience has raised awareness of another confounding characteristic of pandemic-level outbreaks: the appearance of disease mutations that may be resistant to existing treatments or about which the effectiveness cannot be anticipated. The reason is it is impossible to predict and thus preempt the emergence of different strains before they reach the public and begin to spread. This characteristic makes international efforts at pandemic containment particularly complex and frustrating. As an example, when the "Indian variant" of the virus appeared on the Indian subcontinent around May 2021, it was not clear whether existing vaccines (which were largely unavailable locally anyway) could mitigate or treat the spread of this delta variant to growing portions of the one-billion-plus people who live in India and well beyond.

The Comparative Case: AIDS and COVID

Not all the pandemics that have afflicted the contemporary and historic environments have been the result of the transmission of aerosol-borne variants of various influenza viruses. Virtually all the influenza-type diseases are particularly difficult to deal with because the early appearance of what turns out to be a pandemic-induced outbreak can be spread so easily by simple contact with other humans and acts as simple and apparently innocent as breathing air that the carrier is infected with. Most of the outbreaks beginning at least with the so-called Spanish flu of 1918–1920 were apparently caused by aerosol transmission, and the aerosol method of infection has been the apparent method by which epidemics like SARS (sudden acute respiratory syndrome) and the swine flu have spread. Others are different. The Ebola variant, which is prevalent in parts of Africa, is an example. The Ebola Virus Disease (EVD) is transmitted through the transfer of viruses through human blood after a person has had contact with a wild animal. It is thus a hemorrhagic rather than airborne virus. Those infected have brief but excruciating symptoms, and if they exchange blood with others, they pass it along. Up to 90 percent of those infected die quick but agonizing deaths. The outbreak did not reach pandemic proportions worldwide because it was isolated to rural areas in Africa and because victims generally died before they could travel, contact, and infect others. Ebola variants generally share the common trait of being diseases transmitted from other animal species to humans through physical contact.

Particularly in terms of its impact on Americans and other Westerners, a closer comparison between COVID-19 and the HIV-AIDS pandemic that caught worldwide attention during the early part of this century and remains a major health crisis in parts of the developing world is helpful. The two diseases are different in most ways, but they share deadliness to their victims as a common tie. If untreated, they have the potential to create massive human suffering.

HIV-AIDS (human immunodeficiency virus and acquired immunodeficiency syndrome), of course, is a viral disease the most famous characteristic of which is that it can be passed between humans through intimate sexual contact. It was not identified as a major communicable disease until 1959, when it was observed in Zaire. The occurrence and extent of the disease is particularly widespread in Africa, where most of the cases have been observed. The largest number of the twenty-five to thirty-five million deaths attributed to it have occurred there, and the demographic and medical emergencies are the greatest. As such, it has been a far more deadly disease than COVID.

The suppression of HIV-AIDS is conceptually simpler than COVID, although it has not been in practice. The large-scale outbreaks of the disease occurred first in remote parts of Africa, where medical knowledge and practices are less available to citizens and where sexual practices and taboos are widespread. Male virility and female submissiveness in many of the highly rural, tribal areas of Africa make it both difficult to reach out to and educate people about the consequences of actions that can result in the spread of the disease which, if not treated, is fatal. The problem is thus twofold. Potential victims of HIV-AIDS may well not be aware of the causes of the affliction, and, even if they are, there are strong cultural problems that work against efforts to teach sexual abstinence and protection against the deadly consequences of what is biologically normal behavior.

The second problem is in some ways even more daunting than the first, and it helps point to a major difference between the impacts of HIV/AIDS and COVID-19: the cost of treatment. HIV-AIDS can be treated medically, but the medicines involved in an AIDS "cocktail" are expensive, in the range of $10,000 to $15,000 annually. This cost is simply too much for the governments and individuals affected in poor African states to bear. In fact, such costs exceed the annual gross domestic product (GDP) per capita in many of these countries, and there are simply insufficient international sources of funding to underwrite effective international efforts in most affected areas. Efforts at prevention like abstinence and protection have had a limited impact for cultural reasons, meaning doctors in many African countries can only tell grieving families to take their affected loved ones home to die. By contrast, the AIDS cocktail-based regimen has now been widely adopted in much of the developed world, resulting in the virtual disappearance of AIDS as a major epidemic in those countries. A decade ago, AIDS was a concerning epidemic/pandemic in the developed and developing worlds alike; now it is primarily an affliction of the poorest parts of the world.

Aerosol-based pandemics like COVID-19 pose a different profile as public health problems. Because they are spread by humans breathing in tainted air that has had the virus injected into it, it has the potential for a much more rapid and wide increase if infected and non-infected people intermix and interact. Unlike HIV/AIDS, which basically can be spread from one person to another only through intimate contact that is less "efficient" than spreading an aerosol of tainted air to however many people may be within the effective aerosol range, airborne coronaviruses can infect a population much more "efficiently." This distinction alone suggests some differences in how the two types of viruses can be treated. In both cases, the purposes of action are the same: arrest and reversal of whatever means of transmission are causing the spread to occur. In the case of AIDS, the process is more intimate and personal, convincing individuals and couples to abstain or protect themselves during intimate contact that is biologically natural. In the case of a disease like COVID, the basis of stopping the spread is the isolation of the infected from far more casual contact so that they cannot infect the rest. In some sense, condoms are the symbol of AIDS mitigation; the aerosol-protecting mask and vaccines are the symbols of COVID.

There is a second point of comparison: cost. It begins with the question of whether mitigation and prevention or treatment is the major goal. Keeping people from acquiring the COVID virus is obviously economically cheaper than treating those who succumb, but it is a relative matter. Mitigating AIDS would be easy if access to vulnerable rural African areas was facile and there were adequate numbers of trained personnel to carry it out, but there are not, and cultural and biological factors means there is resistance to the efforts. Due to the massive efforts by pharmaceutical firms working with governments, vaccines have become available to inoculate people from COVID. The fact of aerosol transmission, however, means a chief avenue of mitigation has been to keep populations separated, and this is a difficult health (and international relations) problem, as is the manufacture and distribution of enough vaccine to protect the target population (which is essentially everyone). As mitigation efforts proceeded in 2021, a major barrier to effective control was the reluctance or refusal of parts of populations to take the vaccine, a particular problem in the United States. At the unit level, the cost of dealing with AIDS is higher per capita among the afflicted, but the numbers of the afflicted is lower. Dealing with COVID involves a much more universal target population, but the unit costs may be lower (exactly whether or how much cheaper is a question of accounting that can be assessed adequately only after the crisis has passed). The Biden-led commitment to distribute at least 500 million doses free to developing world countries in June 2021, a pledge matched by the European Union (EU), is a positive step toward addressing this problem.

The comparison between these two most recent human catastrophes has not been coincidental. They represent two physically different forms of pestilence with some commonalities. Both are viruses apparently spread from infested animal species of one sort or another to humans, and both spread widely within the affected human population once they are acquired by people. Each has its own distinct signature in how it emerges, spreads, and the agony it inflicts on those who contract and often die from it. They are also different: HIV/AIDS contraction is the resulting of unwitting but purposive behavior by people, but it is also a death sentence for those who contract it and either do not have access to or cannot afford treatment. COVID spreads more insidiously among its victims, who by and large do not engage in overt acts that would cause them to be sickened, but not all the victims die from the disease. In both cases, the numbers are large enough that one feels the need to ask and try to answer tentatively, will

AIDS or COVID be the model for the next affliction that may result in suffering even greater than these pandemics have exacted? What can be done, if anything, to anticipate and prevent the recurrence of similar disasters? It is clearly a worldwide problem, and it almost certainly requires a concomitant response. What will that be?

Application: COVID-19 Eradication and Beyond

Massive pandemics of one sort or another have been occasionally recurring human disasters throughout human history. The instances have increased because populations have multiplied in number and amount of contact. Some have had spectacular impacts, like the effects of the Plague of Athens during the Peloponnesian War, the decimation of much of the European population during the fourteenth-century's bubonic plague that killed up to 200 million, or the smallpox pandemic that killed an estimated 50 million in 1520. Between February 1918 and April 2020, the H1N1 virus killed millions of participants in World War I (estimates range from 18 million to 100 million). More American service members were killed by this Spanish flu, as it was mistakenly named (the name comes because King Alfonso of Spain contracted it and not because Spain was the point of origin), than died in combat during the war.

Highly communicable diseases with influenza bases have become an increasing part of life in a world where population has exploded and there are thus many more people who can catch them and transmit them to others. Not all reach the human proportions of some of history's most deadly outbreaks, but they are becoming more frequent. The COVID-19 crisis that began in China in 2019 has been one of the deadliest versions, surpassed since 1900 by only a handful of other examples in terms of lives lost. The toll stood at 3.5 million dead in May 2021 and was still growing; no one knows what the final count of those killed by it will be.

Dealing with the Pandemic

At the most obvious, intuitive level, there are two major conceptual matters framing how to deal with the pandemic. The first is scientific and technical, and it focuses on the dual goals of eradicating the current spread of the virus and developing protocols and conventions that can more rapidly identify future outbreaks and thus contain them more rapidly. At its most ambitious level, discovering means to eradicate the coronavirus problem for the future dominates. Whether the latter goal is attainable is an open scientific question that entrances many medical researchers, but its feasibility and secrets remain beyond contemporary science. The outbreak of numerous pandemics/epidemics in recent history suggests, however, that it is a quest that might occupy a higher global priority than epidemiology has heretofore occupied. The alternative may be increasing periodic outbreaks of pandemics like COVID-19 and the global and personal dislocations that have accompanied them. No one who has experienced the stresses of the current pandemic can disagree that the avoidance of an equivalent—or worse—outbreak of some communicable disease should be a high priority.

The problem is that it is not entirely clear what kind of commitment and goal is being pursued. There are two broad possibilities, both of which are probably being investigated with differing levels of intensity and expectation. One is that the effort should focus on the mitigation of the effects of the current virus, which has been the public focus of the efforts of pharmaceutical companies in the United States and elsewhere and which has succeeded in producing vaccines that prevent virtually all of those inoculated with them from contracting the current COVID-19 virus. Unresolved short-term questions include what can be done to recruit and treat people who are reluctant to be inoculated and how many people in other countries should receive how many doses of the vaccine. Both are political questions addressed in the next section. The other goal, presumably also being explored within the privacy of research laboratories, is whether to try to devise a vaccine that insulates recipients from a broader range of influenza viruses and that can thus be an effective preventative against future outbreaks and thus effectively avoid future pandemics. This would seem an obvious long-term goal, but it is also subject to political considerations that make its pursuit and implementation (if that is scientifically feasible, itself a scientific question) matters of concern. When one first thinks of the COVID pandemic or any of the pestilences that have preceded it, one does not immediately think of them as "cases in international relations," but that concern is part of the overall question of the current and possible future pandemics.

International and Domestic Politics of Health Efforts

The international organizational focus on things like pandemics falls under the broad purview of an international organization, the World Health Organization (WHO). Its statement of objectives is "the attainment by all peoples of the highest possible level of health," and its motto, captured in the subtitle of this chapter, is that "disease knows no frontiers." It is a simple and intuitively obvious description that clearly applies to the spread of diseases, and thus pandemics, from country to country, but the efforts of WHO are rarely at the center of public discussion of the current problem or how to deal with it. The fact that WHO is not central in the discussion points toward the political nature of dealing with international medical problems.

The WHO is one of the specialized agencies of the United Nations system. It was established in 1948 with its world headquarters in Geneva, Switzerland, and it has broad responsibility in the collection and analysis of health conditions and problems worldwide and has had a lead role in the eradication of smallpox and the development of the COVID vaccine. It is active in the area of other communicable diseases like HIV-AIDS and Ebola. It has an annual budget of $7.2 billion for 2020–2021. In addition to contributions from member states, it also receives private donations, including a large amount (11.65 percent of its budget) from the Bill and Melinda Gates Foundation.

The WHO's motto captures both the nature of internal pandemics and the necessary parameters of efforts to attack and solve them. The COVID-19 virus, like all those that preceded it (and future varieties that will succeed it), is not tied to international boundaries and pays no attention to whether it violates the national sovereignty of individual states. States under siege from pandemics may exercise the sovereign right to exclude individuals they suspect may be spreaders of diseases from their territories, but the disease itself knows no such inhibition. Because the nature of the diseases is truly international, one would think that efforts to contain and destroy it would be truly international as well, but such an inference would be at least partially incorrect. International and domestic politics both intrude in efforts to mitigate and to work on solutions coterminous with the problem where the major, even sole criterion would be defeat of the disease. Such an assumption would be at least partially false, to the probable harm to the collective effort.

International Barriers. One of the most striking characteristics of COVID-19 is the universality of its appearance in most countries of the world. To some significant extent, this is a simple artifact of the modern world: there are more people on Earth today than there ever have been before, they inhabit more territory adjacent to one another than before, they tend to travel from one place to another more than previously, and both their commercial and geopolitical interactions encompass more of the world than previously was the case. The Spanish flu, which spread over much of the United States and Europe, and more recent outbreaks like SARS, Ebola, and HIV-AIDS have spread more widely across the world than older outbreaks limited geographically in a less populous world.

Because so much more of the world is in use so much more of the time by more humans and other species, one of the international problems that has multiplied is the spread of various viruses and other sources of pestilences and pandemics. In a recent *Foreign Affairs* article, Brilliant and his colleagues point to the consequences of the world becoming a smaller place. "The COVID-19 pandemic is not going away," they write. "SARS-CoV2 cannot be eradicated, since it is clearly growing in more than a dozen species. The virus will likely ping-pong across the globe for years to come." Part of the reason for this dire assessment is the current inadequacy of international efforts to cooperate in dealing with diseases that transcend national boundaries, a problem that is a likely feature of the future. The article concludes, among other things, that "the international system for responding to pandemics must be substantially strengthened."

The pandemic has also become a geopolitical phenomenon, thereby politicizing it and making cooperation more difficult. The center of concern has focused on China, both because the pandemic began there and because the Chinese government was allegedly too slow to recognize and act on it internally, thereby losing any ability to keep it localized. The result has been a spate of blame being heaped on the Chinese at a time when their experience and accumulated expertise could probably have been applied to the international effort with better results.

The international politics of vaccine distribution has also been a source of international power politics. The international effort to develop and distribute vaccines to inoculate people against contracting the disease has been impressive, but the sheer geographical and demographic extent of the potential recipient population has clearly outstripped the production capacity of the pharmaceutical efforts to produce and distribute the vaccine. The simple fact is that large numbers of people in many, often heavily populated developing world countries are suffering and dying without hope of assistance, and this is a problem that must be addressed if the international system is to prepare adequately—and humanely—for a future pandemic that seems likely at some point. Politically influenced domestic resistance to the vaccine in places like the United States has only added to the difficulty of containment.

Domestic Barriers. There has also been substantial resistance to efforts to mitigate and suppress the pandemic in the United States. Although the reasons for resistance are often idiosyncratic, they are basically the result of the toxic political divisions in the country. Resistance has become the mantle of many conservatives, whereas compliance to requirements like vaccination has become the rallying cry of many more liberal and progressive Americans. Turning pandemic mandates into a battleground of domestic political wars may be understandable given the political climate as it has evolved in the early twenty-first century, where seemingly every issue is framed in partisan terms. It almost certainly is not helpful in the fight against COVID-19. Early in the pandemic, there was some hope that some reconciliation would accompany the common, global effort. It has not yet decisively occurred.

The heart of the problem is diffuse, but it has some common themes that are offered as examples, not in a partisan way. The first is the populist strain that has been a legacy of the 2010s and which tends to resist calls for mandated actions like immunization as infringements on the basic freedoms of Americans. Closely related is the matter of partisan politics. A massive government push to contain the virus has become symbolically linked to restrictive requirements like vaccination and the wearing of masks, and these have become negative symbols for those who fear the expansion (often phrased as overreach) of the government into private lives. Maximum freedom from regulation of behavior and pandemic suppression are at odds in terms of suppressing and eliminating the pandemic, and the American (and other) political cultures would be well advised to resolve those issues before the next outbreak. Some opposition is inevitable in a political democracy where medically advisable actions have negative impacts on free people. Minimizing or reconciling the accompanying sacrifices in advance would clearly have facilitated mitigating actions in this crisis and would be desirable to minimize resistance in the future.

Conclusion

The COVID-19 crisis is by no means the first viral outbreak to ravage humankind, and if virtually all projections are correct, it will not be the last. The global environment has changed the context and problems involved: in ancient times, there were less people living farther apart. Their ability to treat their afflictions was virtually nonexistent, and all the Athenians and others could do was let the pandemics run their course. Today, there are much greater numbers of potential victims in the world, and they are closer together and thus far more capable of spreading the deadly effects. At the same time, modern medicine (and notably epidemiology) is much further advanced than in previous periods, meaning the appearance of a pandemic is not automatically a death sentence for all exposed. How can these advantages and disadvantages be reconciled to reduce or, most hopefully, eliminate the deadly suffering of the past and even the present?

The discussion in this chapter has touched only on a small portion of the complex range and difficulty both of eradicating the current COVID-19 pandemic and learning from that experience how to confront future pandemic conditions. Because of the nature of this book, it has, in the end, raised more questions about the politics of the pandemics than it has answered. The world will, hopefully, emerge from the COVID-19 with significant knowledge that one hopes will be applied to mitigate future pandemics. Although the problem and its answer are largely epidemiological in nature, politics, as always, plays a role in the equation as well.

Study/Discussion Questions

1. What is a pandemic? Have they been common historical occurrences? Have they been important international events? Explain.

2. What factors surrounding the occurrence, nature, and consequences of epidemiological disasters have existed and changed over time? Contrast the traditional phenomenon with the current COVID-19 pandemic.

3. Compare and contrast the impact of demographics and the state of epidemiology in past epochs and today. What pandemics have marred the human situation since 1918? Briefly describe.

4. Discuss the nature and evolution of the COVID-19 crisis. Compare it to the HIV-AIDS pandemic, including how each may contribute to planning for massive health disasters in the future.

5. Compare COVID-19 and past pandemics in terms of their surrounding circumstances and consequences. What might the differences mean for the future?

6. The motto of the World Health Organization (WHO) is "disease knows no frontiers." What is the implication of this observation for organizing and thinking about future global pandemics?

7. What are the main international and domestic barriers to planning for and organizing future efforts to avert or minimize the impacts of pandemics? Discuss.

8. Should primarily political considerations in dealing with international catastrophes be reduced or, if possible, eliminated in this highly politicized domestic and international political environment? Defend your position in light of projections about the certainty of future world pandemics.

Bibliography

Arnold, Catharine. *Pandemic 1918: Eyewitness Accounts from the Greatest Medical Holocaust in Modern History*. New York: St. Martin's Press, 2018.

Bacci, Massimo Livi. *A Concise History of World Population* (sixth edition). New York: Wiley-Blackwell, 2017.

Barry, John M. *The Great Influenza: The Story of the Deadliest Pandemic in History*. New York: Penguin Books, 2005.

Bashford, Allison. *Global Population: History, Geopolitics, and Life on Earth* (Columbia Studies in International and Global History). New York: Columbia University Press, 2016.

Benedictow, Ole J. *The Black Death, 1346–1353: The Complete History*. Woodbridge, UK: Baydell Press, 2006.

Brilliant, Larry, et al. "The Forever Virus: A Strategy for the Long Fight against COVID-19." *Foreign Affairs* 100, no. 4 (July/August 2021): 76–91.

Cantor, Norman F. *In the Wake of the Plague: The Black Death and the World It Made*. New York: Simon and Schuster, 2014.

Chakraborty, Arup, Andrew Shaw, and Philip J. S. Stork. *Viruses, Pandemics, and Immunity* (MIT First Reads). Cambridge, MA: MIT Press, 2020.

DeWaal, Alex. *AIDS and Power: Why There Is No Political Crisis—Yet*. Amsterdam: Zed Books, 2006.

Garrett, Laurie. "The Lessons of HIV/AIDS." *Foreign Affairs* 84, no. 4 (July/August 2005): 51–64.

———. "The Next Pandemic?" *Foreign Affairs* 84, no. 5 (September/October 2005): 3–23.

Howard, Jacqueline. "What Is a Pandemic?" New York: CNN News, February 25, 2020.

Kelly, John. *The Great Mortality: An Intimate History of the Black Death, the Most Devastating Plague of All Time*. New York: Harper Perennials, 2012.

Kim, Richard. "The People Versus AIDS." *The Nation* 283, no. 2 (July 6, 2006): 5–6.

Macip, Salvador, and Julia Wark. *Modern Epidemics: From Spanish Flu to COVID-19*. Cambridge and Oxford, UK: Polity Press, 2021.

Mackenzie, Deborah. *COVID-19: The Pandemic That Never Should Have Happened and How to Stop the Next One*. New York: Hatchette Books, 2020.

Oldstone, Michael B. A. *Viruses, Plagues, and History: Past, Present, and Future*. Oxford, UK: Oxford University Press, 2009.

Patterson, Amy S. *The Politics of AIDS in Africa*. Boulder, CO: Lynne Rienner Publishers, 2006.

Quammen, David. *Spillover: Animal Infections and the Next Human Infection*. New York: W. W. Norton, 2012.

Quinlan, Heather E. *Players, Pandemics, and Viruses: From the Plague of Athens to COVID-19*. Detroit, MI: Visible Ink Press, 2020.

Rabadan, Raul. *Understanding Coronavirus*. Oxford, UK: Oxford University Press, 2020.

Shah, Raj. "COVID's Haves and Have Nots: To End the Pandemic, Rich Countries Must Pay to Vaccinate Poor Ones." *Foreign Affairs* (online), June 4, 2021.

Shah, Sonia. *Pandemic: Tracking Contagions, from Cholera to Coronaviruses and Beyond*. New York: Macmillan, 2016.

Slavitt, Andy. *Preventable: The Inside Story of How Leadership Failures, Politics, and Selfishness Doomed the U.S. Coronavirus Response*. New York: St. Martin's Publishing Group, 2021.

Snow, Donald M. *Cases in International Relations* (fourth edition). New York: Longman, 2010.

Thucydides. *The History of the Plague of Athens*. New York: Palula Press, 2015.

United State Census Bureau. *Historical Estimates of World Population*. Washington, DC: U.S. Census Bureau, 2021.

Waltner-Toews, Daniel. *On Pandemics: Deadly Diseases from Bubonic Plague to Coronavirus*. Vancouver, BC: Greystone Books, 2020.

World Health Organization. *What Is a Pandemic? Emergencies, Preparedness, Response* (www.who.int/csr/disease/swineflu/frequently asked questions). February 24, 2010.

Worldometer. *World Population by Year*. www.worldometers.info/world-population/world-population-by-year/, 2021.

Wright, Lawrence. *Plague Year: America in the Time of Covid*. New York: Knopf Doubleday, 2021.

Zakaria, Fareed. *Ten Lessons for a Post-Pandemic World*. New York: W. W. Norton, 2020.

Index